7-04

D0394961

The
Beverly Lewis
Amish Heritage
COOKBOOK

By Beverly Lewis

ABRAM'S DAUGHTERS

The Covenant

The Betrayal

The Sacrifice

❖ ❖ ❖

THE HERITAGE OF LANCASTER COUNTY

The Shunning

The Confession

The Reckoning

❖ ❖ ❖

The Postcard

The Crossroad

❖ ❖ ❖

The Redemption of Sarah Cain

October Song

Sanctuary*

The Sunroom

❖ ❖ ❖

The Beverly Lewis Amish Heritage Cookbook

*with David Lewis *www.beverlylewis.com*

The

Beverly Lewis
Amish Heritage
COOKBOOK

BETHANYHOUSE
PUBLISHERS
MINNEAPOLIS, MINNESOTA

The Beverly Lewis Amish Heritage Cookbook
Copyright © 2004
Beverly Lewis

Cover design and photography by Dan Thornberg
Interior design by Jennifer Parker
Interior illustrations by Jennifer Horton
Back cover photo by Daryl Martin/Gene Photography

Scripture quotations are from the King James Version of the Bible.

Grateful acknowledgment is given for permission to reprint the following items:
    Songs of the Ausbund, the English translation of O Gott Vater, from Das Lob Lied—
"Song of Praise," copyright 1998. Reprinted by permission of the Ohio Amish Library,
Millersburg, Ohio. Contact Ohio Amish Library, Inc., 4292 SR 39, Millersburg, OH 44654
to order Songs of the Ausbund (History and Translations of Ausbund Hymns).
    "New Mercies" by Alice Reynolds Flower, from Along a Gentle Stream, copyright 1987,
Gospel Publishing House, Springfield, Missouri. Used with permission.
    Date Pudding, Chocolate Peanut Butter Frosting, Katie Fisher's Beef Stew, Broccoli and
Cauliflower Salad, Salad Dressing, Grape Mush Dessert, Baby Pearl Tapioca, Cauliflower
and Broccoli Soup from Katie's Kitchen, by Katie S. Fisher of Lancaster County,
Pennsylvania. To order her Amish cookbook, write to: Emmanuel and Katie Fisher, 338
N. Ronks Road, Bird-in-Hand, Pennsylvania 17505.

All rights reserved. No part of this publication may be reproduced, stored in a retrieval
system, or transmitted in any form or by any means—electronic, mechanical,
photocopying, recording, or otherwise—without the prior written permission of the
publisher and copyright owners.

Published by Bethany House Publishers
11400 Hampshire Avenue South
Bloomington, Minnesota 55438

Bethany House Publishers is a Division of
Baker Book House Company, Grand Rapids, Michigan.

Printed in the United States of America
ISBN 0-7394-4257-0

Dedication

To Priscilla Stoltzfus,
wonderful-good friend.

Christian Aid Ministries of Berlin, Ohio, is the recipient of the author royalty earnings from *The Beverly Lewis Amish Heritage Cookbook*. CAM's specific endeavors include distribution of food, clothing, and medical supplies for the needy in Eastern Europe, Liberia, Haiti, and Nicaragua, as well as aid for orphanages in both Romania and Liberia.

Acknowledgments

To the superb (and generous) cooks who shared family recipes or helped in a variety of ways less visible, I am sincerely grateful. They are the following contributors:

Fay Landis, Ruth Mellinger, Darlene Smoker, Rhoda Dombach, Irene Nolt, Mary Jane Hoober, Dorothy Brosey, Julie Buxman, Priscilla Stoltzfus, Leon and Joyce Hershey, Cherie Lynn Hershey, Aleta Hirschberg, Iris Jones, Judy Verhage, Sharon Johnson, Cheryl Ann Clow, Glenda Cooper, Cheryl Zimlich, Omar and Dorothy Buchwalter, Barbara Birch, Jane Buchwalter Jones, John and Ada Reba Bachman, Verna Flower, Katie S. Fisher, Sarah Ebersol, Susie Stoltzfus, Geraldine (Gerry) Goshert, Emma Ebersol, Diana Horgen, Denise Kerr, Hank Hershberger, Dale Gehris, and David Lewis.

My splendid editors, Carol Johnson, Julie Smith, and Cheri Hanson, made the editorial process seem nearly effortless. My heartfelt thanks!

Contents

A Personal Glimpse

ADA BUCHWALTER
1886–1954

My maternal grandmother, Ada Groff (Ranck) Buchwalter, was the youngest of five children, born to Amos and Barbara Ranck of Strasburg, Pennsylvania. They were farmers and devout Old Order Mennonites.

During her teen years Ada was courted by a handsome young man with chestnut hair and blue eyes—Omar Neff Buchwalter, who lived with his Mennonite family across the narrow road that in those days divided the villages of Strasburg and Paradise. Sometimes as Ada set about doing her daily farm chores, her cheerful whistling reached Omar's ears. (The name *Ada* means *joyful* in German.)

When Ada told her parents of her engagement to Omar (who was more interested in preaching than farming, and who by now had attended one year as a ministerial student at non-Mennonite Nyack Bible Institute in New York), Ada's father was strongly opposed to the couple's plans. Nevertheless, Omar and Ada were wed on September 13, 1906, and Ada and her new husband were no longer welcome in her family home. (My first novel, *The Shunning*, is loosely based on Ada's life.)

Yet my grandmother, young as she was, drew strength and courage from God. Her life was a testament of grace, and her quiet and gentle spirit influenced each of her eight children, including my mother, Jane. Many of Ada's offspring—children, grandchildren, and great-grandchildren—have been involved in Christian ministry at home and abroad. (Daughter Beulah is buried in Ghana, West Africa, having died as a young missionary while writing a Bible primer in a tribal language.)

As a minister's wife, Ada's gift of warm hospitality meant offering her "wonderful-good" cooking and cozy bedrooms to a steady stream of American pastors and British missionaries, including Smith Wigglesworth, a faith healer and evangelist of the early 1900s. This was during the Great Depression, yet my grandparents happily opened their home and hearth to many. Ada Buchwalter went home to her heavenly reward on June 14, 1954.

I am truly indebted to my grandmother for her shining example—as well as for the wealth of recipes she has passed on to the family . . . and now to you, my loyal readers!

Letter to Readers

My Dear Reader,

Happy cooking and baking!

If you have already read my comments about Ada Buchwalter, my grandmother, you can imagine the joy and near childlike wonder I experienced when my dear mother offered Ada's old wooden recipe box to me last year! For weeks I simply cherished it, looking at it fondly on my dresser where it sat—front and center. I found myself hesitant to even open the lid and investigate the many handwritten recipes I knew were tucked inside.

When I did sit quietly reading each faded recipe card, I felt as if I had been given a heartwarming glimpse into the past. Some months later I decided—with the enthusiasm and encouragement of my publisher, Gary Johnson, and my editor, Carol Johnson—that these wonderful old recipes must see the light of day yet again and be joyfully shared with you. Not only do they come from the hand of master cook and baker Grandmother Ada, but I, along with my tireless helpers, have taken great care to test these delicious dishes, along with oodles of Amish recipes and other scrumptious dishes unique to the Plain community, much to the delight of my own immediate and extended family.

Included are kitchen hints and tips, as well as Amish lore, poetry, and pertinent Scriptures, favorites of the Plain people. Also scattered throughout, you'll find personal notes from me to you . . . hopefully helpful comments, as well as family anecdotes and warm memories of bygone days.

In addition, certain recipes have been modified or updated from the Old Order way of doing things (such as cooking on woodstoves and beating batter by hand—and feeling or tasting one's way through a recipe instead of jotting it down) for the benefit of non-Amish cooks who may have less time to spend in the kitchen. If you find yourself wondering about various ingredients listed, please know that present-day Amish *do* go to the store; they don't necessarily cook *everything* "from scratch."

Truly, this cookbook would not have been possible without the help of my wonderful daughter Julie and my dear cousins Joyce and Cherie Lynn Hershey, who cheerfully kitchen-tested and/or typed endless recipes.

Joyfully yours,

Beverly

Appetizers and Beverages

Mary Ruth hurried with Hannah to help Mamma, Leah, and Lizzie with a smorgasbord-style spread laid out on long tables in the sunny kitchen. Today being a perfect day for a picnic, the People would eat and fellowship on the grounds. Bread and homemade butter, sliced cheeses, dill and sweet pickles, strawberry jam, red beets, half-moon apple pies, and ice-cold lemonade—the standard light fare for a summer Sunday go-to-meeting. Not that a body could eat himself full on such a menu. It was merely intended to squelch growling stomachs till the People could ride horse and buggy back home.

—from *The Betrayal*

(Note: See OLD-TIME LEMONADE on page 17.)

Therefore if thine enemy hunger, feed him; if he thirst, give him drink. —ROMANS 12:20

SEAFOOD-FILLED MUSHROOMS

⅓ c. butter, melted
½ c. (rounded) plain un-
    seasoned bread crumbs
8 oz. imitation crabmeat,
    finely chopped
½ c. (rounded) very finely
    chopped onion

1 clove garlic, minced
⅓ c. butter, melted
32 medium mushrooms
    (approximately), stems
    removed
10 oz. Swiss cheese, grated

Heat ⅓ c. butter in cast-iron frying pan; sauté bread crumbs, crabmeat, onion, and garlic until lightly browned. Allow to cool until stuffing mixture can be handled easily.

Spray 9×13 glass baking dish with olive oil cooking spray; add ⅓ c. melted butter to cover bottom of baking dish. Place mushroom caps in baking dish and fill firmly with stuffing mixture. Fill in spaces in baking dish with any extra stuffing mixture. Top with Swiss cheese.

Bake at 400 degrees for 20–25 minutes; serve immediately. Leftovers are delicious, also! May be reheated.

Note: For two 10×15 glass baking dishes, triple this recipe.

Kissin' don't last; cookin' do!

REFRIED BEAN DIP

2 16-oz. cans refried beans
¼ tsp. garlic powder
½ large white onion, finely
  chopped
1 16-oz. jar chunky medium
  salsa

1 6-oz. can pitted black olives,
  sliced
2 16-oz. containers sour
  cream
12 oz. sharp white Cheddar
  cheese, grated

Mix refried beans, garlic powder, and chopped onion; spread in the bottom of a 9×13 glass baking dish. Spread salsa on top of bean mixture. Add layer of sliced black olives, reserving some for garnish. Spread sour cream on top of olives; top with grated cheese. Garnish with reserved olive slices.

Refrigerate. Serve with tortilla chips.

Note from Bev

A well-loved dip among the present-day Plain community in Lancaster County!

CHEESE BALLS

2 8-oz. packages cream
  cheese, softened
10 oz. extra-sharp white
  Cheddar cheese, grated
10 oz. extra-sharp Cheddar
  cheese, grated
8 oz. Monterey Jack cheese,
  grated
8 oz. Colby cheese, grated

8 oz. blue cheese, crumbled
4 tsp. Worcestershire sauce
½ tsp. lemon juice
¼ c. grated onion
2 tsp. dry mustard
½ tsp. salt
Pecans (optional)

Whip the cream cheese; add all other ingredients except pecans and mix well. Shape into three or four cheese balls. Top with finely chopped pecans if desired.

Note: These keep for several weeks in the refrigerator.

CREAMY GARDEN DELIGHT

8 oz. fresh mushrooms, sliced	42 saltine crackers (approximately)
1 large red bell pepper, cut into strips	1 lb. grated cheese—Pepper Jack or sharp Cheddar
2 small zucchini, sliced	¼ tsp. ground black pepper
1 large onion, sliced	5 eggs
2+ Tbsp. butter or olive oil	1¾ c. milk
1½ tsp. salt, divided	

Sauté sliced mushrooms, pepper strips, zucchini, and onion slices in the butter or oil. Sprinkle with ½ tsp. salt.

Grease a 9×13 glass baking dish. Spread approximately 18 crackers in the bottom. Layer with half of the cooked vegetables, then half of the grated cheese. Sprinkle approximately ⅛ tsp. ground black pepper on top. Add another layer of approximately 24 crackers on top of cheese—then another layer of remaining vegetables, cheese, and black pepper. Beat eggs, milk, and remaining salt, and pour over mixture. Gently push vegetables, cheese, and crackers down into egg mixture until all is moistened. Bake at 350 degrees for approximately 40 minutes or until a sharp knife inserted in the center comes out clean.

LEMON JUBILEE PUNCH

1 6-oz. can frozen lemonade concentrate
1.5 6-oz. cans frozen orange juice concentrate (9 oz. total)
1 c. ginger ale, chilled

Prepare fruit juices as directed on cans and pour into punch bowl. Just before serving, add ice blocks and pour ginger ale slowly down inside of bowl. Makes 3 quarts.

East, west, home's best.

PEACHES-AND-CREAM MILK SHAKE

1 c. sliced peaches
1 pt. peach ice cream
1 c. milk, divided

Additional peach slices for
  garnish

Place peaches, ice cream, and ¼ cup milk in blender. Blend until softened. Add remaining milk and blend until mixed. Sweeten with a little sugar if desired. Pour into large glasses. Garnish each with fresh peach slice.

When April showers bring May flowers,
And tulips by the dozen,
A boy starts thinking of a girl,
One that's not his cousin.
—Author Unknown

PINEAPPLE-LIME FLOAT

1 12-oz. can pineapple juice
1 c. lime juice
⅔ c. sugar
Green food coloring

1 pt. lime sherbet
2 7-oz. bottles of ginger ale,
  chilled
Fresh mint (optional)

Combine pineapple juice, lime juice, sugar, and a few drops of food coloring; chill. Fill six glasses half full with juice mixture. Add a scoop of sherbet to each. Fill with ginger ale and garnish with fresh mint if desired.

HOT WASSAIL

1 gallon apple cider
1 cinnamon stick
½ tsp. nutmeg
1 tsp. whole cloves
1 can frozen orange juice
  concentrate

1 can frozen lemonade
  concentrate
Juice and rinds from 2 oranges
  and 1 lemon
Sugar to taste

Combine all ingredients and simmer for 3 hours. *Do not boil.*

Note from Bev

This lovely, warming drink was a welcome sight when Mother served it to my sister and me on blustery Pennsylvania nights. We especially enjoyed it at Christmastime and on New Year's Day.

Serve sun tea in mason jars for fun.

OLD-TIME LEMONADE

3 lemons   1 qt. water

½ c. sugar

Wash lemons. Squeeze juice from lemons into a large pitcher. Add sugar; fill pitcher with 1 qt. water. Chop rinds into 8–10 pieces and let soak in lemonade. Stir well until juice gets syrupy. Strain rinds out of juice and refrigerate.

Note from Bev

This homemade lemonade was always a big favorite at Buchwalter family picnics and all during the summer. Any time, really. The chopped lemon rinds make all the difference!

BIRD-IN-HAND EGGNOG

1 egg   1 c. milk

2 Tbsp. sugar   ½ tsp. vanilla

Dash of salt   Nutmeg

Beat egg until thick. Stir in sugar and salt until sugar is dissolved. Mix milk and vanilla in with egg mixture, chill, and enjoy. Dust each serving with nutmeg for a spicy flavor.

PARTY PUNCH

1 46-oz. can pineapple juice, chilled

3 c. cranberry juice, chilled

1 qt. ginger ale, chilled

1 lemon, thinly sliced

Combine all liquids in a large punch bowl. Float lemon slices on top.

Thou preparest a table before me in the presence of mine enemies . . . my cup runneth over. —PSALM 23:5

AUNT GLADYS'S CHOCOLATE MILK SHAKE

1$^{1}/_{2}$ c. whole milk

$^{1}/_{2}$ c. cold water

10 Tbsp. chocolate milk mix

2 oz. whipped topping

4 handfuls ice cubes

2 tsp. vanilla extract

Combine all ingredients in blender; blend until smooth. Serve cold.

Note from Bev

One of my aunt's mouth-watering recipes from the early 1930s.

FRUIT PUNCH

1 6-oz. can frozen orange juice concentrate

2 6-oz. cans frozen limeade concentrate

1 6-oz. can frozen lemonade concentrate

1 can (1 lb., 14 oz.) pineapple juice, chilled

2 c. cranberry juice, chilled

2–4 c. cold water

2 qts. ginger ale, chilled

1 qt. plain soda water, chilled

Fruit and mint for garnish

Empty all juices and water into large container; thaw and stir well. Pour mixture into punch bowl. Add ice cubes. Before serving, gently pour in ginger ale and soda water. Top with fruit ice ring (see recipe below) and sprigs of mint or fruit slices to garnish.

Makes 30 servings.

Note from Bev

I have served this delectable punch at various church and family gatherings, as well as at piano recitals throughout the years when I taught both voice and piano students. People always ask for the recipe. Enjoy!

FRUIT ICE RING

Use any combination of lime, lemon, or orange slices. Arrange in a pattern in bottom of 8-inch ring mold. Add water to cover the fruit; freeze. To remove ice ring from mold, dip bottom of mold into warm water. Float the ring on top of punch. Garnish with mint leaves and, if available, fresh strawberry slices.

IDA'S HOMEMADE TOMATO JUICE

1 peck (½ bushel) tomatoes
 or a 2-gallon crock full
4 large peppers, chopped
4 large onions, chopped

3 stalks celery, chopped
1 c. sugar
2 Tbsp. salt

Combine all ingredients in a large pot. Cook until soft, then strain. Bring to a rolling boil; bottle for canning.

Note: If unfamiliar with the canning process, a good resource is the *Ball Blue Book of Preserving* (available by calling 1-800-392-2575, option 1).

HOT COCOA

1 16-oz. can baking cocoa
32 c. powdered instant milk
(1 lb., 9.6 oz. box)

8 oz. instant coffee creamer
1 lb. powdered sugar

Mix together all ingredients and store in a large container.
For a single serving, use 1–3 tsp. dry mix per cup of hot water.

Let not the sun go down upon your wrath.

—EPHESIANS 4:26

Breakfast Specialty Dishes

She headed downstairs to cook the usual breakfast for her dear ones. Abandoning thoughts of the past, she turned her attention to the future as she scrambled up nine large eggs, made cornmeal mush and fried potatoes, and set out plenty of toast, butter, grape jelly, and apple butter. Just knowing that she and Jacob and the children could move so far from home, that a Bible-based conservative group was expecting their arrival—or so Esther had said—filled her heart with gladness. The future was ever so bright.

—from *The Postcard*

(Note: See CORNMEAL MUSH on page 24.)

Fritters (Apple or Zucchini)

Apple fritters:

2 c. dry pancake mix

⅓ c. oil

1 c. yogurt or sour milk

1 tsp. soda

Pinch of salt

1½ c. cut-up apples

Prepare batter by mixing together first five ingredients; stir in apples. Fry on lightly greased griddle. Serves 4.

Zucchini fritters:

Prepare batter as above, omitting apples and salt. Grind up 2 or 3 small zucchini, as well as ½ c. grated Parmesan cheese; add to batter. Fry by dropping ½ c. of batter on greased griddle. Serve hot and eat with syrup.

Grandma's Corn Fritters

1 c. ground corn*

1¼ c. milk

½ tsp. sugar

½ tsp. salt

1 tsp. baking powder

½ c. chopped cauliflower

1 egg

Combine corn and milk; let stand 30 minutes. Add remaining ingredients and fry until golden brown.

*Use ground corn or corn cut from the cob. It doesn't necessarily need to be ground; I've eaten corn fritters with whole, tender kernels of corn.

Note from Bev

It has been said no one could make a lighter, more delicate corn fritter than my own grandmother, Ada Buchwalter. She certainly had that innate "touch" every cook strives for in the kitchen.

CORNMEAL MUSH

6½ c. yellow cornmeal

½ c. flour

1 Tbsp. salt

4 c. cold water

2 c. cold milk

10 c. boiling water

olive oil

Mix cornmeal, flour, and salt together in a 6-qt. slow cooker. Gradually add cold water and milk; mix until smooth. Slowly add boiling water; stir in. Heat on high for approximately 2 hours, stirring with a wooden spoon every 10–15 minutes. Mixture will be thick and will not separate when done.

Fill 3 loaf pans with mixture; smooth tops. Cover each pan with plastic wrap, leaving two corners slightly open to let steam escape. Cool to room temperature; refrigerate overnight. (These will keep in refrigerator at least a week.)

Remove mixture from loaf pans; slice in pieces approximately ¼" thick.

Spray frying pan with olive oil cooking spray; add olive oil. Fry slices until nicely browned—approximately 5–8 minutes on first side, approximately 3–5 minutes on second side. Serve immediately with maple syrup or a thick corn syrup.*

*King's Syrup and Old Barrel table syrup are ideal for creating the true Pennsylvania Dutch taste. Other syrups are usually much too runny and will not create a satisfactory outcome.

I have esteemed the words of his mouth more than my necessary food.   —JOB 23:12

BAKED EGGS

Cut out a round shape from a piece of toast and place in a muffin tin. Moisten slightly with milk. Break egg onto it and put in a slow oven (300 degrees) until desired consistency.

WAFFLES

2 c. flour	3 eggs, separated
2 tsp. baking powder	1¹/₂ c. milk
1 tsp. salt	3 Tbsp. shortening, melted
2 c. sugar	

Sift flour, baking powder, salt, and sugar together. Beat egg yolks well; gradually add yolks and milk to dry ingredients, mixing well. Add melted shortening. Beat egg whites until stiff; fold into batter. Bake on an evenly heated, well-greased waffle iron.

Note from Bev

This well-loved recipe came from my grandmother Ada's recipe file. Her wonderful waffles were served not only at breakfast but frequently at suppertime, as well, with tender pieces of cooked chicken and rich gravy.

BAKED OATMEAL

¹/₄ c. cooking oil	1 tsp. cinnamon
¹/₂ c. sugar (white or brown)	1¹/₂ c. quick oats (or rolled
1 egg	oats)
1 tsp. baking powder	1 c. milk
¹/₂ tsp. salt	

Beat together all ingredients with mixing spoon; pour into greased 9×13 pan.

Bake at 275 degrees for 30 minutes or until done. Serve with milk.

Variations: Top baked oatmeal with ¹/₂ c. blueberries, raisins, diced bananas, or apples for a succulent option.

EASY BREAKFAST SOUFFLÉ

8 slices whole wheat bread,
cut in cubes
1 lb. cheese, grated
1½ c. chopped lean sausage,
pre-cooked (lean ground
beef can be used as a substitute)

6 eggs
3 c. whole milk
¾ tsp. dry mustard
Salt and pepper

Layer bread cubes in a greased 9×13 pan, followed by a mixture of cheese, beaten eggs, milk, sausage, and seasonings to taste. Set overnight in refrigerator. Start in a cold oven; bake at 350 degrees for 45 minutes. Serve piping hot.

Note from Bev

What a way to begin the day! Your overnight guests will think you stayed up all night preparing this mouth-watering offering. I like to serve this with a variety of fresh seasonal fruit, along with apple juice and hot tea or coffee.

Do all the good you can,
By all the means you can,
In all the ways you can,
In all the places you can,
At all the times you can,
To all the people you can,
As long as ever you can.
—John Wesley's Rule

Honour thy father and thy mother: that thy days may be long upon the land which the Lord thy God giveth thee.

—EXODUS 20:12

BIRD'S NEST (OR EGG IN THE MIDDLE)

Bread slices (one per serving)
Eggs (one per slice of bread)
Salt and pepper
Honey
Cinnamon

Butter the sliced bread on one side. Place as many slices as desired on a greased cookie sheet, buttered side up. Using round cookie cutter, cut a hole in the middle of bread; set cutouts aside. Crack a raw egg into each cut-out circle; salt and pepper to taste.

Spread honey and cinnamon on the reserved cut-outs; place on the cookie sheet. Bake at 350 degrees for 10–15 minutes or until egg is firm.

Note from Bev

My mother often baked this tasty breakfast for my younger sister, Barbara, and me when we were growing up. She also served it on special days like Christmas morning or Thanksgiving Day. Mother created the recipe title, as well. Interestingly, it has stuck all these years.

Add diced or ground meat to omelets and soufflés.

CHOCOLATE WAFFLES

½ c. shortening

1 c. sugar

2 eggs, separated

2 1-oz. squares unsweetened
chocolate

1½ c. cake flour (sifted before
measuring)

2 tsp. baking powder

¼ tsp. salt

½ c. milk

¼ c. evaporated milk

¼ c. water

½ tsp. vanilla

Cream together shortening and sugar. Add well-beaten egg yolks; mix well. Melt chocolate in double boiler over hot water and add to creamed mixture; mix thoroughly.

Sift together the pre-sifted cake flour, baking powder, and salt. Mix milk, evaporated milk, and water together; add alternately with dry ingredients to chocolate mixture. Add flavoring; fold in stiffly beaten egg whites.

Serve with hot syrup, whipped cream, or ice cream. Makes 4 servings.

 Haste makes waste.

PERFECT PUMPKIN BREAD

3½ c. unsifted flour

3 c. sugar

2 tsp. baking soda

1½ tsp. salt

1 tsp. cinnamon

2 c. cooked fresh (or canned)
pumpkin

1 c. vegetable oil

⅔ c. water

4 eggs

2 c. (12-oz. pkg.) peanut
butter chips

1 c. chopped nuts

1 c. raisins (optional)

Grease and flour three loaf pans (8½×4½×2½ inches).

In medium mixing bowl, combine flour, sugar, baking soda, salt, and cinnamon; set aside. In large mixing bowl, blend pumpkin with oil, water, and eggs. Mix the dry ingredients in gradually until well blended. Stir in the peanut butter chips, nuts, and raisins.

Pour mixture into prepared pans and bake at 350 degrees for 50–60 minutes or until cake tester (or toothpick) comes out clean. Cool loaves in pans at least 10 minutes.

Serve with honey butter or whipped cream.

Note from Bev

Folks will ask for your recipe when you serve this. Also makes a nice light dessert at lunchtime or a midnight snack!

NO-BAKE GRANOLA BARS

Mix together the following ingredients:

5 c. oats	Nuts
4½ c. Rice Krispies cereal	Sunflower seeds
Raisins	Coconut

Mix the following in a separate bowl:

2 bags of small marshmallows*	½ c. peanut butter
1 c. butter	¼ c. honey

Melt marshmallows and butter together; stir in peanut butter and honey. Add to dry ingredients; mix well. Press into greased 9×13 pan. Cut into squares and serve.

*Marshmallow crème may be substituted; mix in with melted butter.

She riseth also while it is yet night, and giveth meat to her household, and a portion to her maidens. —PROVERBS 31:15

Breads

Tomorrow, the Lord's Day, would be another story yet. There'd be no extra chores, just what had to be done in the barn—milkin' and whatnot. She would be cookin' food ahead for her siblings today. A right-gut baking ham was just the thing. She'd slice and serve it with other cold cuts tomorrow, along with strawberry-banana Jell-O, cup cheese, and homemade bread. Josiah had been beggin' for Apple Dapple Cake here lately, so she'd prob'ly go ahead and bake some for the whole family.

—from *The Redemption of Sarah Cain*

(Note: See Priscilla's Homemade Amish Bread on page 35.)

WHOLE WHEAT ROLLS

1½ c. milk

½ c. sugar

2 tsp. salt

½ c. oil

2 Tbsp. dark molasses

2 c. whole wheat flour

2 ¼-oz. packages of yeast

1 c. warm water

4 eggs, beaten

7–7½ c. unbleached all-
  purpose flour

Mix together milk, sugar, salt, oil, molasses, and whole wheat flour; let soak overnight in the refrigerator.

In the morning, dissolve yeast in warm water. Remove milk and flour mixture from refrigerator; stir in dissolved yeast and beaten eggs. Mix in unbleached flour; knead. Let rise until approximately doubled in size, about one hour. Punch dough down and let rise again until doubled, about one hour. Roll dough out and cut with circle cookie cutter to desired size. Place on greased sheet. Let rise until approximately doubled in size. Bake at 350 degrees for 8–10 minutes.

Note: Makes a large quantity, but the rolls freeze very well.

MORNING GLORY MUFFINS

6 eggs

2½ c. sugar

2 c. oil

4 c. grated carrots

1 c. coconut

1 c. raisins

1 c. chopped nuts

2 c. grated apples

4 tsp. baking soda

1 tsp. salt

4 tsp. cinnamon

4 c. flour

Stir all ingredients together. Make as many muffins as desired, baking at 375 degrees for 20 minutes.

Note: This recipe makes quite a lot of batter. Extra batter will keep in refrigerator for up to 4 weeks.

Keep your eyes wide open before marriage, half shut afterwards.
—Benjamin Franklin

GREEN TOMATO BREAD

1 c. oil	3 c. flour
3 eggs, beaten	½ tsp. baking powder
2 c. sugar (or 1 c. honey)	¼ tsp. baking soda
1 tsp. vanilla	1 c. chopped nuts
2 c. diced green tomatoes	1 c. raisins (optional)

Add oil to eggs, sugar or honey, vanilla, and tomatoes. Add dry ingredients to mixture and blend well. Stir in nuts and raisins. Pour into 2 greased loaf pans. Bake at 350 degrees for 40–45 minutes.

Man doth not live by bread only, but by every word that proceedeth out of the mouth of the Lord doth man live.

–DEUTERONOMY 8:3

PLAIN BISCUITS

1 c. sifted flour	3 Tbsp. margarine
2 tsp. baking powder	⅓ c. milk
½ tsp. salt	

Preheat oven to 400 degrees. Sift together dry ingredients. Add margarine and milk; mix quickly. Knead on floured board and roll out ½-inch thick; cut into rounds or squares. Bake on ungreased baking sheet for 20 minutes.

PRISCILLA'S HOMEMADE AMISH BREAD

2 ¼-oz. pkgs. active dry yeast   ½ c. sugar

1 Tbsp. sugar   1 c. boiling water

1 c. warm water   2½ c. warm water

¼ c. shortening   10 c. (or more) flour

2 Tbsp. salt

Dissolve yeast and 1 Tbsp. sugar in 1 c. warm water (not too hot). Set aside.

In a large mixing bowl, combine shortening, salt, sugar, and boiling water. Mix together until shortening is dissolved. Add 2½ c. of additional warm water. Now add the yeast mixture, and blend thoroughly in large bowl.

Next, add 5–6 cups of flour, gradually mixing until dough can no longer be mixed. Knead dough for 20 minutes, continuing to add the remaining flour until the dough becomes soft and is no longer sticky. Let rise for 2 hours.

Place dough in four bread pans, cover with a heavy cloth, and let rise for an additional two hours.

Bake at 350 degrees for 30 minutes.

Note from Bev

This bread is very appetizing!

*Hospitality is making guests feel
at home, even though
you wish they were.
—Author unknown*

PECAN ROLLS

Syrup:

2 Tbsp. butter

¹/₂ c. brown sugar

¹/₄ c. molasses

1¹/₂ c. pecans

Rolls:

1 ¹/₄-oz. pkg. yeast

¹/₄ c. warm water

1 c. scalded milk, cooled to
   lukewarm

¹/₄ c. sugar

1 tsp. salt

1 egg, beaten

3¹/₂ c. flour, divided

¹/₄ c. margarine, melted

Butter and cinnamon

Syrup: Heat butter, sugar, and molasses until sugar is dissolved; stir in nuts. Pour syrup into two 9×13 pans; set aside.

Rolls: Dissolve yeast in warm water. Stir in milk, sugar, and salt. Add beaten egg, 1³/₄ c. flour, and melted margarine; mix well. Stir in remaining flour. Knead dough; let rise until double in size. Roll dough out to ³/₄-inch thickness; spread with butter and cinnamon. Roll up and cut into 18 rolls. Place on top of syrup in prepared pans; let rise for 2 hours.

Bake rolls at 375 degrees for 25–30 minutes. Remove from oven; invert pans over a cookie sheet, allowing the remaining topping to drizzle over rolls.

Note from Bev

Pecan rolls bring back fondest memories of early Christmas morning and birthday time, as well. It's nearly impossible to eat only one! Also delicious served with hot tea or coffee!

*The hurrier I go,
the behinder I get.*

BANANA NUT BREAD

½ c. shortening	1 c. walnuts
1 c. sugar	2 c. flour
2 eggs, beaten	½ tsp. baking soda
1 c. mashed bananas	2 tsp. baking powder

Cream together shortening, sugar, eggs, bananas, and nuts. Add flour, soda, and baking powder; mix well. Bake in greased loaf pan at 350 degrees for 1 hour.

Variations:

(1) Substitute 1 c. applesauce for mashed bananas. Add ½ tsp. cinnamon and a dash of nutmeg or cloves. Optional: add raisins.

(2) Substitute 1 c. cooked rhubarb instead of mashed bananas.

Note from Bev

The light texture will convince banana bread connoisseurs on the very first bite!

CINNAMON SQUARES

2 8-oz. pkgs. crescent rolls	1 egg
2 8-oz. pkgs. cream cheese, softened	1 Tbsp. vanilla
1 c. sugar	¼ c. cinnamon-sugar

Unroll first package of crescent rolls; press into 9×13 pan. Mix together cream cheese, sugar, egg, and vanilla; spread over rolls. Unroll second package of rolls and arrange over top of mixture. Sprinkle with cinnamon-sugar. Bake at 350 degrees for 25 minutes.

The Lord is my light and my salvation; whom shall I fear? The Lord is the strength of my life; of whom shall I be afraid?
                                              —PSALM 27:1

GRANDMA'S NUT LOAF

1 lb. dates

1 lb. English walnuts, shelled

1 c. flour, sifted

1 c. granulated sugar

2 tsp. baking powder

1/2 tsp. salt

4 eggs, separated

Mix together dates, walnuts, and dry ingredients. Beat egg yolks; stir in. Beat egg whites; fold into mixture. Bake in a greased loaf pan at 325–350 degrees for 1 hour.

HUSH PUPPIES

2 c. cornmeal

1 Tbsp. flour

1/2 tsp. baking soda

1 tsp. salt

1 egg, beaten

1 c. buttermilk

1/3 c. finely chopped onion

Oil

Mix together dry ingredients. Stir in egg, buttermilk, and onion. Pour oil 1/2-inch deep in skillet and heat to 400 degrees. Drop batter by spoonfuls into oil and fry, turning occasionally. Drain on paper towels and serve piping hot. Recipe makes about 20 hush puppies, depending on size of spoonfuls.

PEANUT BUTTER BREAD

2 c. flour

4 tsp. baking powder

1/2 c. sugar

1 tsp. salt

2/3 c. peanut butter

1 c. milk

Sift together dry ingredients. Blend peanut butter and milk; add to dry ingredients. Pour batter into loaf pan that has been greased or lined with wax paper. Bake at 350 degrees for 45–50 minutes.

Use for sandwiches of cream cheese and tart jelly, such as grape or currant.

Honey Wheat Rhubarb Muffins or Cake

½ c. brown sugar, firmly
   packed

⅓ c. bran (optional)

½ c. raw honey

⅓ c. wheat germ

½ c. oil

⅓ c. whole wheat flour

2 tsp. vanilla

1½ c. white flour

1 c. buttermilk

1 tsp. baking soda

1½ c. diced rhubarb

1 tsp. baking powder

½ c. chopped walnuts or
   pecans

Topping:

1 Tbsp. butter, melted

1 tsp. cinnamon

2 Tbsp. honey

In a large bowl, mix together first five ingredients. Stir in rhubarb and nuts. In a second bowl, combine remaining ingredients. Fold slowly into the rhubarb mixture until well blended. Spoon batter into greased muffin tins, filling each cup two-thirds full. Mix together topping ingredients and sprinkle over each muffin. Bake at 400 degrees for 20–25 minutes. Makes 20 muffins.

Cake: Pour batter into greased loaf pans and bake at 400 degrees for 30–35 minutes or until done. Makes 2 cakes.

Judge not, and ye shall not be judged: condemn not, and ye shall not be condemned: forgive, and ye shall be forgiven: Give, and it shall be given unto you; good measure, pressed down, and shaken together, and running over. . . . For with the same measure that ye mete withal it shall be measured to you again.

—LUKE 6:37–38

AMISH FRIENDSHIP BREAD STARTER

Method 1: Covered glass or plastic container

1 c. flour   1 c. milk

1 c. sugar

Mix all ingredients together in a glass or plastic container and follow the steps below. Do not refrigerate. Keep securely covered at room temperature from Day 1 through Day 10.

* Day 1: Make or receive starter.
* Day 2: Stir and cover—do not use a metal utensil to stir.
* Day 3: Stir.
* Day 4: Stir.
* Day 5: Add 1 c. each of flour, sugar, and milk.
* Day 6: Stir.
* Day 7: Stir.
* Day 8: Let stand—do not stir.
* Day 9: Let stand—do not stir.
* Day 10: Make Friendship Bread (see following recipe); do not stir or disturb until making bread.

Method 2: Ziplock freezer bag

½ c. flour (regular or   ½ c. milk (store-bought or
   unbleached)   raw goat's milk)

½ c. sugar (white granulated
   or raw)

Mix all ingredients together and put in a 1-gallon ziplock freezer bag, making sure the zipper is clean and seals well. Follow the steps below. Do not refrigerate; let sit at room temperature in a place where it can rise.

* Day 1: Make starter and put in sealed bag.
* Day 2: Squish bag to mix thoroughly.*
* Day 3: Squish bag to mix thoroughly.
* Day 4: Squish bag to mix thoroughly.
* Day 5: Squish bag to mix thoroughly.

❧ Day 6: Add 2 c. flour, 1 c. sugar, and 1 c. milk. Squish bag to mix thoroughly.

❧ Day 7: Squish bag and let air out—be careful that the zipper is clean before resealing. (Note: you may have to let air out before squishing bag.)

❧ Day 8: Squish bag and let air out—be careful that the zipper is clean before resealing. (Note: you may have to let air out before squishing bag.)

❧ Day 9: Squish bag and let air out—be careful that the zipper is clean before resealing. (Note: you may have to let air out before squishing bag.)

❧ Day 10: Make Friendship Bread (see following recipe); do not squish or disturb bag until making bread.

Starter can be used to make approximately 4 cups of new starter. On Day 10, you can make four batches of Friendship Bread or make one batch of bread and give three 1-cup starters to friends. Alternatively, you can make three batches of Friendship Bread and save 1 cup starter for yourself.

*Starting with Day 2, it may be necessary to let excess air out of the bag one or more times per day; be careful not to disturb starter while doing so.

FRIENDSHIP BREAD

Cinnamon

Sugar

1 c. oil

3 large eggs

1/2 c. milk

1 tsp. vanilla

2 c. flour

1 c. sugar

1 1/2 tsp. baking powder

1/2 tsp. salt

1/2 tsp. baking soda

2 tsp. cinnamon

1 large box of instant vanilla pudding (or 3/4 c. [rounded] bulk instant vanilla pudding)

1 c. baking raisins (or soak raisins 5 minutes in hot water, then drain well)

1 c. flour

1 c. sugar

1 c. milk

Preheat oven to 325 degrees. In a small bowl, make a mixture of sugar and cinnamon. Prepare two loaf pans, one Bundt pan, or a 9×13 baking dish by greasing the pans and coating with the cinnamon-sugar mixture, reserving some for topping. (Note: Tin loaf pans are excellent for making Friendship Bread.) Set aside.

Combine oil, eggs, ½ c. milk, and vanilla in a large glass or nonmetal bowl, mixing well. Add 2 c. flour, 1 c. sugar, baking powder, salt, baking soda, cinnamon, pudding, and raisins to egg mixture; do not mix.

In separate medium glass or nonmetal bowl, using wooden spoon, mix together 1 c. flour and 1 c. sugar. Gradually add 1 c. milk, keeping mixture smooth. Add Amish Friendship Bread Starter from container or plastic bag, mixing in gently with a wooden spoon. Add approximately 1 cup of the resulting mixture into the egg/flour/raisin mixture. With a wooden spoon, mix egg/flour/raisin/starter mixture together well.

Pour batter into the prepared pans; sprinkle reserved cinnamon-sugar mixture on top. Bake at 325 degrees for approximately 1 hour or until toothpick inserted in center comes out clean. Do not over-bake. Allow to cool in pans. This bread freezes well.

Of the remaining new starter mixture, put 1 c. each into three plastic or glass containers or gallon ziplock freezer bags. Keep one starter for yourself and give two starters to friends with the instructions for Amish Friendship Bread Starter (today is Day 1), or make additional batches of Friendship Bread to give away.

One batch Friendship Bread makes two loaf pans, one Bundt pan, or one 9×13 cake pan.

Variations: Add chopped nuts, dates, or chocolate chips to the batter before baking. For a different flavor, a pudding mix other than vanilla may be used.

Note from Bev

The original idea of this unique recipe was to share either starter or baked bread with friends or family. A thoughtful gift!

DATE AND NUT BREAD

1 c. boiling water	³/₄ c. sugar
1¹/₂ c. pitted dates, cut fine	1 tsp. vanilla
with scissors	¹/₂ tsp. salt (scant)
1 tsp. soda	2 c. sifted flour
1 egg	³/₄ c. chopped nuts

Pour boiling water over dates. Add soda and let mixture cool. In separate bowl, beat egg; add sugar and mix well. Stir in date mixture and remaining ingredients; mix well. Bake in loaf pan, greased or lined with wax paper, for 1 hour or more at 350 degrees. Ice with plain frosting if desired.

Note from Bev

Very nice sliced thin and served with Velveeta cheese.

BARBIE'S ZUCCHINI BREAD

3 eggs	1 tsp. cinnamon
1³/₄ c. sugar (or ¹/₂ c. honey)	1 tsp. baking soda
1 c. oil	1 tsp. baking powder
2 c. grated zucchini	3 c. flour
1 tsp. vanilla	

Combine first five ingredients until smooth. Add cinnamon, baking soda, and baking powder. Gradually add flour and mix until thoroughly combined. Pour batter into 2 large, greased loaf pans. Bake at 375 degrees for 55 minutes.

Note from Bev

Barbara, my sister, passed this recipe along to me years ago. My granddaughter, Ariel, likes to put jelly or honey on top . . . sometimes whipped cream. I know you'll love it, too!

Whither thou goest, I will go; and where thou lodgest, I will lodge: thy people shall be my people, and thy God my God.

—RUTH 1:16

IRENE'S HOMEMADE BREAD

5 c. whole wheat flour

1 c. sugar

1 Tbsp. salt

¼ c. yeast

2 eggs, beaten

⅔ c. oil

5 c. very warm water

9 c. high-gluten white flour or bread flour

Combine 3 cups whole wheat flour, sugar, salt, and yeast and mix with wooden spoon. Add eggs, oil, and water; mix well. Add remaining whole wheat flour and mix in. Add high-gluten or bread flour, 3 cups at a time, till approximately 8 cups are stirred in. Save the ninth cup to add while kneading dough.

Dump dough on floured board and knead about 10 minutes, adding reserved flour as needed until dough is a smooth consistency. Put a little oil in mixing bowl and put dough back in, oiling both sides lightly. Let rise 20 minutes. Punch down and let rise approximately 1 hour. Punch down; shape into 6 (1½ pounds each) loaves. Place in greased bread pans and let rise about 1 hour or until dough rises above pans. Bake at 300 degrees for 25 to 30 minutes. Cool on wire rack about 30 minutes or until cool enough to bag.

Note from Bev

The Mennonites first developed the type of wheat for high-gluten white flour in Russia and brought it with them when they migrated to ``Penn's Woods''—Pennsylvania—in the early 1700s.

Salads and Salad Dressings

Ida went about her kitchen work, sweeping and washing the floor. She began cooking the noon meal for Abram and the girls, knowing how awful hungry her husband, and Leah, too, would be when they came in from the barn around eleven-thirty or so, eager for a nice meal. Today it was meatball chowder, homemade bread and butter, cottage cheese salad, and chocolate revel bars, Abram's favorite dessert.

—from *The Covenant*

(Note: See COTTAGE CHEESE AND PEPPER SALAD on page 55.)

GRANDMA BUCHWALTER'S TUNA SALAD

6 hard-boiled eggs, mashed   ½ c. diced celery

Mayonnaise   Lettuce

1 6-oz. can tuna   Paprika

Mix eggs and desired amount of mayonnaise together; stir in tuna and celery. Using an ice cream dipper, make balls of tuna mixture and place on lettuce "cups." Sprinkle with paprika.

Note from Bev

This is my grandmother's exquisite recipe. The amount of eggs makes the tuna salad delicate and light as a feather!

WALDORF SALAD

1 celery stem, chopped   1 Tbsp. raisins

1 apple, diced   Lettuce

2 Tbsp. mayonnaise

Stir celery, apple, mayonnaise, and raisins together; dish onto washed and dried lettuce cups. Add your choice of garnish.

PERFECTION SALAD

1 c. boiling water   1 c. finely diced celery

1 3-oz. package lemon-   1 c. finely shredded cabbage

   flavored gelatin   2 Tbsp. finely chopped

2 Tbsp. lemon juice or vinegar   pimiento

1 tsp. salt   ⅓ c. chopped sweet pickles

1 c. cold water

Pour boiling water over gelatin in bowl, stirring until dissolved. Stir in lemon juice, salt, and cold water. Chill until slightly thickened but not set. Stir in celery, cabbage, pimiento, and pickles. Pour into 6 to 8 individual molds; chill until firm.

CHICKEN SALAD

2 c. diced cooked chicken	1/4 tsp. onion powder
1 1/2 c. sliced celery	1/4 tsp. pepper
3/4 tsp. salt	1/3 c. mayonnaise
1/2 tsp. powdered mustard	2 tsp. lemon juice

In a large bowl, combine chicken, celery, salt, mustard, onion powder, and pepper. Stir in mayonnaise and lemon juice. Cover and refrigerate until chilled and ready to serve.

To frost grapes: Dip tiny bunches of washed grapes into lemon juice. Then sprinkle with granulated sugar. Dry on wire rack. A tasty garnish for that special fruit salad or other dishes.

CRANBERRY GRAPE SALAD

1 lb. cranberries, fresh or frozen	1 c. chopped nut meats
1 2/3 c. sugar	12 large marshmallows, quartered
2 c. Tokay grapes or other red grapes, halved and seeded	1 c. whipped cream
1 c. sliced celery	Lettuce

Grind cranberries through fine blade of food chopper into a medium bowl; drain. Add sugar to ground cranberries; set aside. Combine all other ingredients except lettuce and fold together thoroughly; fold in cranberries. Chill for several hours. Serve in lettuce cups.

And the fruit of righteousness is sown in peace of them that make peace. —JAMES 3:18

GINGER ALE SALAD

Salad:

1 20-oz. can crushed
   pineapple
2 Tbsp. unflavored gelatin
2 Tbsp. water
³⁄₄ c. sugar

1 c. hot water
Juice of 1 lemon
1 pt. ginger ale
1 c. seedless red grapes,
   halved

Dressing:

2 Tbsp. flour
¹⁄₂ c. sugar
2 eggs, beaten
1¹⁄₂ Tbsp. butter, melted

Pineapple juice (reserved from
   canned pineapple, above)
1 c. whipped cream

Salad: Drain pineapple, reserving juice; set aside. Dissolve gelatin in 2 Tbsp. water; stir well. Add sugar and hot water to gelatin, mixing well. Stir in lemon juice and ginger ale; refrigerate until almost firm. Fold in pineapple and grapes. Chill. Serve topped with dressing.

Dressing: Mix flour and sugar well. Add eggs, butter, and reserved juice; cook until thick. Let cool. Fold in whipped cream.

LIME PINEAPPLE CHEESE

1 8-oz. can crushed pineapple,
   undrained
1 3-oz. box lime Jell-O

1 lb. cottage cheese
1 c. heavy cream, whipped

Heat crushed pineapple to a boil. Dissolve Jell-O in hot pineapple. Cool. Fold in cottage cheese and whipped cream. Pour in salad bowl; chill.

MOLDED CUCUMBER SALAD

1½ Tbsp. gelatin

1 c. boiling water

½ c. cold water

2 c. heavy cream, whipped

2 cucumbers, washed

1 tsp. salt

1 sweet pimiento, chopped

1 tsp. lemon juice

½ green pepper, chopped

Lettuce

Pimiento

Parsley

Dissolve gelatin in boiling water; add to cold water and let sit for 5 minutes. Fold the whipped cream into the gelatin.

Pare and dice the cucumbers; mix together with salt, pimiento, lemon juice, and green pepper. Fold into gelatin mixture. Pour into a chilled wet mold. When set, serve on lettuce, garnished with pimiento and some parsley.

Waste not; want not.

BROCCOLI AND CAULIFLOWER SALAD

2 c. mayonnaise

1 c. sugar

½ tsp. salt

¼ c. vinegar

2 Tbsp. mustard

1 medium head broccoli,
   florets only

1 medium head cauliflower,
   florets only

Mix all ingredients except vegetables together until smooth. Chop broccoli and cauliflower very fine; toss with dressing.

Note from Bev

This dressing is also good for potato or macaroni salads or coleslaw. For a cucumber and onion salad, add a little sour cream to the dressing, mix with chopped cucumbers and onions, and garnish with raisins.

SALMON AND EGG SALAD

1 8-oz. can salmon (or tuna if preferred)

3 hard-boiled eggs, chopped

1 stalk celery, chopped

2 Tbsp. mayonnaise

Lettuce (optional)

Mix all ingredients together lightly with fork. Serve on lettuce, or spread on toast for sandwich.

In quietness and confidence shall be your strength.

—ISAIAH 30:15

SUNSHINE SALAD

1 3-oz. box orange Jell-O

1/4 tsp. salt

1 c. boiling water

1 c. cold water

Juice of 2 lemons

1/2 c. crushed pineapple

3/4 c. grated carrots

Stir all ingredients together. Chill until firm; serve.

MISTY MINT SALAD

1 20-oz. can crushed pineapple

1 pkg. unflavored gelatin

1/2 c. mint-flavored apple jelly

2 c. whipped cream

Grated carrots (optional)

Drain pineapple, reserving juice. Set aside. Use the juice to soften gelatin. After gelatin is softened, place in a saucepan over low heat, stirring constantly until dissolved. Add jelly and stir until melted. Remove from heat; add pineapple. If desired, grated carrots may be added for color. Chill until thick and syrupy. Fold in whipped cream; turn into a lightly oiled 4-cup mold. Chill until set.

SIMPLE SALADS

Arrange the following salads on a salad plate:

Salad #1:

1 large lettuce leaf (cup
   shape)
1 sliced tomato
1/2 hard-boiled egg, sliced
Grated cheese on top
Add a dab of homemade
   mayonnaise.

Salad #2:

1 large lettuce leaf (cup
   shape)
1 slice pineapple
2 slices peach or apricot
Top with dab of whipped
   cream.

Salad #3:

1 large lettuce leaf (cup
   shape)
1 dip of potato salad (use ice
   cream dipper to shape)
Top with a green olive.

Salad #4:

1 large lettuce leaf (cup
   shape)
1 slice pineapple
1/2 banana (slices arranged on
   edge of pineapple)
Whipped cream or homemade
   mayonnaise
Top with a cherry.

HOMEMADE MAYONNAISE DRESSING

1 Tbsp. flour
3 Tbsp. sugar
2 eggs
Big pinch of salt (less than
   1/2 tsp.)

1/2 c. vinegar (scant)
Butter

Mix together flour and sugar. Beat eggs thoroughly; add to flour and sugar. Mix in salt and vinegar.

Melt butter the size of an egg in saucepan. Pour egg mixture in and let cook until thick, stirring constantly. When mixture has thickened, remove pan from heat, pour mixture into bowl, and beat with egg beater until light and smooth. Refrigerate.

The fruit of the Spirit is love, joy, peace, longsuffering, gentleness, goodness, faith, meekness, temperance.

—GALATIANS 5:22–23

MIXED VEGETABLE SALAD

Grind young, raw carrots, turnips, cabbage, sweet pepper, onion, and radishes through a food processor, using the finest setting. Mix with mayonnaise and serve on lettuce.

RAW BEET AND CARROT SALAD

1 c. grated young carrot $^1/_3$ c. mayonnaise
$^1/_2$ c. grated young beet

Mix and serve on lettuce.

SPINACH AND CARROT SALAD

$^1/_2$ c. finely chopped raw   1 c. grated raw carrot
   spinach $^1/_3$ c. mayonnaise

Mix and serve on lettuce.

CABBAGE, PEPPER, AND CARROT SALAD

$^1/_2$ c. ground cabbage $^1/_2$ c. ground sweet pepper
$^3/_4$ c. ground carrot $^1/_3$ c. mayonnaise

Mix and serve on lettuce.

EGG, CABBAGE, AND SWEET PEPPER SALAD

1 c. chopped cabbage   1 Tbsp. chopped pepper
2 hard-boiled eggs, chopped $^1/_3$ c. mayonnaise

Mix and serve on lettuce.

'Tis the gift to be simple,
'Tis the gift to be free,
'Tis the gift to come down
Where we ought to be.
—Shaker Hymn, 1848

STUFFED TOMATOES WITH COTTAGE CHEESE

Scald and peel firm tomatoes. Lay each one on a plate, stem end down. Cut two slits from top down toward the stem end in such a way as to remove a wedge-shaped piece. Then cut out similar wedged-shaped pieces from the sides of the tomato midway between the bottom and the opening made in the top. Fill openings with cottage cheese. Place on lettuce and surround with plenty of mayonnaise.

PEACH SALAD

Peel large ripe peaches. Halve; remove pits. Place on lettuce and fill peach cavities with red raspberries. Serve with whipped cream.

PINEAPPLE FRUIT SALAD

4 slices pineapple	4 thin orange slices
4 lettuce leaves	4 red cherries
1/3 c. mayonnaise	

Place pineapple on lettuce leaves and spread with mayonnaise. Add orange slices and top with cherries. Makes 4 servings.

Add garden mint to fruit salads or a
sprig atop a bowl of blueberries.

COTTAGE CHEESE AND PEPPER SALAD

2 c. cottage cheese

1/2 c. sour cream

1 small onion, diced

1 green pepper, diced

Salt and pepper

Crisp lettuce "cups"

1 Tbsp. chopped watercress or
parsley

Blend cottage cheese and sour cream with a fork. Add vegetables and mix well. Season to taste. Serve cold on crisp lettuce "cups." Garnish with watercress or parsley.

PAPPA'S POTATO SALAD

3 lbs. potatoes

3 stalks celery

1/2 onion

2 Tbsp. sugar

2 Tbsp. vinegar

1 tsp. salt

1/8 tsp. pepper

1 c. mayonnaise

1 c. sour cream

Cook potatoes in salted water until tender; drain and cool. Peel potatoes and cut into small squares. Cut celery and onion into very small pieces and add to potatoes; set aside.

In saucepan, mix together sugar, vinegar, salt, and pepper. Cook, stirring, until sugar dissolves; remove from heat. Cool. Stir in mayonnaise and sour cream.

Toss sour cream mixture with potatoes, celery, and onion. If salad is too dry, cream may be added. Refrigerate until ready to serve.

Let your moderation be known unto all men.

–PHILIPPIANS 4 5

INDIANA AMISH SALAD

Salad:

2 6-oz. pkgs. lemon Jell-O

4 c. boiling water

1 20-oz. can crushed
   pineapple

2 c. whipping cream

1 8-oz. package cream cheese

Topping:

3 egg yolks, lightly beaten

1 c. granulated sugar

Pineapple juice (reserved from
   salad) plus water to equal
   3½ cups

2 rounded Tbsp. cornstarch

1 c. water

Salad: Dissolve Jell-O in boiling water; refrigerate until partially set. Meanwhile, drain pineapple, reserving juice. Stir pineapple into slightly set Jell-O. Beat whipping cream and cream cheese together in a large mixing bowl until light. Gradually fold Jell-O into cream cheese mixture. Pour into a 9×13 pan; cover and chill.

Topping: Beat egg yolks and sugar together in a large saucepan. (Be careful not to let mixture boil over.) Combine reserved pineapple juice with water to make 3½ cups of liquid; gradually stir into the sugar and egg yolks, keeping mixture smooth. In a separate small bowl, slowly stir in 1 c. water to cornstarch, stirring until smooth. And water and cornstarch to mixture in saucepan and bring to a boil; reduce heat. Simmer over medium heat until thick, about 30 minutes, stirring frequently. Cool to room temperature and spread evenly on chilled salad. (Topping will thicken.) Keep refrigerated until ready to serve.

Too soon old, too late smart.

AVOCADO AND EGG SALAD

4 hard-boiled eggs, chopped

4 slices crisp bacon, crumbled

1 Tbsp. finely chopped green onion

2 large avocados, halved and pitted

2 Tbsp. mayonnaise

2 tsp. lemon juice

1 tsp. prepared mustard

1/4 tsp. salt

Dash of pepper

Lettuce

Bacon for garnish

Combine eggs, bacon, and onion. Carefully scoop out avocado halves, leaving shells firm, and brush insides of shells with a little lemon juice. Mash avocado and stir in remaining ingredients. Add egg mixture and spoon into avocado shells. Serve each shell on lettuce with a bacon curl.

Note from Bev

Mm-m! Lunchtime doesn't get better than this. Nice and light!

STUFFED TOMATO SALAD

4 medium tomatoes (1 per serving)

2 hard-boiled eggs (one half per serving)

1/4 c. diced cucumber

1 stalk celery, chopped

Chopped radish

Mayonnaise to taste

Fresh parsley

Lettuce

Carve out top of tomato with a sharp knife. Scoop out the contents and set aside. Halve eggs; remove and mash egg yolks. Chop egg whites. Mix diced cucumber, chopped celery, chopped egg white, and radish with the tomato contents, adding mayonnaise to moisten. Fill each tomato with the mixture and sprinkle egg yolk on top. Add spray of parsley and serve on lettuce.

MANDARIN ORANGE SALAD

Salad:

¼ c. slivered almonds	2 stalks celery, sliced
4 tsp. sugar	2 onions, thinly sliced
¼ head iceberg lettuce	1 11-oz. can mandarin
¼ head romaine lettuce	oranges, drained

Dressing:

¼ c. canola oil	1 Tbsp. chopped parsley
2 Tbsp. sugar	½ tsp. salt
2 Tbsp. vinegar	Dash pepper

Salad: Cook almonds and sugar over low heat until sugar is melted. Cool.

Tear lettuce into bite-size pieces. Add celery, onion, oranges, and almonds. Top with dressing just before serving.

Dressing: Mix all ingredients together thoroughly and serve over salad.

PINEAPPLE SHERBET SALAD

1 3-oz. box orange Jell-O	1 banana, sliced
1 c. hot water	1 20-oz. can crushed pine-
1 pt. pineapple sherbet	apple, drained
1 8-oz. can mandarin oranges, drained	

Combine all ingredients. Chill and serve.

Note from Bev

One of my mother's favorites . . . mine, too!

APPLESAUCE SALAD

2 c. sweetened applesauce

1 3-oz. box lime Jell-O

1 7-oz. bottle 7-Up

1 c. chopped celery

1/2 c. chopped nuts

Heat applesauce until hot enough to dissolve gelatin. Remove from heat and stir in Jell-O. Allow to cool but not thicken. Add 7-Up, celery, and nuts. Mix well, pour into molds, and chill.

HICKORY HOLLOW SALAD

1 large pineapple

1 c. shredded lettuce

4 oz. cooked ham (cut into strips)

4 oz. cooked turkey (cut into strips)

4 oz. sharp cheese (cut into strips)

Cut pineapple in half lengthwise. Remove hard center core. Using a small knife, cut around edge of fruit, leaving 1/2-inch rim. Remove and dice loosened fruit. Arrange in pineapple shells with lettuce, ham, and turkey strips. Top with cheese strips.

LETTUCE SALAD

Salad:

1 head of lettuce, rinsed, drained, and torn up

1/2 large white onion, chopped

4 hard-boiled eggs, sliced

10 oz. Swiss cheese, grated

Dressing:

1 c. Miracle Whip Light

1/2 c. sugar

1 Tbsp. apple cider vinegar

3–4 Tbsp. milk

Mix dressing ingredients together; set aside. Starting with lettuce, layer all salad ingredients. Pour dressing over the top; toss together. (Lettuce will wilt.) May also serve the salad layered and add salad dressing to taste.

Look before you leap.
—English Proverb

DAWDI FISHER'S POTATO SALAD

Salad:

5 lbs. potatoes, unpeeled	1 large white onion
2 stalks celery	5 hard-boiled eggs

Sauce:

2 c. Miracle Whip Light	2 Tbsp. (or less) apple cider
⅔ c. sugar	vinegar
¼ c. stone-ground mustard	2–3 tsp. salt

Salad: Cook potatoes in salted water until firm-soft; peel and cut into small pieces. Cut celery, onion, and eggs into very small pieces and add to potatoes; mix together lightly. Add sauce; mix lightly. Refrigerate.

Sauce: Mix together Miracle Whip and sugar. Add mustard, vinegar, and salt; blend well. Keep refrigerated.

Variation: Spaghetti Salad
Boil 1 lb. angel hair spaghetti according to directions on package, breaking pasta in half before putting into boiling water. Run cold water over cooked spaghetti until cool. Drain well and use in place of potatoes.

CUCUMBER SALAD

1 cucumber, peeled and sliced fine	½ c. Miracle Whip Light
	¼ c. sugar
1 onion, sliced fine	½ tsp. vinegar

Combine cucumbers and onion in bowl. Mix together remaining ingredients and add to vegetables. Chill.

BLUE CHEESE DRESSING

1 c. mayonnaise

$1/2$ c. crumbled blue cheese

$1/2$ c. sour cream

$1/3$ c. milk

1 Tbsp. sugar

2 Tbsp. white vinegar

1 tsp. Worcestershire sauce

$1/2$ tsp. salt

$1/8$ tsp. black pepper

1 garlic clove, minced

Stir together all ingredients in medium bowl; cover and chill. Serve over tossed greens or mixed vegetables. (Stir in additional milk if dressing thickens upon standing.)

A fat wife and a big barn never did a man any harm.

OLD-FASHIONED SOUR CREAM DRESSING

$1/2$ c. sour cream

2 Tbsp. vinegar

$1/2$ tsp. salt

2 Tbsp. sugar

Paprika

Beat all ingredients together until mixture is stiff. Serve with shredded cabbage or as a dressing for salads.

Soups and Stews

And my, oh my, Sadie could clean and cook like a house a-fire. Nobody around these parts, or in all of Lancaster County for that matter, could redd up a place faster or make a tastier beef stew. But those were just two of Sadie's many talents.

—from *The Covenant*

(Note: see SADIE's BEEF STEW on page 65.)

SADIE'S BEEF STEW

3 lb. beef (round or rump)

Salt and pepper to taste

1/4 tsp. crumbled saffron
  threads

2 Tbsp. gelatin

2 carrots, diced

3 Tbsp. uncooked rice

2 Tbsp. barley

1 c. pinto beans (boiled soft)

2 stalks blanched celery,
  chopped

1 head of cabbage, chopped

1 onion, chopped

1 ear of corn (kernels only)

1½ Tbsp. alphabet pasta

2 potatoes, peeled and diced

Cut beef into stew-size pieces; add enough water to cover by an inch. Boil beef for 2 hours. Add salt, pepper, saffron, and gelatin; boil for an additional hour. Stir in all remaining ingredients except for potatoes; boil for 15 minutes. Add potatoes and boil for an additional 30 minutes or until vegetables are tender.

Her children arise up, and call her blessed; her husband also, and he praiseth her. —PROVERBS 31:28

SATURDAY SOUP

2 lbs. soup bones or stewing
  meat

Salt and pepper

4–5 large potatoes, diced

1 c. diced carrots

1 c. diced onion

1½ c. green beans (frozen or
  canned)

Dash curry powder

2 bay leaves

In kettle, cover soup bones or stewing meat with water; add salt and pepper to taste. Simmer for at least 1 hour; remove soup bones from liquid. Add remaining ingredients; mix together with broth. Simmer for several hours.

CORN CHOWDER

6 medium potatoes

1/2 lb. bacon

2 small onions, diced

4 c. milk

1 tsp. salt

1 1/2 c. corn

1/2 tsp. pepper

2 tsp. parsley flakes

Potato flakes (optional)

Cut potatoes into bite-size pieces, boil until soft, drain. Dice bacon and fry until almost crisp; drain. Add onions to bacon; cook until tender. Heat milk, but do not boil. Add bacon and onions to warming milk; stir in potatoes and remaining ingredients. Add potato flakes to thicken if desired. Let simmer for 1 hour.

Let us therefore follow after the things which make for peace, and things wherewith one may edify another.

–ROMANS 14:19

HEARTY VEGETABLE SOUP

6–8 potatoes, peeled and chopped

1 1/2 c. diced carrots

1 1/2 c. sweet peas

2 10.75-oz. cans tomato soup

1 10.75-oz. can cream of mushroom soup

1 c. brown rice

1 Tbsp. oregano

1/2 tsp. chili powder

1 tsp. celery seed

1 tsp. tarragon

1/2 tsp. garlic powder

1 beef bouillon cube

1/2 c. cornstarch

8 c. hot water

In a large kettle, combine all ingredients. Bring to a boil for 10 minutes. Simmer for 1 hour or until vegetables are soft. Salt and pepper to taste. Enjoy!

Save meat bones for making soup stock with vegetables.

WISE WOMAN'S SOUP

5–6 large potatoes, peeled and
  diced
1 10.75-oz. can cream of
  mushroom soup
1 10-oz. can chicken broth
3 bay leaves
1 10.75-oz. can chicken and
  rice soup
1 Tbsp. oregano
1 tsp. parsley flakes

1 tsp. celery seed
3/4 c. whole milk
2 cups corn (frozen or
  canned)
1 c. green beans
1/2 c. diced carrots
1/2 c. diced celery
1 medium onion, diced
Salt and pepper

Fill a large kettle two-thirds full of water, add potatoes, and bring to a rolling boil. Add remaining ingredients. Let boil 10 minutes more. Simmer 2–3 hours. Salt and pepper to taste.

KATIE FISHER'S BEEF STEW

2 Tbsp. butter
2 lbs. beef (cubed)
1 large onion
1 clove garlic
4 c. boiling water
1 Tbsp. salt
1 Tbsp. lemon juice
1 tsp. sugar
1 tsp. Worcestershire sauce
1/2 tsp. pepper

1/2 tsp. paprika
1 or 2 bay leaves
Dash of cloves or allspice
6 carrots, chopped
1 lb. small onions
6 med. potatoes, peeled and
  diced
1/2 c. cold water
1/4 c. flour

Brown meat in butter. Add next 11 ingredients and simmer for 2 hours. Add carrots, onions, potatoes, and paste made of water and flour; cook an additional 30 minutes.

CREAMY POTATO SOUP

10 potatoes, diced

2 c. water

1 c. chopped onions (or more)

1 tsp. salt

1 stalk celery, finely chopped

2 c. whole milk

Butter

3–4 hard-boiled eggs

Parsley (optional)

Combine potatoes, water, onion, salt, and celery in large saucepan; bring to a boil. Do not drain. When potatoes are soft, add milk and a large pat of butter; heat through. Season with salt and pepper. Meanwhile, peel the hard-boiled eggs, chopping the egg whites and fork-mashing the yolks.

To serve, sprinkle each serving with a couple of tablespoons of finely mashed egg yolk. Add the chopped whites to the individual servings, as well. Sprinkle with parsley if desired.

Note: The hard-boiled eggs help to round out the meal, along with either toasted or buttered whole grain bread.

ASPARAGUS SOUP

2 c. asparagus

¼ c. butter

¼ c. flour

¼–½ tsp. salt

2 c. milk

8 oz. sharp white Cheddar
cheese, shredded

Cut asparagus into 1" pieces (cut with a sharp knife from the top down to where stalk gets tough). Cover with salted water and cook until tender; do not overcook. Do not drain.

Melt butter in saucepan; mix in flour and salt. Simmer mixture while gradually adding milk, stirring constantly. Boil mixture until smooth and fairly thick. If necessary, add a bit of extra milk to keep smooth. Add cheese. After cheese is melted, mix some of the liquid from the asparagus into the cheese mixture to thin it down. Add cheese sauce to asparagus and water; mix until well combined. Heat soup through but do not boil. Serve immediately.

MEATBALL STEW

1 lb. lean ground beef
1/4 c. fine dry bread crumbs
1/4 c. chopped onion
1 egg
1 tsp. salt
2 Tbsp. oil
2 c. tomato sauce

1 c. thinly sliced carrots
1 Tbsp. sugar
1/8 tsp. basil leaves (or parsley
    flakes)
1 lb. small potatoes (approxi-
    mately 4), cut up
2 Tbsp. flour

Mix the first 5 ingredients well and shape into 16 meatballs. Brown in oil in skillet; pour off the fat. Add 1½ c. tomato sauce along with the next 3 ingredients. Cover and cook over low heat for 15 minutes, stirring occasionally. Add potatoes and cook 5 minutes longer or until potatoes are tender. Blend remaining tomato sauce into flour until smooth. Slowly stir this into the sauce and cook, stirring, until thickened. Serves 6.

MAMMA'S CABBAGE PATCH STEW

1–2 lbs. extra-lean ground
    beef
1 medium onion, chopped
1 c. diced celery
2 c. finely shredded cabbage
2 c. water
2 Tbsp. Worcestershire sauce

2 tsp. chili powder
2 tsp. salt
2 Tbsp. sugar
1 14.5-oz. can stewed toma-
    toes, cut up
1 8-oz. can kidney beans

Brown the meat in a large skillet; drain. Add onions, celery, and cabbage; cook until wilted. Add water, Worcestershire sauce, chili powder, salt, and sugar. Add tomatoes and beans. Cover and cook for 30 minutes.

Note from Bev

I always serve this lip-smacking stew piping hot and with a variety of cheeses and specialty crackers.

OYSTER STEW

4 c. whole milk	2 Tbsp. butter or margarine
24 oysters, shucked	Salt and pepper

Bring milk to boil and remove from heat. In a separate saucepan combine the oysters, butter, and salt and pepper to taste. Cover and cook for 3–4 minutes. Remove the lid and add the boiled milk to oysters. Bring to a boil for 1 full minute.

Note from Bev

Very appetizing when served along with buttered toast or grilled cheese sandwiches. Yummy!

 Put a pinch of baking soda in tomatoes before adding milk when making tomato soup. This keeps milk from curdling.

PENNSYLVANIA DUTCH CHICKEN CORN SOUP

6 c. chicken broth	1 tsp. salt (unless broth is
2 c. corn (fresh or frozen)	already seasoned)
1 c. noodles	¼ tsp. freshly ground pepper
1 c. chopped celery	2 c. cooked, diced chicken
2 Tbsp. chopped parsley	

Bring the broth to a boil; add the corn, noodles, celery, parsley, salt, and pepper. Boil 5 minutes or until corn and noodles are tender. Add chicken and heat through.

Note from Bev

This soup is so hearty and tasty! It's the Pennsylvania Dutch version of chicken noodle soup.

CAULIFLOWER AND BROCCOLI SOUP

1 or 2 med. onions, chopped
1 Tbsp. butter
1 qt. water
1 head cauliflower, chopped
1 head broccoli, chopped
1 Tbsp. onion salt
¹/₄ tsp. pepper

¹/₃ c. flour
¹/₂ c. water
1 qt. hot milk
1 pound Velveeta or American
cheese, broken into small
pieces

Fry onion in butter (just a little); add 1 qt. water, cauliflower, broccoli, onion salt, and pepper. Boil until vegetables are soft; mash with potato masher. Make a paste with flour and ¹/₂ c. water and stir into soup. Remove from heat and add hot milk and cheese. Return to stove and heat through until cheese is melted; do not boil. If soup is not salty enough, add regular salt or more onion salt.

Variations: For potato soup, use potatoes instead of cauliflower and broccoli.

For clam chowder, use 6–8 oz. canned clams and omit the cheese, cauliflower, and broccoli.

Too many cooks spoil the broth.

Main Dishes

Mam was smart thataway. There were times when she enticed her daughters to redd up the bedrooms, changing sheets and dusting, with the promise of chicken and dumplings for lunch. "The sooner we finish cleanin', the quicker we'll eat." Mamma's gentle, persuasive prodding taught them by example that work was, indeed, fun.

—from *October Song*

(Note: See Rebecca Lapp's Homemade Dumplings on page 80.)

AMISH MEAT LOAF

2 lb. ground beef

1 c. cracker crumbs

1 Tbsp. chopped onion

1 c. milk

1 tsp. salt

1/4 tsp. pepper

Flour

1 10.75-oz. can cream of
    mushroom soup

1/2 c. steak sauce

Mix first six ingredients together and shape into loaf; refrigerate overnight. Cut loaf into 1/2-inch slices and dip in flour. Brown slightly on both sides; place in casserole dish. Mix cream of mushroom soup with steak sauce; pour over meat loaf. Bake at 250 degrees for 2 hours.

PORK CHOPS WITH RICE

5 pork chops

1/2 c. uncooked rice

1/2 c. diced green pepper

2 c. strained tomatoes

1 1/2 tsp. salt

1/8 tsp. pepper

Fry chops slightly in a hot pan. Move chops to one side and add rice to the fat; allow rice to brown. Push rice to side of pan and finish browning chops. Add pepper, tomatoes, and seasoning. Cover; cook slowly over low heat for 1 hour.

LAMB LOAF

1 lb. ground lamb*

1 c. fine bread crumbs

1/2 c. V8 juice

1/2 c. water

1 tsp. salt

1 tsp. ground cumin

2 eggs, beaten

1 large onion, finely chopped

Mix all ingredients together and put into a glass loaf pan. Bake at 375 degrees for 1 hour.

*May substitute ground beef to make meat loaf.

And he took butter, and milk, and the calf which he had dressed, and set it before them; and he stood by them under the tree, and they did eat. —GENESIS 18:8

DINNER IN A DISH

1 medium onion, minced	3 c. fresh or frozen corn
1 green pepper, minced (optional)	1/2 tsp. salt
	Pepper
2 Tbsp. shortening or margarine	2 tomatoes, sliced
	1 c. bread crumbs
1 lb. lean ground beef	

Sauté onion and green pepper in shortening until tender. Add ground beef; brown. Place a layer of meat into a greased casserole dish. Add a layer of uncooked corn, sprinkle with salt and pepper, and add tomatoes. Repeat layers again, ending with tomato slices. Top with bread crumbs. Bake at 350 degrees for 45 minutes or until bubbly and corn is tender.

Note from Bev

Grandmother Ada was known to "scare up a meal in a hurry." Here's one of the many I especially love to this day.

BAKED SALMON

1 11-oz. can salmon	Dash of salt
1/2 c. cooked rice	Dash of pepper
2 eggs	Dash of sugar
2 c. milk	Onion to taste

Mix all ingredients together and press into a greased loaf pan. Bake at 350 degrees for 1 hour.

Veal Ring

Ring:

2 lbs. ground veal	1/8 tsp. pepper
1 lb. ground pork	1 tsp. mustard
1/4 c. minced onion	1 tsp. salt
1/4 c. horseradish	2 eggs
1/2 tsp. sage	1/2 c. catsup

Bread sauce:

1 c. milk	1/3 tsp. pepper
1/3 c. bread crumbs	1 1/2 Tbsp. butter
1/3 tsp. salt	1 small onion, finely chopped

Ring: Mix veal and pork together; add onion, horseradish, seasonings, and eggs. Pour catsup in the bottom of a well-greased ring mold. Pack in the meat mixture. Bake at 350 degrees for 1 hour.

When finished baking, turn out catsup side up. Serve with bread sauce.

Bread sauce: Mix together ingredients and bake at 350 degrees for 20 minutes.

But we all, with open face beholding as in a glass the glory of the Lord, are changed into the same image from glory to glory, even as by the Spirit of the Lord.

–2 CORINTHIANS 3:18

Shredded Corn Beef

1 c. shredded corn beef	1 onion, chopped
2 c. peas	1 c. stewed tomatoes

Boil all ingredients together for 1 hour and serve.

Ways to serve beef: in stew, meatloaf,
patties, and with gravy.

MACARONI GOULASH

Butter and shortening
1/4 c. diced celery
1/4 c. diced onion
1 lb. ground chuck steak or
  lean ground beef

1 10.75-oz. can tomato soup
2 c. cooked macaroni

Melt a pat of butter and a bit of shortening in a large skillet. Add the diced celery and onion; sauté until tender. Brown the hamburger in the sautéed mixture; add tomato soup. Mix together with cooked macaroni and serve hot.

Note from Bev

This dish was the "talk of the town" when visiting ministers and their families spent time in Ada's homey kitchen during the Depression years.

AMISH FRIED CHICKEN

1 c. crushed saltine crackers
  or bread crumbs
1/4 c. flour
2 tsp. salt
1 tsp. oregano
1/2 tsp. Frontier Veggie pepper*

1/2 tsp. garlic granules or
  garlic powder
2 chickens, cut in pieces
2 eggs, mixed with 1/4 c. water
1 c. water

Combine crackers or bread crumbs, flour, and seasonings. Dip each piece of chicken in egg and water mixture; coat with crumb mixture. Fry quickly in butter until brown. Place chicken pieces in a single layer in roasting pan or 4-qt. casserole dish. Add 1 c. water; cover with foil. Bake at 350 degrees for approximately 90 minutes.

*If Frontier Veggie pepper is unavailable, use mixture of 1/4 t. ground black pepper, 1/4 t. onion salt, 1/4 t. red pepper, and 1/8 t. celery seed.

Baked Macaroni and Cheese

4 c. uncooked macaroni	5 c. milk
5 Tbsp. butter	10 oz. sharp Cheddar cheese,
1/3 c. flour	cut in pieces
2 rounded tsp. salt	10 oz. extra-sharp white
2 rounded tsp. dry mustard	cheese, cut in pieces

Bring large pot of salted water to a boil; slowly add macaroni. Boil for 10 minutes, stirring occasionally. Drain; place macaroni in a buttered 4-quart glass baking dish.

While macaroni is boiling, melt butter in another saucepan. Remove pan from heat; blend in flour, salt, and mustard. Return to heat and gradually add milk, stirring constantly, until sauce thickens and is smooth. Bring to a boil. Carefully add cheese pieces to boiling milk mixture, stirring until all cheese is melted. Pour cheese mixture over cooked macaroni; mix evenly. Bake at 350 degrees for 45 minutes or until golden brown and bubbly.

Rice and Eggs for Two

1/3 c. uncooked enriched	1/2 large white onion, chopped
converted long-grain rice	1/4 tsp. salt
1 Tbsp. olive oil	2 eggs
1 c. water	

In saucepan, fry rice in olive oil until golden brown, stirring constantly. Add water, onion, and salt. Cover pan and bring to a boil. Simmer for 20 minutes, stirring about every 5 minutes. Add a bit of water if needed. Top each serving with an egg "over light." Mix all together, adding salt to taste. Serve immediately.

Note from Bev

A nice alternative for a light lunch or can be served as an appetizer.

TUNA CASSEROLE

1 6.5-oz. can tuna, drained

1 3-oz. can french fried onions

1 c. thinly sliced celery

¼ tsp. onion powder

4 oz. canned or fresh mush-

rooms, sliced

1 10.75-oz. can cream of

celery soup

Combine tuna and ½ can fried onions with remaining ingredients; place in greased casserole dish. Bake at 350 degrees for 25 minutes. Sprinkle remaining onions on top; bake for 5 more minutes.

RUTH'S ELEGANT CHICKEN

8 boneless chicken breasts

16 slices boiled ham

4 oz. dried beef

1 c. sour cream

1 10.75-oz. can cream of

mushroom soup

Paprika

Cut chicken breasts in half; wrap each half with a slice of ham. Cover bottom of baking dish with dried beef; place chicken breasts on top. Blend together sour cream and cream of mushroom soup; pour over chicken. Sprinkle with paprika. Bake at 375 degrees for 60–75 minutes, covered; uncover and bake 15 minutes longer.

REBECCA LAPP'S HOMEMADE DUMPLINGS

1 c. sifted flour

1 tsp. salt

2 tsp. baking powder

1 egg, beaten

Mix together dry ingredients; pour beaten egg over mixture. Add drops of cold tap water, but be careful not to get too much! Stir together. Drop by big spoonfuls into a deep pot of simmering chicken stew, as dumplings tend to boil up. (Or simply place dumplings in boiling water for 5 minutes.) Either way, boil for 5 minutes without lifting lid. Serve dumplings in stew or gravy or with cooked chicken.

TURKEY LOAF

1 egg

1 c. whole milk

1 lb. skinless ground turkey

6 slices white bread, cubed

½ c. chopped celery

¼ c. chopped onion

Beat egg and milk with a fork. Mix together with remaining ingredients and press into loaf pan. Bake at 350 degrees for 1 hour.

Note from Bev

If mixture seems too moist, sprinkle a few dried bread crumbs on top. Sure to satisfy!

CHICKEN CASSEROLE

6 Tbsp. butter

6 Tbsp. flour

3 c. chicken broth

½ tsp. salt

¾ tsp. celery salt

1 10.75-oz. can cream of chicken soup

1 10.75-oz. can cream of celery soup

8 oz. Velveeta cheese (cut up)

1 12-oz. pkg. noodles, cooked

4 c. diced cooked chicken

Dry stuffing mix

In a saucepan, melt butter over medium-low heat. Stir flour in slowly, using a wire whisk, until the butter and flour mixture begins to bubble. Continue cooking and stirring for about two minutes; remove from heat.

In a separate pan, heat chicken broth; stir in salt and celery salt. Once broth is fully heated, add it to the butter and flour mixture, stirring quickly. Return the saucepan to heat; stir over medium heat until sauce begins to thicken (don't allow it to boil). Add soups and Velveeta cheese; cook until creamy and smooth. Mix sauce, noodles, and chicken together; pour into greased 9×13 casserole pan and cover with stuffing mix. Bake at 300 degrees for 1 hour. Makes 8–10 servings.

Cooked at low temperatures, meats shrink less. This also provides more broth and better flavor.

AMISH ROAST[1]

1 5-7 lb. chicken, 8-10 lb. capon, or 12–15 lb. turkey (if using a turkey, make a double batch of stuffing)

Stuffing:

3 cups chopped celery

1–3 c. chopped onion (to taste)

1 c. butter

1 Tbsp. shortening

1½ gal. bread cubes (approximately 24 cups—use 2 24-oz. loaves white bread)

4 eggs

1 tsp. salt

¼ rounded tsp. pepper

Pinch of lemon pepper

Pinch of Spike seasoning

Pinch of Mrs. Dash seasoning

Pinch of Italian seasoning

1 Tbsp. olive oil

Fry celery and onion in butter and shortening until tender; toss lightly with the bread cubes. Beat eggs; mix in seasonings and olive oil. Pour over bread cubes. Mix well and stuff chicken, capon, or turkey.

For chicken, bake in a covered roaster at 325 degrees for 2½ to 3¼ hours.* For capon, bake in a covered roaster at 325 degrees for 2½ to 3¼ hours, checking for doneness after 3 hours.* For turkey, bake in a covered roaster at 300 degrees for 8 hours or overnight.* Bake extra stuffing in a covered casserole dish at 325 degrees for 1 hour.

*Alternative: Bird may be baked in Reynolds Oven Bag according to directions in box.

When chicken, capon, or turkey is done, remove from oven and let

_____

[1]The "roast" is the mixture of stuffing and finely chopped meat.

sit, covered, for 30 minutes—meat will be more moist. Set broth aside and cool. After 30 minutes, remove meat from bones. Grind the skin in a meat grinder and mix in with cooked stuffing. Chop meat in very small pieces—the smaller the better—and mix in with cooked stuffing.

After broth is cool, remove "fat" layer from the top and reserve for when the stuffing is reheated; reserve broth for making gravy (see recipe below). Spread fat over the top of the stuffing mixture when reheating. Reheat stuffing and meat mixture in a 4-qt. covered greased casserole dish at 325 degrees for 45 minutes to 1 hour, checking center for doneness before serving.

Note: Make several days ahead of time. The flavor gets through better this way.

Note from Bev

On Christmas morning, the Buchwalter kitchen was always "redd up" first and everyone dressed for the day before they gathered in the front room for family worship. After prayer and Bible reading, Mother, her seven siblings, and their parents presented simple gifts to one another, often homemade. Before sitting down to dinner they joined their voices in song with a rousing "Joy to the World."

GRAVY FOR AMISH ROAST

Place 1 c. flour in a small bowl and gradually stir in enough water to form a smooth paste. Add some turkey or chicken broth into flour/water mixture until it is a "watery" consistency so the gravy doesn't get lumpy as additional flour is added. Simmer gravy until thickened to desired consistency, adding more flour if needed and stirring to keep smooth. Add salt to taste if needed.

Practice makes perfect.

Homemade Hamburger Helper

1 lb. ground beef	2 c. uncooked macaroni
2 10.75-oz. cans tomato soup	1 can peas and carrots,
4 soup cans of water	drained

Brown the ground beef; add both cans of tomato soup, 2 cans water, and the macaroni. Cook until macaroni is soft, adding the other 2 cans of water as needed when cooking, stirring occasionally. When macaroni is soft, stir in peas and carrots; remove from heat. Let mixture sit for about 15 minutes to thicken.

Pork Chops

4 pork chops	¼ tsp. poultry seasoning
¼ c. butter, melted	1 10.75-oz. can cream of
3 c. soft bread crumbs	mushroom soup
2 Tbsp. chopped onion	½ c. milk
¼ c. water	

Brown pork chops on both sides in melted butter; place in ungreased casserole dish. Mix bread crumbs, onion, water, and poultry seasoning together; place a mound of "stuffing" on each pork chop. Blend cream of mushroom soup with milk; pour over chops and stuffing. Bake, uncovered, at 350 degrees for 1 hour.

Chicken and Waffles

Make waffles. Mix 2 Tbsp. cornstarch with water until dissolved. Add cornstarch mixture to chicken broth or gravy containing small pieces of chicken; thicken. Pour over waffles.

Make hay while the sun shines.

A good name is rather to be chosen than great riches, and loving favour rather than silver and gold. —PROVERBS 22:1

AMISH HAYSTACKS

1 box Ritz crackers, crushed ¼ box
1 28-oz. box Minute Rice, cooked ¼ box
8 lbs. ground beef, browned, mixed with spaghetti sauce and taco
    seasoning mix* ½ jar ①

Choice of toppings: chopped tomatoes (8), green peppers (oodles),
    grated carrots (lots), raisins (mounds), black and green olives
    (plenty), walnuts (many), onions (several diced), sunflower
    seeds (an ample amount), and salsa (several jars)

Stack ingredients on plates in layers, using cracker crumbs first,
then rice, followed by ground beef. The order of the other ingredients is not important. Top with grated cheddar cheese or cheddar
cheese soup.

*Use approximately 1 package taco seasoning per pound of ground
beef and four large cans spaghetti sauce, adjusting to taste.

Note from Bev

Talk about feeding a multitude! This recipe is commonly used at fundraiser dinners in Amish and Mennonite communities. Quite tasty, and additional condiments can be added (or deleted) to suit your taste buds. The meal is not only delicious but very filling.

CREAMED CHIPPED BEEF

Melt 2 Tbsp. butter in a skillet; stir in 2 Tbsp. flour and mix well. Add 2 c. milk and 1 c. chipped beef cut up in tiny pieces. Stir well until hot and thickened. Pour over waffles or mashed potatoes.

RICE PILAF TURKEY STUFFING

½ c. pine nuts or slivered almonds

½ c. butter

1 c. finely chopped onion

3 c. uncooked long-grain rice

¼ tsp. cinnamon

½ c. chopped parsley or celery

¼ tsp. allspice

2 tsp. salt

¼ tsp. pepper

5 c. chicken broth

Toast nuts in 350-degree oven for 5 minutes. In a wide frying pan, heat butter and sauté onion for about 5 minutes. Add rice and cook, stirring, over medium heat for 4 minutes. Blend in cinnamon, parsley, allspice, salt, pepper, and toasted nuts.

In another pan, boil broth and pour over rice mixture; stir lightly. Cover and reduce heat to low. Simmer until moisture is absorbed (about 25 minutes).

EASY CHICKEN DIJON

2 16-oz. pkgs. broccoli spears, cooked

2 c. diced cooked chicken

1 10.75-oz. can cream of chicken soup

⅔ c. mayonnaise

½ c. grated cheese (optional)

1 tsp. lemon juice

¼ tsp. curry powder

1 4-oz. can mushrooms

1 c. croutons, cereal, or bread crumbs for topping

Place broccoli spears in a greased casserole dish, layering with pieces of chicken. Combine remaining ingredients except for croutons, cereal, or bread crumbs; mix well. Pour sauce over broccoli and chicken; sprinkle with topping. Bake at 350 degrees for 30–45 minutes or until bubbly.

Early to bed and early to rise, makes a man healthy, wealthy, and wise.
— *Benjamin Franklin*

FISH À LA WORCESTER

1½ lb. halibut, flounder, or cod fillets
3½ tsp. Worcestershire sauce, divided
½ c. melted margarine
½ c. soft bread crumbs
¼ c. finely minced onion

¼ c. finely minced green pepper
¼ c. finely minced red pepper
¼ tsp. salt
¼ tsp. minced garlic
Parsley sprigs

Sauce:

2 Tbsp. melted butter
1 tsp. Worcestershire sauce
1 tsp. lemon juice
½ c. sour cream

¼ c. grated Cheddar cheese
Salt and pepper to taste
Paprika to top

Fish: Preheat broiler to 500 degrees. Wash fish and place on ungreased pan. Brush fillets with ½ tsp. Worcestershire sauce. Set aside. In small bowl combine margarine, crumbs, onion, green and red peppers, salt, garlic, and remaining Worcestershire sauce. Spread mixture over fish.

Broil 6 inches from heat until fish "flakes" easily when tested with a fork. Arrange fish on heated platter; top with sauce and garnish with parsley. Serves 4.

Sauce: Blend melted butter with Worcestershire sauce, lemon juice, sour cream, and grated cheese in a small saucepan. Stir continually until sauce is smooth and thick. Add salt and pepper to taste; sprinkle with paprika.

Note from Bev

Sauce is great on halibut steaks, flounder, perch, and fillets of white fish.

BAKED SHAD

Place 3 or 4 slices of bacon in a roaster. Cut the shad in half, length-wise, and lay in roaster with skin side down. Dot with butter and salt generously. Spread evenly with 2 Tbsp. milk. Bake for 45 minutes at 350 degrees. Top with dressing (below).

Dressing:
1 c. whole milk, warmed

1 level tsp. flour, moistened
with a bit of water

Butter, pepper, and salt to taste

Simmer dressing ingredients together and spread on meat.

Note from Bev
My dad recalls shad as being a popular ``catch`` with our friends in Quarryville, Pa. (Shad fish travel in large schools in the Susquehanna River.) Be careful when eating this baked fish, akin to herring, as there are often small bones.

CHICKEN AND BROCCOLI QUICHE

3 Tbsp. butter

1 small onion, chopped

3 Tbsp. flour

1¼ c. milk

3 eggs, beaten

1 unbaked pie shell

¾ c. cubed cooked chicken

¾ c. chopped cooked broccoli

Dash of basil

Salt

Grated cheese

Sauté onions in butter until transparent. Stir in flour until thick; add milk and blend. Add eggs and stir but do not cook. Pour mixture into unbaked pie shell; add chicken, broccoli, a dash of basil, and salt to taste. Top with grated cheese. Bake at 350 degrees for 40 minutes. Serve hot.

Note from Bev
This dish is really satisfying and so delicious!

TURKEY CASSEROLE

1½ c. milk
1 10.75-oz. can cream of
mushroom soup
3 eggs, beaten
2¼ c. uncooked fine egg
noodles

2–2½ c. cooked, cubed turkey
1 c. shredded sharp American
cheese
¼ c. chopped green pepper
2 Tbsp. chopped pimiento
⅓ c. grated Parmesan cheese

Blend milk into soup. Stir in remaining ingredients except Parmesan cheese. Pour into shallow baking dish; top with Parmesan cheese. Bake at 350 degrees for 30 minutes or until a knife inserted in center comes out clean.

Prove all things; hold fast that which is good. Abstain from all appearance of evil. —I THESSALONIANS 5:21–22

CHICKEN MUSHROOM BAKE

⅓ c. flour
1 tsp. salt
½ tsp. pepper
1 tsp. paprika
2–3 c. cubed chicken
⅓ c. butter

1 10.75-oz. can cream of
mushroom soup
1 c. sour cream
½ c. sliced mushrooms
⅔ c. shredded Cheddar cheese

Combine flour, salt, pepper, and paprika in a paper bag. Shake chicken in flour mixture. Melt butter in large skillet and brown chicken on all sides. Place in a 9×13 baking dish. Combine soup, sour cream, and mushrooms; pour over chicken. Bake at 350 degrees for 1 hour or until chicken is tender. Sprinkle with cheese and return to oven until cheese is melted.

TUNA MELTS

3 or 4 Tbsp. light olive oil

6-oz. can of tuna

¼ large white onion, chopped

¼ tsp. salt (or to taste)

10 oz. Swiss cheese

4 pieces bread, buttered on one side

Garlic granules or garlic powder (optional)

Put approximately 1 Tbsp. olive oil in a small cast-iron frying pan; add the tuna, chopped onion, and salt. Cook on medium-low heat until tuna is lightly browned and onion is tender.

Thinly slice the cheese, cutting enough slices to cover each piece of bread. Heat large cast-iron frying pan for 10 to 15 seconds, then turn the heat off. Put 2 or 3 Tbsp. oil in the pan. Sprinkle some garlic granules on the buttered side of 2 pieces of the bread, then put them buttered side down in the oil. Place cheese slices on each, then put half of hot tuna mixture on each slice of bread. Place remaining cheese slices over the top of the hot tuna mixture, then cover with the remaining pieces of bread, buttered side up. Sprinkle garlic granules on the bread. Cover the pan and fry on medium heat for approximately 3–5 minutes on the first side, or until golden brown. Turn sandwiches and fry on the second side for 1–2 minutes, or until golden brown. (Second side gets brown much quicker because the pan is already hot.) Makes 2 tuna melts.

Note: These instructions are for a gas stove; the heating times may vary a bit for an electric one.

GRANDMOTHER BUCHWALTER'S MEAT LOAF

1 lb. lean ground beef

1 tsp. salt

1 c. bread crumbs

1 c. milk

1 egg, beaten

Finely chopped onions to taste

Mix all ingredients thoroughly; place in loaf pan. Bake at 350 degrees for 1 hour.

Vegetables and Side Dishes

A careful look at her pantry—each shelf lined with freshly canned vegetables, fruit, and preserves—and she spied parsley and ground pepper needed for her scalloped potatoes recipe, as well as some coconut and nutmeg for the coconut squash dish. Her eyes caught sight of a row of tall glass jars of asparagus and she decided, then and there, to add creamed asparagus to her menu for Saturday night. She also planned to make Mary's lime salad, a recipe from their teen years, which called for marshmallows and cream cheese, two ingredients she had written on her list. She would make sure she squeezed in a quick trip to the grocery store sometime today for those items.

—from *October Song*

(Note: See SCALLOPED POTATOES WITH CHEESE SAUCE on page 96.)

AMISH BROCCOLI DISH

2 10-oz. bags frozen chopped
  broccoli
4 oz. Velveeta cheese
1 10.75-oz. can cream of
  mushroom soup

½ tsp. salt
2 c. crushed croutons
5 Tbsp. melted butter

Boil and drain broccoli. Cream together cheese and cream of mushroom soup; mix in broccoli and salt. Place in greased 3-qt. casserole dish. Mix croutons and melted butter together and pour evenly on top of casserole. Bake at 350 degrees for 20 minutes.

Note from Bev

Another wonderful-good Amish recipe—the ultimate way to describe it.

JANE'S CELERY CASSEROLE

4 c. diced celery
¼ c. slivered almonds
½ c. sliced water chestnuts
5 Tbsp. butter, divided
3 Tbsp. flour

1 c. chicken broth
¾ c. half-and-half cream
½ c. canned mushrooms
½ c. grated Parmesan cheese
½ c. dry bread crumbs

Boil celery for 5 minutes; celery should still be crisp. Drain and place into a greased 1.5-qt. baking dish with almonds and water chestnuts. Melt 3 Tbsp. butter. Add flour; stir and cook for a few minutes over low heat. Slowly stir in broth with half-and-half. Simmer over low heat for 5 minutes. Add mushrooms to sauce, then pour over celery. Sprinkle with Parmesan cheese and dot with remaining 2 Tbsp. of butter. Finish with bread crumbs. Bake at 350 degrees until bubbly, approximately 30 minutes.

SWEET POTATOES DELUXE

2 c. cooked, mashed sweet potatoes	Scant pinch of pepper
3 Tbsp. butter or margarine	1 egg, beaten
½ tsp. salt	Corn flakes cereal
	Olive oil

To mashed sweet potatoes, add butter, salt, pepper, and egg; mix well. Shape into small balls and roll in crushed corn flakes. Fry sweet potato balls in olive oil and drain. If sweet potatoes become too dry before shaping into balls, simply add hot milk to moisten.

ASPARAGUS CASSEROLE

2 8-oz. cans or 1 15.5-oz. can asparagus	1 10.75-oz. can cream of chicken soup
4 hard-boiled eggs, sliced	Crumble of potato chips

In a greased 2-qt. casserole dish, place asparagus, eggs, and cream of chicken soup. Top with crumbled chips. Bake at 350 degrees for 45 minutes.

Put salt water on cabbage or spinach to drive out bugs or worms.

GREEN BEANS THE PENNSYLVANIA DUTCH WAY

Cook green beans until just tender to fork. In a small frying pan, put 2 or 3 Tbsp. of flour; stir constantly. When flour is light brown, stir in ¼ c. butter and ½ c. whole milk. Pour over beans and serve.

Note from Bev

I never tire of this delicious way to cook and serve green beans. It's one of those tried and true dishes you'll see at oodles of gatherings in and around Lancaster County.

BEETS

1 32-oz. can beets (1 qt.)   ³/₄ tsp. salt (or to taste)
2 Tbsp. butter   ¹/₂ c. sugar
2 rounded Tbsp. flour   Juice of 1 orange

Drain beets, reserving juice. Set aside. Melt butter in saucepan; mix in flour, salt, and sugar. Add the juice of the orange, then add reserved beet juice very gradually. Simmer until thickened. Add beets last. Serve.

Note from Bev

Incredibly delicious, and the ideal side for a luncheon or a lighter meal.

*Everything in life only lasts
for a season.*

SPINACH CASSEROLE

3 Tbsp. butter   ¹/₄ tsp. pepper
3 Tbsp. chopped onion   ¹/₄ tsp. nutmeg
1 lb. mushrooms, finely   2 c. half-and-half cream
   chopped   3 10-oz. pkgs. frozen spinach,
3 Tbsp. flour   thawed
2 tsp. salt   ¹/₄ c. grated Swiss cheese

Sauté onions and mushrooms in butter until transparent. Blend in flour, salt, pepper, and nutmeg. Gradually add in the half-and-half and stir until thick. In a well-buttered baking dish, spread half the uncooked spinach. Cover with half of the mushroom sauce. Repeat layers. Bake at 350 degrees for 15 minutes. Sprinkle the cheese on top and return to oven until cheese is melted.

Baked Beans

1 lb. dry pinto beans
½ tsp. prepared mustard
½ onion, diced
1 14-oz. bottle catsup

⅛ c. brown sugar
½ lb. smoked meat, chopped
¼ tsp. pepper
3 Tbsp. vinegar

Cook beans in Dutch oven until soft. Add the remaining ingredients, including smoked meat. Bake, covered, at 350 degrees for one hour.

Scalloped Potatoes With Cheese Sauce

3 Tbsp. mild Cheddar cheese, grated
3 Tbsp. butter or margarine
1 tsp. salt
2 Tbsp. flour
2½ c. whole milk
6 large potatoes

2 Tbsp. minced white onion
1 c. diced cooked ham or 1 c. fried bacon pieces for flavor
Additional butter
Pepper to taste
1 tsp. dried parsley

Melt cheese and butter in a saucepan on low heat. When melted, add salt and flour. Continue cooking until smooth. Add milk gradually, stirring until well blended. Cook until thickened.

Pare and thinly slice potatoes. In a greased casserole dish, make a layer of potatoes and sprinkle with part of the minced onion and part of the diced ham or bacon pieces. Repeat layers until all ingredients are used.

Pour the melted cheese and butter mixture over the layers. Dot with butter; sprinkle with pepper and dried parsley. Bake, covered, for one hour at 375 degrees. Uncover and continue baking for approximately 10–15 minutes or until top layer forms a brown crust.

Let your speech be alway with grace, seasoned with salt.

—COLOSSIANS 4:6

DRIED CORN CASSEROLE

½ c. milk

2 eggs, beaten

1 c. dried sweet corn, previously soaked in 1 c. hot milk (I use Cope's toasted dried sweet corn)

2 Tbsp. butter

2 Tbsp. sugar

1 tsp. salt

Dash of pepper

Mix all ingredients together; place in a buttered baking dish. Bake at 375 degrees for 40 minutes.

Note from Bev

Dried corn is unique to Lancaster County and has a much different flavor than fresh corn, canned, or frozen. Pennsylvania Dutch cooks toast the corn in woodstoves. The process caramelizes the natural sugars, giving it a slightly nutty flavor. I remember enjoying this casserole from early childhood when Mother served it at Thanksgiving and Christmas Day dinners. My Swedish husband, however, has been known to season dried corn with catsup! An interesting and tasty twist, to say the least.

SCALLOPED ASPARAGUS

3 c. fresh asparagus, trimmed, tips reserved

4 hard-boiled eggs, chopped

¼ c. flour

1 c. milk

¼ c. butter

½ c. grated cheese

1 c. bread crumbs

Put half of asparagus in greased casserole dish; place eggs on top. Combine flour, milk, and butter; pour onto asparagus and eggs. Add grated cheese and bread crumbs. Dress with asparagus tips. Brown at 425 degrees for 20 minutes.

BAKED POTATOES

Prepare 1 baked potato per person.

Poke skin of baking potatoes (Idaho, red potatoes, etc.) with fork 4 times and coat with olive oil; sprinkle with salt. Place on a cookie sheet or put foil on the rack below the potatoes, as the oil may drip just a bit. Bake on center rack at 375 degrees for 1 hour (longer for larger potatoes). When done, potato should be fairly soft when jabbed with a fork. After potatoes are baked, allow to sit a couple minutes before cutting open. Then, being careful not to burn your fingers, quickly and gently push all around, or squeeze the potato to soften the inside. Cut open and serve with butter, sour cream, and salt.

Optional: Serve with snipped chives and grated cheese.

Home is home,
be it never so homely.
—Old English Proverb

AMANDA'S TOMATO ZUCCHINI CASSEROLE

1 lb. zucchini	1½ tsp. salt
2 medium onions, thinly sliced	¼ tsp. black pepper
5 medium tomatoes, sliced	1 c. grated cheese
¾ c. fine dry bread crumbs	

Wash but do not peel zucchini. Cut into ⅛-inch slices, then cook in boiling salted water for 5 minutes and drain. In a buttered casserole dish, arrange alternate layers of zucchini, onions, tomatoes, bread crumbs, and seasoning. Top with tomato slices. Cover and bake at 400 degrees for 1 hour. Remove cover and sprinkle with cheese. Return to oven until cheese is melted.

Note from Bev

Mm-m, good!

Delicious Baked Sweet Potatoes

Bake sweet potatoes in oven at 375 degrees for 45–60 minutes (depending on size of potato). Place foil on rack underneath the potatoes, as juices may ooze during baking time. Bake until soft when jabbed with fork. Cut open and mash with fork. Cover with butter and salt, then add brown sugar to taste.

Susanna's Creamy Cabbage

4 c. shredded cabbage

½ c. water

2 Tbsp. flour

1 c. milk

1 tsp. salt

⅛ tsp. pepper

Cook cabbage in water for 5 minutes. Sprinkle flour over cabbage; mix well. Add remaining ingredients and cook, stirring occasionally, until thickened.

Baked Corn

8 Tbsp. butter

7–8 cups frozen corn, thawed (excellent if frozen fresh)

2 Tbsp. sugar

2 tsp. salt (rounded)

¼ tsp. ground black pepper

24 saltine crackers, crushed

4 eggs

2 c. milk

Melt butter in large saucepan. Add corn, sugar, salt, and pepper; heat through. Add crushed crackers. Beat eggs and milk together and add to corn mixture; heat to almost boiling. Pour into buttered 9×13 glass baking dish. Bake at 350 degrees for 50 minutes or until lightly browned.

Add a little milk to water in which cauliflower is cooking; the cauliflower will remain attractively white.

BROWNED BUTTER

Melt 1 regular stick of real butter (not unsalted) in a watched skillet until brown. Stir with dry fork, as water will make the butter "spritz" (spit). Drizzle browned butter over corn, carrots, peas, lima beans, green beans, mashed potatoes, noodles, or stewed crackers. May also be spread over bread crumbs for stuffing.

Note from Bev

Browned butter can be used on almost any vegetable imaginable and is uniquely Pennsylvania Dutch. Very tasty and makes for a pretty presentation.

MASHED POTATOES

5 lb. potatoes, peeled and
  quartered
3 tsp. salt, divided
3 Tbsp. butter

2 c. milk, heated
¼ c. butter, browned
Sour cream and/or cream
  cheese (optional)

In large saucepan, nearly cover potatoes with water. Add 1 tsp. salt to the water and bring to a boil, then simmer until potatoes are soft enough to mash easily. Pour off all water. Mash well, then add 3 Tbsp. butter and mash. Add remaining salt and milk, ½ cup at a time, mashing well after each addition. Pour hot browned butter over the top. Serve immediately with gravy.

To reheat leftovers:
(1) Add a bit of sour cream and/or cream cheese and milk.
(2) Make potato cakes by patting refrigerated mashed potatoes into a small flat "cake" and frying on both sides until dark golden brown. Serve with "eggs over light."

"A Friend Indeed" (excerpt)
–Dedicated to the memory of Edna Keller

A cook par excellence—few could compare,
Though I'm sure there are some who would try.
Edna's feasts were like a country fair,
When you thought you were finished,
She'd serve you the pie!
She was a "Martha"—extremely hospitable,
Anyone knows who has sat at her table!
But a "Mary" she was in her heart,
As she chose the better part.
Because she loved God's Holy Word,
Edna is now forever with the Lord.
She was loving and giving,
In the true sense of the word.
Ever cheerful, diligent, and faithful . . .
Living a life that wholly pleased our Lord
—Jane Buchwalter Jones

Note from Bev

My mother wrote this poem on the day of Edna's heavenly homegoing. She was "Aunt Edna" to my sister and me for as long as I can remember. Aunt Edna made the best mashed potatoes, and I was always eager to help her by licking off the beaters when we were invited for Sunday dinner.

MARBLE MASHED POTATOES

2 lb. sweet potatoes, peeled and chunked

8 oz. cream cheese, divided

2 lb. white potatoes, peeled and chunked

Cook potatoes in separate pots until soft enough to mash. Drain, saving ¾ c. cooking water from each potato pot. Mash potatoes and sweet potatoes, adding 4 ounces cream cheese to each. Add cooking water, salt, and pepper to taste. Spoon potatoes, alternating each kind, into shallow 2½-quart microwave-safe dish. Lightly mix with tip of fork. Either bake at 350 degrees, covered, for 40 minutes to 1 hour, or microwave on high for 8 minutes. Potatoes can be refrigerated up to 2 days.

Let nothing be done through strife or vainglory; but in lowliness of mind let each esteem other better than themselves.

–PHILIPPIANS 2:3

CORN PUDDING

1 c. fresh or frozen corn

2 Tbsp. sugar

2 c. milk

1 Tbsp. flour

2–4 eggs, slightly beaten

Butter and salt to taste

Soak corn in milk for 1 hour. Mix in the remaining ingredients. Bake in moderate oven—350 degrees—for 45 minutes or until a table knife inserted near the center of the pudding comes out clean.

Note: Omit flour or add more eggs if desired.

GRANDMA FISHER'S OYSTER FILLING

2 12-oz. jars oysters,
  undrained
3 c. milk
¾ tsp. salt

Dash pepper
4 c. flat 6-sided oyster
  crackers
½ c. browned butter

Place oysters with their juice, milk, salt, and pepper in a saucepan. Heat just to boiling, then immediately remove from heat. Butter a 4-qt. (covered) baking dish. Layer oyster crackers and oyster/milk mixture. Crackers will float, so gently push them into the milk, distributing oysters as evenly as possible. Bake, covered, at 325 degrees for 1 hour. Drizzle with browned butter before serving.

A pint's a pound the world around.

STEWED CRACKERS

30 saltine crackers
2¼ c. scalded milk

¼ c. butter, browned

Place saltine crackers in an ungreased 1½-pt. covered baking dish. Pour scalded milk on top of crackers, gently pressing them into milk. Cover and let sit for 10 minutes or put in the oven at 300 degrees for 30 minutes to keep warm. Pour browned butter on top, cutting down through mixture so the browned butter gets mixed through. Makes 4 servings.

NOODLES AND BUTTER

Cook 16 oz. noodles in water until soft; drain. Melt ¼ c. of butter in frying pan until slightly brown. Add noodles and cut up fresh parsley. Mix and serve.

Note from Bev

My sister, Barbara, and I often asked for seconds of this mouth-watering dish when we were girls.

Sour Cream Salmon Mold

1 Tbsp. unflavored gelatin	2 tsp. lemon juice
1/2 c. cold water	1/4 tsp. dried dillweed
1 envelope sour cream sauce mix	1 16-oz. can salmon
	1/2 c. diced celery
1/2 c. mayonnaise	Carrot curls or tomato slices

Soften gelatin in cold water, stirring over boiling water until gelatin dissolves; cool. Prepare sour cream sauce according to package directions. Blend in mayonnaise, lemon juice, and dillweed; gradually stir in gelatin. Drain salmon, discarding skin and large bones. Fold salmon and celery into sour cream mixture; turn into a 3-cup mold. Chill until set—4 to 5 hours. Unmold; then garnish with carrot curls or tomato slices. Serves 4.

Farmer's Rice

1 1/2 c. flour	1/2 c. sugar
1 small egg	1 tsp. vanilla
3 1/2 c. milk	Cinnamon (optional)

Add egg to flour. Mix together and form small rivels by rubbing the mixture between your hands. Stir rivels into almost boiling milk. Boil 5 minutes, stirring constantly. Add sugar and vanilla plus cinnamon if desired.

Note from Bev

An inexpensive dish to make, but it is filling and "sticks to the bones." Farmers' wives used this recipe to stretch their food budget, especially during the Depression, I'm told.

Desserts

Leah and Sadie had dressed for bed rather quickly, accompanied by their usual comments, speaking in quiet tones of the ordinary events of the day, of having especially enjoyed Mamma's supper of barbecued chicken, scalloped potatoes with cheese sauce, fried cucumbers, lima beans, and lemon bars with homemade ice cream for dessert.

—from *The Betrayal*

(Note: see LEMON BARS on page 107.)

LEMON BARS

½ c. butter

1 c. flour

½ c. pecans, chopped

1 c. powdered sugar

8 oz. cream cheese, softened

1¾ c. whipped cream, divided

2 small boxes instant lemon
   pudding mix

3 c. milk

Nuts, optional

Melt butter; mix with flour and pecans. Press into a 9×13 pan. Bake at 350 degrees for 15 minutes. Cool.

Mix together powdered sugar, cream cheese, and 1 c. whipped cream; spread over cooled crust. Blend lemon pudding mix and milk until thick; spread over the cream cheese layer.

Spread remaining whipped cream over mixture. Nuts can be sprinkled on top if desired. Cover and refrigerate. Cut into bars when chilled.

ANGELS' SALAD

1 20-oz. can pineapple

1 large can white cherries

¼ lb. small marshmallows

¼ lb. slivered almonds

2 c. whipped cream

1 c. milk

1 tsp. cornstarch

1 egg, beaten

2 Tbsp. vinegar

Combine all ingredients except for vinegar in saucepan; cook. Remove from heat; stir in vinegar. Cool. Chill in refrigerator for 2–4 hours before serving.

Note from Bev

Sweets for the sweet . . . from Grandma Ada's wooden recipe box to you!

We came unto the land whither thou sentest us, and surely it floweth with milk and honey; and this is the fruit of it.

—NUMBERS 13:27

FROSTED CAROB BROWNIES

Brownies:

1¼ Tbsp. butter

⅔ c. light oil

¾ c. carob powder, divided (sifted after measuring)

2 c. raw sugar (sifted before measuring)

5 eggs

2½ tsp. vanilla

1 c. unbleached flour (sifted after measuring)

Icing:

¾ c. creamy peanut butter

6 Tbsp. carob powder, sifted

½ c. honey

5–6 Tbsp. milk

Brownies: Spray saucepan with olive oil cooking spray, then melt butter. Add oil and ¼ c. carob powder; heat only until mixed and barely at a boil. Mix in sugar. Beat eggs slightly; add eggs and vanilla to mixture in saucepan; mix just until smooth. Mix in flour and remaining carob powder. Bake in a greased and floured 9×13 cake pan at 325 degrees for 30 minutes if glass pan, 350 degrees for 30 minutes if metal pan. Ice brownies immediately after removing from oven.

Icing: Mix peanut butter, carob powder, and honey together. Gradually add milk; mix well. Immediately after spreading icing on brownies, before icing sets, swirls may be added with the tip of a smooth table knife.

Pretzels are often served with ice cream.

FRUITY DESSERT

Mash ½ c. each of strawberries, raspberries, and sliced peaches. Cut ½ c. marshmallows into small pieces and add to fruit. Beat 1 c. cream until stiff; mix together with fruit and marshmallows. Sweeten to taste.

CHOCOLATE CRUNCH SURPRISE

1 c. sugar
1 c. light corn syrup
1 c. peanut butter
6 cups Rice Krispies
½ c. peanuts

1 6-oz. pkg. semisweet choco-
    late chips
1 6-oz. pkg. butterscotch
    morsels

Mix together sugar and light corn syrup; bring to a boil in a 3-qt. saucepan. Remove from heat; blend in the peanut butter, Rice Krispies, and peanuts. Press into a buttered 9×13 pan. Melt chocolate chips and butterscotch morsels over very hot (but not boiling) water. Spread over top of cereal mixture. Chill for 5 minutes or until top is firm. Cut into squares.

Two heads are better than one.

BERRY TAPIOCA

Crush 2 c. fresh berries and sweeten to taste. Set aside. Combine 5 Tbsp. minute tapioca, ½ c. sugar, ¼ tsp. salt, and 2 c. water in top of a double boiler. Place over rapidly boiling water, bring to scalding point and cook about 5 minutes, stirring frequently. Remove from heat. Add berries, 1 Tbsp. lemon juice, and 1 tsp. butter. Chill. Serve with whipped cream and whole berries.

CREAM PUFFS

Puffs:

1 c. water	1 c. flour
2 pinches of salt	3 eggs
½ c. shortening	

Creamed filling:

¼ c. flour	1½ c. scalded whole milk
⅔ c. sugar	2 tsp. vanilla
¼ tsp. salt	1 c. heavy cream, whipped (or
2 eggs, beaten	whipped topping)

Puffs: Bring water to a boil; add shortening and salt. Stir until the mixture returns to a boil. Add all the flour at once. Stir heartily until the mixture pulls away from the side of the pan. Add one unbeaten egg at a time, thoroughly beating it in. Shape into round or oblong forms on an ungreased baking sheet, using 1 Tbsp. of the mixture for each one.

Bake at 450 degrees for 20 minutes. Reduce oven heat to 350 degrees and bake 20 minutes longer. Remove puffs from baking sheet; cool. When completely cooled, slit one side and fill with whipped cream or creamed filling.

Creamed filling: In the top of a double boiler, mix the flour, sugar, and salt. Stir in well-beaten eggs. Add scalded whole milk and blend thoroughly. Cook over boiling water, stirring constantly, for 4–5 minutes. Do *not* allow mixture to stick to bottom. Continue to cook at a medium heat for another 5 minutes, stirring less often. Cool in refrigerator. When chilled, add vanilla and fold in whipped cream.

 Watermelon is tasty with salt.

Blessed is every one that feareth the Lord: that walketh in his ways. For thou shalt eat the labour of thine hands: happy shalt thou be, and it shall be well with thee. Thy wife shall be as a fruitful vine by the sides of thine house: thy children like olive plants round about thy table. —PSALM 128:1–3

RHUBARB SAUCE

3 c. diced rhubarb
1½ c. sugar (raw is fine)
2 Tbsp. cornstarch
⅛ tsp. salt
Juice of 1 orange

Boil all ingredients together until mixture is thickened and rhubarb is cooked.

Note from Bev

Delicious over vanilla ice cream!

GRANDMA'S APPLE CRISPETT

1 qt. peeled and sliced apples
½ c. water
¾ c. sugar
¾ c. brown sugar
1 c. flour
5 Tbsp. butter

Place apples in shallow baking dish; pour water over apples. Mix together remaining ingredients to make crust; sprinkle over apples and water. Do not stir together. Bake at 350 degrees for 45 minutes. When cool, cut in squares and serve with ice cream or whipped cream.

The best mirror is an old friend.
—German Proverb

Many hands make light work.

MOTHER'S CHERRY COBBLER

2 c. sour cherries	1 tsp. baking powder
½ c. honey	¼ tsp. salt
2 Tbsp. flour or tapioca	1 Tbsp. honey
½ c. fruit juice (orange or apple)	2 Tbsp. butter
1 c. flour	6 Tbsp. milk

Mix cherries, honey, flour or tapioca, and fruit juice together and let stand 5 minutes. Pour into deep 10×16 baking dish.

Mix flour, baking powder, salt, and honey. Cut in the butter with pastry blender or fork. Add milk and mix until a soft dough is formed. Shape dough with hands (dust mixture and hands with flour first) until it fits over the cherries. Make slits in the dough to permit steam to escape.

Bake at 375 degrees for 30 minutes. Serve plain or with whipped cream, whipped topping, or ice cream.

Note from Bev

My mother and her whole family often picked cherries "on the halves" at her grandfather's farm in Strasburg. But the "cherry-seeding party," especially, was the most memorable. The red juice stained her fingers and nails, and ran down her elbows. (Lemon juice and soapy water removed the stains.) This cobbler recipe is one of my mother's outstanding desserts. It's sure to bring smiles and requests for seconds.

Coconut Squares

½ c. butter	2 Tbsp. flour
1½ c. brown sugar, divided	¼ tsp. salt
1 c. flour	½ tsp. baking powder
2 eggs, beaten	1½ c. coconut flakes
1 tsp. vanilla	1 c. walnuts, chopped

Cream together butter and ½ c. brown sugar. Add 1 c. flour and work into crumbs with hands. Bake in a very slow oven—250 degrees—for 10 minutes or until done.

Meanwhile, add remaining brown sugar and vanilla to beaten eggs. Sift 2 Tbsp. flour and blend with salt and baking powder. Mix dry ingredients with egg and sugar mixture. Blend in coconut flakes and chopped walnuts. When crust is finished baking, pour mixture over the top. Return pan to oven and continue baking for an additional 25 minutes.

Favor is deceitful, and beauty is vain: but a woman that feareth the Lord, she shall be praised. —PROVERBS 31:30

Chocolate-Covered Strawberries

Melt semisweet chocolate. Hold strawberry by the stem and dip in chocolate. After the bottom is set, the top (including the stem) may be dipped in melted white chocolate—or the entire strawberry may be dipped in white chocolate.

Decorate with little swirls or patterns by using the opposite color chocolate or white chocolate tinted with food coloring.

Note from Bev

Delicious and elegant.

APPLE BETTY

Apple Betty:

7 c. tart baking apples
(approximately 9 apples),
peeled, cored, sliced, and
cut into small pieces

¼ c. raw or granulated sugar

1½ c. (packed) brown sugar

1 Tbsp. cinnamon

⅛ tsp. salt

5 Tbsp. butter

3 c. tiny bread cubes (3–4
pieces of white bread, cut in
⅛" slivers, then cut the
opposite way)

¼ c. lemon juice

¼ c. boiling water

Icing:

½ c. butter, softened

2 tsp. vanilla

1¾ c. confectioners' sugar,
sifted (measure before
sifting)

1 tsp. milk

Apple Betty: Mix apple pieces with ¼ c. sugar; set aside. Mix brown sugar, cinnamon, and salt; set aside. (Note: after mixing, spoon brown sugar mixture lightly into measuring cup to measure.)

In saucepan, melt butter; add bread cubes and mix well. Set aside 1 c. of the buttered bread cubes; spread remaining bread cubes in the bottom of a buttered glass 9×9 baking dish. Arrange 3 c. of the sugared apples on top of the bread cubes; sprinkle with ¾ c. of the loosely spooned brown sugar mixture. Spread ½ c. of the remaining buttered bread cubes over the brown sugar mixture. Layer the rest of the apples over bread cubes; sprinkle with all but ½ c. of the loosely spooned brown sugar mixture. Mix remaining brown sugar mixture with the remaining bread cubes and place on the top.

Mix lemon juice and boiling water. With a large spoon, sprinkle over the whole top. Bake dessert at 350 degrees for 1 hour. After removing from oven, allow to cool for 10–15 minutes. Add icing while still warm but not hot.

Icing: Cream butter with vanilla. Gradually add the sifted confectioners' sugar, beating until fluffy after each addition. Add the milk, beating until fluffy. Place spoonfuls on warm (but not hot) apple betty, spreading gently with a smooth table knife. (A spoon tends to create a bit of suction and would bring up some of the crumbs into the icing quicker than a smooth knife.)

Note from Bev

Absolutely tasty served with milk or light cream.

APPLE CRISP

3 lbs. baking apples (a bit tart)	2 c. flour
	3 c. brown sugar
1 Tbsp. (rounded) granulated sugar	1 Tbsp. cinnamon
	1 c. butter, softened
2/3 c. water	1/2 c. chopped pecans

Peel and slice apples; arrange in a buttered 9×13 glass pan. Lightly sprinkle with sugar; top with water.

Mix flour, brown sugar, and cinnamon in a bowl. Cut in butter with a pastry knife. Sprinkle crumbs over apples; sprinkle chopped pecans over the top. Bake at 375 degrees for approximately 45 minutes or until browned and bubbly.

Note from Bev

Serve hot with vanilla ice cream and hot tea or coffee.

PEACH DELIGHT

5–6 fresh peaches	4 vanilla wafers

Pit and slice peaches. Put vanilla wafers in a paper bag and crush with rolling pin. Put crumbs on piece of waxed paper; roll peaches in crumbs till peaches are covered. Serve in dessert dishes with whipped cream.

NUT BARS

¾ lb. dates, chopped   ¼ tsp. salt

1 c. nutmeats, chopped   3 eggs, beaten

¾ c. oats   1 c. brown sugar

¼ c. flour   Granulated sugar

1 tsp. baking powder

Mix together dates, nutmeats, oats, flour, baking powder, and salt. Add brown sugar to beaten eggs; stir into flour mixture. Pour into greased 9×11 baking dish. Bake at 350 degrees for 25–30 minutes. When cool, cut into bars. Roll in granulated sugar.

A little house well filled, a little field well tilled, and a little wife well willed, are great riches.
—Benjamin Franklin

Puddings and Custards

Mary Ruth volunteered quickly when Mamma asked for someone to take one of two batches of graham-cracker pudding over to the Peacheys' the Thursday following Elias's funeral. Glad for an excuse to clear her head in the chilly air, she headed across the cornfield to the neighbors', low in spirit and dressed in the black garb of a mourner. Spying Adah's younger sister driving into the lane, she hurried to deliver the pudding to Miriam, then returned to help Dorcas unhitch the horse from the carriage.

—from *The Sacrifice*

(Note: See GRAHAM CRACKER PUDDING on page 119.)

GRAHAM CRACKER PUDDING

1 14-oz. can sweetened condensed milk, chilled, plus
enough regular milk to total
3 c.

¾ tsp. vanilla

1 large box instant vanilla
pudding mix (or ¾ c. bulk
instant vanilla pudding mix)

3 Tbsp. butter

1 c. crushed graham crackers,
divided

2 c. heavy whipping cream,
divided

Strawberries or blueberries,
optional

Mix cold milk (including sweetened condensed milk) and vanilla together. Gradually add pudding mix, stirring continually for 2 minutes; put in refrigerator.

Melt butter in saucepan and add crushed graham crackers. Stir over medium heat until lightly browned. Remove from heat.

Beat 1 c. heavy whipping cream until peaks form; fold together with ½ c. browned graham cracker crumbs and cooled pudding mixture. Pour into a 2-qt. serving dish. Reserving 1 Tbsp. crumbs, sprinkle remaining browned graham cracker crumbs over the pudding mixture; refrigerate.

Before serving, beat the remaining 1 c. of whipping cream and spread over the chilled mixture, making peaks with the whipped cream. Sprinkle reserved crumbs over the top to decorate. Serve immediately if possible; refrigerate leftovers.

Optional: Serve with sweetened strawberries or blueberries.

Banana Pudding: Fold 2 sliced bananas into pudding mixture before pouring into serving dish.

*To make eggs beat more quickly, add
a tiny pinch of salt to the whites.*

BUTTERSCOTCH PUDDING

Crust:

1½ c. flour   ⅔ c. pecans, chopped

¾ c. melted butter

Mix these ingredients and press into a 9×13 pan. Bake at 350 degrees for 20 minutes. Cool completely.

Second layer:

1 8-oz. package cream cheese,   1 c. powdered sugar

softened   1½ c. whipped topping

Beat these ingredients until smooth; spread onto cooled crust.

Third layer:

1 large pkg. instant butter-   3 c. milk

scotch pudding

Beat until thick; pour over second layer.

Fourth layer:

Spread additional whipped topping (as much as you wish) over pudding layer. Sprinkle with chopped pecans. Let stand several hours in fridge before serving.

RICE PUDDING

4 c. milk   ¼ tsp. salt

⅓ c. uncooked rice   ¼ tsp. nutmeg

⅓ c. sugar   ¼ tsp. cinnamon

Combine all ingredients; mix well. Spoon mixture into buttered baking dish. Bake at 250 degrees for 2 hours, stirring occasionally while baking.

Optional: add ⅓ c. raisins during the baking process.

CHOCOLATE CREAM PUDDING

2 c. milk

3 Tbsp. cornstarch

$\frac{1}{2}$ c. sugar

3 Tbsp. cocoa

$\frac{1}{4}$ tsp. salt

1 tsp. vanilla

Scald milk by placing in the top of a double boiler and heating until a skin is formed over top of milk. Remove skin. Mix cornstarch, sugar, cocoa, and salt in a bowl. Add a small amount of scalded milk to form smooth paste. Gradually add rest of milk and vanilla. Chill.

DATE PUDDING

Syrup:

3 c. brown sugar

5 c. water

5 Tbsp. butter

Batter:

4 c. flour

1 tsp. salt

8 tsp. baking powder

2 c. brown sugar

2 c. milk

4 c. dates, chopped

4 c. walnuts, chopped

Whipped cream

Syrup: Combine sugar and water. Boil for 2 minutes and add butter. Pour into 2 greased 9×13 inch pans.

Batter: Combine flour, salt, and baking powder. Add sugar and milk; mix well. Fold in dates and walnuts. Pour over syrup in pans; bake at 350 degrees for 40 minutes. To serve, alternate layers of date pudding and whipped cream in a glass dish.

Note from Bev

Makes an attractive dish to serve at Christmastime or other special occasions. Delicious any other time, as well.

Not that we are sufficient of ourselves to think any thing as of ourselves; but our sufficiency is of God.

—2 CORINTHIANS 3:5

BABY PEARL TAPIOCA

2 c. milk
2 rounded Tbsp. pearl tapioca
1/3 c. sugar
1/8 tsp. salt (optional)

1 egg, beaten
Whipped cream or whipped
    topping

Put milk and tapioca in top of double boiler; cook until tapioca is clear. Add sugar and salt. Add a little hot mixture to egg and stir, then mix all together, cooking until slightly thick. Allow to set until cool. Fold in whipped cream or whipped topping to taste.

GRAPE MUSH DESSERT

4 c. water
2 c. pure (100%) grape juice
1 1/2 c. sugar
1 small box raspberry Jell-O
2/3 c. instant Clear Jel*

1 c. water
1/2 tsp. salt
Juice of 2 lemons

Heat first 4 ingredients; stir in Clear Jel, 1 c. water, and salt. Mix in lemon juice. Chill. This makes a large amount!

*Instant Clear Jel can be purchased where canning supplies are available. Tapioca can be substituted if necessary.

Note from Bev

Delicious over Baby Pearl Tapioca.

EGG CUSTARD

4 c. milk   3 Tbsp. sugar

4 or 5 eggs   1 tsp. vanilla

Mix all ingredients together in order given. Bake in lightly greased custard cups at 350 degrees for 15–20 minutes.

PINEAPPLE CUSTARD

Pastry for a single-crust pie   1 c. sugar

1 20-oz. can crushed pine-   2 Tbsp. cornstarch

   apple, drained   15 large marshmallows,

1 c. water   halved

Bake pie shell for 10 minutes; let cool. Boil pineapple, water, sugar, and cornstarch together until thick; pour into pie shell. Top with cut marshmallows. Bake at 350 degrees for 15 minutes or until topping is light brown.

FROZEN CUSTARD

1½ c. sugar   1 Tbsp. vanilla

1 Tbsp. flour   1 small can evaporated milk,

⅓ tsp. salt   chilled and whipped stiff*

3 c. boiling water   Crushed fruit of choice

2 eggs, beaten

Mix sugar, flour, and salt. Add water and boil for three minutes, stirring constantly. Pour mixture over eggs slowly to prevent curdling. Return to heat and cook 2 more minutes. Cool. Add vanilla and fold in whipped evaporated milk; stir in crushed fruit of choice. Place in the freezer. For a smoother texture, whip again after the custard has just begun to freeze.

*Use more or less evaporated milk depending on how thick you want the custard to be.

CRACKER PUDDING

2 eggs, separated
½ c. plus 3 Tbsp. sugar,
   divided
4 c. whole milk
1 c. finely ground cracker
   crumbs (my grandmother
   used Eagle Butter crackers,
   but I substitute Le Petit
   Beurre golden toasted butter biscuits)

½ c. shredded coconut (or
   flakes)
Pinch of salt
1 tsp. vanilla

Beat egg yolks and ½ cup sugar; set aside. Scald milk in top of double boiler, stirring slowly. Gradually add egg yolk mixture to scalded milk, stirring continually. Cook for one full minute; then add cracker crumbs, coconut, and salt. Keep stirring! Once cracker crumbs are soft and the entire mixture is thick, remove from heat and add vanilla. Pour the mixture into a buttered 9×13 baking dish.

Create meringue by beating 3 Tbsp. sugar into stiffly beaten egg whites; spread over top of cracker pudding. Bake at 350 degrees for 30–40 minutes or until meringue is golden brown. Makes 6–8 servings.

Note from Bev

This is a very old, as well as scrumptious, Pennsylvania Dutch recipe. It was commonly served at Plain gatherings in Lancaster County, including our Ranck family reunions. I discovered it recently in my aunt Gladys Buchwalter's recipe notebook from the 1930s, written in her own hand when she was nineteen. In the autumn of that year, she was hired by a Lancaster dentist and his wife—the Paul Herr family—to cook, as well as to care for their young children.

OLD-FASHIONED BREAD PUDDING

4 slices stale bread, buttered
  and cut into small cubes
4 c. whole milk
4 eggs

¼ c. sugar
Pinch of salt
1 Tbsp. vanilla or pinch of
  nutmeg

Place bread cubes in milk and soak until very soft. Heat mixture until almost boiling. Set aside.

Beat eggs until light. Add eggs to sugar, salt, and vanilla or nutmeg. Mix well; stir into bread and milk mixture. Pour into greased medium baking dish and set in a pan of water. Bake at 300 degrees for 45 minutes.

Optional: Add ½ cup raisins to milk-soaked bread cubes for variety.

SNOW PUDDING AND DRESSING

Pudding:

2 c. water
¾ c. sugar
2 Tbsp. cornstarch

1 egg white, beaten until
  frothy
1 tsp. vanilla

Dressing:

½ c. sugar
1 Tbsp. cornstarch
1 big c. milk or water

1 egg yolk, beaten
Vanilla

Pudding: Bring water to boil. Mix sugar and cornstarch together; stir into boiling water. Cook until thickened, stirring constantly. Remove from heat. Beat in egg white and vanilla; chill. Serve cold— the colder the better.

Dressing: Mix sugar and cornstarch with milk or water; bring to a boil and cook until thick, stirring continually. Remove from heat and let cool slightly; stir in beaten egg yolk and a touch of vanilla. Serve over chilled pudding.

Cakes and Frostings

Lydia and Anna Mae got up to clear the table, bringing over an angel food cake for dessert. "Anna Mae baked this just for you, Aunt Sarah," Lydia said.

Anna Mae stood at Sarah's side, close enough to touch. "I want you to have the first piece." The girl grinned, showing her gums slightly.

"How nice of you," Sarah said, holding her plate while Anna Mae cut into the spongy white dessert.

—from *The Redemption of Sarah Cain*

(Note: see GOLDEN ANGEL FOOD CAKE on page 129.)

The ear that heareth the reproof of life abideth among the wise. —PROVERBS 15:31

GOLDEN ANGEL FOOD CAKE

9 eggs, separated, room temperature

1 tsp. vanilla

1 c. sugar,* divided

1 c. flour* (measure before sifting)

1/2 rounded tsp. cream of tartar

In small mixing bowl, beat egg yolks until thick and lemon colored (5 minutes or more, depending on beater). Add vanilla. Mix on low until blended. Gradually add 1/2 c. sugar. Continue to mix on low until blended, then beat 5 minutes more on high. Sprinkle part of the flour over yolk mixture; fold in by hand. Continue until all flour is folded in. Set aside and cover so batter doesn't dry out.

Thoroughly wash and dry beaters. Then, in a large mixing bowl, beat egg whites with cream of tartar on high until soft peaks form. Gradually add remaining 1/2 c. sugar. Beat on high until stiff peaks form. Take some of the egg whites and fold into the yolk mixture to soften. Add yolk mixture to stiff egg whites; fold together.

Gently pour batter into ungreased 10" tube pan with removable sides. Bake on lowest oven rack at 350 degrees for 50–60 minutes. When done, top will spring back when gently touched near the center. Immediately turn upside down until completely cool.

*Raw sugar and unbleached flour work very well.

Optional: Serve with fruit such as strawberries, peaches, or blueberries and whipped cream or milk.

CRUMB CAKE WITH FRESH APPLESAUCE

½ c. flour

¼ c. brown sugar

⅔ c. butter, divided, softened

¼ c. sugar

1 egg

1 c. sour milk or yogurt

1 tsp. baking soda

1 tsp. baking powder

Pinch of salt

2 c. flour

1 tsp. cinnamon

Mix flour, brown sugar, and 2⅔ Tbsp. butter by hand until crumbly; set aside. Cream together remaining ½ c. butter and remaining ingredients except for cinnamon; pour into greased 9×9 cake pan. Sprinkle with crumb mixture and cinnamon. Bake at 350 degrees for approximately 30 minutes or until the cake rises. Serve warm with applesauce.

When there's room in the heart, there's room in the house.

RAISIN CAKE

2 c. hot water

2 c. seedless raisins

3 c. flour

1 tsp. salt

1 tsp. cinnamon

1 tsp. cloves

2 Tbsp. lard

2 c. brown sugar

2 eggs, stirred a bit with fork

1 tsp. baking soda, dissolved
  in a little hot water

Bring water and raisins to a boil. Sift together flour, salt, cinnamon and cloves. In separate bowl, cream together lard and brown sugar. Add the hot water, raisins, and eggs; mix well. Stir in dry ingredients and baking soda. Pour batter into two greased 9-inch round cake pans and bake at 350 degrees for 30 minutes.

CREAM CAKE AND FILLING

Cake:

1 Tbsp. butter	2 c. flour
1 egg	2 heaping Tbsp. baking
1 c. sugar	powder
1 c. sweetened condensed milk	Vanilla extract

Filling:

1 egg, beaten	1 c. milk plus a little extra
1/4 c. flour or cornstarch	1/2 tsp. vanilla

Cake: Cream together the butter and egg. Gradually add the sugar, sweetened condensed milk, flour, baking powder, and vanilla to taste. Pour into two greased 8-inch layer pans. Bake at 350 degrees for 35–40 minutes. Cool. Spread filling between layers and on top of cake.

Filling: Stir flour or cornstarch together with beaten egg; moisten with a little milk. Bring 1 c. milk to boil; stir in flour and egg mixture until thick. Flavor with vanilla.

SHOOFLY CAKE

4 c. flour	2 c. boiling water
1 c. oil	1 c. molasses
1 lb. brown sugar	2 tsp. baking soda

Mix together flour, oil, and brown sugar; work into crumbs. Reserve 1/2 c. of crumbs for topping. Stir remaining crumbs together with water, molasses, and baking soda until mixture is very thin. Pour into greased and floured 8×12 pan. Top with reserved crumbs and bake at 350 degrees for 45 minutes or until nice and brown.

Note from Bev

My family loves this cake. It is reminiscent of shoofly pie but is a completely different taste experience!

MAYONNAISE CAKE

1 c. boiling water	2 c. flour
1 c. chopped nuts	1 tsp. vanilla
2 tsp. baking soda	1/2 c. brown sugar
1 c. sugar	1/2 c. nuts, chopped
1 c. mayonnaise	1 c. chocolate chips

Combine first seven ingredients and mix well. Put in a greased and floured 9×13 pan. Combine brown sugar, nuts, and chocolate chips; sprinkle over batter. Bake at 300 degrees for 45 minutes.

GINGERBREAD

2 Tbsp. molasses	1 tsp. salt
2 Tbsp. melted butter	1 egg, well beaten
1 c. sugar	1 c. sour milk
1 tsp. cinnamon	1 tsp. baking soda
1/2 tsp. cloves	2 c. flour
1/4 tsp. ginger	

Cream together molasses, butter, and sugar. Add spices and salt; mix well. Add egg, sour milk, baking soda, and flour, stirring slowly. Pour into a greased 8×8 pan. Bake at 350 degrees for 40 minutes.

GRANDMA'S GINGERBREAD

1/4 c. butter	2 1/2 c. flour
1/4 c. lard	1 1/2 tsp. baking soda
1/2 c. sugar	1 tsp. ginger
1 c. hot water	1 tsp. cinnamon
1 egg	1/2 tsp. cloves
1 c. molasses	1/2 tsp. salt

Cream together butter, lard, and sugar. Add hot water to creamed mixture; beat smooth. Add remaining ingredients; beat until smooth. Bake in greased shallow pan at 325–350 degrees for 35 minutes.

Serve applesauce on warm
gingerbread instead of
whipped cream.

HOT WATER SPONGE CAKE

4 eggs, separated
2 c. sugar, divided
1 c. hot water
1 tsp. lemon juice
1 tsp. vanilla extract

2¹/₂ c. sifted flour (measure
   after sifting)
1¹/₂ tsp. baking powder
¹/₂ tsp. salt

Beat egg whites by hand until stiff but not dry. Slowly stir in ¹/₄ c. sugar. In separate bowl, beat egg yolks until light to lemon colored. Slowly add hot water and beat until mixture fills a large bowl. Gradually add in remaining sugar; then lemon juice and vanilla extract. Sift together dry ingredients; stir into egg yolk mixture. Gently fold in the egg whites. Pour into an ungreased tube cake pan. Start in cold oven and bake at 350 degrees for approximately 1 hour or until lightly browned.

SPICE CAKE

1 egg
3 egg yolks
2 c. brown sugar
¹/₂ c. butter, softened
¹/₂ c. milk
2 c. flour

1 tsp. baking soda
2 tsp. cream of tartar
2 tsp. cinnamon
¹/₂ tsp. cloves
1 tsp. nutmeg

Beat egg and egg yolks. Cream together brown sugar, butter, and milk; stir in beaten eggs. Mix dry ingredients together and blend well with creamed mixture. Pour batter into a greased tube or Bundt cake pan. Bake at 375 degrees for 30–40 minutes or until done.

CHOCOLATE CAKE

1 c. brown sugar	1 c. buttermilk
1 c. granulated sugar	2½ c. sifted flour
½ c. butter, softened	1 tsp. cream of tartar
4 eggs, separated	1 tsp. baking soda
½ c. baking cocoa, dissolved	Big pinch of salt
in ½ c. boiling water	1 tsp. vanilla

Cream together the sugars and butter for 15 minutes, beating by hand. Beat egg yolks; stir into creamed mixture. Mix in cocoa, buttermilk, and dry ingredients; add vanilla. Fold in beaten egg whites. Bake in greased pans at 375 degrees for 35 minutes or until done. Makes 2 large or 3 medium layers.

Note from Bev

Ideal with Butter Icing (see recipe on page 137).

WHITE CHOCOLATE CAKE

Cake:

¾ c. chopped or grated white chocolate	1 c. butter, softened
½ c. hot water	1½ c. sugar
2½ c. flour	3 eggs, separated
½ tsp. baking powder	1 c. buttermilk
½ tsp. baking soda	½ c. chopped nuts
½ tsp. salt	½ c. grated coconut
	1 tsp. vanilla

Icing:

½ c. butter, softened	3 Tbsp. milk (use more or less
1 lb. confectioners' sugar	for desired consistency)
Pinch of salt	2 Tbsp. flour
1 tsp. vanilla	Chopped nuts

Cake: In a small saucepan, melt white chocolate in hot water; set aside to cool. Sift together flour, baking powder, baking soda, and salt; set aside. Cream butter; add sugar and egg yolks. Cream well.

Slowly stir in white chocolate. Add dry ingredients alternately with buttermilk. Fold in nuts and coconut. Beat egg whites until they stand in peaks; add vanilla. Fold gently into batter. Line three 8-inch cake pans with wax paper. Pour batter into prepared pans and bake at 350 degrees for 30–35 minutes. Cool on wire racks.

Icing: Combine all ingredients except for nuts; beat well with electric mixer. Spread icing between cake layers and on top and sides; sprinkle with chopped nuts.

Gossip seems to travel faster over grapevines that are a slight bit sour.

GUMDROP CAKE

2 c. brown sugar	1 tsp. cinnamon
2 c. hot water	Peel and pulp from ¼ orange,
½ c. shortening	ground
1½ c. golden raisins	Peel and pulp from ½ lemon,
½ tsp. salt	ground
2 eggs, beaten	Juice from ½ lemon

Boil above ingredients together for 5 minutes; cool.

Mix together in a separate bowl:

½ tsp. baking soda, dissolved in 1 Tbsp. hot water	¾ lb. pitted dates, cut in pieces with scissors
3½ c. flour	1 c. pecans, chopped and
1 lb. gumdrops (no black gumdrops)	browned in butter

Stir both mixtures together. Pour into greased loaf pans, filling each half full. Bake at 250 degrees for 2–3 hours. Let cool before serving.

PINEAPPLE UPSIDE-DOWN CAKE

Canned sliced pineapple

3 Tbsp. melted butter

1/2 c. brown sugar

1/3 c. shortening

1/2 c. sugar

1 egg

1 tsp. vanilla

1¼ c. flour

2 tsp. baking powder

¼ tsp. salt

1/2 c. pineapple juice

Press pineapple slices between paper towels. Line the bottom of a greased 9-inch square cake pan with slightly moist pineapple slices. Cream together melted butter and brown sugar; pour over pineapple to make syrup. Mix together remaining ingredients; pour resulting batter gently over pineapple slices and syrup. Bake at 350 degrees for 30–35 minutes.

Be not overcome of evil, but overcome evil with good.

—ROMANS 12:21

OATMEAL CAKE

Cake:

1½ c. boiling water

1 c. unflavored instant oatmeal

1 c. brown sugar

1 c. sugar

1/2 c. oil

2 eggs

1½ c. flour

1 tsp. cinnamon

1 tsp. baking soda

1 tsp. salt (or a bit less)

Frosting:

1/2 c. butter

1 c. brown sugar

1/2 c. sweetened condensed milk

1 tsp. vanilla

1 c. angel flake coconut

Cake: Pour boiling water over oatmeal; let stand to cool. Cream together sugars, oil, and eggs. Sift together dry ingredients; add to creamed mixture and blend well. Add oatmeal and mix again. Pour batter into greased and floured loaf pan. Bake for 35–40 minutes at 350 degrees.

Frosting: Melt together butter, brown sugar, and sweetened condensed milk in a small saucepan. Cook, stirring constantly, until thick; remove from heat. Add vanilla and coconut; stir until well mixed. Spread over cake.

Watch and pray, that ye enter not into temptation: the spirit indeed is willing, but the flesh is weak. —MATTHEW 26:41

MIDNIGHT CAKE

1½ c. sugar	2 eggs
¼ c. butter, softened	1 tsp. vanilla
¼ c. lard	2 c. flour
½ c. baking cocoa	1 tsp. baking soda
⅛ tsp. salt	1 c. buttermilk

Cream together sugar, butter, and lard. Mix in cocoa and salt. Add eggs and vanilla; beat well for 3 minutes. Gradually mix in flour and baking soda, then buttermilk. Beat well for 5 minutes. Pour into two 8-inch round greased and floured pans. Bake at 350 degrees for 30–35 minutes or until toothpick inserted near center comes out clean. Cool. Frost with CHOCOLATE PEANUT BUTTER FROSTING (page 138).

BUTTER ICING

¼ c. butter, melted	Whole milk (enough to make
2 c. confectioners' sugar	a heavy paste when blend-
3 drops vanilla extract	ing with butter and sugar)

Beat all ingredients together well and spread on cake.

Chocolate Peanut Butter Frosting

3 heaping Tbsp. creamy
   peanut butter
3 heaping Tbsp. soft butter
1 tsp. vanilla

2 c. powdered sugar
3 heaping Tbsp. cocoa
⅛ tsp. salt
2–4 Tbsp. milk

Mix together peanut butter, butter, and vanilla. Stir in sugar, cocoa, and salt. Add milk, stirring, until desired consistency is reached.

Note from Bev

Really terrific on Midnight Cake. Ideal frosting for a two-layer cake.

Cocoa Fluff Icing

6 Tbsp. butter, softened
1½ tsp. vanilla
½ c. baking cocoa

½ c. milk*
3 c. confectioners' sugar

Cream the butter; stir in vanilla and cocoa. Add the milk and confectioners' sugar alternately, beating until light and fluffy after each addition. Spread on cake, making swirls with the tip of a smooth table knife.

*Use less milk if necessary; icing should be thick enough to hold its form.

Pies

Especially now, at summer's onset, when strawberries are ripe and ready for pies and preserves, I think of Jonas. He loved strawberry-rhubarb pie like nobody's business, and both his mamma and mine made it for him with sugar and raw honey, so it was nothing short of wonderful-good. "Desserts are s'posed to be plenty sweet," Mamma has said for as long as I can remember. This, with her irresistible wide-eyed smile. These days Sadie is the one baking such delicious fruit pies for Jonas.

—from *The Sacrifice*

(Note: See STRAWBERRY-RHUBARB PIE on page 143.)

PIE CRUST

3 c. flour

2 c. shortening

1/4 c. sugar

1/2 c. water

Pinch of salt

Mix ingredients together until they form a soft ball. Use plenty of flour when rolling out dough. Makes 1 double crust or 2 single crusts.

Note: Placing the dough on a piece of wax paper makes it easier to put in the pie tin.

"New Mercies"

After the sowing of springtime,
After the showers of rain,
Cometh the blossoms of summer,
Cometh the fruit and the grain.
After the summer comes autumn
And harvest of seed early sown;
After the richness of autumn
A welcome of winter's white gown!
Just so our lives know unfolding:
After each turn of our way
Always a blessed revealing
Of God's new purpose each day.
New ev'ry morning His mercies,
Never an end to His care;
After our pilgrimage journey,
Fullness of glory to share.
—Alice Reynolds Flower

PIE DOUGH

4 c. flour	1 egg
1½ tsp. salt	½ c. cold water
1 Tbsp. sugar	1 Tbsp. vinegar
1½ c. shortening	

Mix flour, salt, sugar, and shortening together to form crumbs. Beat egg, water, and vinegar; add to crumbs and stir with fork until mixture forms a ball. Roll crusts out and place in pans. Makes 5–6 single crusts.

Note from Bev

This recipe makes quite a few crusts, but they store nicely in the freezer for quick use later.

LEMON SPONGE PIE

3 eggs, separated	¼ c. flour
2 c. sugar	2 c. warm milk
5 Tbsp. lemon juice	9-inch unbaked pie crust
3 Tbsp. melted butter	

Beat egg yolks. Add sugar, lemon juice, and melted butter; mix well. Stir in flour and milk.

In separate bowl, beat egg whites until they form stiff peaks; fold into the first mixture. Pour into unbaked pie crust and bake at 425 degrees for 10 minutes. Reduce heat to 325 degrees and continue baking for 35 minutes.

Note from Bev

One of my all-time favorite Amish pies!

Spread butter or margarine on both sides of knife when cutting a meringue pie.

STRAWBERRY-RHUBARB PIE

1½ c. diced rhubarb
½ c. water
½ c. raw honey
½ c. sugar

1 3-oz. pkg. strawberry Jell-O
1 generous c. vanilla ice cream
Pre-baked pie shell for 9-inch
  pie

Cook rhubarb in water until tender; sweeten with honey and sugar. Cool; puree in blender.

Prepare Jell-O as directed on package and chill until almost set. Remove from refrigerator and add pureed rhubarb and vanilla ice cream. Beat thoroughly. Place mixture in pre-baked pie shell and refrigerate until firm. Makes one 9-inch pie.

Optional: Slice a few fresh strawberries on top. Also, strawberry ice cream can be used instead of vanilla ice cream.

Note from Bev

One of my mother's well-loved pie recipes. She often makes this without the rhubarb and serves it with or without a pie crust. It is delightful and refreshing either way!

SNITZ PIE

3 gallons apple butter
3 gallons applesauce
5 c. sugar
½ c. lemon juice
1 rounded Tbsp. cinnamon
1 rounded Tbsp. cloves

½ c. butter, melted
1 c. Clear Jel* or minute
  tapioca
1 tsp. salt
Pastry for 20–24 double-crust
  pies

Stir all ingredients together and fill unbaked pie shells; top with crust. Bake pies at 350 degrees for 1 hour or until done. Makes 20–24 pies.

*Clear Jel is available where canning supplies are sold.

INDIANA SHOOFLY PIE

1 c. flour

²⁄₃ c. brown sugar

1 rounded Tbsp. shortening or margarine

1 c. molasses

³⁄₄ c. hot water

1 egg

1 tsp. baking soda dissolved in ¼ cup hot water

Pastry for 9-inch single-crust pie

Combine flour, brown sugar, and shortening; make crumbs either by hand or using a pastry blender. Set aside ½ c. crumbs to put on top of finished pie.

Combine molasses, hot water, egg, and baking soda dissolved in water; mix well. Stir crumbs into liquid. Pour resulting mixture into pie crust and top with reserved crumbs. Bake at 375 degrees for 35 minutes.

Note from Bev

Delicious served slightly warm with ice cream or whipped cream. This makes an excellent pie and won first prize many times at farm show judging. It was also a popular choice at Mary Jane Hoober's family restaurant for many years.

LANCASTER COUNTY WET-BOTTOM SHOOFLY PIE

Syrup Mixture:

2 large eggs

2²⁄₃ c. Ole Barrel syrup*

1½ tsp. baking soda

2 c. boiling water

In a small mixing bowl, beat eggs with electric mixer until thick. Beat in syrup. Stir in baking soda. Gradually add boiling water, stirring continually until mixed. Set aside until completely cool. If in a hurry, set bowl in cold water and stir gently until cool.

*Ole Barrel syrup will produce the best results. However, if it is unavailable in your area, a thick corn syrup may be substituted.

Crumbs:

2½ c. flour	⅛ tsp. salt
1½ c. brown sugar	2 Tbsp. shortening

Pastry for two 9.5-inch single-crust pies

In a large bowl, mix together flour, brown sugar, and salt. Cut shortening into flour mixture with a pastry blender. Set 1⅓ c. crumb mixture aside in a small bowl. Pour approximately 1 c. syrup mixture into remaining crumb mixture; mix by hand to make a thick, smooth paste. Add remaining syrup mixture approximately 1 c. at a time, stirring well after each addition to keep mixture as smooth as possible.

Pour syrup and crumb mixture into pie crusts; sprinkle half of reserved crumbs evenly on each pie. Bake at 375 degrees for 10 minutes; reduce heat to 350 degrees and bake for 30 more minutes. If center of pie is not set at the end of this time, turn oven off and leave pies in the oven for 5–15 minutes more. Delicious served hot with vanilla ice cream. Shoofly pie seems even better the day after it is made.

Note from Bev

There are many recipes for shoofly pie. However, the best pies are those with a gooey or wet bottom. I distinctly remember eating this delicious pie at church and family gatherings in Lancaster County. There's really nothing to compare with this sweet offering. Makes my mouth water just remembering. . . .

*B*lessed are the meek: for they shall inherit the earth.

—MATTHEW 5:5

PEANUT BUTTER PIE

8 oz. cream cheese, softened

12 oz. confectioners' sugar
  (approximately 1½ c.)

7½ oz. creamy peanut butter

1 c. whole milk

16 oz. whipped cream

2 graham cracker pie crusts,
  baked

Beat the cream cheese on low speed until soft and fluffy. Stir in sugar and peanut butter. Slowly add milk, beating constantly. Fold in whipped cream. Pour mixture into graham cracker pie crusts; freeze until firm, about 4 hours.

Note from Bev

A chocolate pie crust with a sprinkling of walnuts is also an option. So tasty!

PUMPKIN CHIFFON PIE

1 envelope unflavored gelatin

¼ c. cold water

3 eggs, separated

1 c. sugar, divided

1¼ c. canned pumpkin

½ c. milk

½ tsp. salt

½ tsp. ginger

½ tsp. nutmeg

½ tsp. cinnamon

Pastry for single-crust pie,
  baked

Soften gelatin in cold water; set aside. Beat egg yolks slightly; add ½ c. sugar, pumpkin, milk, salt, and spices. Cook in double boiler until thick. Add softened gelatin to hot pumpkin mixture; mix thoroughly and cool. Beat egg whites until stiff; stir in remaining sugar. When pumpkin mixture begins to thicken, fold in egg whites. Pour into baked pie shell; chill in refrigerator.

Note: Pie may be garnished with whipped cream before serving.

APPLE MINCEMEAT PIE

2 c. apples, coarsely ground
$^3/_4$ c. raisins
$^1/_2$ lb. lean ground beef, browned
$^1/_2$ tsp. cloves

2 c. sugar
Water
Pastry for two 9-inch double-crust pies
2 Tbsp. vinegar

In saucepan, blend together apples, raisins, browned ground beef, cloves, and sugar. Add a little water and bring to a boil; place mixture into pie shells. Sprinkle 1 Tbsp. vinegar on each pie before covering with top crust. Bake pies at 350 degrees for 50–60 minutes. Serve warm with vanilla ice cream.

A fresh egg will sink to the bottom on its side in a deep pan of water. If it is not good, it will stand on end or float.

BLUEBERRY PIE

2 c. sour cream
1 c. sugar
$^1/_4$ c. sifted flour
$^1/_2$ tsp. salt
$^3/_4$ tsp. almond extract
2 eggs

1 unbaked graham cracker pie crust
2 c. canned, ready-to-use blueberry pie filling
$^1/_2$ c. whipped cream

Combine first six ingredients; beat well and pour into pie crust. Bake at 375 degrees for 25 minutes. Remove from oven and spread with blueberry pie filling. Cool and refrigerate. When chilled, spread whipped cream on top.

RICH CHOCOLATE PIE

Cream ½ c. butter with ¾ c. sugar. Stir in 2 squares of unsweetened baking chocolate, melted and cooled. Add 2 eggs, one at a time, beating for 5 minutes on high speed after each addition. Fold in 2 c. whipped cream. Pour into baked 9-inch pie crust. Chill until firm, about 2 hours. Can be frozen, as well.

Note from Bev

A very rich pie, but so luscious. It makes 12 small portions. Enjoy!

PUMPKIN TORTE

2½ c. graham cracker crumbs	3 egg yolks
⅓ c. sugar	½ c. sugar
½ c. butter, softened	½ c. milk
2 eggs, beaten	½ tsp. salt
¾ c. sugar	1 Tbsp. cinnamon
8 oz. cream cheese, softened	3 egg whites
1 envelope gelatin	¼ c. sugar
¼ c. cold water	1 c. whipped cream
2 c. pumpkin (cooked or canned)	

Mix together graham cracker crumbs, ⅓ c. sugar, and butter; press into 9×13 baking pan. Mix together beaten eggs, ¾ c. sugar, and cream cheese; pour over graham cracker crust. Bake at 350 degrees for 20 minutes. Cool.

Dissolve gelatin in cold water. Cook pumpkin, egg yolks, ½ c. sugar, milk, salt, and cinnamon until mixture thickens. Remove from heat and add dissolved gelatin; cool.

Beat egg whites and ¼ c. sugar together; fold into pumpkin mixture. Pour over cooled, baked crust. Top with whipped cream.

Vanilla Pie

Bottom part:

1/2 c. brown sugar	1 egg
1/2 c. molasses	1 c. water
1 Tbsp. flour	1 tsp. vanilla

9-inch unbaked pie crust

Top part:

1 c. flour	1/2 tsp. soda
1/2 c. brown sugar	1/2 tsp. baking powder
1/4 c. butter-flavored shortening	

In saucepan, combine ingredients for bottom part of pie, except the vanilla, and cook till thickened. Allow to cool; stir in vanilla. Pour into unbaked pie crust. In separate bowl, combine ingredients for top part, mixing until crumbly. Spread over bottom layer of pie. Bake at 350 degrees for 40–45 minutes. (Depending on the oven, pie might be done in only 30 minutes.)

Pecan Pie

3 eggs	1 c. dark corn syrup
1/2 c. sugar	1 c. broken pecans
1/2 tsp. salt	Pastry for 9-inch pie
1/3 c. melted butter	

Beat eggs, sugar, salt, melted butter, and corn syrup until well mixed. Add pecans and pour into a 9-inch pastry-lined pie pan. Bake at 350 degrees for 40–50 minutes.

Note from Bev

I can't recall a single Christmas dinner while I was growing up that did not include this fantastic pie. Pecan pie, to my mind, equals the warm and fond memory of family, friends, and delightful fellowship.

WEEPLESS PIE MERINGUE

1 Tbsp. cornstarch   2 egg whites
2 tsp. water   2 Tbsp. sugar
½ c. boiling water

Moisten cornstarch with 2 tsp. water. Stir in boiling water; cook over low heat until thick, stirring constantly. Set aside to cool. Beat egg whites and sugar until slightly stiff. Gradually beat in cooled cornstarch mixture until it forms peaks. Pile meringue on pie; brown.

Note from Bev

``Weepless´´ means this meringue never fails.

When ye come together to eat, tarry one for another.

—I CORINTHIANS 11:33

Cookies and Candies

Together, she and Lizzie had made a big batch of peanut-butter balls dipped in melted chocolate, several dozen sand tarts, candied dates, and crystal stick candy at Lizzie's house yesterday. They'd had a laughing good time doing so. The best part of all was there were still plenty of sweets to go around, even having shared a considerable portion with Cousin Peter and Fannie's wee ones.

—from *The Sacrifice*

(Note: see SAND TARTS, PEANUT BUTTER BALLS, CRYSTAL STICKS, and CANDIED DATES on pages 158, 167, 169, and 170.)

Butterscotch Icebox Cookies

1½ c. melted shortening   4½ c. flour

1 c. brown sugar   2 tsp. baking soda

1 c. sugar   1 tsp. cinnamon

3 eggs, well beaten   ½ tsp. nutmeg

1 c. chopped nuts   ½ tsp. cloves

1 tsp. salt

Cream melted shortening with sugars. Gradually stir in eggs, then mix in nuts. Sift dry ingredients together and add to creamed mixture; mix well. Shape into a 2½-inch-thick roll. Wrap in waxed paper and refrigerate overnight or until firm. Slice cookie dough into ⅛-inch slices with sharp knife.

Preheat oven to 425 degrees. Bake on ungreased cookie sheets for 5 to 6 minutes. Makes 75 cookies.

Pineapple Cookies

½ c. shortening   1 tsp. baking powder

½ c. brown sugar   ½ tsp. salt

½ c. sugar   1 c. crushed pineapple

1 egg   ½ c. chopped walnuts

2 c. sifted flour

Cream shortening and sugars. Add egg; beat thoroughly. Sift together dry ingredients; add to creamed mixture alternately with pineapple. Stir in nuts. Drop by teaspoonfuls on greased cookie sheets, allowing 4 inches between each cookie.

Bake at 350 degrees for 15–18 minutes. Makes about 3½ dozen cookies.

And it was in my mouth as honey for sweetness.

—EZEKIEL 3:3

DROPPED AMISH CHURCH SUGAR COOKIES

3½ c. flour

1 tsp. baking powder

1 tsp. baking soda

1 tsp. ground nutmeg

1 tsp. salt

1½ c. margarine (no substitutes)

2 c. white sugar

1 tsp. vanilla extract

1 tsp. almond extract

2 eggs, slightly beaten

1 c. sour cream

Sugar

Preheat oven to 375 degrees. Stir together flour, baking powder, baking soda, nutmeg, and salt. In large bowl, beat margarine, sugar, and extracts until creamy. Add eggs and sour cream; beat well. Gradually add dry ingredients, mixing well.

Grease cookie sheets or line them with parchment paper. Using medium-sized cookie scoop, drop cookies 2 inches apart. Sprinkle with sugar.

Bake cookies for 10–15 minutes or until set. Don't allow cookies to get too golden. Remove from cookie sheet and place on cooling rack. When completely cool, store between sheets of waxed paper.

Note from Bev

The perfect cookie for holiday gatherings of any kind . . . and for all ages, from Indiana Amish country!

OLD-FASHIONED WALNUT OR PECAN DROPS

4 egg whites, room temperature (approx. ⅔ c.)

3½ c. powdered sugar (measure before sifting)

1 lb. black walnuts or pecans, finely chopped

2 Tbsp. flour, sifted (measure before sifting)

Beat the egg whites until very light and soft peaks form. Sprinkle some of the sifted powdered sugar over the beaten egg whites; beat in. Repeat until all the powdered sugar is mixed in and the mixture is very light; then add nuts and sifted flour. Mix gently.

Drop by half spoonfuls onto buttered cookie sheets. (Drops should be about the size of a silver dollar.) Bake at 325 degrees for 20 minutes. Serve cool.

HERMITS

1½ c. granulated or brown
    sugar
1 c. shortening or butter
2½ c. flour
3 eggs
1 tsp. cinnamon

1 tsp. baking soda, dissolved
    in 2 Tbsp. boiling water
1 lb. English walnuts, chopped
¾ c. chopped raisins, boiled
    until soft

Mix together all ingredients except walnuts and raisins. Drain off the water from raisins; add both raisins and walnuts to mixture and blend thoroughly. Drop by teaspoon onto greased cookie sheet, about 1½ inches apart. Bake at 325 degrees for 15 minutes or until lightly browned.

Note from Bev

A very old recipe from Grandmother Ada, as well as her mother's recipe files. This cookie is quite popular in Amish country.

CHOCOLATE CHEER-UP COOKIES

½ c. butter
1 egg
⅓ c. sugar
½ c. brown sugar
½ tsp. vanilla
1 c. sifted flour

½ tsp. salt
½ tsp. baking soda
1½ oz. semisweet chocolate,
    melted
½ c. M&M's

Cream together butter, egg, sugars, and vanilla. Sift together dry ingredients; combine with creamed mixture. Stir in melted chocolate and M&M's. Drop on greased cookie sheets and bake at 375 degrees for 12–14 minutes or until brown.

Note from Bev

The perfect encouragement gift for a shut-in or sad friend. This is my daughter Julie's original recipe. Delicious!

The fear of the Lord is the instruction of wisdom; and before honour is humility. —PROVERBS 15:33

CHOCOLATE CHRISTMAS COOKIES

Cookies:

4 c. flour	2 tsp. instant coffee granules
1 tsp. baking soda	³/₄ c. baking cocoa
¹/₂ tsp. salt	¹/₄ c. olive oil
1 c. butter, softened	1¹/₃ c. sour cream
2 c. light brown sugar	2 c. angel flake coconut
2 eggs	2 c. English walnuts, chopped

Icing:

6 Tbsp. baking cocoa	¹/₂ c. butter, softened
2 Tbsp. olive oil	4 c. confectioners' sugar
¹/₂ c. sour cream	

Cookies: Mix together flour, baking soda, and salt; set aside. Beat together butter, sugar, eggs, coffee, cocoa, olive oil, and sour cream. Gradually stir in the dry ingredients. Add coconut and walnuts; mix well. Drop by tablespoons onto greased baking sheets; bake at 350 degrees for 10 minutes. Spread with the following icing when completely cool.

Icing: Mix together cocoa, olive oil, sour cream, and butter. Stir in confectioner's sugar until desired consistency is reached.

Baking powder removes tea and coffee stains from cups and porcelain pots.

"My Christmas Wish for You"

This year at blessed Christmastide,
My dearest wish for you
Comes wrapped in love and peace and joy,
God's precious gift to make us new.
Courage in the midst of fear.
Joy in the midst of sorrow,
Healing for pain,
Hope for tomorrow.
This Christmas wish I offer you,
Came as Mary's babe, God's only Son.
This blessed gift so dear, so true—
For you and everyone.
—Beverly Lewis

PUMPKIN COOKIES

$1/2$ c. shortening	$1/2$ c. raisins
1 c. sugar	1 tsp. salt
1 egg	$1/2$ tsp. baking soda
$1 \ 3/4$ c. flour	$1/2$ tsp. baking powder
1 c. pumpkin	1 tsp. cinnamon
1 c. All-Bran cereal	$1/2$ tsp. ground cloves
$1/2$ c. chopped nuts	$1/4$ tsp. nutmeg

Mix together shortening, sugar, and egg. Stir in remaining ingredients until well blended. Drop onto lightly greased cookie sheet; bake at 375 degrees for 7–10 minutes.

Note from Bev

The lovely smell of these cookies, freshly baked, brings back happy memories of returning home from school and finding Mother waiting, all smiles.

Take heed that ye do not your alms before men, to be seen of them: otherwise ye have no reward of your Father which is in heaven.   —MATTHEW 6:1

SAND TARTS

½ c. butter, softened
1 c. sugar
1 Tbsp. whole milk
1 tsp. vanilla
2 eggs, separated
½ tsp. salt

1 tsp. baking powder
1½ c. flour
Blanched almonds, halved
¼ tsp. cinnamon
2 Tbsp. sugar

Cream butter and sugar; stir in whole milk, vanilla, and egg yolks. Mix until well blended and light. Sift together salt, baking powder, and flour; stir into creamed mixture and mix well. Chill for 3 hours.

On lightly floured surface, roll dough out exceptionally thin. Cut out cookies, using 3-inch star or heart cookie cutters. Place cookies on greased cookie sheet with an almond half centered on each cookie. Beat egg whites into a glaze. Mix together cinnamon and sugar. Brush cookies lightly with beaten egg whites and sprinkle with cinnamon-sugar topping. Bake at 375 degrees for 8 minutes or until cookies are slightly brown on the edges. (They burn easily, so watch carefully). Makes 30 cookies.

Note from Bev

What a cookie—none are more delicate than this! My sister and I liked to help Mother bake them on Christmas Eve afternoon so we could nibble on them while we trimmed the tree with our parents that evening.

CARROT COOKIES

Cookies:

1 c. shortening

¾ c. sugar

1 egg

2 c. flour

2 tsp. baking powder

½ tsp. salt

1 c. cooked, mashed carrots

1 tsp. vanilla

Frosting:

3 c. confectioners' sugar

Juice of 1 orange (approx. ¼ c.)

1–2 Tbsp. grated orange rind

Cookies: Blend shortening, sugar, and egg. Sift together dry ingredients; stir into creamed mixture along with carrots and vanilla. Mix thoroughly; drop on cookie sheet. Bake at 375 degrees for 15 minutes. Makes 5 dozen.

Frosting: Mix confectioners' sugar into orange juice until very smooth and right consistency for frosting. Mix in grated orange rind. Spread on cooled cookies.

Note from Bev

Watch guests light up when they bite into these lovely cookies!

ZUCCHINI COOKIES

½ c. butter

½ c. honey

1 egg

½ tsp. vanilla

1 c. raw zucchini, skinned and grated

2 c. flour

1 tsp. cinnamon

1 tsp. cloves

1 tsp. baking soda

Nuts or raisins

Cream butter, honey, egg, and vanilla together. Stir in zucchini. Sift together dry ingredients; stir into creamed mixture. Stir in nuts or raisins. Bake as drop cookies on greased cookie sheets at 325 degrees for 12–15 minutes.

CRANBERRY CRUNCHIES

1 c. uncooked rolled oats	½ c. butter or margarine
½ c. flour	1-lb. can cranberry sauce (jel-
1 c. brown sugar	lied or whole)

Mix oats, flour, and brown sugar in a bowl. Cut in the butter with a dull knife until mixture is crumbly. Place half the mixture in an 8×8 greased baking dish; cover with all the cranberry sauce. Spread the rest of the crumb mixture over the top. Bake at 350 degrees for 45 minutes. Cut into squares and serve hot or cold topped with vanilla ice cream.

Therefore all things whatsoever ye would that men should do to you, do ye even so to them: for this is the law and the prophets. —MATTHEW 7:12 (The Golden Rule)

CHOCOLATE CHIP COOKIES

1 c. butter, softened	1 tsp. baking soda
1 c. sugar	1 tsp. salt
½ c. brown sugar, packed	12 oz. chocolate chips
1 tsp. vanilla	1 c. chopped walnuts
2 eggs	(optional)
2¼ c. flour, sifted	

Cream together butter, sugars, and vanilla until light and fluffy. Beat in eggs. Sift together flour, baking soda, and salt; gradually add to creamed mixture, mixing until well blended. Fold in chocolate chips and walnuts. Drop on greased cookie sheets and bake at 375 degrees for about 10 minutes. Makes 5 dozen 3-inch cookies.

SUGARLESS COOKIES

1 c. raisins	1 Tbsp. honey
1/2 c. chopped dates	1 tsp. vanilla
1/2 c. chopped apples	1 tsp. soda
1/2 c. water	1 c. flour
1/2 c. shortening	1/2–3/4 c. chopped nuts
2 eggs, beaten	

Boil raisins, dates, and apples in 1/2 cup water for 3 minutes. Mix in shortening; cool. Add beaten eggs, honey, vanilla, and soda to mixture, then stir in flour and nuts. Refrigerate until chilled. Drop by teaspoons on well-greased cookie sheet; bake at 350 degrees for 10–12 minutes. Refrigerate in airtight containers.

Train up a child in the way he should go: and when he is old, he will not depart from it. —PROVERBS 22:6

ORANGE COOKIES

1/2 c. butter or margarine, softened	1/4 tsp. cream of tartar
	1/2 tsp. baking soda
1 c. sugar, divided	2 Tbsp. whole milk
1/4 c. brown sugar	3 tsp. grated orange rind
1 egg, beaten	8 tsp. orange juice
11/2 c. sifted flour	

Cream together butter, 1/2 c. sugar, and brown sugar; add beaten egg and mix well. Sift together the dry ingredients; stir into creamed mixture along with milk and orange rind. Mix remaining sugar with orange juice; stir into dough. Bake as drop cookies on greased cookie sheets at 375 degrees for 10–15 minutes.

AUNT DOTTIE'S PEANUT BUTTER COOKIES

½ c. margarine, butter, or shortening

½ c. peanut butter

½ c. sugar

½ c. brown sugar

1 egg, beaten

1¼ c. flour

¼ tsp. salt

¾ tsp. baking soda

½ tsp. baking powder

Cream together the margarine, peanut butter, and sugars. Add the beaten egg and mix all together. Sift dry ingredients and add to the mixture. Chill cookie dough. Roll into small balls and place on greased cookie sheets. Press with fork and bake at 375 degrees for 12–15 minutes. Makes about 4 dozen cookies.

SNICKERDOODLES

½ c. butter, softened

¾ c. sugar

1 egg

1⅜ cups sifted flour

1 tsp. cream of tartar

½ tsp. soda

¼ tsp. salt

2 Tbsp. sugar

2 tsp. cinnamon

Mix together butter, sugar, and egg. Sift together flour, cream of tartar, soda, and salt; stir into creamed mixture. Chill dough for 1 hour. Roll into balls the size of small walnuts. Combine sugar and cinnamon; roll balls in mixture. Place cookies 2–3 inches apart on ungreased baking sheets.

Bake at 400 degrees until lightly browned, approximately 6–8 minutes. (Cookies puff up at first, then flatten out with a crinkled top). Makes 3 dozen cookies.

Note from Bev

I'm so fond of these cookies I created a story line around them in one of my books for girls, No Guys Pact (HOLLY'S HEART series). My mother baked them often all the years I was growing up, and I enjoy making them now for my own family.

And be ye kind one to another, tenderhearted, forgiving one another. —EPHESIANS 4:32

FILLED COOKIES

½ c. shortening	1 egg
1 c. sugar	¼ c. milk
¾ tsp. salt	3 c. flour
1 tsp. vanilla	1 Tbsp. baking powder

Combine all ingredients and mix, using slow speed on mixer. Roll dough out and cut into circles. Place a spoonful of desired filling on half of the cookies (see options). Moisten edges of cookies with water; top with remaining cookies. Prick the top cookies and press down around filling to seal. Place cookies on greased cookie sheets and bake at 375 degrees for 10 minutes or until browned.

Filling options: Mincemeat, fig filling, date and nut filling, dried apricots (boil in a bit of water until apricots are soft or desired consistency and sweeten to taste, using approximately 1 c. sugar per 1 c. fruit).

Oven-cleaning tip (for non-self-cleaning ovens): In a cool oven, place 2 c. of soapy water in a shallow porcelain baking pan along with 3 Tbsp. ammonia. Close the oven door and let set overnight. Because the ammonia fumes will dissolve much of the grease, it is possible to clean the oven with little effort.

GINGERSNAPS

1 c. sugar

1/3 c. molasses

1/2 c. butter or margarine

1 egg

1 tsp. ginger

1 tsp. cinnamon

1/2 tsp. cloves

2 c. flour

Pinch of salt

1 tsp. baking soda, dissolved
in approximately 1/4 tsp.
warm water

Sugar

Combine 1 c. sugar, molasses, butter, and egg in a bowl; mix well. Blend in all remaining ingredients except for remaining sugar. Chill dough. Roll into approximately 1-inch balls; roll in sugar. Place about 2 inches apart on lightly greased cookie sheets, as cookies tend to spread. Bake at 350 degrees for 7–9 minutes or until edges are firm.

BUTTERMILK COOKIES

1 c. margarine or butter,
softened

2 c. sugar

3 eggs, beaten

1/2 tsp. salt

1 tsp. baking powder

1/2 tsp. nutmeg

4 1/2 c. flour

1 c. buttermilk

Cream butter and sugar together. Add beaten eggs to the creamed mixture. Combine dry ingredients in a separate bowl; add to creamed mixture alternately with the buttermilk. Drop dough onto a well-greased cookie sheet and bake at 350 degrees for about 15 minutes. For variety, add cooked raisins or nuts to dough.

Note from Bev

This recipe belonged to my paternal great-grandmother, Lettie Jones, mother of nine children and cookie-maker extraordinaire. Baked with her loving touch in each cookie.

Our Father God, thy name we praise
To thee our hymns addressing,
And joyfully our voices raise
Thy faithfulness confessing;
Assembled by thy grace, O Lord,
We seek fresh guidance from thy word.
Now grant anew thy blessing!
—*from* Songs of the Ausbund

DATE OR RAISIN COOKIES

2¹/₄ c. dates or raisins, chopped	2 c. brown sugar
1 c. sugar	3 eggs
1 c. water	4 c. flour
1 c. chopped walnuts	¹/₂ tsp. salt
1 c. shortening	¹/₂ tsp. baking soda

In saucepan, mix chopped dates or raisins, sugar, and water. Boil slowly, stirring continually, for about 10 minutes. Remove from heat and add chopped walnuts; set aside to cool.

In large mixing bowl, cream together shortening and brown sugar. In a separate small bowl, beat eggs well. Add eggs to creamed mixture and beat well for 3 minutes, then stir in flour, salt, and baking soda. Divide dough in half. Cool in refrigerator for approximately 30 minutes, then roll out each half of dough separately, about ¹/₄-inch thick. Spread half of the date or raisin mixture on each. Roll dough up; refrigerate overnight. Cut in ³/₈-inch pieces and place approximately 1-inch apart on buttered cookie sheet. Bake at 375 degrees for 15–18 minutes or until lightly browned. Leave on cookie sheet for about 5–8 minutes, then remove cookies to a rack to finish cooling.

SNOWBALLS

5⅓ c. sifted all-purpose flour (sifted before measuring)

2½ tsp. salt

2¼ c. shortening or butter, softened

2 c. sifted confectioners' sugar

¼ c. orange juice

4 tsp. vanilla

3 c. pecans or almonds, chopped

Additional confectioners' sugar

Cut together flour, salt, and shortening with pastry blender (not too long) until crumbs are the size of peas. Stir in confectioners' sugar. Add orange juice, vanilla, and chopped nuts; blend well (but don't overmix). Dough should be somewhat crumbly.

Mold dough into 1-inch balls. Place an inch apart on ungreased cookie sheet. Bake at 375 degrees for 12–15 minutes or until bottoms of cookies are lightly browned. Using two spoons, roll cookies in sifted confectioners' sugar while still hot. If sugar soaks in, roll balls in sugar again while still warm.

Prepare prunes by rinsing in scalding water, then wash in cold water. Place in cooking vessel, cover with water, and bring to a simmer. Do not boil.

APPLE SNITZ SNACK

Peel 5 apples and cut into slices. Place on cooling rack. Mix a bit of cinnamon and sugar together; spoon on each apple slice. Bake at lowest oven setting—approximately 150 degrees—for approximately 8 hours or more. While baking, make sure a tray is beneath the rack to catch drippings. For a chewier snack, bake for less time. For a crispier snack, leave in oven longer. If apples get too hard, soften by putting in a bag with soft bread.

Peanut Blossoms

5¼ c. flour	1½ c. peanut butter
1 Tbsp. baking soda	3 eggs
1½ tsp. salt	6 Tbsp. milk
1½ c. butter, softened	1 Tbsp. vanilla
1½ c. sugar	Sugar
1½ c. brown sugar	120 Hershey's Kisses (approx.)

Sift flour, baking soda, and salt together; set aside. Cream together butter and sugars. Stir in peanut butter, eggs, milk, and vanilla; mix well. Stir in dry ingredients. Shape dough into small balls—approx. 1- to 1½-inch—and roll in sugar. Place on ungreased cookie sheet. Bake at 375 degrees for 10 to 12 minutes. Cookies should be slightly browned when done. While cookies are baking, remove wrappers from Hershey's Kisses. As soon as cookies are removed from oven, place a Kiss in the center of each. Allow cookies to cool completely before storing. Layer alternately.

Now therefore hearken unto me, O ye children: for blessed are they that keep my ways. —PROVERBS 8:32

Peanut Butter Balls

8 oz. cream cheese, softened	4 c. powdered sugar
½ c. butter, softened	Melted chocolate
2 c. peanut butter	

Mix cream cheese, butter, and peanut butter together by hand. Gradually stir in powdered sugar; mix well. Form into balls and refrigerate overnight. Dip chilled balls in melted chocolate.

PEANUT BUTTER FUDGE

In heavy saucepan, mix together 2 c. sugar, ²/₃ c. milk, and a piece of butter the size of a walnut. Stir over low heat until butter and sugar are melted; then boil briskly until mixture forms a soft ball when dropped in cold water. Remove pan from stove and stir in 2 Tbsp. peanut butter and 2 Tbsp. marshmallow whip. Stir until creamy and pour into buttered pan. Do not beat, as mixture will get hard.

Thou shalt call, and I will answer thee: thou wilt have a desire to the work of thine hands.   —JOB 14:15

TAFFY

1 Tbsp. unflavored gelatin	2 c. light corn syrup
½ c. cold water	Vanilla extract
2 lbs. granulated sugar	Paraffin wax (size of a wal-
2 c. cream	nut)

Soak gelatin in cold water. Boil sugar, cream, corn syrup, vanilla extract, and paraffin wax for 15 minutes; stir in gelatin and boil until a tiny bit of the mixture put in cold water hardens immediately (hard-ball test). Let cool. Pull taffy in a cool place, buttering hands slightly so taffy will not stick to them.

Note from Bev

Lots of fun to make and to eat. A quaint and happy Christmas tradition may await you, just as many Amish folk enjoy this family activity during the holidays and beyond.

POPCORN OR PEANUT BALLS

2 c. brown sugar	¼ c. butter
1 c. light or dark corn syrup	Pinch of salt
1 c. water	Popped corn or peanuts

Blend together the sugar, corn syrup, water, butter, and a pinch of salt until sugar is completely dissolved. Continue cooking until the syrup comes together in a soft ball shape. Pour hot syrup over popped corn or peanuts. Shape mixture into balls, buttering your hands first.

MACAROONS

½ c. sweetened condensed milk	2 c. shredded coconut
	Vanilla (optional)

Mix together sweetened condensed milk and coconut. Add vanilla if desired. Drop on buttered baking sheet and bake at 350 degrees for 10 minutes.

CRYSTAL STICKS

3 eggs, well beaten	1 c. flour
1 c. sugar	1 tsp. baking powder
1 c. chopped nuts	Powdered sugar
1 c. chopped dates	

Mix all ingredients together and spread in a greased shallow pan. Bake at 350 degrees for 20–30 minutes. Cool, cut in strips, and sprinkle with powdered sugar.

Note from Bev

Aunt Ada Reba Bachman was so kind to share this delectable recipe with me, from her childhood memories of growing up at 217 South Queen Street. Her mother, my grandmother Ada, for whom my aunt was named, first created this delicacy for family to enjoy on special occasions.

CANDIED DATES

Slit seedless dates lengthwise. Put smooth peanut butter down inside the dates, plumping them out a bit, enough to widen the dates slightly. Then roll the dates in granulated sugar.

OATMEAL–PEANUT BUTTER–CAROB "FUDGIES"

3 rounded c. quick oats

2 tsp. vanilla

1/2 c. peanut butter

2 c. raw sugar

1/2 c. carob powder (sift after measuring)

1/3 c. olive oil

2/3 c. milk*

Cut oatmeal, vanilla, and peanut butter together with a pastry blender; set aside. Mix together raw sugar, carob powder, olive oil, and milk in a saucepan and bring to a boil over medium heat. Continue cooking at a full boil on medium heat for 2 minutes. Remove from heat and immediately add oatmeal mixture. Mix well and quickly drop by large spoonfuls onto waxed paper. (If mixture starts drying out, it may be heated a bit on low heat, stirring constantly.) Allow "fudgies" to cool for approximately 30 minutes. Makes about 2 dozen.

*Fudgies get especially creamy if raw goat's milk is used.

For the Lord God is a sun and shield: the Lord will give grace and glory: no good thing will he withhold from them that walk uprightly. —PSALM 84:11

Jellies, Jams, Relishes, and Preserves

Hurriedly, she opened the door leading downstairs to the cold cellar. Here, with the help of women from her church district, she'd put up and stored eight hundred quarts of produce. She, in turn, had assisted her neighbors with their canning, as well. Piles of potatoes, onions, turnips, and sweet potatoes were stored separately, more than enough until the next harvest. There were rows and rows of canning jars filled with pickled beets, chow-chow, tomato relish, bean salads, and Rebecca's luscious jams and jellies.

—from *The Shunning*

(Note: see CHOW-CHOW on page 179.)

HOT PEPPER JELLY

2 c. peppers*, finely grated   ¼ cup vinegar

3 c. sugar (raw is fine)   1 pkg. Sure-Jell

Drain peppers, then heat for 5 minutes, stirring constantly. Add sugar and vinegar. Heat to boiling; add Sure-Jell. Let boil for 1 minute, stirring constantly. Immediately put mixture in canning jars. Invert jars for 5 minutes. As the jars cool, you should hear each one pop as it seals.

*Use a combination of regular and hot peppers, as desired. Use rubber gloves when handling hot peppers.

Note: One 5-gallon bucket of regular peppers, grated, equals 14 cups. Add 6 cups of grated hot peppers for a total of 20 cups, which makes 10 batches. This recipe may be made in large quantity, but keep the mixture boiling, stirring constantly, while filling the canning jars. If only a small amount is made, it will keep well in a glass jar in the refrigerator without canning.

He which soweth sparingly shall reap also sparingly; and he which soweth bountifully shall reap also bountifully.

−2 CORINTHIANS 9:6

ADAH PEACHEY'S RHUBARB JAM

5 c. rhubarb, chopped   1 3-oz. box red Jell-O (straw-

3 c. sugar   berry, raspberry, cherry,

1 c. crushed pineapple   etc.)

Mix together rhubarb, sugar, and crushed pineapple; let stand for 2 hours. Boil mixture for 10 minutes or until mushy. Remove from heat and add Jell-O. Mix well and put into jars to cool. After jam is cooled, put jars in the freezer.

APPLE, PEACH, OR PEAR BUTTER

Apple Butter:

6 three-gallon buckets of
  apples

20 gallons sweet apple cider
  (or fresh)

20 lbs. sugar

Peach or Pear Butter:

3 three-gallon buckets of
  peaches or pears

12 gallons water

20 lbs. sugar

Apple Butter: Core and quarter the apples. Place in a large kettle and add the cider; cover and simmer on low for 45 minutes or until soft, stirring frequently.

Press cooked apples through a sieve. Discard the skins, return the pulp to the pan, and stir in the sugar.

Simmer, stirring frequently, until the mixture is thick—about 1½ hours. (Or pour the mixture into a roasting pan and bake uncovered at 350 degrees for 1 hour, stirring occasionally. Reduce the oven to 250 degrees and bake 2–3 hours longer, or until thick.)

Sterilize pint jars. Remove the apple butter from the heat and ladle into hot sterilized pint jars, leaving ¼-inch of space from the top. Use a rubber spatula to release air bubbles inside the jar. Be careful to wipe the rim of the jar with a clean cloth. Cap each jar according to the manufacturer's instructions. Process for 10 minutes in a boiling water bath (consult a cookbook with directions on boiling bath canning).

Peach or Pear Butter: Follow the instructions above, substituting peaches or pears for apples and substituting water for cider.

Note from Bev

My memories of church picnics and large family get-togethers are filled with apple butter. As a girl, I liked to spread it on toast, on crackers, and even on celery sticks.

PINEAPPLE PRESERVES

3 fresh pineapples   3 lbs. granulated sugar
1 qt. water

Core pineapples; grate either by hand or using a food processor. In
a large saucepan, bring water and sugar to a boil. Add grated pineapple and continue to boil another 20 minutes, stirring frequently.
When mixture is thick enough, pour into sterilized jars and seal.

Note from Bev

An exceptionally scrumptious jelly.

QUINCE HONEY

1½ lbs. sugar   2 c. water
1 c. ground quince

Mix together all ingredients and cook for 5 minutes, stirring occasionally. Pour mixture into jars and seal. (Follow home-canning
procedures.)

CATSUP

½ bushel tomatoes   1 c. sugar
½ c. vinegar   1 Tbsp. cinnamon
⅓ c. salt   ½ Tbsp. pepper

Boil tomatoes with the skins on, then rub them through a window
screen. Add remaining ingredients; let simmer for 45 minutes.

For the wisdom of this world is foolishness with God.

—I CORINTHIANS 3:19

HOMEMADE MAYONNAISE

1 c. cream

3 Tbsp. sugar

1 tsp. salt

1 rounded Tbsp. real butter

1 egg

2 or 3 Tbsp. yellow mustard

1 pt. Miracle Whip

Heat cream in top of a double boiler. Add sugar, salt, and butter. Beat egg until thoroughly mixed but not frothy; stir into mixture very slowly. Stir continually until custard-like. Strain any lumps. Cool, then mix in mustard and Miracle Whip. Makes approximately 1 quart of extra-rich mayonnaise.

SANDWICH SPREAD

1 gallon green tomatoes (cut in fourths)

4 yellow peppers

4 red peppers

6 onions

1 pt. sweet pickles, drained and ground (1 c. juice reserved)

3 cups sugar

3 Tbsp. salt

3 Tbsp. cornstarch

1½ c. mustard

1 qt. salad dressing or mayonnaise

Grind together green tomatoes, peppers, and onions. Add juice from sweet pickles, sugar, and salt; boil together for 20 minutes. Dissolve cornstarch in a small amount of water, enough to make a smooth (not heavy) paste. Stir cornstarch paste into tomato mixture; reduce heat. Add ground sweet pickles, mustard, and salad dressing; heat through but do not boil. Can according to home-canning procedures.

Cantaloupe is delicious eaten with pepper.

AUNT LIZZIE'S TARTAR SAUCE

3/4 c. mayonnaise (homemade
   is best; see recipe on page
   176)
1/2 tsp. minced onion
1 tsp. chopped sweet pickle

1 tsp. chopped green olives
1 Tbsp. minced parsley
2 tsp. minced capers
1 Tbsp. tarragon vinegar

Fold vegetables into mayonnaise. Add vinegar; chill. Serve with any type of fish.

The light of the eyes rejoiceth the heart: and a good report maketh the bones fat.   —PROVERBS 15:30

CORN RELISH

5 pts. corn (cooked and cut
   off cob)
5 pts. cabbage, chopped
5 red peppers, seeded and
   chopped

2 qts. vinegar
1 1/2 lbs. sugar
2 Tbsp. salt
1/4 lb. mustard seed

Place all ingredients in a large kettle and boil for 30 minutes. Pour into sterilized canning jars and seal hot.

Note: If unfamiliar with the canning process, a good resource is the *Ball Blue Book of Preserving* (available by calling 1-800-392-2575, option 1).

Note from Bev

This mouth-watering recipe from Grandmother Ada's recipe files makes oodles of succulent relish.

CRANBERRY RELISH

1 20-oz. can crushed pinepple

1 pt. fresh or frozen cranberries

2 oranges, peeled and diced

1 large apple, diced

Honey or sugar

Drain pineapple, reserving and setting aside juice. Mix cranberries, oranges, apple, and pineapple together; chill. Stir in reserved pineapple juice; sweeten to taste with honey or sugar.

She looketh well to the ways of her household, and eateth not the bread of idleness. —PROVERBS 31:27

GREEN TOMATO MINCEMEAT

2 lbs. fresh green tomatoes,
chopped

2 tsp. salt

1 c. suet

½ c. water

4 lb. sugar

3 c. chopped apples

3 lb. raisins

1 lemon, seeds and stem
removed, ground

Grated peel of 1 orange

2 tsp. cinnamon

2 tsp. nutmeg

1 tsp. cloves (optional)

⅓ c. vinegar

Sprinkle salt over tomatoes; let stand 1 hour. Drain, discarding juice. Cover tomatoes with cold water; boil for 5 minutes. Drain, add suet and ½ c. water; simmer for 20 minutes. Stir in sugar until dissolved. Add remaining ingredients and boil until thick. Put in jars and seal.

Timely good deeds are nicer than afterthoughts.

CHOW-CHOW

6 peppers (red and green)

1 qt. small onions, chopped

1/2 head of cauliflower, broken
   into florets

2 qts. waxed beans

2 qts. young beans (waxed,
   lima, and green beans)

2 qts. sweet corn kernels

1 bunch of celery

1 horseradish root, grated

1 oz. celery seed

2 qts. carrots, chopped

1/2 head of cabbage, chopped
   in 1-inch strips

13 small cucumbers, sliced

1/2 qt. lima beans

2 oz. ground mustard

2 oz. turmeric

2 qt. apple cider vinegar

1 1/4 lbs. sugar

1 Tbsp. cornstarch

Sprinkle of salt

In a large kettle, combine all ingredients; bring to a boil. Cook for 5–7 minutes longer or until vegetables are tender. Pack the mixture into canning jars (washed in dishwasher) and follow home-canning procedures.

Note: If unfamiliar with the canning process, a good resource is the *Ball Blue Book of Preserving* (available by calling 1-800-392-2575, option 1).

Note from Bev

Chow-Chow is a staple of any Amish meal.

PICKLED PEARS

6 qts. fresh pears

6 c. cider vinegar

6 c. sugar

Peel, core, and slice pears; place in kettle. Add vinegar and sugar; cook until tender. Remove pears from liquid and place in sterilized canning jars. Continue to boil syrup until it is nice and thick, then pour over pears and seal jars.

Butter and honey shall he eat. —ISAIAH 7:15

PICKLED CANTALOUPE

2 lbs. cantaloupe

½ tsp. pulverized alum

1 pt. vinegar

1 lb. sugar

Cinnamon

Cloves

Peel and seed cantaloupe; cut in 1½-inch square pieces. Boil cantaloupe pieces and alum in water for 10 minutes; drain. Add vinegar, sugar, and cinnamon and cloves to taste. Boil together and place in sterilized canning jars. Seal, following home-canning procedures.

Pickles taste better if allowed to stand at least six weeks before serving.

HANNAH'S DILL PICKLES

4 qts. medium cucumbers

8 sprays of dill

4 garlic cloves

1 qt. vinegar

1 c. salt

3 qt. water

On the day before preparing, wash cucumbers and cover with water. Let stand overnight. The next day, put 1 dill spray in bottom of each of 4 quart jars. Pack cucumbers into jars, being careful not to bruise. Add 1 garlic clove to each jar. Place 1 dill spray on top of each jar. Combine vinegar, salt, and water; bring to a rolling boil. Fill jars to overflowing with vinegar mixture; seal.

Note from Bev

My mother says I loved dill pickles so much that as a young girl, I actually drank the juice at the end of the jar.

MARY RUTH'S PICCALILLI

2 qts. green tomatoes	3 green peppers
2 qts. ripe tomatoes	1 large cucumber
3 onions	2 bunches of celery
3 red peppers	½ c. salt

Put all vegetables through a food chopper. Sprinkle with salt and let stand in refrigerator for 12 or more hours. Drain well and add the following:

3 pts. vinegar	1 scant tsp. pepper
2 lbs. brown sugar	1 tsp. mustard

Simmer for 1 hour and then pour into hot sterilized canning jars; follow home-canning procedures. (The juice can be drained off and canned for soup, as well.)

PICKLED RED BEETS AND RED BEET EGGS

32-oz. can red beets,	¾ c. vinegar
undrained	⅛ tsp. salt
1 c. sugar	12 hard-boiled eggs, peeled

In saucepan, mix red beets and juice, sugar, vinegar, and salt. Bring to a boil.

Pour over whole eggs. Allow to cool to room temperature; place in refrigerator for at least 24 hours.

Note from Bev

Very Lancaster County! One of the "seven sweets and seven sours."

Love not the world, neither the things that are in the world.

—I JOHN 2:15

The secret to enjoying life is to be thankful for what each day brings.

BREAD AND BUTTER PICKLES

24 medium cucumbers, washed and thinly sliced

10 medium-sized onions, finely chopped

1 Tbsp. salt

6 red peppers, seeded, chopped, and stems removed

1 qt. vinegar

2 c. brown sugar

1 tsp. celery seed

1 tsp. mustard

½ tsp. ginger

1 tsp. turmeric

Mix cucumbers together with chopped onions, salt, and red peppers. Let stand at least one hour. Boil vinegar, sugar, and spices. Add cucumber mixture and bring to almost a rolling boil, stirring frequently with wooden spoon. Pack pickles into hot sterilized jars and seal.

Note from Bev

Another one of Grandmother Ada's time-tested recipes. These pickles are especially good on sandwiches or hamburgers. The whole house will smell of this down-home aroma.

CANNED PEACHES

½ bushel peaches = approx. 12 quarts canned

1½ c. honey

4½ c. sugar (raw or turbinado sugar work well)

12 c. water

Follow home-canning procedures for canning peaches. (If you are unfamiliar with the procedure, the *Ball Blue Book of Preserving*, available by calling 1-800-392-2575, option 1, has clear instructions.)

Combine honey, sugar, and water and bring to a boil to form syrup; keep syrup simmering while adding to peaches in jars.

Note: Syrup will not be as clear when using honey and raw or turbinado sugar, but it is delicious.

Note from Bev

Canning peaches was a family affair in the busy Buchwalter kitchen—among the daughters, at least. My mother's job was to thoroughly wash all the canning jars. She also remembers the process of tenderly placing each halved peach into the jar, round side out, to make the jars look "pretty." An art form, to be sure.

My meat is to do the will of him that sent me, and to finish his work.   —JOHN 4:34

Recipe Index
(ALPHABETICAL BY CATEGORY)

I0394968

The 1400s

HEADLINES IN HISTORY

Books in the Headlines in History series:

The 1000s
The 1100s
The 1200s
The 1300s
The 1400s
The 1500s
The 1600s
The 1700s
The 1800s
The 1900s

The 1400s

HEADLINES IN HISTORY

Stuart A. Kallen, *Book Editor*

Bonnie Szumski, *Editorial Director*
Scott Barbour, *Managing Editor*

Greenhaven Press, Inc., San Diego, California

PUYALLUP PUBLIC LIBRARY

y9
940.2
F

Every effort has been made to trace the owners of copyrighted material. The articles in this volume may have been edited for content, length, and/or reading level. The titles have been changed to enhance the editorial purpose.

No part of this book may be reproduced or used in any form or by any means, electrical, mechanical, or otherwise, including, but not limited to, photocopy, recording, or any information storage and re-trieval system, without prior permission from the publisher.

Library of Congress Cataloging-in-Publication Data

The 1400s / Stuart A. Kallen, book editor.
    p. cm. — (Headlines in history)
  Includes bibliographical references and index.
  ISBN 0-7377-0536-1 (lib.)—ISBN 0-7377-0535-3 (pbk.)
  1. Fifteenth century. 2. Civilization, Medieval.
3. Renaissance. 4. Indians. 5. America—History.
I. Kallen, Stuart A., 1955– II. Headlines in history
(San Diego, Calif.)

CB367 .A16 2001
940.2'1—dc21

                  00-052801

Cover photos: (top, left to right) Chimu Indian mummy mask, AKG London; Columbus's ships approaching land, © North Wind Picture Archives; Joan of Arc, AKG London; (bottom) Johannes Gutenberg examining a proof, © North Wind Picture Archives
Dover Publications, 69, 134
Library of Congress, 54, 139, 160, 226
North Wind Picture Archives, 83
Planet Art, 150
Prints Old and Rare, 178

Copyright © 2001 by Greenhaven Press, Inc.
P.O. Box 289009, San Diego, CA 92198-9009

Printed in the USA

CONTENTS

Chapter 1: Empires and Conquest

1. Politics in Fifteenth-Century Europe
by Robert Warnock and George K. Anderson   39
By the end of the fifteenth century, Europe was composed of more than a dozen powerful city-states, many
of them battling one another for control over religion,
trade, and territory.

2. Eyewitness to the Battle of Agincourt
by Jean de Waurin   44
Fifteenth-century writer Jean de Waurin describes a
battle in the Hundred Years' War between the English
and the French armored knights in Agincourt, France.

3. Joan of Arc
by Robin Neillands   50
When the young peasant girl Joan of Arc heard the
voices of the saints telling her to battle the English at Orleans, France, the forces she commandeered helped begin England's defeat during the Hundred Years' War.

4. The Conquest of Constantinople
by Philip Mansel   56
The crown jewel of Western Christianity was Constantinople in present-day Turkey. The fall of that city to
the Ottoman Turks led European Christians to believe
that Muslims might someday rule the entire continent.

5. Eyewitness to Turkish Invasion
by John Bessarion   62
Cardinal John Bessarion witnessed the destruction
caused by the Ottomans when they invaded Constantinople in 1453.

the Medici family who ruled that city. Although their great wealth came from banking and industry, Cosimo, Piero, and Lorenzo de Medici were among the greatest art patrons of their time.

San Salvador, the explorer wrote a detailed letter to his benefactors—the king and queen of Spain—describing the wonders he had seen in the New World.

Chronological time lines of history are mysteriously fascinating. To learn that within a single century Christopher Columbus sailed to the New World, the Aztec, Maya, and Inca cultures were flourishing, Joan of Arc was burned to death, and the invention of the printing press was radically changing access to written materials allows a reader a different type of view of history: a bird's-eye view of the entire globe and its events. Such a global picture allows for cross-cultural comparisons as well as a valuable overview of chronological history that studying one particular area simply cannot provide.

Taking an expansive look at world history in each century, therefore, can be surprisingly informative. In Headlines in History, Greenhaven Press attempts to imitate this time-line approach using primary and secondary sources that span each century. Each volume gives readers the opportunity to view history as though they were reading the headlines of a global newspaper: Editors of each volume have attempted to glean and include the most important and influential events of the century, as well as quirky trends and cultural oddities. Headlines in History, then, attempts to give readers a glimpse of both the mundane and the earth-shattering. Articles on the French Revolution, for example, are juxtaposed with the then-current fashion concerns of the French nobility. This creates a higher interest level by allowing students a glimpse of people's everyday lives throughout history.

By using both primary and secondary sources, students also have the opportunity to view the historical events both as eyewitnesses have experienced them and as historians have interpreted them. Thus, students can place such historical events in a larger context as well as receive background information on important world events.

Headlines in History allows readers the unique opportunity to learn more about events that may only be mentioned in their history textbooks, or may be ignored entirely. The series presents students with a variety of interesting topics that span cultural, historical, and political arenas. Such a broad span of material will allow students to wander wherever their curiosity will take them.

INTRODUCTION

L ooking back on the world of the fifteenth century from the modern age of computers, cars, and strip malls, one would notice a place that was greatly unmarred by human endeavors. Large portions of the globe would be in their natural state, with wildlife abundant in mountains, fields, and forests. Travel across this landscape would be at a horse's pace or determined by the wind in a ship powered by sail.

Even major cities were incredibly small by modern standards. Paris—one of fifteenth-century Europe's largest cities—had fewer than eighty thousand people, compared with 8.7 million today. The population of the entire world was only about 375 million, in contrast to the more than 6 billion people alive today. In fact, the entire population of Europe was only 70 million, 15 million less than the number of people living in modern-day Germany alone.

Despite the fact that most of fifteenth-century Europe was a rural place full of untrammeled forests and natural beauty, human nature remained as it had for centuries. Charismatic leaders gained great power, formed great armies, marched across continents, conquered weaker peoples, and slaughtered the opposition. Then, as now, religious conflicts were the justification for most major wars.

The fifteenth century, however, is different from most other centuries in the last millennium in that it is divided into two segments by historians. Until 1450 or so, the era is classified as part of the Middle Ages. After that time, the fifteenth century is considered part of the Renaissance, literally the "rebirth" in arts, letters, and music. The dividing line is marked by the invention of the European-style printing press, which led to a world-changing revolution in communication and education comparable to the invention of the modern personal computer and Internet. (The Chinese invented the first printing press in the twelfth century, but it was never in widespread use.)

The Late Middle Ages that ended in the fifteenth century was a time of disaster and destruction in Europe. Between 1347 and 1351, the Black Death (bubonic plague) cut a swath of disease and death across Europe, killing 25 to 50 percent of the population, depending on the region. Periodic outbreaks continued to kill millions of people well into the sixteenth century. Meanwhile, between 1337 and 1453, the so-called Hundred Years' War continued intermittently in France—the most populous country in Europe—disrupting life and bringing misery to many average citizens whose villages were already devastated from the recent plague.

In Italy, powerful city-states such as Florence and Venice battled each other for supremacy, while farther to the south and east, Islamic forces associated with the Turkish Ottoman Empire invaded Constantinople, Russia, Hungary, and India.

Although horrible in their scope, the wars and disease that marked the fifteenth century had some beneficial effects. The plague disrupted society, but it also destroyed the feudal social structure of earlier times. With fewer people to compete for food, land, and shelter, peasants—especially those in western Europe—found greater prosperity and freedom. In regions where the wars were concluded, new cultures mingled on former battlegrounds, increasing trade in spices, sugar, dyes, cloth, and other goods that brought new wealth to formerly embattled regions.

The cultural roots of the modern world were significantly advanced during the latter half of the fifteenth century. The art of Leonardo da Vinci, Michelangelo, and others changed the way people looked at the world. And the Renaissance ideal of humanism, the belief in the personal worth of the individual, gave rise to religious reformation and planted the seeds of modern democracy.

As the fifteenth century drew to a close, European explorer Christopher Columbus opened up a new route across the seas to lands where Aztec, Mayan, and Native American peoples were living at the apex of their cultures. The clash of cultures between the Europeans and the indigenous peoples of America would be carried out over the next several centuries.

The affairs of the fifteenth century continue to influence life in modern times—even if in subtle ways. To study these past events is to give context to the present—to frame modern times in the endeavors of those who lived before. While twenty-first-century inventions and technological wonders may shape the everyday lives of people today, by peering into centuries past it is possible to see that people's dreams, hopes, and desires have continued along the same path for hundreds of years.

Gateway to the Modern Age

To the average person living in Europe in the year 1400, life had not changed much for hundreds of years. Daily existence was almost completely given over to growing or gathering food. Agriculture was still in its primitive stages, with farmers using small, inefficient plows that barely scratched the surface of the soil. Feudal lords possessed great landholdings and forced peasants to turn over a large portion of their crops in exchange for the right to farm small strips of land. People supplemented their diets by raising cattle, pigs, and fowl, and by hunting, fishing, and gathering wild food. Those who desired milk or cheese or items such as shoes or furniture generally had to produce such things for themselves. The European printing press would not be invented for another five decades, and the majority of the population had neither the time nor the luxury to learn how to read and write.

The peasants were ruled by emperors, kings, queens, and leaders of the Catholic Church. Within these controlling hierarchies, perpetual battles for influence and supremacy resulted in conflict, wars, and endless scheming to obtain—and retain—power. Each leader had his or her own seat of power and, unlike today, few unified countries existed. Instead, cities formed their own countries known as city-states, which ceaselessly battled one another. For example, in Italy in the early fifteenth century, five major city-states, including Venice, Milan, Florence, Pisa, and Genoa, competed for dominance in the region. Even nobles in small towns and rural areas raised armies of up to one thousand men to fight wars against neighboring towns over petty property disputes. In fact, between 1450 and 1660 there were only four years when there was not an organized war somewhere in Europe.

The Black Death

This way of life—and almost every other matter in the fifteenth century—was profoundly affected by the bubonic plague, known as the Black Death. The plague was a frightening and horrible epidemic.

15

Although it was not understood at the time, the disease was carried by fleas that lived on black rats brought to Europe from Asia on trading ships. Anyone bitten by a plague-infected flea became gravely ill within days. The body temperature would rise to 104 degrees Fahrenheit and the victim would become delirious and experience severe vomiting and muscle pain. The lymph nodes (called buboes—hence the name *bubonic plague*) in the groin and thighs would enlarge and spread the disease throughout the body. The skin would break out in large black spots.

The disease killed an estimated 18 to 35 million people in its first sweep across the continent between 1347 and 1351. Every ten years or so, the Black Death would strike again. Italy alone suffered epidemics in 1400, from 1422 to 1425, from 1436 to 1439, from 1447 to 1451, and from 1485 to 1487. In addition to the plague, dozens of other deadly diseases were rampant, including influenza, smallpox, and scarlet fever.

Poor people who lacked food and sanitary living conditions suffered the most from the Black Death. At the first signs of an epidemic, the rich fled the cities for their country estates. In Fernand Braudel's *Capitalism and Material Life 1400–1800,* one man wrote about a Paris epidemic, saying,

> Death was principally directed towards the poor so that only a very few of the Paris porters and wage-earners who had lived there in large numbers before the misfortune, were left. . . . As for the district of Petiz Champs, the whole countryside was cleared of poor people who previously lived there in large numbers.[1]

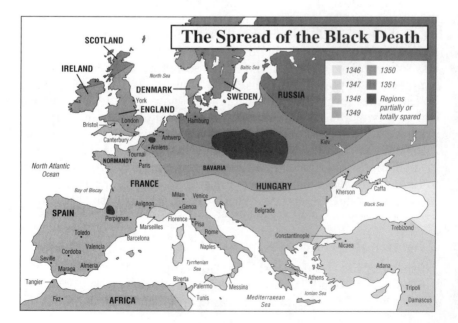

The Spread of the Black Death

As the death toll from the disease mounted, individuals thought only of their own survival. Those suspected of carrying the plague were driven from town. Neighborhoods where the disease was rampant were cordoned off by authorities, and no one was allowed to leave. Houses where the plague had struck were marked with red crosses. The clothing and all household goods of the dead were burned. And, according to William Manchester in *A World Lit Only by Fire: The Medieval Mind and the Renaissance,* "Each night gravediggers' carts creaked down the street as drivers cried, 'Bring out your dead!' and in Germany entire towns . . . had become like cemeteries."[2]

Jewish people, who were less susceptible to the disease—possibly because their homes were cleaner or possibly because they lived in isolated areas—were accused of poisoning the wells of Christians. As a result, some Christians organized violence against the Jewish people, scapegoating them for their troubles.

In addition to killing countless numbers of people, the plague affected the living as well. According to Werner Rösener in *Peasants in the Middle Ages,*

> The immediate effect of the plagues was a kind of existential shock which made itself felt in every sphere of contemporary life as well as in the forms of human behaviour, causing reactions ranging from a fervent religiosity to a large variety of secular excesses. [The] serious drop in the population of the late Middle Ages was one of the turning-points in the history of Europe. . . [It] is literally impossible to understand historical developments in the following centuries without taking . . . into account . . . the plagues. For this was more than death on a massive scale, this was something deeply distressing and incomprehensible, for which the men of the Middle Ages could find no solace. The Black Death was an apocalyptic event, incomparable to all previously known tragedy from famine to war.[3]

Although the plague continued to ravage Europe every ten years until the late eighteenth century, those who survived actually found themselves in a better situation. According to *Voyages of Discovery: Timeframe AD 1400–1500,*

> [The] plague had destroyed humans, not things. Real assets—land and buildings, ships, whatever primitive machinery existed, and of course the gold that nestled in . . . vaults—were untouched, but they were shared by far fewer people. In fact, the Black Death had created a cash surplus that could not easily be spent in the ordinary fashion, for the means of production, being almost exclusively based on human labor, had decreased with the population. But the money could always be spent, given sufficient ingenuity. In a very real sense, the [dead people's] share of the wealth would finance the [coming] expensive artistic display of the Renaissance.[4]

The Rise of Peasant Power

In the centuries before the Black Death, peasants had little control over their lives. Most people survived under an arrangement called manorialism, a system in which land, or "the manor," was owned by lords, known as the landed aristocracy. This land was parceled out to peasants, known as serfs, who farmed it and in return paid the lords with labor or with a large percentage of their money or crops. Serfs, bound by unfair contracts to the lord, lived in virtual slavery.

Marzieh Gail describes a typical serf household in *Life in the Renaissance:*

> The Italian peasant . . . fell at night onto a mattress stuffed with straw. This could be on a floor of packed earth, or possibly on a low, crude wooden platform. His house had few windows and no window glass. Tallow for candles was too expensive, so he lit his hovel with pieces of pitch-filled wood, which gave off a great deal of smoke, or he might place a wick in a dish of olive oil, like the ancient Romans and Greeks. His wife cooked in clay pots. Later on, a peasant might be able to afford pewter or copper. But the food on the plates was all raised by himself, except the salt fish bought or bartered for at the nearest market. He got along with very few spices but used a good deal of salt—for preserving meat through the lean winter months, but also because he liked his food well salted. Honey was much easier to come by than sugar, so he used it for sweetening. And, just as today, wine was his chief drink.[5]

Because of their living conditions, peasant farmers were considered the lowest people in society. Gail continues,

> In Renaissance Italy almost no one had a good word for the man trudging along back of a plow. It did not matter if he rose at dawn and worked as long as there was light; nor that all Italy depended on the farmer for most of what it ate and drank and wore; nor that more people lived on the land than in the towns.
>
> Townspeople considered the farmer as stupid as the oxen pulling his clumsy plowshare through the hard earth. Writers made him the butt of their jokes: it was said, for instance, that a peasant would faint away if he smelled perfume, and could only be revived by a whiff of manure. On the other hand, the nobles whose land he tilled called him shrewd, cunning—a conniver, always looking out for himself. . . . Another charge against the farmers was that they went in for magic rather than prayer and sought to cure themselves and their animals through secret potions and incantations.[6]

When periodic epidemics wiped out great numbers of laborers, however, the system of manorialism changed radically, and corroded the enormous power that the lords had once held. Many farmers who survived abandoned the hard work of the serf and opened businesses in nearby towns, many of which were nearly empty. The lords, facing bankruptcy, were forced to lower rents, offer better working conditions, and otherwise give more power and money to serfs. When those incentives failed, criminals or prisoners who were captured in wars were forced into agricultural slavery.

The fifteenth-century trend favoring peasant farmers had several repercussions. The move away from the land gave rise to a growing number of cities and towns across the landscape. Thus, with more people inhabiting such towns, a new class of merchants emerged to provide these people with food, clothing, and other necessities. This, in turn, hastened the move toward commercialism and capitalism and accelerated the need for foreign trade and imports. The new desire for imported items motivated explorers such as Vasco da Gama, Columbus, and others to seek out new trade routes by the end of the century.

Clash of Powers

During most of the Middle Ages (the period lasting from about A.D. 900 to 1450), the farms and villages of Europe were controlled by three major powers: the church, various monarchs (kings and queens), and the landed aristocracy. According to Joseph Dahmus in *The Middle Ages: A Popular History,* this more or less equal competition began to change in the fifteenth century:

> Until the beginning of the fourteenth century the church could aspire to retain a significant voice in public affairs. And there were moments, even in the fifteenth [century] when the aristocracy appeared about to extinguish the monarchy in both England and France. But in the end the king emerged supreme over much of western Europe. By 1500 he had subordinated both church and feudal aristocracy to his will.[7]

One cause of this shift in power was the move away from manorialism. Another primary cause was the change in the nature of warfare. In earlier centuries, rich noblemen who could afford horses, armor, swords, and the men to use them could raise an army strong enough to challenge a king. During this period, wars were fought by knights in shining armor, who were supported by serfs conscripted into armed service against their will.

The development of newer and more powerful weapons changed this equation. The longbow allowed archers to pierce a knight's armor with deadly arrows from a six-hundred-foot distance. The spearlike pike and the axlike halberd also made armor ineffective. Dahmus explains,

> Pikemen with their twenty-foot spears could stop a charge of knights. If they took the offensive, they could throw a company of knights into panic. The halberd was a fearful weapon some eight feet in length, whose heavy head bore a sharp point at the top, a hatchet on one side, and a wicked hook on the other. When swung like a battle-ax it could cleave

through helmet and armor as though they were matchwood.

To counter these new weapons, the knight kept putting on more armor. In the fifteenth century plate armor covered him from head to toe, and except for the well-aimed shot of a longbowman's arrow, he was reasonably secure. Yet while armor assured him considerable protection, [its heavy weight] almost immobilized him in addition to bankrupting him. Only under ideal field conditions could he fight, and progressively fewer men could afford the necessary outlay.[8]

When gunpowder became increasingly popular in the mid–fifteenth century, the age of the knight was over—and the power of the landed aristocracy along with it.

The king's dominant power came from his ability to afford large armies that wielded expensive artillery. This was the result of the rise of capitalism and commerce—and the taxes these transactions provided the kings. In earlier centuries, kings had no way of raising large sums of money because most of their subjects were serfs, whose labor supported the lords of the manor. In the fifteenth century, however, the rise in the number and size of towns gave monarchs a new source of duties, taxes, and other revenue. With his new wealth, the king could afford to hire the best soldiers, equip them with the finest weapons, and use them to make sure his taxes were collected.

The Hundred Years' War

The radical changes in warfare were accelerated by the so-called Hundred Years' War, which actually lasted 116 years from 1337 to 1453. The war, which was given its name in the nineteenth century, was a long-running battle between England and France, who were the two greatest powers in western Europe at that time.

The Hundred Years' War was really a series of battles fought off and on for different complicated reasons for nearly twelve decades. The central issue was that, beginning in 1327, several English kings believed that they should also be the kings of France.

The kings of England in the fourteenth and fifteenth centuries were descended from French nobles who had invaded and conquered England in 1066. (In fact, when the war began in 1337, most of the English nobility still spoke French, although most knew enough English to rule the country.) These English rulers still owned vast territories in France. Over the centuries, French kings repeatedly attempted to wrest these lands from the now-English rulers.

In 1327, the English throne was taken over by the bold young Edward III. The daring new king claimed that, in order to protect English lands in France, he would also become the king of France. Naturally, the French vehemently disagreed with this position, and soon war broke out.

The war began slowly and centered on various sieges, battles, and signed—and broken—peace treaties. Edward III pursued his dream of becoming the king of France until he died in 1377. Meanwhile, thousands of soldiers died and tens of thousands of peasants suffered the horrors of war. Little changed, however and the English continued to hold lands in France while the French wanted to evict them. In the late fourteenth century, a stalemate developed, and in 1397 France and England agreed to a thirty-year truce.

This truce lasted just sixteen years, however, ending when Henry V, the great-grandson of Edward III, came to power in England. The English renewed the war in France and won several decisive battles, especially the one at Agincourt in 1415. In 1421, the English finally saw Edward III's wish come true: Henry V was declared heir to the French throne. Henry V married the former French king's daughter, and the couple had a child. When Henry V died unexpectedly in 1422, his son Henry VI also became the king of France and England. Unfortunately, the nine-month-old Henry was not old enough to wear two crowns and rule two countries.

Joan of Arc

While Henry VI was growing up, Henry V's brothers attempted to hold on to the English gains. Their hopes were dashed however, by the seemingly divine powers of a French peasant girl named Joan of Arc. Joan was about thirteen in 1424 when she claimed that she heard voices from Saint Catherine, Saint Margaret, and Saint Michael that instructed her to liberate France from the English. In 1429, after revealing her powers to the French authorities, Joan traveled to the city of Orleans, which had been suffering greatly under English siege for eight months. In only eight days, Joan and her troops were able to break the English hold on Orleans and push them out of the Reims region.

In early 1430, Joan continued her campaign against the English, but she was captured and turned over to English authorities in Rouen. The English declared that the voices Joan of Arc had heard did not belong to the saints but to Satan. Joan was put on trial for witchcraft and heresy. She was burned at the stake on May 30, 1431. In her death, Joan of Arc became a heroine to the French people, and she was canonized as a saint in 1920.

In 1453, the Hundred Years' War came to its long, bloody conclusion when the French finally drove the English from their last holdout in the Bordeaux region. The loss of the war—and periodic bouts of insanity—severely weakened the powers of Henry VI, who had assumed the crown at age sixteen in 1437. This and the fact that Henry had no heirs, led to a civil war in England as warring families fought over who would take the throne. This war, known as the War of the Roses, continued off and on until 1485.

The Hundred Years' War permanently changed the nature of war. At its beginning, battles were fought by small bands of armored knights wielding clubs and bows and arrows. At its end, the war was waged by large armies using artillery.

The use of ships and navies also became more important, as Christopher T. Allmand writes in *Society at War: The Experience of England and France During the Hundred Years War:*

> Naval warfare . . . was beginning to assume a role of importance in international conflict. The numbers involved in fighting at sea; the use made of naval forces to carry out lightning raids on coastal districts; the importance of keeping the sea-passages open in certain circumstances; the avowed aim of disrupting the enemy's trade and conveyance of military goods and personnel are all a clear indication that the war at sea was regarded as having an increasing role to play in war.[9]

The Great Schism

As the Hundred Years' War raged between two of the greatest Christian powers in the world, the papacy—which governed the church—was itself engaged in a major conflict known as the Great Schism. Unlike an invasion from an outside force, according to Manchester, this "wound to the prestige of the Vatican was self-inflicted."[10]

The problems began for the church in 1305 when Pope Clement V, because of conflicts in Rome, moved the papacy to Avignon in what is now southeastern France. The Holy See resided in France for more than seventy years. By 1377, when Pope Gregory XI returned the papacy to Rome, the College of Cardinals (the body that elects the pope) had a strong French majority. When Gregory died in 1378, the French cardinals wanted to elect a French pope. The Italian cardinals wanted an Italian pope. The Italians, backed by a throng of angry Romans, won the day and elected Urban VI from Naples.

The choice of Urban soon proved to be a mistake. He was a ruthless man who quickly reduced the powers of the cardinals who had elected him. The French majority of cardinals fled back to their homeland and declared Urban's election fraudulent. The French then elected Pope Clement VII, and for nearly four more decades, the church was ruled by two vicars of Christ, one in Avignon and one in Rome. Over the years, the Roman branch saw the election of three more popes, while the French replaced Clement with Benedict XIII.

The schism continued until 1417, when the cardinals met at the Council of Constance and elected Martin V, who was generally accepted by everyone as the only pope.

The petty battles concerning the pope had opened the church up to great criticism from religious scholars as well as the general public. This occurred despite the fact that, at that time, anyone who dared to question church leaders or criticize the church could face the death penalty. With the Great Schism behind it, the church turned its attention to solidifying its power and ridding itself of any dissidents. One major critic had been Oxford theologian John Wycliffe, who, according to Dahmus,

> [attacked] the wealth of the church, the political influence of bishops, and assorted abuses. Then he became a revolutionary, and in voluminous writings shifted his assault to such fundamental practices and doctrines as monastic vows, [and] indulgences [forgiving sins in exchange for money][11]

The Hussite Revolution

Wycliffe died in 1383, and the church ordered all of his books burned. Wycliffe's ideas, however, had been adopted by John Hus, a priest and religious reformer in Prague, Bohemia (the present-day Czech Republic). Like Wycliffe, Hus criticized the church's wealth. Unlike Wycliffe, who was a wealthy academic, Hus was born a peasant and had the ability to attract large numbers of followers from the lower classes. This was a direct threat to the hierarchy of the church.

Hus became the rector of the University of Prague in 1409, but because of his outspoken views, he was excommunicated in 1411. In 1415, Hus was arrested, convicted of heresy, and burned at the stake. As a result, according to C.W. Previté-Orton in volume 2 of *The Shorter Cambridge Medieval History,*

> Hus became a martyr for the liberty of the individual conscience, and his death was as powerful as his life. His cause had become identified with that of the Czech nation which was inspired by him. . . . The news of his execution . . . roused a storm of indignation among nobles and peoples.[12]

Hus's followers, called Hussites, began a national reform movement in Bohemia and Moravia. Unfortunately, they were divided into two warring camps, the conservatives and the radicals. The radicals proposed open warfare against the church and ignited the Hussite Revolution in 1420.

Pope Martin V ordered a crusade against the Hussites, and in the wars that followed, the crusading armies were repeatedly beaten by the Hussites, led by Jan Zizka. In May 1434, however, the power of the radicals was broken, and the Hussite Revolution came to an end. Although they had been beaten, the writings of Hus and the demands of the reformers would be revived in the sixteenth century by Martin Luther and would result in the founding of the Protestant religion.

The Ottoman Empire and the Fall of Constantinople

While the Catholic Church was engaged in internal battles, Christianity faced a more serious threat from Islamic armies to the south.

The same year that the Hundred Years' War ended, the great city formerly known as Constantinople was invaded by the Ottoman Turks. The city, now renamed Istanbul, is located on both sides of the Bosporus, a narrow strait known as the Golden Horn between Europe and Asia. The Bosporus connects three major waterways—the Black, Aegean, and Mediterranean Seas. For more than a thousand years, this strategic location helped make the city a prosperous center of trade between the Asian, European, and African continents.

The wealth of the city, originally founded in 657 B.C. and named Byzantium, made it vulnerable to dozens of invasions over the years. Byzantium was captured by the Romans in A.D. 196. It was renamed Constantinople by Roman emperor Constantine I in 330. The city flourished as the capital of the Byzantine Empire and as a continuation of the Roman Empire, which converted to Christianity in the fourth century. By the sixth century, the powerful Byzantine Empire dominated the Mediterranean region. Over the centuries, however, the power of the city slowly evaporated, and by the fifteenth century Constantinople was only a minor player on the world stage.

Throughout the years, Constantinople had become isolated as a religious center as well. The city had adopted the Eastern Orthodox branch of Christianity, which clashed with the customs of the western, Catholic Church. As such, Constantinople was invaded and sacked by western crusaders in 1204. The city was retaken by the Byzantine forces in 1254 but was seriously weakened. Over the next several centuries, the city's population would drop from over 1 million to less than 100,000.

Meanwhile, the Muslim power of the Ottoman Empire had grown considerably during the fourteenth century. At the beginning of the century, the Ottomans, descendants of Turkoman nomads, were a small tribe living on the edges of the Byzantine Empire. But by 1389 the Ottomans had consolidated their power in Anatolia (present-day Turkey) and crossed into eastern Europe, conquering Serbia, Bulgaria, and Bosnia. By the mid–fourteenth century, Constantinople was surrounded by Ottoman-held lands.

In 1453, Muslim soldiers of the Ottoman Empire led by sultan Mehmed II invaded Constantinople. Although the Turks had superior forces, the city had already withstood twenty-two sieges over the centuries. It was surrounded by high stone walls interspersed with 188 towers that stood sixty-five-feet high. These medieval walls eventually fell to the withering fire of the Ottoman cannon, however, and on May 29, the victorious Mehmed II rode into the vanquished Constantinople. The loss of the city was a major blow to eastern Christendom and was called by *The Shorter Cambridge Medieval History,* "the greatest tragedy of the [fifteenth] century, [for it represented] the [final] fall of the Roman Empire, which had preserved ancient civilization, however tarnished, throughout the Middle Ages."[13]

A Christian Spain Unites

Constantinople was not the only place where Christians clashed with Muslims. In present-day Spain, centuries of conflict had finally left Catholic forces victorious over the Muslims.

By the fifteenth century, Spain, located on the Iberian peninsula on the far western reaches of Europe, had been a place of military contention between Muslims from Africa and Christians from Europe for more than six hundred years. In fact, Barnet Litvinoff writes in *1492*, "It could not be said for certain whether the Iberian peninsula constituted the south-western extremity of Europe or the northernmost outpost of Africa."[14]

By the twelfth century, the country was splintered into several kingdoms controlled by different factions. Arab Muslims from Africa known as Moors had conquered a large part of the peninsula and were firmly entrenched in Iberian society, as were Jews who had been driven out of the Holy Land by the Crusades of earlier times. In the meantime, two Christian kingdoms, Castile and Aragon, maintained a strong foothold in the northern and central regions. The present-day country of Portugal was also recognized as an independent Christian kingdom. By 1248, the Christians had driven the Moors out of every region except Granada, where Islamic culture continued to thrive.

Although the Muslims in Granada had little power compared with the Christian kingdoms, the region was used as a base of operations for Muslim invasions from North Africa, which continued to threaten Catholic Spain. In 1469, Ferdinand of Aragon wed Isabella, princess of Castile, and the two most important kingdoms of Spain were joined. Finally, on January 2, 1492, Boabdil, the last Moorish ruler in Europe, was forced to surrender Granada to King Ferdinand and Queen Isabella, uniting Spain into one Christian country.

The Spanish Inquisition

Ferdinand and Isabella were known as the "Catholic Kings," and they used the church to centralize their power by driving out or killing anyone who was not a Christian. Beginning in 1480, the church, at the insistence of the king and queen, created a council to investigate the religious activities of people in Spain. Known as the Spanish Inquisition, this council quickly branded thousands of people as heretics—most of them Jews or Muslims.

In order to gain confessions from the alleged heretics, the council, led by the Grand Inquisitor Tomas de Torquemada, tortured people by whipping them, stretching their limbs on the rack, burning their skin with red-hot pokers, and squeezing their fingers and toes in "thumbscrews." After such tortures, the accused were burned at the stake in town squares while thousands of spectators jeered and yelled as the victims went up in flames.

The main targets of the Spanish Inquisition were Jews who had converted to Christianity. These people were known as crypto-Jews, New Christians, Judaisers, or *Marranos* (a word that meant "pig"). They were greatly resented in Spanish society because many of them were successful in business and other matters. In fact, some Jewish converts had risen to the highest levels of the Catholic Church. For instance, the Bishop Pablo de Santa Maria, who served the royal household of Castile, was the former Rabbi Solomon Halevi.

In the fifteen years that Torquemada was grand inquisitor, about eight thousand Spanish crypto-Jews were burned at the stake. Countless others died in torture chambers and prisons. (Before the Inquisition officially ended in 1820, thirty-two thousand heretics were killed.)

In 1492, the same year that Christopher Columbus sailed from Spain to America, Jews in Spain were forced to accept baptism or be banished from the country. Soon thirty thousand to sixty thousand Jews were expelled from Spain, their property confiscated by the government.

The Inquisition spread to Portugal. Manchester writes,

> [The] king of Portugal, finding merit in the Spanish decree, ordered the expulsion of *all* Portuguese Jews. His soldiers were instructed to massacre those who were slow to leave. During a single night in 1506 nearly four thousand Lisbon Jews were put to the sword.[15]

The Humanist Movement

During the era of great religious schisms, intellectuals and artists in Italy began to question the rigid orthodoxy of the all-powerful church. Instead of confronting the church as Wycliffe and Hus had done, these thinkers enhanced their educations with ancient Latin (Roman) literature and philosophy. These students of classical literature were called humanists: their philosophy valued the personal worth of the individual—and human values—over strict religious dogma. The study of so-called pagan, or pre-Christian, Latin culture was known in Latin as *studia humanitatis* (studies of mankind), or the humanities. And while Renaissance humanists promoted secular ideals and Latin philosophy, they remained devout Christians.

The Italian poet Francesco Petrarca (1304–1374), known as Petrarch, is one of the men credited with reviving the humanist movement, which had its roots in the eleventh century. Petrarch searched the dusty old libraries of Italian monasteries where ancient Latin books had been stored—unread—for centuries. This led to a revival of study in math, philosophy, rhetoric, geology, astronomy, and lit-

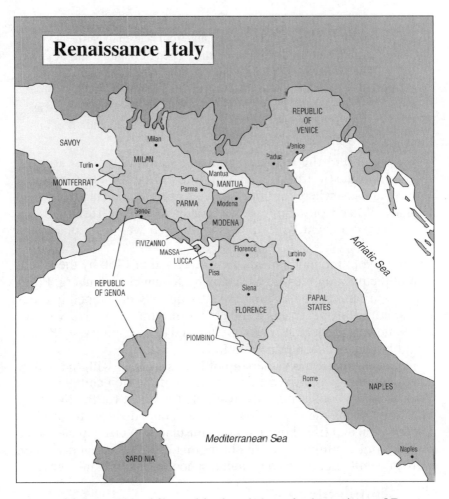

Renaissance Italy

SAVOY

Turin

MONTFERRAT

Milan

MILAN

Genoa

FIVIZANNO
MASSA
LUCCA

Pisa

REPUBLIC
OF GENOA

PIOMBINO

SARDINIA

Mantua

MANTUA

Parma

PARMA

Modena

MODENA

Florence

Siena

FLORENCE

REPUBLIC
OF
VENICE

Venice

Padua

Urbino

PAPAL
STATES

Rome

Mediterranean Sea

Adriatic Sea

NAPLES

Naples

erary criticism. The philosophical and rhetorical treatises of Roman leader Cicero (106–43 B.C.) became important humanities texts.

Petrarch and his colleagues had little understanding of ancient Greek, but in the early fifteenth century, a Greek scholar named Manuel Chrysoloras moved from Constantinople to Florence and began teaching the ancient language to aristocrats and nobles. After learning Greek, the humanists began to revive the works of Greek philosophers Plato and Aristotle, along with the literature of Homer, Plutarch, and others.

The city-state of Florence, Italy, was an important center of humanism. The powerful man who ruled the city, banker and industrialist Cosimo de Medici, cared as much for literature, art, music, and philosophy as he did for business and industry. The rule of Cosimo was followed by that of his son Lorenzo the Magnificent, whose dedication to arts and learning was legendary. According to *The Renaissance* by Will Durant,

It was under the Medici . . . that the humanists captivated the mind of Italy, turned it from religion to philosophy, from heaven to earth, and revealed to an astonished generation the riches of pagan thought and art. . . . The proper study of mankind was now to be man, in all the potential strength and beauty of his body, in all the joy and pain of his senses and feelings, in all the frail majesty of his reason; and in these as most abundantly and perfectly revealed in the literature and art of ancient Greece and Rome. This was humanism.[16]

By the end of the fifteenth century, scholars were searching through monastic libraries and private collections in Germany, France, and elsewhere for priceless works by the ancient Greeks and Romans. When Constantinople was conquered by the Turks in 1453, thousands of ancient Greek books made their way from that fallen city to Italy.

This revolution in learning was accelerated in 1450 by the invention of the printing press in Germany by Johannes Gutenberg. Printing presses and the publishing industry quickly developed in cities throughout Europe. In Italy, the center of humanism, every major city-state was producing books. By the end of the century, 4,987 different books had been printed in Italy.

In earlier times, the ownership of books—along with the luxury of education—was only within the realm of the rich and powerful. With so many books suddenly available for study, for the first time in history, young men of the lower classes could dedicate themselves to education and rise above their circumstances to take a place in the burgeoning community of the humanist elite. (Girls and women were generally not allowed to attend school in the fifteenth century.)

The Renaissance

The revival of the study of ancient Greece and Rome also spawned a rebirth in art and music. As with the humanist movement, the Italian city-states were at the heart of what the Italians called *la Rinascita* (rebirth) and what is today referred to as the Renaissance. These city-states included Rome, Milan, Ferrara, Mantua, and others, but the wealthy cities of Florence and Venice were the most vital to the Italian Renaissance. This was a favorable time to be an artist in Italy, as explained in *Voyages of Discovery: Timeframe AD 1400–1500:*

Throughout most of the century, there was plenty of work for all [artists]. Commissions were numerous; it was a time when every important family—and not just in Florence—was engaged in the politics of conspicuous display. Fine art enhanced the prestige. When in the years after 1436 Cosimo de' Medici spent lavishly on the restoration and reconstruction of churches and other buildings, it was a not-so-subtle assertion of Medici power that was well understood by his fellow citizens, some of whom responded with commissions of their own. The city's great guilds all contributed, too, and even ordinary, reasonably well-off merchants found that their judiciously exercised patronage [of the arts] could draw favorable attention to themselves in the city's ruling circles. The combination of sophisticated taste and civic ostentation was an unprecedented gift for the epoch's artists.[17]

Many of the legendary artists who benefited from such merchant patronage are still well-known today, including Donatello, the luminary of Renaissance sculpture, and Leonardo da Vinci, the artist and scientist whose portrait of the *Mona Lisa* is one of the most well known paintings in the world. Other artists such as Raphael, Titian, and Michelangelo utilized fifteenth-century Renaissance ideals in the sixteenth century.

Under the tutelage of patrons such as the Medicis, the intellect and culture of Italy—and eventually the rest of Europe—grew and blossomed even as wars and the Black Death continued to leave a dark footprint on human affairs.

Opening New Trade Routes

The Renaissance spawned a culture that desired the finest material goods money could buy. Unfortunately, many of these goods came from a far distance and at a great expense. Fine quality silks had to be imported from Persia and China; cotton, rubies, and emeralds from India; garnets, sapphires, and other precious stones from Ceylon. Only the wealthy could afford many of these items, but spices were in great demand by almost everyone.

The European diet consisted mainly of meat, but in the days before mechanized farming, winter food was scarce for cattle. Thus cows were slaughtered in the fall and the beef was preserved by salting so that it could be consumed in the winter. By January and February, the meat was tough and unpalatable. Spices helped make the meat edible. In addition, spices were believed to heal the sick and help cure disease. They were also used in perfumes, which were very popular among the merchant classes. The spices most in demand were pepper, cinnamon, nutmeg, cloves, and other substances from the East.

In earlier centuries, these exotic trade goods were brought to markets along the Persian Gulf and then carried overland by pack animals to Venice and other European markets. Those who traded in such goods became incredibly wealthy. Political changes and wars often centered around control of these trade routes. In 1453, when the Ottomans took control of Constantinople, a major trade route to the East was virtually cut off from European traders. As a result, it became necessary for Europeans to find other trade routes to India and the East.

There were only two ways an explorer could sail a ship away from the western edge of the European continent. One way was south, down the rugged and inhospitable coast of Africa. The other was to sail west, into the unknown. Europeans knew they could reach India by sailing around Africa, but many feared the unknown of sailing west.

According to William Manchester in *A World Lit Only by Fire,* "When the cartographers [mapmakers] of the Middle Ages came to the end of the world as they knew it [while drawing maps], they wrote: *Beware: Dragons Lurk Beyond Here.*" [18]

The Portuguese Explorers

At its strategic location on the western edge of Europe, Portugal was perfectly situated for southern and western exploration. Portuguese sailors were experienced navigators and had long traded Portugal's wine, olives, and fruits with Mediterranean countries. Portugal was also an extremely religious country, and their wish to export Christianity to Africa and beyond motivated their desire to explore.

Portuguese explorations began in 1419 when Prince Henry, the third son of Portugal's King John I, sponsored several forays down Africa's rocky and inhospitable coast. In 1434, Henry's captain Gil Eanes sailed 200 miles south of the Canary Islands to the wind-swept Cape Bojador. In 1436, another captain went 125 miles past Bojador, killed a few

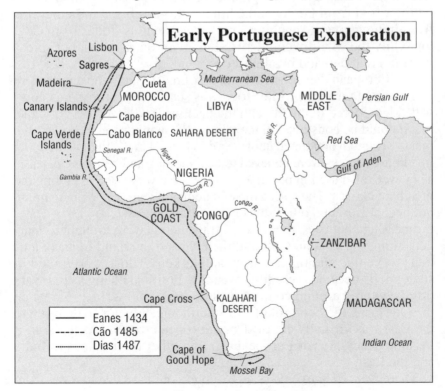

Early Portuguese Exploration

seals, and brought their skins back to the king. Then, according to *Voyages of Discovery: Timeframe AD 1400–1500,*

> Four years later, a two-vessel expedition returned to Portugal with a more sinister load—a dozen Africans. To Henry, the prisoners were merely a source of information, but others quickly saw that the discovery could be put to a different use: As slaves the Africans would solve a labor shortage that had been paralyzing the country since the devastating plague of the previous century. That was the start of a trade that was to be the economic backbone of the subsequent process of discovery. In 1448, the Portuguese established a fort on the island of Arguin, about 500 miles south of Bojador, and soon another 200 black captives appeared back in Portugal, where they were sold at a public auction. . . . Slavery was to remain an essential part of Portugal's economy for the following 400 years.[19]

Henry died in 1460, but Portuguese explorers continued their attempts to circumnavigate Africa. Finally in 1488 Bartolomeu Dias rounded the southermost tip of Africa. Although Dias returned to a hero's welcome in Portugal, his joy was short-lived. The Portuguese explorers had been surpassed by an Italian navigator working for the king and queen of Spain.

The Voyages of Christopher Columbus

For decades Christopher Columbus had been pursuing a dream of reaching India by sailing west instead of south around Africa. In fact, he had spent twelve years in Portugal trying to convince the king to back his proposition with money, men, ships, and supplies. Having failed to do so, Columbus finally convinced King Ferdinand and Queen Isabella to supply him with three ships, the *Niña, Pinta,* and *Santa María.* Columbus believed that Japan was 2,400 miles west of the Canaries, and China no more than 3,500 miles. In reality, Japan is 10,600 miles beyond the Canaries, but no one in Europe knew that North, South, and Central America lay between Europe and Asia.

Columbus left the southern region of Spain, known as Andalusia, on September 6, 1492. Thirty-three days later he landed on the islands he named San Salvador in the Bahamas. Later, Columbus and his men sailed to Cuba and Hispaniola. Believing that he had landed in India, Columbus named the indigenous Taino people who lived on the islands "Indians." He also claimed the islands for Spain.

After Columbus returned to Spain, he told his sponsors that the islands he had found were rich in gold and spices. In a letter to the king and queen, Columbus wrote,

> Doubters may say I exaggerate the amount of gold and spices to be found, and, in truth, we have only yet seen a hundredth of the splendor of these kingdoms. . . . I know that huge mines of gold will be found if your Highnesses allow me to return.[20]

In fact, there was very little gold to be found on the islands. But Columbus's letter worked. He soon returned to the New World with seventeen ships and fifteen hundred men. These new arrivals wreaked destruction on the Tainos. Earlier, Columbus had written about the Tainos, they are "so free with what they possess, that no one would believe it" and "they invite a person to share . . . and show as much love as if they were giving their hearts." [21]

When the Spanish returned to San Salvador, however, the loving Tainos were unmercifully forced into slavery as the conquistadors (conquerors) demanded that they search everywhere for gold. Many of those who did not obey had their hands chopped off. Others were killed outright. Sixteenth-century historian Fernández de Oviedo wrote about one Taino chief who the Spanish named Quemando, or "Burnt One," "because in fact and quite without cause they burned him, because he did not give them as much gold as they asked him for." [22] Historian Bartolomé Las Casas wrote,

> In this time, the greatest outrages and slaughterings of people were perpetrated, whole villages being depopulated. . . . [The Tainos] saw themselves each day perishing by the cruel and inhuman treatment of the Spaniards, crushed to the earth by the horses, cut in pieces by swords, eaten and torn by dogs, many buried alive and suffering all kinds of exquisite tortures. [23]

In addition, the natives had little resistance to European diseases. Within a decade of Columbus's discovery, the indigenous population of the island was all but annihilated.

Meanwhile, on July 8, 1497, Vasco da Gama sailed out of Portugal with three ships and 170 men, determined to find a true sea route to India. For five months the expedition worked its way around the coast of Africa. On May 20, 1498, da Gama finally reached the city

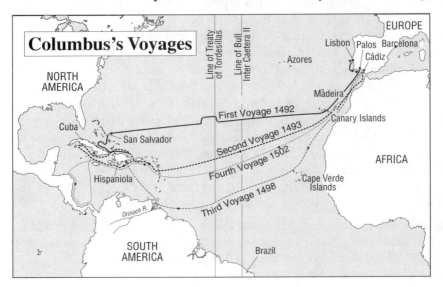

Columbus's Voyages

of Calicut, India. Unfortunately, da Gama was greeted with hostility by the Muslim merchants who traded with the Hindus there. In addition, there was little demand for the cheap Portuguese goods that had been brought, because the Indians had been trading fine silks, porcelains, and spices with the Chinese for years. On the way home, da Gama ran into headwinds, and it took his crew months to sail around Africa. Diseases such as scurvy wracked da Gama's ships, and the expedition did not arrive back in Portugal until late 1499. Of the 170 men who began the voyage, only 54 survived.

The Americas

While the Spanish conquistadors were building their first primitive settlements in the Americas, the Aztec, Mayan, and Inca tribes had been building grand empires there for centuries. In Central America, the Aztecs ruled over a prosperous empire based in Tenochtitlán, a city of about 150,000 on Lake Texcoco near present-day Mexico City. The Aztecs had risen to great power in the fourteenth century, conquering local tribes and building a society that was as advanced in science, art, and architecture as any other in the world at the time.

The Aztecs were ruthless warriors who created the largest empire in Mesoamerica, but they were also responsible for many sophisticated improvements within their society. Aztec rulers oversaw a highly efficient government system in which administrators collected taxes and maintained an intricate economy based on trading and agriculture. Their religious beliefs, while promoting human sacrifice, also expressed the integral connection the Aztecs had to nature and the universe.

Aztec society was also rich in art and architecture. Towering pyramids decorated with serpents carved from stone dominated the skyline. The city of Tenochtitlán was crowded with merchants and shoppers, according to sixteenth-century conquistador Bernal Diaz:

> [There were] dealers in gold, silver, and precious stones, feathers, mantles, and embroidered goods . . . traders who sold great pieces of cloth and cotton, and [those] who sold cacao. . . . [There] were skins of tigers and lions, of otters and jackals, [and] deer . . . [and those] who sold beans . . . vegetables . . . fowls . . . hares, deer . . . young dogs—the eating variety—and every sort of pottery made in a thousand different forms . . . those who sold honey . . . lumber, boards . . . and vendors of firewood.[24]

South of the Aztec empire, in southern Mexico and present-day Guatemala and Belize, lay the great cities of the Mayan culture. Like their neighbors to the north, the Mayans built great pyramids and practiced advanced math, astronomy, and chronology (the science of time and calendars). Between 900 and 1100, the Mayan city of Chichén Itzá, in northern Yucatan, Mexico, was the largest city in Mesoamerica. By the fifteenth century, for reasons unknown, the great Mayan culture of earlier times had fragmented into dozens of smaller, less advanced societies.

Farther to the south, in present-day Peru in South America, was one of the largest and best-organized empires in the world: the Inca empire, consisting of about 12 million people.

The Incas built cities and towns using advanced stone masonry and engineering methods. Their streets were marked by wide avenues and open squares lined with temples and public buildings. Tall pyramids made of huge stone blocks were pieced together with amazing accuracy. As with the Mesoamerican cultures to the north, the Incas excelled at art and music.

It the first decades of the sixteenth century, the arrival of the Spanish to what the Europeans called the "New World" proved to be disastrous for the advanced cultures of the Americas. The Spaniards possessed three things the native cultures, no matter how prosperous, did not have—the gun, the wheel, and the written word. With these weapons, small forces of conquistadors quickly overwhelmed the large populations of Aztecs, Mayans, and Incas. Those natives not killed in wars of conquest were wiped out by previously unknown diseases such as smallpox, tuberculosis, scarlet fever, and others. The riches of the Aztec and Inca empires were quickly looted, while priceless works of art made from gold and silver were simply melted down and minted into coins. Native species of the New World were replaced with the European cow, pig, sheep, and goat, which trampled native grasses and destroyed habitat for indigenous plants and animals.

As the 1400s began, the civilizations of Europe were still mired in the primitive wars and social practices of the Middle Ages. As the century ended, a new, unspoiled world was ripe for conquer. The balance of powers shifted away from France and England and the Ottomans in Constantinople to whatever powers could exploit the Americas and Africa. This task fell mainly to the Spanish and the Portuguese, who, with a Bible in one hand and a musket in the other, set the course of world history for the next two hundred years.

Notes

1. Quoted in Fernand Braudel, *Capitalism and Material Life 1400–1800*. New York: Harper and Row, 1973, pp. 48–49.
2. William Manchester, *A World Lit Only by Fire: The Medieval Mind and the Renaissance*. Boston: Little, Brown, 1992, p. 34.
3. Werner Rösener, *Peasants in the Middle Ages*. Chicago: University of Illinois Press, 1992, p. 258.
4. Editors of Time-Life Books, *Voyages of Discovery: Timeframe AD 1400–1500*. Alexandria, VA: Time-Life Books, 1989, p. 48.
5. Marzieh Gail, *Life in the Renaissance*. New York: Random House, 1993, p. 76.

6. Gail, *Life in the Renaissance,* p. 72.
7. Joseph Dahmus, *The Middle Ages: A Popular History.* Garden City, NY: Doubleday, 1968, p. 347.
8. Dahmus, *The Middle Ages,* p. 348.
9. Christopher T. Allmand, ed., *Society at War: The Experience of England and France During the Hundred Years War.* New York: Barnes & Noble, 1973, p. 126.
10. Manchester, *A World Lit Only by Fire,* p. 19.
11. Dahmus, *The Middle Ages,* p. 383.
12. C.W. Previté-Orton, *The Shorter Cambridge Medieval History,* vol. 2. Cambridge, England: Cambridge University Press, 1952, p. 966.
13. Previté-Orton, *The Shorter Cambridge Medieval History,* vol. 2, p. 1,010.
14. Barnet Litvinoff, *1492.* New York: Charles Scribner's Sons, 1991, p. 21.
15. Manchester, *A World Lit Only by Fire,* p. 35.
16. Will Durant, *History of Civilization, Part V: The Renaissance.* New York: Simon & Schuster, 1953, pp. 77–78.
17. Editors of Time-Life Books, *Voyages of Discovery,* p. 54.
18. Manchester, *A World Lit Only by Fire,* p. 27.
19. Editors of Time-Life Books, *Voyages of Discovery,* p. 21.
20. Quoted in Desmond Wilcox, *Ten Who Dared.* Boston: Little, Brown, 1977, p. 49.
21. Quoted in Julian Mates and Eugene Cantelupe, eds., *Renaissance Culture.* New York: George Braziller, 1966, p. 273.
22. Quoted in Kirkpatrick Sale, *The Conquest of Paradise: Christopher Columbus and the Columbian Legacy.* New York: Penguin, 1991, p. 158.
23. Quoted in Sale, *The Conquest of Paradise,* p. 159.
24. Quoted in Victor Wolfgang von Hagen, *The Ancient Sun Kingdoms of the Americas.* Cleveland, OH: World Publishing, 1961, p. 40.

Chapter

1

Empires and Conquest

The 1400s were a time of great conflict between religions, kings, and wealthy aristocrats. The Hundred Years' War, which began in 1337, pitted the great empires of England and France against each other, while leaders of small regions, such as the duke of Burgundy, played the two countries off one another for their own benefit. This was an era when knights clad in shining suits of metal armor fought with bows and arrows, pikes, and axes. Before the century was over, however, gunpowder, artillery, and navies would permanently change the nature of war for all time.

The fifteenth century was also marked by broad religious schisms. Even the institution of the Catholic Church was ripped by destructive forces. In 1305 a papacy was established in Avignon in modern-day France to compete with the Holy See in Rome. The establishment of two popes, who bitterly opposed each other for more than a century, caused many religious thinkers to question other practices of the powerful church. At that time, the church owned 80 percent of the farmable land in England, owned huge expanses of property elsewhere, and flaunted gold, jewels, and other riches while the majority of people lived in poverty.

After the papacy was once again united in Rome in 1417, the church decided to persecute those who had questioned its ways. This resulted in a holy crusade against the followers of John Hus, known as Hussites, in the present-day Czech Republic. This harsh and divisive war eventually led to a complete split within the church when the Protestant sect of Christianity was established in the sixteenth century.

Meanwhile, to the south, another religious conflict brought about the fall of the Christian city of Constantinople to the Islamic Ottoman Turks. This battle, pitting Eastern Orthodox Christians against Muslims, had its roots in previous centuries and would remain a source of political conflict in the region for centuries to come. After the fall of Constantinople, the center of the Eastern Orthodox religion moved to Moscow, where Ivan the Great used his power to unite the scattered territories of Russia into one country whose capital was based in the Kremlin.

Present-day Spain, to the west of Constantinople, was another flash point for Islamic-Christian hostilities. Isolated from the rest of Europe on the Iberian peninsula, Spain had been a cultural center for Catholics, Islamic Moors from Morocco, and Jews who had earlier been driven out of the Middle East by the Crusades. When Spain was united near the end of the century under the "Catholic Kings" King Ferdinand and Queen Isabella, they consolidated their power by driving the Muslims from Granada and instituting a program of persecution and murder against Spanish Jews.

By the end of the fifteenth century, the world had moved from the Middle Ages, which began around A.D. 400, into a new age now defined by historians as the modern period. Even as empires rose and fell and religions struggled for dominance, the roots of today's culture were being developed by small enclaves of artists, philosophers, writers, and musicians—and by the explorers who would carry the best and the worst of European culture to the Americas and beyond.

Politics in Fifteenth-Century Europe

Robert Warnock and George K. Anderson

By the fifteenth century, Europe was composed of more than a dozen powerful city-states, many of them battling one another for control over religion, trade, and territory. To the south, soldiers of the Islamic Ottoman Empire—the Turks—had overrun the Christian city of Constantinople and appeared to be on the verge of sweeping north onto the European continent, where they threatened to replace Catholic culture with their Islamic beliefs. To the north, warring factions of French and English had been fighting epic battles in the Hundred Years' War since the fourteenth century. In the middle of the continent, powerful Italian city-states such as Venice and Genoa—the home of Christopher Columbus—battled one another even as a new age of creativity and cultural enlightenment known as the Renaissance was spreading throughout an otherwise confused and warring continent.

Robert Warnock is a historian and professor at Yale University. George K. Anderson is a professor at Brown University.

The agricultural economy of the Middle Ages with its barter of goods and services worked against the power of national sovereigns and in favor of the barons living in close contact with their retainers on feudal estates. Without a money economy the kings could not readily collect taxes, and without the power of wealth they could not force their rule on the nation as a whole. The self-sufficient and virtually independent estates that dotted the map of Europe discouraged the rise of national feeling among the people as well as any strong national rule.

Excerpted from Robert Warnock and George K. Anderson, *Centuries of Transition,* revised edition. Copyright © 1950, 1967 Scott, Foresman and Company. Reprinted with permission from Addison-Wesley Educational Publishers, Inc.

But the revival of trade in the late Middle Ages restored the money economy of the ancient world, and there emerged a powerful merchant class, which, in order to pursue its farflung trading, demanded a more stable government than the petty feudal rulers could provide with their limited resources. Money enabled the national sovereign to collect taxes, develop a national army, and assert a personal rule over his country as a whole. The merchants readily supported the power of the throne in return for a stable national law and uniform conditions of trade throughout the land. But the national monarchies of the Renaissance rose out of bitter civil struggles in which the kings finally destroyed the power of feudal nobles and the entire system of feudalism.

Small States in Italy

In Italy, the first area to feel the force of the Renaissance, special conditions produced a peculiar political evolution. During the thirteenth and fourteenth centuries the Italian cities in the north formed part of the [German] Holy Roman Empire, the international agglomeration of many little states that was theoretically ruled by a German royal house. There was no native king of Italy in the Middle Ages comparable to the feudal kings of England and France. Consequently, when the authority of the emperors declined in Italy in the thirteenth and fourteenth centuries, the Italian city-states were bent on securing independence from imperial rule rather than union under an Italian sovereign. The growth of their wealth through commerce owed nothing to the protection of a king, and they used it to strengthen their independence. The presence in Italy of the Church and the Pope also discouraged a national spirit, since the Church was an international force and the Pope laid claim to being an international ruler, who was therefore in frequent conflict with the Emperor. Moreover, the temporal rule of the Pope over large states of his own in central Italy discouraged the unification of the northern, central, and southern sections of the peninsula.

Except for the southern Kingdom of Naples, Italy was cut up into numerous small states, each focused on a large city—Venice, Genoa, Pisa, Florence, Milan, Bologna—which controlled its politics and sought through ultimately disastrous little wars to extend its power over its neighbors. The turbulent political history of the oligarchic city-states during this period recalls the tumultuous careers of the Greek cities of antiquity. This internal strife interfered with the commercial prosperity of the states and led the ruling classes in the fourteenth century to sacrifice their power to despots who would guarantee peace and orderly government for a period of years. Since the dictator was often a leader of an army of mercenary soldiers, he might continue his rule indefinitely and bequeath it to a member of his family. Thus, remarkable dynasties of despots were established in several Italian states and eventually took on the magnificence of royalty in other countries. The famous Medici rule of Florence was founded by Cosimo de' Medici in 1434 and produced in his grandson, Lorenzo the Magnificent (1449–1492), the greatest patron of scholarship, art, and literature in Renaissance Italy. Men did not inquire into the morality of dictatorship but assumed the pragmatic view that any means, however dishonest or inhumane, was justified if it achieved the end of increasing the prosperity and power of the state. This cynical, if realistic, view of state dictatorship was brilliantly enunciated by Machiavelli in his treatise, *The Prince*. Yet, though it might carry the states to remarkable prosperity in the fourteenth century, this sordid philosophy destroyed patriotism and the citizen's sense of responsibility for the welfare of the state, so that in the sixteenth the states were an easy prey to the imperialistic designs of France and Spain.

The Holy Roman Empire

Germany too failed to achieve unification under a national monarchy, and for somewhat similar reasons. The many small German states were theoretically united under the Holy Roman Emperor, but since he was elected by seven local rulers called Electors, his office until 1438 lacked the dynastic continuity of the kingships of France and England and did not inspire ambitions to effective monarchy. Moreover, the Holy Roman Emperor was usually more interested in pursuing his international claims or advancing his family holdings than in unifying the German states. The decline of the Empire in the thirteenth century enfeebled central government still further. Nevertheless, some states were gradually consolidated in clusters, as the powerful ones absorbed the weaker, so that several large states emerged from the medieval confusion, although there were still over three hundred states until the nineteenth century. There undoubtedly was national feeling in Germany of the Renaissance, but it expressed itself in the religious Reformation of Luther rather than in a national monarchy, and was thereafter weakened by the religious differences engendered by the Reformation.

Strong English Government

It was in the countries along the Atlantic seaboard that the great monarchies of the Renaissance developed. The time was the fifteenth century, when the little Italian states were enjoying their last period of commercial supremacy. England was the first to evolve a strong central government, perhaps because the power of the king had been stronger in England since the days of William the Conqueror

(1028–1087) than in France and elsewhere. The greater power of the king explains why England was the first to achieve a strong monarchy; the importance of the parliament of nobles, church dignitaries, and commoners explains why the English monarchy was never so absolute as the French. When the authority of the king weakened, as in the fourteenth century, the national parliament rather than individual nobles assumed his powers. Yet the fifteenth century brought a civil struggle in which the nobles supporting the rival houses of Lancaster and York fought the War of the Roses (1455–1485) to decide the kingship and in the process dissipated their own authority and paved the way for a dynasty of strong monarchs, who temporarily eclipsed the power of parliament.

After a long period of war and devastation the populace welcomed the firm rule of the Tudors. Henry VII established the line in 1485 and quickly shaped the national monarchy that England was to become. . . .

Restored Prestige in France

The rise of national monarchy in France was at first inhibited by the claim of the English kings to huge sections of the land. In the Hundred Years' War (1339–1453) the English, using new methods of warfare unknown to the backward French, won brilliant victories at Crécy, Poitiers, and Agincourt and even secured the aid of the Dukes of Burgundy, the most powerful of the feudal nobles in France, against the French king. But in 1429 a naïve peasant girl, Joan of Arc, inspired by what she thought to be divine voices, rallied the French and led an army herself to relieve the siege of Orleans and restore the prestige of the French crown. Soon after, the English evacuated nearly all of France and left that unhappy country to fifty years of slow revival. The process of unifying France as a strong nation was begun by Louis XI, the ugly but able king from 1461 to 1483 who finally established the authority of the French crown over Burgundy. But his successors interrupted French recovery by four expensive and unsuccessful wars with Spain for control of Italy. . . .

The Unification of Spain

Early in the eighth century the Arabs of the East had extended their power from northern Africa over virtually all of the Iberian peninsula (which contains modern Spain and Portugal). The history of this region for the seven centuries that followed is chiefly the gradual liberation of the land from the Moslems by the dogged persistence of the Christians in pushing them ever farther south toward Gibraltar. By the twelfth century the Moslems controlled merely the southern third, and four powerful feudal states had emerged in the north— Portugal, Leon, Castile, and Aragon. In the thirteenth century the

Moslems were reduced to the kingdom of Granada, and Castile had absorbed Leon to become the largest state in the peninsula. The marriage of King Ferdinand of Aragon and Queen Isabella of Castile in 1469 and their conquest of Granada in 1492 completed the political unification. But little Portugal remained an independent kingdom, except for a brief Spanish conquest, and in the late fifteenth and early sixteenth centuries amassed a fantastic empire in South America, Africa, and Asia. Her national poet, Camoëns, preserved the glory of her great century in his magnificent epic, *The Lusiads* (1572), which told in heroic fashion of the voyage of Vasco da Gama around Africa to India in 1498.

The long struggle with the Moslems gave Spain a unique national fervor in the Renaissance that blended with the Christian ardor of her holy wars. Catholic mysticism was nowhere so intense as in the land of Spain [which] led the Catholic Reformation with the militant zeal of the Jesuits under Ignatius Loyola and the heresy hunts of the Inquisition. When the national monarchy appeared under Ferdinand and Isabella, the absolute authority of the Spanish monarchs was enforced for several generations by their profound piety, so that the Spaniard's devotion to "dios y el rey" (God and the king) was centered in his Most Catholic Majesty. . . .

The rise of aggressive national states and the decline of chivalry, with its idealistic codes of warfare, destroyed for a time the moral basis of international law as the new nations competed in a ruthless struggle for empire. War took on a new horror with more deadly weapons, and respect for treaties and moral obligations declined. The Hundred Years' War ended without a treaty. The English crown actually sanctioned piracy against Spain on the high seas. But humanitarian forces gradually came to demand a regulation of warfare, and even the grasping monarchies began to realize that they all stood to gain from some recognized control of their savage competition.

Eyewitness to the Battle of Agincourt

Jean de Waurin

War at the beginning of the 1400s was a hand-to-hand experience carried out by men wearing suits of armor that weighed up to seventy-five pounds. The following description by fifteenth-century writer Jean de Waurin details the disadvantages of this type of combat as he describes the famous battle of Agincourt in 1415 where the English beat the French in a decisive battle in the Hundred Years' War.

Even as these soldiers fought with swords and axes, gunpowder in cannons made armor obsolete. Naval warfare, however, had assumed a new importance as military expert Vegetius explains in the excerpt that describes the outfitting of ships for battle at sea.

Jean de Waurin was fifteen years old and serving with his father in the French army at the time of the battle of Agincourt. His descriptions of this and other battles remain some of the most vivid—and well-known—eyewitness accounts of the Hundred Years' War.

[In 1415] this eye-witness account [by Jean de Waurin] of the battle of Agincourt shows how physical conditions conspired with the skill of the English archers to defeat the numerical superiority of the French

The fact of the matter is that the French had drawn up their battle formations between two small woods, one close to Agincourt, the other by Tramecourt. The place itself was narrow, [thus] greatly favouring the English, while acting very much against the French interest; for the said French had spent all the night on horseback in the

Excerpted from Jean de Waurin in *Society at War: The Experience of England and France During the Hundred Years' War,* edited by C.T. Allmand. Copyright © 1973 Oliver & Boyd. Reprinted with permission from Boydell & Brewer Ltd.

rain; their pages, grooms and many others, while exercising their horses, had turned up the earth which had become very soft, so that only with some difficulty could the horses pick their hoofs up from the ground. In addition, the French themselves were so burdened with armour that they could hardly bear it nor move forward. For they were armed with coats of steel which were very heavy, right down to the knees or below, in addition to their leg harnesses; and besides this plate armour, the majority also had hooded helmets. Together, this weight of armour and the softness of the sodden earth, as has been said, held them almost immobile, so that it was only with the greatest difficulty that they lifted their weapons; to crown all these mischiefs was the fact that not a few [of the French] were worn out by hunger and lack of sleep. It was wonderful to see all the banners, some of which, it had been decided, were to be displayed. The French agreed among themselves to shorten their lances so that they should be less likely to yield when the time for attacking and closing with the enemy should come; quite a number, too, commanded archers and crossbowmen, but they would not let them use their weapons since the ground was so confined, and there was really only sufficient room for the men-at-arms.

On turning to the English we find that, after the parleying between the two sides, already described, was over, and the delegates had each returned to his own side, the king of England ordered a knight called Sir Thomas Erpingham to arrange his archers in front of the two wings (he and Sir Thomas were to be in charge of the operation), and exhorted all his men to fight well and with vigour in his name against the French, so as to secure and save their very lives. Then the knight, who was riding in front of the formation with only two others, on seeing what the hour was and that all was ready, threw up a stick which he was holding in his hand, shouting "Nestrocq" ["Now Strike"], which was the sign to advance; he then dismounted and came over to join the king, who, likewise, was on foot in the midst of his retinue, his banner being carried before him. The English, seeing this signal, suddenly began to advance, and let out a great cry, at which the French greatly wondered. When the English saw that the French were not coming out to meet them, they moved towards them in very good order, once again giving out a very loud cry, and then stopping to regain their breath. Thereupon the English archers who, as I have said, were on the wings, seeing that they were now within range, began with vigour to shoot arrows upon the French; the majority of these archers had no armour but were only wearing doublets [long close-fitting tunics], their hose rolled up to their knees, with hatchets and axes or, in some cases, large swords hanging from their belts; some of them went barefooted and with nothing on their heads, while others wore caps of boiled leather, while yet others still had simply back plates covered with pitch or leather.

Arrows Fell Thick and Fast

The French, seeing the English coming towards them in this way, drew themselves into rank, each man beneath his banner, and wearing his basinet [steel cap] upon his head. The constable, the marshal, the admirals and the other princes strongly admonished their men to fight bravely and valiantly against the English. As they came together, the trumpets and clarions made a great noise on all quarters; but the French soon put their heads down, especially those who were not shielded in any way, such was the effectiveness of the English arrows, which fell so thick and fast that no man dared to uncover himself nor even to look up. They advanced a little, then made some slight retreat; but before the armies could get together again, many of the French were either hurt or wounded by the arrows. When they finally reached the English they were, as reported, so tightly packed together that they could not raise their arms to strike their enemies, except those who were out in front, who struck forcefully with lances which had been shortened so as to be more rigid and in order to come to closer grips with the enemy.

The French, as I shall describe, had made the following plan. The constable and the marshal had chosen a thousand or twelve-hundred men-at-arms, some of whom were to go on the Agincourt side, the remainder through Tramecourt, the intention being that they should split the two wings of English archers. But when they finally approached [the English], those under the leadership of Sir Clugnet de Brabant, who had charge over on the Tramecourt side, now numbered only one hundred and twenty, while Sir Guillaume de Saveuse, a most valiant knight, had charge on the Agincourt side with about three hundred lances. He advanced, with only two others, against the English, followed by all his men and attacked the English archers who were behind their stakes which, however, scarcely stood up since the ground was so soft. Thus the said Sir Guillaume and his two companions came in to attack, but their horses fell upon the stakes, and they themselves were soon killed by the archers, which was a great shame; most of the remainder, out of fear, turned and moved back upon the vanguard, where they caused much disorder and gaps in the ranks, causing them to retreat and lose their footing in the newly-sown ground, for their horses had been so badly wounded by the arrows that they found themselves unable to hold or control them. It was by these, chiefly, that the French vanguard was put into disorder: countless persons began to fall and their horses, feeling the arrows falling upon them, started to bolt behind the enemy, many of the French following their example and turning to flight. Then the English archers, seeing the advance-guard in such disarray, emerged from behind their stakes, threw their bows and arrows aside and, taking up their swords, hatchets, hammers, axes, falcon-beaks [scyth-like weapons] and other weapons, rushed into those places where they saw gaps, killing and laying low the French without mercy, not ceasing to kill until the said advance-guard, which had fought but little or not at all, was completely wiped out. They came through, striking to right and to left, to the second squadron which was behind the advance-guard, and here they were joined by the king in person, together with his own retinue. And Antoine de Brabant, who had been sent for by the king of France, was in such a hurry to flee that his men could not keep up with him, for he would not wait for them: he took a banner from one of his trumpeters, made a hole in the middle, and wore it as if it were a tabard [he was probably hoping to secure for himself the immunity due to a herald], but soon afterwards he was killed by the English. Then began what was both a fight and a great slaughter of Frenchmen, who defended themselves but little since their formation had been broken up, as related above, by their own cavalry, so that the English were able to attack them with greater and greater success, breaking the ranks of the first two squadrons in several places, bringing down men and killing cruelly and mercilessly; some got up again with the help of their grooms, who were then able to lead them out of the skirmish for the English were so concerned with killing and taking prisoners that they did not pursue anybody. Then the whole rearguard, which was still mounted, seeing the confusion in which the other two squadrons found themselves, turned and fled, all except a few of the leaders. It should also be stated that, while all this was going on, the English had captured a certain number of valuable French prisoners. . . .

Killing the Prisoners

At this moment, when they were the least expecting it, the English experienced a moment of very great danger, for a large detachment from the French rear-guard, among them men from Brittany, Gascony and Poitou, having grouped themselves around some standards and ensigns, returned and, in good order, advanced with determination upon those holding the field. When the king of England saw them coming, he immediately ordered that every man who had a prisoner should kill him, something which they did not willingly do, for they intended to ransom them for great sums. But when the king heard this, he ordered a man and two hundred archers to go into the host to ensure that the prisoners, whoever they were, should be killed. This esquire, without refusing or delaying a moment, went to accomplish his sovereign master's will, which was a most terrible thing, for all those French noblemen were decapitated and inhumanly mutilated there in cold blood, and all this was done on account of this worthless company of riff-raff who compared ill with the nobility who had been taken prisoner, men who, when they saw the English preparing to receive them, just as suddenly turned in flight, so as to save their lives; several of them, in fact, managed to get away on horseback, but there were many killed among those on foot.

When the king of England saw that he was master of the field and had overcome his enemies, he graciously thanked the Giver of Victories; and he had good reason to, for of his men there died but about sixteen hundred of all ranks, among whom was the duke of York, his great uncle, which was a great blow to him. Then the king called together those closest to him, and asked them the name of the castle which was close by; and they told him, 'Agincourt.' To which he replied: 'It is proper that this our victory should always bear the name of Agincourt, for every battle should be named after the fortress nearest to which it has been fought.' When the king of England and his army had stood there, defending their claim to victory, for more than four hours, and neither Frenchmen nor others appeared to challenge them, seeing that it was raining and that evening was drawing in, the king went to his lodgings at Maisoncelles. The English archers went out to turn over the bodies of the dead, beneath whom they found some good prisoners still alive, of whom the duke of Orléans was one. And they took away many loads of equipment from the dead to their lodgings. . . .

Advice for Naval Warfare

Naval warfare, by the end of the middle ages, was beginning to assume a role of importance in international conflict. The numbers involved in fighting at sea; the use made of naval forces to carry out lightning raids on coastal districts; the importance of keeping the sea-passages open in certain circumstances; the avowed aim of disrupting the enemy's trade and conveyance of military goods and personnel are all a clear indication that the war at sea was regarded as having an increasing role to play in war, a fact which was recognised by all parties in their search for allies, Castilian or Genoese, who might supply valuable maritime support for those unready to provide it themselves.

> The traditional, strongly-built, high-sided vessel of northern European waters enabled ships, even merchantmen, to be temporarily modified and strengthened so as to make it possible to fight what at times seemed like a land war fought at sea, employing tactics such as those suggested in this extract.

On the subject of fighting at sea, or on rivers, Vegetius speaks, first of all, of how one should build ships and galleys: [he says that] in the months of March and April, when the trees begin to have plenty of sap, one should not cut those from which one wishes to build the ships, but rather that this should be done in August, or in July, when the sap of the trees begins to dry; and from these trees planks should then be cut and left to dry, so that they will not warp.

Those who fight on ships and in galleys should be better armed than those who fight on battlefields, for they are less mobile, and yet must receive great hurt from missiles. They must be well supplied with containers filled with black pitch, resin, sulphur and oil, the whole mixed up and enveloped in tow. These containers must be ignited, and then thrown on to the enemies' ships and galleys, which should then be strongly attacked so that they shall have no time to extinguish the fire.

Item, spies should be used to ascertain when the enemy is lacking in anything.

Item, those who fight must always endeavor to manoeuvre the enemy towards the shore, while keeping themselves on the open sea.

Item, to the ship's mast there should be attached a large beam, protected by iron on both sides; this should be used to attack an enemy ship, a mechanism ensuring that this beam is raised so as to be dropped with great force upon the enemy ship, which is damaged by the impact.

Item, there should be an ample stock of large arrows, which should be shot at sails so as to pierce them, so that they can no longer retain wind, and ships may therefore not escape.

Item, there should be a piece of metal, with a good cutting edge, rounded like a sickle and tied to a long pole, so that with it the yards may be cut; in this condition, the ship will no longer be in a proper condition to fight.

Item, with iron hooks and crampons, the enemy ship should be attached to one's own, so that it may not escape when it is at a disadvantage.

Item, one should have several containers, which must be easily breakable, filled with lime or powder, to be thrown on to enemy ships; when these break, their contents blind the enemy.

Item, one should have pots filled with soft soap, for throwing upon the enemies' ships; when these pots break, the soap makes everyone slip so that they can no longer stand on their feet, and fall into the water.

Item, one should be provided with sailors who can swim for long periods under water; these should have well-sharpened instruments with which to hole the [enemies'] ships in several places, so that the water will enter; and on to the side which lists the more, quantities of large stones and sharp iron rods should be thrown, so as to pierce the ship and cause it to sink.

Joan of Arc

Robin Neillands

The following excerpt details the adventures of Joan of Arc in the Hundred Years' War that helped her French countrymen prevail over the English. Joan was a seventeen-year-old French peasant girl who claimed to hear voices from the saints telling her to lead her countrymen into battle against the English. By the time this happened in 1429, the French had been more or less losing the Hundred Years' War for ninety-two years. Called the Maid of Orléans by the French, Joan was eventually captured by English allies in Burgundy and sold to the English who put her on trial for heresy and witchcraft. Joan was burned at the stake on May 30, 1431. In spite of her death, Joan's actions had revived French morale and the French went on to win the war. Today, Joan is considered one of the greatest war heroes of France. She was canonized as a saint in 1920.

Robin Neillands is a journalist and travel writer who has written more than forty books.

It is more than curious that the [English] dominion in France . . . came to an end through the actions of a saint, but that is what happened. A girl [Joan of Arc] came riding out of the east and within one short summer, sent the English on a retreat which continued until they were expelled from the kingdom, years after her death.

Perhaps the most remarkable thing about the entire saga is not that a young girl heard voices and believed she had a divine mission, but that [Charles VII] the king of France believed her and entrusted her with an army. There is now a popular belief, fuelled by [playwright George Bernard] Shaw among others, that when Joan arrived at [the city of] Chinon the Dauphin [heir to the French throne] was living in penury, his soldiers disillusioned and unwilling to fight, his courtiers

Excerpted from Robin Neillands, *The Hundred Years War.* Copyright © 1990 Robin Neillands. Reprinted with permission from John Pawsey Literary Agency.

nothing but effete fops. None of this is true. The Dauphin already had plenty of money and would experience no great difficulty in raising more. His soldiers, if as yet none too successful in battle, were still in the field, swiftly regaining any territory the [English and their allies] captured and stoutly defending the walls of Orléans, while a stream of defector knights arrived daily from [English] holdings in the north. The Dauphin still ruled in much of France, and among his supporters were . . . warlike captains . . . a host of knights and burghers and a mass of common people.

He still needed [Joan of Arc] but the reason for this need must therefore be a cause of speculation. She never actually commanded the army; her role was more that of a living standard [banner], charging recklessly at the head of the troops. Indeed, her only tactic was the charge, her only policy a relentless determination to attack the English wherever they could be found. Perhaps it was this that made Charles support her; he was well aware that he lacked what we now call charisma, while this girl dazzled his court, his captains, and all who met her. Maybe, with her at their head, his troops could defeat an English army in the field and put the 'Goddams' [English] on the road back to their foggy island of Albion [England]. Anyway, it was worth the risk.

Jeanne d'Arc, St Joan, . . . the Maid of Orléans was, however, much more than a romantic creation, or a useful tool of kings. She was and remains the embodiment of patriotic France. Her chief appeal lay not with the King and his court, who first used her, then ignored her, and finally abandoned her, but the common people and the common soldier. In Jeanne, people saw the hand of God, fulfilling all their hopes; hopes of an end to this interminable war, the final expulsion of the English and the Free Companies [soldiers], and the creation of a France in which they, too, might have some share in the future peace and prosperity.

Voices of the Saints

According to some of those who knew her . . . Jeanne was born in Domrémy, a hamlet of Lorraine, on 6 January 1412, of fairly well-to-do peasant stock, and was christened in the village Church of St Rémy. The land around Domrémy was held for the Armagnacs [French political faction] by an experienced captain of the Dauphin, Robert de Baudricourt, who commanded the castle at nearby Vaucouleurs and led the garrison out from time to time on punitive raids against . . . the roving bands of English . . . who were then ravaging the surrounding countryside.

Sometime in the autumn of 1428, when she was aged about 17, Jeanne presented herself at the castle of Vaucouleurs and told her tale to the sceptical captain. Since her childhood, she said, she had heard heavenly voices. They spoke to her in the wind and in the bells of the village church, and they told her of the Dauphin Charles, of the plight of his kingdom, of how she must go to see him at Chinon. There the Dauphin would give her an army with which she would raise the siege of Orléans and then she would lead the Dauphin to his coronation at Rheims, and all of France would rise up singing and drive the 'Goddams' from the land they had usurped. It took several visits before Robert agreed to help her, and it was the first of her miracles that she finally convinced this grizzled old soldier of the French wars to risk his command and reputation by giving her his support. He found horses, helped her to disguise herself as a boy, sent a messenger to Chinon to give the Dauphin warning of her coming, and provided a small escort. If she could make her way to the court across hundreds of miles of hostile, harried territory, that in itself would be another miracle, and if not, there was little lost. Like his sovereign a little later, Robert de Baudricourt thought it was worth the risk. . . .

Accused of Witchcraft

Jeanne was not alarming [in appearance]. She was a small, rather plain girl, with a sturdy peasant frame, her short, cropped hair a dark frame to an open face. Only her enthusiasm for the war and her fervent faith marked her out from a hundred others who followed in the train of the armies. [King] Charles admitted her to his presence on 8 March, and though he found her fascinating, he sensibly sent her first to [the city of] Poitiers, where she was carefully examined by the *Parlement* and by a number of clerics, who finally attested to her chastity, sincerity and orthodoxy. Jeanne returned to Chinon in early April, where the King supplied her with armour and horses and sent her on to the army outside Orléans, where matters were not going well.

The English [siege] had continued throughout March and by early April the English were ready to advance on the battered walls of the city and take it by storm. It was only then, when the English were massing to assault the city, that they heard some incredible news. A new French army was marching upon them from Blois and at its head rode a *girl*.

This Maid—doubtless a witch of Satan [according to the English]—announced her intentions in letters to Lord Talbot and the Regent of France, John, Duke of Bedford [the brother of English King Henry V]:

> 'You, the English captains, must withdraw from the Kingdom of France and restore it to the King of Heaven and his deputy, the King of France, while the Duke of Burgundy should return at once to his true allegiance. Take yourself off to your own land, for I have been sent by God and his Angels, and I shall drive you from our land of France. If you will not believe the message from God, know that wherever you happen to be, we shall make such a great Hahaye as has not been made in France these thousand years.'

It is fair to say that the English captains and their Burgundian allies were quite unimpressed by this missive. English heralds promptly put it about that the Dauphin's new army was led by a witch, but to the French soldiers besieged inside the city, the coming of the Maid was a miracle.

A Rapturous Welcome

The army sent to Orléans was actually commanded by the Duke of Alençon, recently released after his capture by Bedford at Verneuil. Most of the force, including Jeanne, entered the city on 30 April. The rest followed, and Alençon's whole army was inside the city by 4 May. The English had now been battering the walls of Orléans for six solid months and were greatly discouraged by the arrival of fresh supplies and more troops for the garrison. Exactly why [English commander John] Talbot was unable to prevent the French entering Orléans is still unclear, but apparently the eastern gate, the Burgundian Gate, was unguarded, and some slipped in there while others crossed the river by night in barges.

On the very day that Alençon entered the city, Jeanne rode out again with diversionary forces which overran the Bastille Saint-Loup. . . . The English and Burgundians in Saint-Loup were massacred and a large convoy of food entered the city. Two days later, on 6 May, Jeanne was in action again when, at the head of 4,000 troops, she crossed the river to storm the English forts along the south bank. This battle on the south bank took two days and on the first day Jeanne was struck in the shoulder by an arrow and carried weeping from the field, the English archers dancing about and shouting out delightedly 'The witch is dead!'

In fact, she had only received a flesh wound, for the arrow had barely penetrated her armour, and next day, to the dismay of the English, Jeanne was back in the fray. The last English troops on the south bank were soon penned up in the shattered ruins of the Tourelles, which fell on 7 May to a combined assault from Jeanne's forces on the southern side, and the city militia advancing from the city. On the following day, Talbot lifted the siege and Jeanne rode back in across the repaired Tourelles bridge to receive a rapturous welcome from Alençon, the soldiers of the garrison and the citizens of Orléans, an event which has been repeated at Orléans on 8 May every year from that day to this.

English Retreat

The command of the large French army, numbering 8,000 men, and now assembled at Orléans, passed to [Jean, Comte de] Dunois, but even with Dunois' intelligent command and Jeanne, a living *Oriflamme* [symbol worthy of devotion], the French were still wary of engaging English archers in open battle and held back when, having burned what they could not carry away, the English army left its camp and halted just north of the city, inviting combat. When the French declined to attack, the English army fell into column and began to withdraw sullenly

Joan of Arc's actions revived morale and helped the French prevail over the English in the Hundred Years' War.

across the Forêt d'Orléans, with the French army now dogging their footsteps. . . .

Jeanne took the field again in the early months of 1430, attacking the English garrisons north of Paris . . . but her successes were limited. Her forces were composed of mercenary companies . . . quite unsupported by the main royal army. John of Bedford . . . was forced by circumstance to hand over more and more English towns to [French] troops. . . . Bedford was quite unable to maintain all the territory he had previously conquered, for he lacked both the men and the money and blamed much of his misfortune on the Maid. 'These blows', he told the young King Henry later, 'were caused in great part by that limb of the fiend called *Pucelle*, or the Maid, who used false enchantments and sorcery.'

It is strange that so level-headed a prince as the Duke of Bedford, should place any belief in witchcraft, but witchcraft was not unknown, even in circles close to the throne. His stepmother, Henry IV's Queen Joan, had been accused of sorcery, and his sister-in-law, Eleanor, Duchess of Gloucester, was to be found guilty of witchcraft and forced to do public penance. Besides, Jeanne claimed to be guided by God, so it was simple and sensible propaganda to claim that she was, in fact, an agent of the Devil. . . .

Captured and Burned

In April 1430, Philippe the Good ordered his vassal, Jean of Luxembourg, to seize Compiègne. . . . Jeanne entered the town on 13 May with a small body of reinforcements. On 23 May she led a sortie to attack a small group of Burgundians blockading the gate and on returning, with the Burgundians in hot pursuit, she found the gates closed against her. Fighting wildly, she was hauled from the saddle by a Burgundian soldier and handed over to Jean of Luxembourg. He sold her to the English for 10,000 *livres*, and her fate was sealed.

The capture of the Maid . . . delighted the English, not least because with her capture their string of reversals suddenly stopped. This was taken, for so it must seem, as further evidence that she was indeed a witch. . . .

Loaded with chains, Jeanne d'Arc was conveyed across France and imprisoned in Rouen to await her trial on charges of witchcraft and heresy, and Bedford held hopes that her trial would both restore English morale and blast the prospects of Charles VII.

The English declared Jeanne to be a witch, or at best a whore and a heretic, who had scandalized religion by dressing in men's clothes and wearing armour. Her trial for heresy and blasphemy, before a clerical court, was conducted by French clerics led by Pierre Cauchon, the Bishop of Beauvais, but it was seen by the English and Burgundians as the chance to demonstrate that her victories at Orléans and Patay and elsewhere were the work of the Devil. Jeanne's trial began on 21 February 1431, and on 21 May, worn down by weeks of interrogation, Jeanne submitted to the court and was sentenced to life imprisonment. When the full horror of what was meant by a lifetime's incarceration dawned upon her, she quickly recovered her nerve and recanted. On 28 May 1431, she was declared a relapsed heretic, handed over to the secular power—the English—and burned to death in the market place in Rouen two days later. The English declared they had destroyed a witch; the French believed the English had martyred a saint and would suffer for it. History was to prove them right.

The Conquest of Constantinople

Philip Mansel

The following excerpt examines the importance of Constantinople and its fall to the Islamic Ottoman Turks in 1453. For centuries, Constantinople had been considered the crown jewel of western Christianity. After the city was conquered by the forces of Ottoman Sultan Mehmed II, many in the west feared that the Turks would initiate a campaign to conquer all of Europe using Constantinople as a base of operations.

Philip Mansel is a historian of courts and royal dynasties and a professor of history and French at Oxford University. Mansel has written biographies of French and Turkish royalty and is a Fellow of the Royal Historical Society.

On the afternoon of 29 May 1453 Mehmed II, the Sultan [of the Ottoman Empire,] entered the long-desired city. Riding a white horse, he advanced down an avenue of death. The city of Constantinople was being put to the sack by the triumphant Ottoman army. According to an observer from Venice, blood flowed through the streets like rainwater after a sudden storm; corpses floated out to sea like melons along a canal. An Ottoman official, Tursun Beg, wrote that the troops 'took silver and gold vessels, precious stones, and all sorts of valuable goods and fabrics from the imperial palace and the houses of the rich. In this fashion many people were delivered from poverty and made rich. Every tent was filled with handsome boys and beautiful girls.' On rode the Sultan, until he reached the mother church of Eastern Christendom and seat of the Oecumenical Patri-

Excerpted from Philip Mansel, *Constantinople: City of the World's Desire, 1453–1924.* Copyright © 1995 Philip Mansel. Reprinted with permission from St. Martin's Press, LLC.

arch, the cathedral of the Holy Wisdom built 900 years earlier by the Emperor Justinian with the largest dome in Europe. He dismounted and bent down to pick up a handful of earth, which he poured over his turban as an act of humility before God.

Inside the shrine which Greeks considered 'the earthly heaven, throne of God's glory, the vehicle of the cherubim', a Turk proclaimed: 'There is no God but Allah: Muhammad is his Prophet.' The cathedral of Haghia Sophia had become the mosque of Aya Sofya. As the Sultan entered, hundreds of Greeks who had taken refuge in the cathedral hoping to be saved by a miracle, were being herded out by their captors. He stopped one of his soldiers hacking at the marble floor, saying, with a conqueror's pride: 'Be satisfied with the booty and the captives; the buildings of the city belong to me.' Below golden mosaics of Jesus Christ and the Virgin Mary, Orthodox saints and Byzantine emperors, he prayed to Allah. After receiving the congratulations of his retinue, he replied: 'May the house of Osman there forever continue! May success on the stone of its seal be graven!'

A Natural Object of Desire

Mehmed II, Sultan of the Ottoman Empire, known in Turkish as *Fatih*, the Conqueror, was only 20 in 1453. Born in Edirne, the Ottoman capital 200 miles north-west of Constantinople, he had, according to a chronicle which he himself commissioned, been possessed since his childhood with the idea of conquering Constantinople, and constantly insisted on the necessity of taking the city without delay. The opportunity to realize his ambition came after he inherited the throne in 1451 on the death of his father Murad II.

Constantinople was a natural object of desire, for it appeared to have been designed by geography and history to be capital of a great empire. Situated at the end of a triangular peninsula, it was surrounded by water on three sides. To the north lay a harbour a kilometre wide and six kilometres long, called the Golden Horn, probably because it turns golden in the rays of the setting sun; to the east the Bosphorus, a narrow waterway separating Europe and Asia; to the south, the Sea of Marmara, a small inland sea connecting the Aegean to the Black Sea. The city was both a natural fortress and a matchless deep-water port, enjoying easy access by sea to Africa, the Mediterranean and the Black Sea. In addition it was situated on the crossroads of the mainland routes between Europe and Asia, the Danube and the Euphrates. Its site seemed to have been expressly created to receive the wealth of the four corners of the earth.

Founded as a Greek colony, allegedly in the seventh century B.C. Byzantium had been re-founded in 324 A.D. by Constantine the Great as New Rome, a new capital in a better strategic position than the old Rome on the Tiber. For over a thousand years thereafter, it had been capital of the Roman Empire in the East. In the sixth century the Emperor Justinian, the builder of Haghia Sophia, had ruled in Constantinople over an empire which stretched from the Euphrates to the Straits of Gibraltar. To the grandeur of Rome, the city added the magic of time: ninety-two emperors had reigned in the 'Queen of Cities'. No other city in the world has such a continuous imperial history. Moreover, for much of its thousand years of empire it had been the largest and most sophisticated city in Europe, a treasure-house of the statues and manuscripts of the classical past, and the nerve-centre of Eastern Christendom. Its wealth had led one medieval traveller, Benjamin of Tudela, to write: 'The Greek inhabitants are very rich in gold and precious stones and they go clothed in garments of silk with gold embroidery, and they ride horses and look like princes. . . . Wealth like that of Constantinople is not to be found in the whole world.'. . .

A Historic City

Constantinople was surrounded by the most majestic city walls in Europe, built between 412 and 422 A.D. Moated, battlemented, interspersed by 192 towers, and of treble [triple] thickness throughout, the walls marched a distance of six kilometres from the Golden Horn to the Sea of Marmara, rising and descending with the inequalities of the ground. They also extended along the Sea of Marmara and the Golden Horn, completely enclosing the city. . . .

The walls had been built because Constantinople was, as one Byzantine had written, 'the city of the world's desire'. No city has endured more attacks and sieges: by Slavs (540, 559, 581), Persians and Avars (626), Arabs (669–79 and 717–18), Bulgarians (813, 913 and 924) and Russians (four times between 860 and 1043). It had never recovered from its sack by a Western crusade in 1204, organized by its commercial rival Venice. After the city reverted to the Byzantines in 1261, repeated defeats of the Byzantine Empire by Muslim enemies, and civil wars between rival emperors, had reduced the city's population from a peak of 400,000 inhabitants to about 50,000 Greeks—or 'Romans', as they were still proud to call themselves. By 1400 it had shrunk to a collection of small towns, separated by farms and orchards.

In 1453 the last Emperor, Constantine XI, ruled over no more than the city, a few islands and coastal districts and the Peloponnese [region]. Commerce had passed into the hands of Venetians and Genoese. The classical statues had been sold or stolen. The lead on the roof of the imperial palace had been used to mint coins. From the roof of Aya Sofya, surveying the ruined palace, the Sultan thought of other fallen empires, and emperors. . . .

Quest for Domination of Europe

Constantinople had been taken by the sword; and until the end of the Ottoman Empire 469 years later force remained the Ottomans' principal means of control, as it did for other dynasties. Already in 1452, in preparation for the siege, the Sultan had designed and built the great fortress of Rumeli Hisari on the Bosphorus. 'In all haste', between 1453 and 1455 the massive seven-towered citadel of Yedi Kule (Turkish for 'seven towers') was built in the west of the city, where the land walls meet the Sea of Marmara. Its present abandoned condition gives no indication that once the Seven Towers was more feared than the Bastille or the Tower of London. It was a citadel where treasure was stored, enemy ambassadors imprisoned, the Sultan's enemies—and on occasion the Sultan—executed. . . .

No poet or traveller has been as intoxicated by Constantinople as the Conqueror. The Ottoman sultans already used *Khan*, Turkish for 'emperor', in their title—as well as the Persian titles *Padishah* (Great King) and *Shahinshah* (King of Kings), and the Arabic *Sultan* (ruler). From 1453 Mehmed II, like his successors, also saw himself as heir to the Roman Empire and the only true Emperor in Europe. A few days after the siege, a Genoese living in the city wrote: 'In sum he has become so insolent after the capture of Constantinople that he sees himself soon becoming master of the whole world and swears publicly that before two years have passed he intends to reach Rome.' Europe and Rome interested the Ottomans, as a field of expansion, more than Turkish-speaking territory in central Asia or the Caucasus. The Turkish metaphor for worldly dominion was the Red Apple. Before 1453 the Red Apple was believed to be the globe held in the right hand of a giant statue of the Emperor Justinian in front of Haghia Sophia. After the statue's destruction in 1453, the apple moved west and came to symbolize the Ottomans' next goal: the city of Rome. 'To Rome! To Rome!' was the constant cry of Mehmed II's great-grandson Suleyman the Magnificent. For later sultans the Red Apple was Vienna, capital of the Habsburg Holy Roman emperors. Ottoman ambition had no rival. In comparison, the Shah of Persia was restrained, the King of France modest, and the Holy Roman Emperor provincial. . . .

Repopulating the City

Constantinople was a creation of the Ottomans and they required a world city, worthy of their empire. Mehmed II and his successors called themselves 'world conqueror', 'the King of the World'. One of the favourite epithets, both of the sultans and their city, soon became *alem penah*, 'refuge of the world'. It appeared appropriate to create a multinational capital for an empire which, it was later calculated, contained seventy-two and a half nationalities [Gypsies were considered half a nationality].

Multinationalism became the essence of Constantinople. A common literary device of Ottoman writers would be to compare the merits and looks of the many nationalities in the empire and its capital. In the fifteenth century national differences, based on history and geography more than race, could be acutely felt. . . . Mustafa Ali, a prominent sixteenth-century historian, extolled as a source of strength the number of nationalities in the empire—Turks, Greeks, Franks, Kurds, Serbs, Arabs and others. In the nineteenth century a minister of the Sultan, Cevdet Pasha, called the Ottoman Empire a great society 'because its people spoke many languages and because it selected the best talents, customs and manners from among its various nations.'. . .

[An expansionist national policy known as] *realpolitik* . . . was the principal reason for Constantinople's variety of nationalities. In his new capital the Conqueror needed a large and prosperous population to service the palace and the state machine. Yet there were not enough Muslim Turks for Constantinople to be a wholly Turkish city. The majority of the empire's population, at this stage, was Christian. Turks were needed throughout the empire, to people Balkan cities and the Anatolian countryside. Accordingly, so the historian Kritovoulos wrote, after 1453 the Sultan gathered people in Constantinople 'from all parts of Asia and Europe, and he transferred them with all possible care and speed, people of all nations, but more especially of Christians. So profound was the passion that came into his soul for the city and its peopling, and for bringing it back to its former prosperity.' In the new capital each *mahalle* or quarter (the basic living unit of the city, with its own places of worship, shops, fountains and night-watchmen) kept, with the name of its inhabitants' city of origin, its special customs, language and style of architecture.

Turks were the first and largest group whom the Sultan brought to Constantinople. In the years following its capture in 1453 the city remained a ruin devastated by plague. The Sultan had to use an Ottoman technique known as *surgun*, or forced transfer of populations, to move Turks to his new capital. The chronicler Ashikpashazade wrote that the Sultan

> sent officers to all his lands to announce that whoever wished should come and take possession in Constantinople, as freehold, of houses and orchards and gardens. . . . Despite this measure, the city was not repopulated; so then the Sultan commanded that from every land families, poor and rich alike, should be brought in by force. And they sent officers with firmans to the kadis and prefects of every land . . . and now the city began to become populous.

Mehmed II personally went to Bursa to force artisans and merchants of this rich trading city to move to the capital. Laments still exist for the fate of the artists and craftsmen brutally transported from the comforts of the old Seljuk capital of Konya in Anatolia to the blood-stained city on the Bosphorus. At moments the Conqueror himself had qualms about his new prize, and withdrew to the former capital Edirne. Edirne had the treble attraction of tranquillity, proximity to hunting grounds and geography: it was the natural mobilization centre for Ottoman campaigns in Europe. However, the Sultan's doubts did not last.

Like Constantine the Great eleven hundred years earlier, when he summoned senators from Rome to Constantinople . . . the Sultan ordered 'the pillars of the empire' to move to his new capital. He told them 'to build grand houses in the city wherever each chose to build. He also commanded them to build baths and inns and market-places and very many and very beautiful workshops, to erect places of worship.' Mahmud Pasha, the ablest statesman of his reign, was one of the first to build his own mosque, now embedded in the warren of *hans* (inns) and alleys beside the Grand Bazaar.

Eyewitness to Turkish Invasion

John Bessarion

Christians who had ruled the city of Constantinople for centuries were contemptuous of the Islamic Ottoman invaders. The following letter was written by John Bessarion—a Christian cardinal in Constantinople and an eyewitness to the invasion. Bessarion describes the destruction caused by the Ottomans to Francesco Foscari, the Doge (magistrate) of Venice, and implores Foscari to provide Christian soldiers to retake the city.

Cardinal John Bessarion was the Greek archbishop of Nicaea, delegate to the Council of Florence.

M ost illustrious and excellent prince, I have put off until this day commending to your highness my unhappy and wretched city of Constantinople. This I have done partly because I was restrained by a certain provincial modesty, lest in asking something for her advantage and welfare, I should seem to seek my own profit; I have also held back because, of its own accord, your renowned Senate, as it has been most merciful to all those who are suffering, had prepared so much aid and assistance that all doubtless might think it sufficient, indeed more than enough, to save this city, to hold back the barbarians from the walls, to contain the attack of a most cruel enemy. Would that it might have been brought to bear at the proper time! Would that we had not been deprived of hope and deceived in our judgment; but truly it was not through any negligence on your part, of which, in so great a crisis, there was never a shadow.

But it so happened, because of the proximity of the enemy and the

Excerpted from Cardinal John Bessarion, "The Turkish Menace," in *The Portable Renaissance Reader,* edited by James Bruce Ross and Mary Martin McLaughlin. Copyright © 1953 The Viking Press, renewed © 1981 Viking Penguin, Inc. Reprinted with permission of Viking Penguin, a division of Penguin Putnam, Inc.

unfavourable season of the year, and by the will of the fates, that, while your fleet was in midcourse, while in hope of victory fresh forces were being brought against the enemy, the barbarians conquered the city [May 29, 1453]. This city which was most heavily protected by its situation, its walls and supplies, and by all manner of defence, this city which, it was hoped, would be able to withstand a total siege for an entire year, the barbarians stormed and overthrew. A thing terrible to relate, and to be deplored by all who have in them any spark of humanity, and especially by Christians.

A City Ravaged and Enslaved

Wretched me! I cannot write this without the most profound sorrow. A city which was so flourishing, with such a great empire, so many illustrious men, such very famous and ancient families, so prosperous, the head of all Greece, the splendour and glory of the East, the school of the best arts, the refuge of all good things, has been captured, despoiled, ravaged, and completely sacked by the most inhuman barbarians and the most savage enemies of the Christian faith, by the fiercest of wild beasts.

The public treasure has been consumed, private wealth has been destroyed, the temples have been stripped of gold, silver, jewels, the relics of the saints, and other most precious ornaments. Men have been butchered like cattle, women abducted, virgins ravished, and children snatched from the arms of their parents. If any survived so great a slaughter, they have been enslaved in chains so that they might be ransomed for a price, or subjected to every kind of torture, or reduced to the most humiliating servitude. The sanctuaries and shrines of the saints have been defiled by curses, scourgings, bloodshed, and all kinds of shameful acts. They have made camps of the churches of God, and have exposed the sacred things of God in their camps. O unhappy, O wretched, and so swift and manifold a transformation of a city! If anyone reads this, ignorant of what has been done, he will not believe that these things have happened.

But I do not wish to lament the calamities of my fatherland to you, to whom these things are perhaps better known than to me, and especially lest I should seem to reopen your wound, whom the fates decreed should share our miseries. So many Venetian citizens and most noble gentlemen were besieged in that city, so many men of patrician rank. Would that they have experienced better fortune than ours, and may return unharmed to their native city. Certainly it is to be feared that, tossed in the same tempest, they may have perished in the same way.

Crush the Madness

To me, however, has been given the opportunity freely to implore aid, not for my fatherland, not for the good of my city, but for the safety of all, for the honor of Christians. On this occasion I could explain in great detail how much danger threatens Italy, not to mention other lands, if the violent assaults of the most ferocious barbarians are not checked. But I am not sure that these arguments are not better known to your Senate than to me. And this letter hastens to its close. I say but this one thing briefly. One of two things must happen: either your Highness, together with other Christian princes, must curb and crush the violence, not to say madness, of the barbarian, in these very beginnings, not only to safeguard yourselves and your own, but also in order to take the offensive against the enemy; or the barbarian, when he has shortly become master in what remains of Greece, which is now still subject to our rule, and in all our islands and also in Pannonia and Illyricum, may bring Italian affairs to a most dangerous crisis.

There is no one who may not hope, however, that Christian princes will take the offensive the more readily, seeing that there are such important reasons, so grave, so serious, so urgent. They would act for the common good, for the Christian religion, and for the glory of Christ, especially if they were summoned by your Highness and your Senate, whose authority is very great.

Therefore I exhort you, renowned and most illustrious prince, and I entreat, beseech, and implore you, with what prayers I can, that, when Italian affairs have finally been settled, and those wars ended in which Christian princes have attacked each other, you will direct your attention to greater matters and behold the enemy raging on the boundaries of Christian territories and destroying everything savagely.

Rise Up, Renowned Prince

Why do you think the barbarian has burst forth with such great insolence? Doubtless because he has learned that Christian princes, waging wars against each other, have stained their hands with the blood of their own people, have defiled their arms with the blood of Christians. These things make the enemy bold; relying on them, he has lately assaulted the chief city of Greece, and has conquered, ravaged, and destroyed it. But if he should learn that, with our own hostilities resolved, united and harmonious as Christian princes should be, we would rise up to defend the Christian religion, believe me, he would not only refrain from invading foreign lands, but would withdraw to that place within his own territories which is most favourable for defence.

Rise up then, renowned prince, and when the mutual animosities of Christians have been extinguished (and this will be easy for you, who are exceedingly influential in authority and wisdom), awaken, awaken at once, and arouse their peaceful and tranquil spirits. Exhort them, challenge them, induce them to join you, before the enemy takes the Peloponnesus, in dedicating themselves to avenging the violence of the barbarian, to destroying the enemy of the Christian faith, to recovering that city which formerly belonged to your republic, and which would be yours again once victory had been achieved. Nothing you could do would be more profitable for your empire, more advantageous for Italy, and for the whole commonwealth of Christians; nothing more acceptable to the immortal God; nothing more glorious for your own fame. If your highness knows anything that my smallness can contribute to this task either by calming the spirits of our people or by exhorting them to wage war on the barbarians, I shall spare no labour, no care or solicitude.

The Spanish Inquisition

Cecil Roth

The following excerpt explains how the Inquisition was used to persecute Jewish people who had recently converted to Christianity in fifteenth-century Spain.

The Inquisition was a Christian church court procedure that was first used in the twelfth century to find and persecute heretics. Originally used by the church to imprison heretics, it was later used in Spain and Portugal to target *Marranos*—converts to Christianity from Judaism—and *Moriscos*—converts from Islam.

Spanish Jews had been assimilated within Christian society for centuries and many Jews were wealthy businesspeople who held positions of great power. During periodic outbreaks of anti-Semitism, many of these Jews converted to Christianity and some even became priests and bishops.

When the Spanish Inquisition began in 1480, many of these converted Jews, or *conversos*, were falsely accused of practicing Judaism in secret. These people were called Judaisers or, alternately, *Marranos*, a slur meaning "pig." These Judaizers were the first to be accused of heresy and burned at the stake. By 1492, all Jews were targeted by the Inquisition and were ordered to leave Spain or die. At about the same time—following Spain's example—similar oppressive measures were enforced in England, France, and Germany. The techniques used in the Inquisition were later used against people falsely accused of witchcraft.

Dr. Cecil Roth is a leading expert on Jewish history and a professor of Jewish studies at Oxford University, England.

Excerpted from Cecil Roth, *The Spanish Inquisition.* Copyright © 1937 Cecil Roth. Reprinted with permission from W.W. Norton & Company, Inc.

The Inquisition may be defined as an institution brought into being by the Church for the purpose of dealing with heresy in all its forms. The conception that dissent should be punished by force was indeed almost as old as Christianity itself. . . .

The history of mediæval heresy followed lines which are only too familiar to the student of modern racial or religious persecution. The first step was the working up, by those who had the power to mould public opinion, of popular hatred of non-conformists; then followed riots and massacres of heretics at the hands of the infuriated populace; and, finally, special tribunals and legislation had to be introduced ostensibly in order to preserve law and order. . . .

Torture and Punishment

The use of torture, though long opposed by the Church, was officially authorised by a Papal Bull of 1252. The Inquisitor was maintained by the confiscation of the property of the victim—a particularly forceful argument, in most cases, against acquittal. When a person was arrested, his property was immediately sequestered. The prisoner was not allowed the use of counsel for his defence, and the names of witnesses were concealed from him. We have here all the features which were later to distinguish the Spanish Inquisition, though that institution developed them to a high pitch of ingenuity and perfection.

So, too, with the punishments. The Inquisition nominally dealt, not with acts, but with spiritual affairs, and its titular object was the salvation of souls, which it hoped to bring about by the imposition of penances sufficient to wash away sin. Sentence was passed, not by the Inquisitors alone, but by a larger body containing a number of experts on theological and doctrinal points, including some delegate of the bishop to whose see the accused belonged. Impenitent heretics were generally burned [at the stake]. Relapse, which was frequent in the thirteenth century, was indeed generally punished by imprisonment, but absolute refusal to submit to penance was bound to lead to the stake. The Inquisition did not itself carry out the death penalty, for it was a spiritual body, but handed the victim over to the secular authorities. The public reading and execution of the sentence was an early institution, and soon became a popular spectacle, like anything else which involves the loss of life. . . .

Isabella the Catholic, [King] Henry's half-sister, came to the throne in 1465, amid a maze of civil war. Although for some time after her accession her attention was absorbed by more pressing problems, she was surrounded by ecclesiastics and notables who were constantly dinning into her ears the necessity for taking action against the [Jews who had converted to Catholicism known as] *conversos*, whether on political or on spiritual grounds. Chief among them was a gaunt, sunken-eyed Dominican friar named Thomás de Torquemada, born at

Valladolid in 1420, and now at the height of his extraordinary powers. He . . . was bitterly opposed to the Jews in spite (or because) of the fact that he was himself said to be of partly Jewish extraction. It was reported, in fact, that long ago he had made Isabella take a vow that, should she reach the throne . . . she would devote herself heart and soul to the [eradication] of heresy and the persecution of the Jews. Even he was outdone in virulence by Fray Alonso de Hojeda, Prior of the Dominican Convent of S. Pablo in Seville, who lost no opportunity of urging extreme and if necessary violent measures against the enemies of the Faith. The ruling Pope, Sixtus IV., was less eager, but hopefully invested his legate to Castile with full Inquisitorial authority. . . .

Passover Celebration Used as Excuse

On the night of Wednesday, March 18th, 1478, a young cavalier penetrated into the *judería* for the purpose (or in the hope) of carrying on an intrigue with a young Jewess who had captivated his fancy. Gaining admission into the house by stealth, he surprised a number of Jews and *conversos* who had come together for some mysterious celebration. That night was the eve of the Jewish Passover, and it is pretty clear that they had assembled in order to celebrate the traditional *Seder* service. By an unfortunate but by no means uncommon coincidence, it happened to be Holy Week. The accidental conjunction conveyed its own story: and the report immediately spread like wild-fire throughout the city, that these miscreants had gathered in order to blaspheme the Christian religion and its founder, at the season of his Passion.

When the news reached the ears of the Prior of S. Pablo, he saw his opportunity and, hastening to Court, laid the evidence before the scandalised young Queen. This, it is said, finally decided her to take action. The Spanish Ambassadors to the Holy See were immediately instructed to obtain a Bull authorising the establishment of an Inquisition. Pope Sixtus hesitated—prompted not so much by humanity as by the desire to keep the body under his own control. But he could not very well maintain his opposition: and at last, in the following November, a Bull was issued noting with horror the existence of many [Jewish] Christians in Spain and empowering the Spanish sovereigns to appoint three bishops or other suitable persons learned in theology or the common law, being priests and above the age of forty, whom they might remove or replace at will, to have complete jurisdiction over heresy within the kingdom of Castile. In these seemingly innocuous terms, the Spanish Inquisition was founded.

The victims enjoyed a respite of nearly two years before the tribunal was actually inaugurated. It was only on September 17th, 1480, that commissions were issued to Miguel de Morillo, Master of Theology, and Juan de San Martin, Bachelor of Theology, both friars of the Dominican Order, with instructions to begin their activities forthwith. . . .

On Christmas Day, they arrived in Seville. A solemn procession was arranged for the following Sunday, so as to inaugurate their activities with that pomp which has always constituted an integral part of Catholic zeal. . . .

The Place of Burning

A *quemadero*, or Place of Burning, had been constructed for the purpose just outside the city walls, in the Campo de Tablada. At the four corners, huge plaster figures of the four major prophets had been set up, as it were to preside over the sufferings of those among their descendants who dared to remain faithful to their teachings according to their own lights. The cost of this tactful embellishment was defrayed by a local dignitary named Meza, whose zeal won for him the highly lucrative position of Receiver to the Holy Office, to administer the confiscated property. He did not live long to enjoy his emoluments, however, for he too was subsequently discovered to be a Judaizer [a Jew who had converted to Christianity, but who practiced Judaism in secret], and was burned on the pyre which he had helped to adorn. . . .

Immediately news had spread of the approaching establishment of the Inquisition, many [Jews] had fled from Seville and the immediate neighbourhood into the surrounding territory, in the hope of finding

Originally established to find and imprison heretics, the Inquisition was later used to persecute Islamic and Jewish converts to Christianity.

refuge under the protection of the local magnates. Peremptory demands were addressed forthwith to the latter, however great their rank or influence, ordering them to surrender the fugitives. Such was the terror which the new tribunal had already excited that, in most cases, these demands were immediately obeyed. From the Marquisate of Cadiz alone, for example, some eight thousand persons were sent back: and the Marquis was notoriously one of the most refractory of all Castilian noblemen. To such an extent did the number of prospective victims increase, that the Inquisitors removed their headquarters from the Dominican Convent of S. Pablo in the centre of the town (where they had established themselves in the first place at Hojeda's invitation) to the great Castle of Triana, just outside the city walls. The accommodation here should have sufficed for any purpose: but, before long, the dungeons were filled to overflowing with suspects.

During the Plague, even those *conversos* who were of the most blameless reputation were forbidden to leave the city except if they abandoned all their property, so as to prevent any possibility of evasion. The Inquisitors themselves took up their residence during this period at Aracena, where they found plenty to engage their attention until the pestilence showed signs of diminishing, when they returned to Seville. [Burnings] continued without intermission; it seldom happened that a month elapsed in which none was held. Even the dead were not spared, their bones being exhumed and burnt after a mock trial. (This, of course, was no meaningless formality, since condemnation automatically led to confiscation.) By November 4th, 298 persons had been burned, while 98 had been condemned to perpetual imprisonment. Vast numbers of others had come forward spontaneously to confess their guilt on the understanding that they would be dealt with mercifully: but even they were made to parade as penitents. At one of these solemnities, no less than fifteen hundred men and women were exhibited. There were still some among the *conversos* who believed that they might be able to find superior authority willing to protect them. They appealed to the Pope, who, in January, 1482, wrote expressing his disapproval of the excessive severity of the methods employed; but this communication had no effect upon the independent rulers of Spain.

Finding All Jews

From the beginning the Spanish Inquisition elaborated certain rules of procedure which were followed throughout its existence. A list was drawn up and published of the signs (many of them grotesque) by which a Judaizer could be recognised; from washing the hands before prayer to changing linen on the Sabbath, and from calling children by Old Testament names to turning the face to the wall at the moment of death. Wholesale denunciations were encouraged by the policy of

promising a free pardon in return for full confession within a stipulated time, and placed thousands in the power of the dreaded Tribunal.
Even the Jews themselves were called upon to help in the work, their
rabbis being compelled to enjoin their congregations, under pain of
excommunication, to reveal everything in their knowledge concerning Judaizers. . . .

The volume of work grew apace, meanwhile, and it soon became
evident that additional tribunals were necessary. By a papal brief of
February 11th, 1482, seven other Inquisitors were nominated, among
them Thomás de Torquemada, the Queen's confessor, who had hitherto been content with being the power behind the scene. Other appointments followed at frequent intervals, and further tribunals were
set up at Córdova, Jaen, Ciudad Real, and possibly also at Segovia.
One of the earliest victims at the first-named city was the lovely mistress of the Treasurer of the Cathedral, who was himself burned in the
following year. The tribunal of Ciudad Real was intended for the
province of Toledo. Four persons only figured in its first *auto* [*da-fé*,
Inquisition hearing], which was held on February 6th, 1484; but at the
second, which followed on the 23rd and 24th of the same month,
thirty men and women were burnt alive, as well as the bones or effi-
gies of forty more who had anticipated proceedings by death or flight.
In the two years of its existence, this Tribunal burnt fifty-two heretics
and condemned 220 fugitives, as well as sentencing 183 persons to
perform public penance.

Burning Fifty Persons a Day

In 1485, the seat of the Tribunal was transferred to Toledo. The *conversos* of this city, who were both wealthy and numerous, followed
the example of those of Seville, and formed a plot to prevent the Holy
Office from entering upon its functions. They planned to raise a tu-
mult while the procession of Corpus Christi was going through the
streets on June 2nd, with the intention of despatching the Inquisitors
during the disorder. Subsequently they proposed to seize the city gates
and the tower of the Cathedral, and hold the town even against the
crown if it should be necessary. But, as at Seville, they proved singularly incapable of reaping any benefit from their wealth and influence,
and the plot was betrayed. If it had any effect, it was only to make the
proceedings more determined.

Seven hundred and fifty persons figured in the first *auto*, which was
held on February 12th, 1486. Carrying unlighted tapers and surrounded
by a howling mob, which had streamed in from the countryside for
miles around to enjoy the spectacle, they were compelled to march bare-
headed and barefoot through the city to the door of the Cathedral, where
they were marked on the forehead with the symbol of the Christian
faith, with the words: "Receive the sign of the Cross which ye have de-

nied and lost." They were fined one-fifth of their property, the proceeds being assigned towards the cost of the war against the Moors; they were subjected to a perpetual incapacity to hold honourable office or to wear any but the coarsest clothes; and they were required to go in procession on six successive Fridays, flagellating themselves with hempen cords. In addition, it was decreed (a deadly corollary) that any disobedience to these injunctions would be treated and punished as a relapse into heresy. Nine hundred penitents appeared at the second *auto* and a further 750 at the third. Before the year had elapsed, the total of those thus treated with relative humanity had approached five thousand. In addition, large numbers were burned—as many as fifty persons sometimes in one day. Among the victims were several friars and ecclesiastical dignitaries, who had hitherto enjoyed a reputation of unblemished sanctity. At this interval of time, it is impossible to tell whether they were martyrs to a concealed faith, or victims of personal or (as seems most likely) racial spite.

Torquemada Takes Over

To perfect the organisation, Thomás de Torquemada was placed at the head of a supreme council established in order to co-ordinate the work of the local tribunals of Castile and of Leon [in October 1483]. . . . Thus the Spanish Inquisition was unified under one central control, and its head had the unenviable distinction of becoming the first Grand Inquisitor. . . .

Under [Torquemada's] direction, the Inquisition rapidly took shape, and extended its activity throughout the country. It was owing to his personal zeal, it is said, that verdicts of acquittal were so infrequent in these early days. . . .

Torquemada was himself an ascetic [one who renounces earthly possessions]. None the less, in order to maintain the dignity of his office, he resided in palaces, and surrounded himself with a princely retinue. He maintained a bodyguard of fifty mounted [soldiers] and two hundred infantry: his subordinates were allowed ten horsemen and fifty archers apiece. Where this train of death appeared, city gates were flung open, the resources of flourishing districts were placed at their disposal, and magistrates swore fealty. He accumulated vast wealth, but lived in perpetual fear of assassination. So mighty did he become that the Roman *curia* itself took alarm, and there were frequent quarrels between him and the Papal nominees. But the victory rested invariably, or nearly so, in the hands of the sunken-eyed ascetic.

The acme of Torquemada's activities in Castile was reached when he took proceedings against two prelates, of high character and great learning, who happened to be of Jewish descent. One was Pedro de Aranda, Bishop of Calahorra and President of the Council of Castile; the other was the venerable Juan Arias Dávila, Bishop of Segovia, who had given proof of his zeal for the faith by the ferocity with which he had persecuted the Jews of his diocese, this being the only indication of Jewish interest which he showed. One of the charges brought against him was the improbable one that, on the introduction of the Holy Office into his diocese, he had the remains of his forebears exhumed, in order to destroy proof of the fact that they had been interred in accordance with Jewish rites. Both these ecclesiastics were sent to Rome for trial. Dávila had the good fortune to pass away before sentence was promulgated; Aranda was deposed and degraded from Holy Orders, dying a prisoner in the Castle of S. Angelo. It is obvious that in both cases the accusations were based on nothing but spite or prejudice. . . .

The history of [Spanish Jews], thus left in isolation, entered now on a new phase, and with it that of the Holy Office as well. Cut off from all contact with Jewish thought, inevitably becoming less and less attached to the faith of their fathers, they were yet doomed to remain suspect for centuries by a majority which (as has happened again in our own day) was imperceptibly turning from religious to racial persecution. The task of the Inquisition, on the other hand, was simplified. There was now, at last, a clean-cut division between the two elements, the unconverted Jews and the converted. The former had gone into exile; the relatively simple task (as it seemed) remained, of forcing the latter into conformity.

The Life of John Hus

George Hodges

The following excerpt explores the life and times of John Hus, whose ideas for religious reform resulted in his death and ignited a religious war in Bohemia. In the early fifteenth century, the Christian church was divided by the Great Schism, with a Roman pope and a French pope each claiming ultimate authority over the powerful institution.

The Great Schism and certain church practices were attacked by Czech professor and religious reformer John Hus. Hus rejected the absolute infallible powers claimed by the church and believed in the authority of the Scriptures over that of the popes. When he refused to be silenced, Hus was condemned for heresy and burnt at the stake. After his death, he became a martyr and his followers, known as Hussites, called on the church to denounce materialism, sell its expensive land-holdings, and return to its traditional roots as described in the New Testament.

In 1420, radical Hussites began a revolution in which open warfare was declared on the powerful Catholic Church. Lands were seized and churches were destroyed before a crusading army raised by Pope Martin V defeated the Hussites.

George Hodges is an expert in religious history.

Unhappily, for three hundred years, from the beginning of the thirteenth century to the beginning of the sixteenth, hardly a pope was . . . strong, or wise, or good. Some were politicians, who

Excerpted from George Hodges, *Saints and Heroes: To the End of the Middle Ages* (New York: Books for Libraries Press, Inc., 1911).

made bargains for money and power with kings. Some were well-meaning but weak men. Some were persons whose wicked lives were a scandal to religion; thieves, adulterers. and murderers.

At the beginning of the fourteenth century, the pope moved from Italy to France, from Rome to [the French city of] Avignon. There he lived under the control of the French king. At the end of that century, on the occasion of a papal election, the cardinals chose an Italian, who took up his residence in Rome. He proved, however, to be so bad a pope that they immediately chose another, who took up his residence in Avignon. So there were two popes. A part of the Church held with the one, another part with the other. The two fought with curses, exchanging excommunications. [English scholar John] Wycliffe compared them to two dogs snarling and growling over a bone. This state of things continued for nearly forty years.

A Man of Wicked Life

At last a council was held which declared that a general conference of Christian men representing the Church is superior to all popes. An attempt was made to get both popes to resign for the good of the Church. When they refused, the council put them both out, and chose another, Alexander V. He died after a short time, and John XXIII, who is thought to have poisoned him, became pope in his place. Thus, although two scandals were amended,—the scandal of the papal court at Avignon. and the scandal of the papal schism,—the worst of the scandals remained: the pope was still a man of wicked life.

John XXIII is said to have begun his career as a pirate. The record of his misdeeds was such that before it was read to the Council which finally deposed him, all outsiders were put out and the doors were locked. It was John who began that public and shameless sale of indulgences, . . . [an] ingenious idea of making money by sending agents all over Europe who promised to release sinners from the punishment due to their sins on the payment of certain specified prices. Of course, there were still good Christians. There were faithful ministers who lived devout lives, and tried to help their people to do right. But the great Church, as represented by the pope at the head, and by the bishops, the monks, and the friars, was teaching men, by constant example, to break the Ten Commandments.

The Greatest Preacher in Prague

It was against this dreadful situation that Wycliffe had protested, but the remedies which he had proposed seemed as bad as the disease. When he said that the trouble with the Church was wealth and power, many agreed; but when he proposed to take away the wealth by giving up the property of the Church . . . [people] would not follow him.

Neither would they follow Hus.

John Hus was a professor in the University of Prague, and the greatest preacher in that part of the country. Born on a farm, and getting his education in spite of such poverty that he begged in the street, Hus had made himself a scholar and a leader. He was a man of simple mind, and righteous life and plain speech. He saw the evils in the Church about him, and made it the business of his life to put an end to them. The books of Wycliffe came to his knowledge and he liked them greatly.

Now, there are two ways in which to deal with evil. One way is to attack in general, without making mention of any names. The other way is to attack it in particular, singling out certain offenders and denouncing them. The first way is easy and safe; the second is full of danger. Hus took the second way.

For example, at the town of Wilsnack, the priests of one of the churches had announced a miracle. They said that it was now proved that the bread in the Lord's Supper is indeed the Body of Christ because pieces of it on their altar had shed blood. And the Holy Blood of Wilsnack began to work miracles. Pilgrims came from all directions, bringing their sick, to the great advantage of the Wilsnack church. Hus was sent to look into the matter, and he found that it was all a fraud. The result was that the pilgrimages to Wilsnack stopped. But the Wilsnack clergy hated Hus.

A Hated Man

And other clergy, for like reasons, hated him. The man was absolutely outspoken. He had no "tact." . . . He never considered whether his words would have a pleasant sound or not. He paid no heed to his own interest. Every day, he made enemies. . . .

Hus was therefore summoned by his enemies to defend himself before the council which was called to meet at Constance. Over this council the Emperor Sigismund was to preside. Hus in his simplicity and innocence, knowing himself to be opposed to nothing in the Church except its sins, agreed to appear before the council, and the emperor gave him a safe-conduct. This was a paper signed by the emperor himself promising that Hus should be safe from violence and should be brought back from the council to his home by the emperor's own guard, if necessary. Thus he went.

Charged with Heresy

The council immediately arrested Hus, and put him in prison. They paid no heed to the safe-conduct of the emperor, and the emperor, on his side, made no serious protest. The theory was that any man accused of heresy was to be accounted a heretic until he had proved himself innocent, and that no faith was to be kept with heretics. No matter what promises had been made, what safe-conducts given, what oaths solemnly sworn, all went for nothing in the case of a heretic.

So Hus was put in prison before his trial had begun, and then was moved to another prison where he was chained by the arms in the daytime and by the arms and legs at night. These were some of the more gentle measures of the Inquisition.

When he was brought at last before the council, he was hooted down whenever he began to speak. Charges were read against him; passages were taken from his books and from the books of Wycliffe, which were held to be against the faith and order of the Church. Some of these he denied as not expressing his beliefs; some he said he would gladly change if anybody could show him that they were not true. He refused to change any opinion by reason of compulsion. He declared the independence of man's conscience, and held that belief is a matter of persuasion and conviction, not of authority.

Condemned to Burn

This was his chief fault. He had won the hatred of the Church by his free speech concerning the sins of churchmen; he was condemned and sentenced because he maintained the right of a man who is in error to be shown his error. His only error was that of insisting that a Christian minister, even a pope, ought to be a good man. That that was an error, nobody could convince him. As for heresy, he had none of it.

Nevertheless, they condemned him to be burned. That was the answer of the council to the man who tried to bring back into the Church the plain righteousness of true religion. They agreed that the Church needed to be reformed, and had assembled for the purpose of reforming it. But they did not like John Hus's way.

They degraded him from the ministry, dressing him in the garments of a priest, and putting a chalice and paten in his hand, and then taking them away with curses. "We commit thy soul," they said, "to the devil." "And I commit it," he answered, "to the most sacred Lord Jesus Christ."

Then they put a paper cap upon his head, with a writing on it saying that he died for heresy. He was taken out and tied to a stake, with a chain about his neck. [Burning logs] were heaped about him, and he was burned to death.

Ivan the Great Unifies Russia

Harold Lamb

Between 1462 and 1505, Ivan III, known as Ivan the Great, was the grand duke of Moscow. Ivan initiated a bold unification of Russian lands under a centralized government in Moscow, making that city the center of trade and culture in Eastern Europe.

In order to elevate Russia as a cultural center, Ivan's soldiers had to repel invasions from the superior armies of the Turkish-speaking Muslim Tatars. From the beginning of his reign, Ivan tried to bribe the Tatars to leave his country in peace, while at the same time attempting to draw them into war with the rival armies of Mongolians. When his machinations failed in 1480, Ivan reluctantly led his army into battle with the Tatars.

Later, Ivan conquered Moscow's rival cities such as Novgorod, Tver, and other territories in order to centralize Russian government in Moscow. Under Ivan's reign, Moscow was rebuilt under the supervision of Italian artists and architects.

Harold Lamb was born in 1892 and wrote more than a dozen books on Russian and European history that included such subjects as Genghis Khan, the Crusades, and Ivan the Great.

For nearly eighteen years Ivan had made sacrifices to avoid a decisive war. To the Tatar khanates [princes] he paid bribes, while he endeavored to stir up conflict between the remnant of the [Mongol] Golden Horde on the Volga and the stronger . . . Krim [Crimea] Tatars. . . .

Meanwhile the European powers had been approaching the Krim khans—the omnipresent Venetians endeavoring to secure the aid of

Excerpted from Harold Lamb, *The March of Muscovy: Ivan the Terrible and the Growth of the Russian Empire, 1400–1648.* Copyright © 1948 Harold Lamb. Reprinted with permission from Random House, Inc.

the Tatars against the advancing Turks [from Constantinople]. And what Ivan dreaded most came to pass, a combination [of forces aligned] against Moscow. In this case it was the Polish King and the Volga Tatars.

In 1480 . . . the Khan with a large field army advanced across the Don to the Oka [rivers], menacing Moscow.

Ivan's agents worked among the Krim Tatars to persuade those ready pillagers to raid the half-deserted cities of the Volga and so compel the invaders to return to protect their homeland. But time lacked for that.

In spite of all his efforts, Ivan was compelled to take command of an army and to march out to a defensive battle that he dreaded. He sent [his wife] Sophie and his children away to safety, then journeyed out to where his armed forces were mustering along the Oka. There, in sudden hopelessness, he abandoned the camp and raced back to Moscow, where he found the citizenry moving into the walled enclosure of the Kremlin to stand a siege.

Before his gates, a panicky crowd blocked his way, shouting at him: "You, the Tsar who rule over us—you have milked us of money in peacetime. Now, because you have paid him no tribute, the Khan is angered, and you fly away from him, betraying us!"

Accustomed to appeasing such mobs, Ivan protested that he had come back to consult the high boyars [aristocrats] and clergy. But the nobles present and the clerics added their voices to the crowd's, clamoring at [the] sight of their prince leaving the battlefront. A patriarch cried at Ivan: "Why do you try to avoid your fate? I am wearied with years, yet I will not turn away. I will go to face the Tatar lances."

Confronted by the panic of his people, Ivan controlled himself and said briefly that he was going back. He busied himself with some attempt to order the defense of the Kremlin, while the Metropolitan [head bishop] of the cathedral came out in robes to bless him, calling him a soldier of Christ, a shepherd of his flock—until the people were calmed and Ivan had no recourse but to return to the camp.

"Go Against the Tatars"

As he rode back the bells of the Kremlin tolled, and the great bell of Novgorod pealed its warning. Ivan went back to the camp because he was helpless to do otherwise. Afraid, clearly aware of his own incompetence, he kept to the ornate pavilion, which in Tatar fashion had been prepared to house the prince who was now commander of a great army.

To that pavilion came impatient *voevodes* [soldiers], and officers of newly arrived contingents, which had marched in from far frontiers. They all seemed to have one thought—to advance across the river, and "go against the Tatars."

That was the one thing Ivan would not do. He knew himself to be a coward; this turbulent camp, noisy with altercation, was a torment to him. Across the river waited terror. Ivan's imagination peopled the far bank with dark masses of charging horsemen.

Actually the far bank looked peaceful enough after the first few days. For the Tatars withdrew their encampment, to let their horses graze and to offer the Russian host every opportunity to cross the small river on rafts or makeshift bridges. Some detachments rode down to the water's edge to taunt the Russians—"If your prince would escape harm, let him stand no more in the way of our Tsar!"

The Tatars fired cannon that blazed and smoked, without doing much damage. They sent exploring columns across distant fords, only to be turned back by bands of experienced Muscovite frontiersmen. Still, Ivan would not give his word to cross the river.

Kiss the Stirrup of Khan

Priests sat with him, telling him how David had gone against the Philistines, and Constantine, the Emperor, had carried a cross into battle with his own hands. Ivan made no reply.

When some of his councilors asked why, then, he would not beg for peace from the Khan, Ivan agreed to do that. He sent envoys with gifts, asking for terms. They came back with the demand of the Tatars, that Ivan should come in person to kiss the stirrup of the Khan and pay the tribute he had not paid for nine years. This, however, he would not do. Nor would he send a son, to make submission for him.

A letter was brought him . . . urging him to give battle to the pagans and not to humble himself before one who had shed Christian blood. "The shepherd must not desert his flock. You, our prince, must not bear the name of traitor and coward. Take courage, for there is no God like our God. His strength he gives to warriors, like your ancestors, Igor and Vladimir."

Always Ivan found himself reproached by the name of Dmitri of the Don, and the glory of Kulikovo. "How he fought! He did not say, I have a wife and children and wealth—if my country is lost to me I will go elsewhere."

And boyars came to kneel at his tent entrance, to remind him that the river could be crossed safely. Did not the waters of the Red Sea allow a Christian host to pass? But Ivan's imagination recalled the slaughter of that great citizen army of Novgorod, the dead on the field of Kulikovo; he could not feel any *power* in this camp with its wrangling officers, and he knew himself to be inept and powerless. Now that all these men waited upon his command to give battle, he refused.

Weeks passed in this strange inertia; autumn cold set in. Whether Ivan was wearied past endurance, or whether the first freezing of the rivers made him fear a sudden attack by the Tatars, he gave a command at last. It was to retreat closer to Moscow.

To his surprise the mass of the army, that had been so unmanage-able in camp, showed itself satisfied to be moving, in whatever di-rection. The withdrawal of the undisciplined mass was disorderly, and Ivan must have felt anew that its numbers did not make of it an army.

His action, however, preserved the army, and probably saved Moscow from another devastation.

Immediately the Tatars retreated from their side of the river, and swept back to the Volga [River]. They may have turned back to pro-tect their own cities from the raid of the Krim horsemen; they may have been disturbed by the unaccountable maneuver of the Mus-covites. More probably they had watched the Russian host grow in size, and when it refused to risk the river crossing, they gave up the campaign as useless.

The folk in Moscow beheld the strange spectacle of its armed host returning home without a battle. Long afterward that same folk would speak of this nameless campaign along the line of the Oka and of this year of 1480 as the one that ended the Tatar yoke. . . .

Expanding the Lands of Moscow

Ivan had found himself to be the shepherd of a weak, leaderless flock. . . . He lashed out now to enforce his will while he could do so. After that winter he paid no tribute whatever to the Tatar khans. He intensified his alliance with the Krim khans, even sending his own boyars with contingents of fighting men to aid those friendly Tatars. Very soon thereafter the Krim raided Lithuania and sacked Kiev in the Ukraine.

Within Moscow, he hastened the rebuilding of the Kremlin citadel, and the outer city walls. And those walls were to stand. The outer face of the Kremlin remains today as it was rebuilt then.

No man could have brought order at this time into the disordered lands of Rus [Russia], but Ivan III, in his lashing out against opposition, managed to weaken the authority of any cities distant and strong enough to head a rebellion against Moscow. He had done so with Novgorod by operating on the recalcitrant burghers, removing part of them elsewhere. He operated more gently against other northern cities, Tver and Viatka, by making them subject to the command of Moscow.

Inexorably but without open war, Moscow was gathering in the surrounding cities; having bought one half of Rostov in 1474 and forced Viatka to surrender in 1489, she stretched out farther to Chernigov (1500), to Pskov (1511) and Smolensk (1514)—the last three being gateways to the west. Riazan, the uncertain neighbor, was incorporated in 1517. During this time the lands of Muscovy ex-panded from fifteen thousand to forty thousand square miles.

So, while his own city was strengthened somewhat by the new fortifications, it was actually *protected* even more by the reduction of
possible rivals.

In doing so, Ivan was not carrying out a definite policy. But he was
gaining ideas, and putting them into effect after a fashion.

Moscow Becomes an International Center

Something odd was happening within Moscow. As it had become the
largest city of Rus in numbers, and the greatest in military force, it
was becoming the only international center. Foreigners were arriving there constantly. Besides the Italians like [architect] "Aristotle"
Fioraventi and [Venetian ambassador] Ambrogio Contarini, there
were the engineers; some of the heads of the Usspensky cathedral
were Armenians; merchants inhabiting the quarter by the market
place and river were Tatars, Persians as well as Armenians. Ivan kept
sons of Tatar princes, as guests and hostages, to serve at the state
banquets. Contarini says: "Every winter great numbers of merchants
come to Moscow from German lands and Poland, to purchase furs
of all kinds, which are exceedingly beautiful."

About this time Ivan (and the [governing body of the] Duma)
closed the trading house of the Germans in . . . Novgorod, thus ending the tie-up of that city with Baltic commerce, and making
Moscow the main center of commerce. This move had unexpected
consequences, not all favorable.

It always happened that the most intelligent foreigners were summoned to talk with Ivan, who gained in this way some knowledge of
what was going on in both the west and east.

Within his own citadel, Ivan staged a demonstration. In reality, it
was staged for effect upon the onlookers.

In the Usspensky cathedral, under the great bell of Novgorod, a
grandson was crowned with the jeweled crown of a Byzantine emperor as Ivan's successor.

In full robes the priests performed the ritual—because it was to
the interest of the Church to enhance the personal authority of the
prince of Moscow. The Metropolitan intoned words over the boy's
head: "Great Tsar and Autocrat."

Witnesses to the ceremony testify that the man most impressed by
it was Ivan himself.

Nomadic Tribes Become Settled

Ivan's parade out to the Oka and back had happened at a point in
time when the great balance of human forces was shifting throughout the plain of Eurasia. It had been shifting for generations. . . . By
slow degrees the settlements were becoming stronger in manpower
and experience than the nomad camps. In weapons, the balance per-

Ivan the Great successfully unified Russia and made Moscow the center of trade, government, and culture.

haps was equal now. Soon, with the new firearms, ships and military discipline, it would incline toward the settlers, the westerners. The Muscovite pioneer in his cabin was now the equal of the steppe [plains] horseman.

The rulers of the horsemen, the khans of the Krim, Nogai and Volga peoples, were becoming heads of settled nations; in the Crimea they lived in the garden palaces of Bagche Serai, under a benevolent sun; on the Volga, in the rich trading centers of Kazan and Astrakhan, they thrived more by merchandise than by war. Their control of the silk, carpet and perfume imports from Asia had become more profitable than the slave raiding of the century before. Even the Venetian merchants had ceased buying young slaves because they could no longer be sold publicly to Europeans.

In this generation, when powers balanced, the half circle of nations around the city of Moscow fell into a live-and-let-live rhythm which was not disturbed by a fresh explosion in the east. The Muscovites appeased the military forces so near them, making gifts with open hands, especially to the Krim khans who held the open steppe below them.

Gradually these Krim khans were scattering the Volga armies, driving the last remnants of the Golden Horde into the towns at the mouth and along the upper reaches of the mighty Volga.

In this expedient of bribing and conspiring, the Muscovites were imitating the Tatars themselves. And they were aided by an increasing pressure from the victorious Turks, who threatened the rear of the surrounding nations—the Krim, Moldavians, Hungarians and the Poles themselves. The Turks of Constantinople were not buying slaves so much as they were taking them, and training them to arms.

The generation of troubled truce from Ivan's accession gave Moscow an opportunity to gather not only land, and the subjection of other cities, but some means of defending itself.

Compulsory Military Service

The best defense was, obviously, a strong army.

Having only one model for a new-style military force, the Tatar, the Muscovites imitated that, without great success. They experimented with mounted divisions that could maneuver together, keeping a flying column concealed to strike a decisive blow. With Tatar weapons, the bow, the curved saber, small shield and light lance, they could at least oppose the warriors of the steppe. But their most reliant human force remained on foot—the rivermen, hunters and frontier settlers who could fight over any kind of ground with cunning and endurance. These were not so easily drilled into disciplined regiments. They persisted in acting like partisans.

Under Ivan, military service became compulsory. It was rewarded by grants of land, to those who had served, and those who were now obliged to serve. Much of the new land in the east was parceled out to the soldier-servants, who had to report for mobilization at command.

This in turn created, by degrees, a new military class of both landowners and peasants. It added a heavy expense of upkeep to be paid by the Moscow treasury, and a new *prikaz*, a bureau to be administered. In time it had a peculiar effect on the new soldier homesteaders. They could not very well leave the land allotted to them. In particular, they could not go off as before when the mood came on them, to serve the Swedes in Viborg, or the Lithuanians in Vilna. To do that now would make them deserters and traitors.

And especially on the frontiers, at a distance from Moscow, the homesteaders were bound to labor to maintain their land, each man on his lot, unless serving in the armies. Those in debt had to work out the debt or be imprisoned and cudgeled [beaten with a stick] for failure to pay. In these isolated frontier holdings appeared the first trace of serfdom.

Something else was happening along the frontiers. Here stood fortified monasteries, and blockhouses that served to defend settlers and traders when attacked. These forts along rivers and the network of portages were called *ostrogs*. Clumsily at first, and then carefully, the planners in Moscow tried to link up these scattered frontier strongpoints in a kind of defense cordon. Ostrogs were garrisoned by trained troops, and outposts extended, to give notice of the approach of an enemy.

This rough defense line, manned for the most part by the settlers of the vicinity—especially by the new soldier-homesteader class—served to protect the lands inside and by slow degrees to create a connected frontier of Rus, in the west. It had grown out of the necessity of the frontier lands, chiefly to check the swift and devastating raids of Tatar horsemen, but it became a people's frontier.

Controlling the Rivers

Another idea had been growing more and more clear to the men who pored over maps and accounts in the workrooms of the Kremlin. It was about the rivers.

In the century before, Muscovite territory had grown haphazard outward from the Moskva—down the Kliazma along the Oka to the Volga. And in the same way, it had stretched northerly along the upper Volga, taking in at first the plain of the two rivers. It happened that by controlling the territory around cities like Vladimir, Moscow had brought Vladimir into its fold, with the rest of them. Now, in turn, by holding a city like Nizhni (Lowland) Novgorod, where the Oka flowed into the Volga, the *trade* of the upper Volga became subject to Moscow control.

The taking over, as it were, of all that other Novgorod's network of trade and transport routes, from river to portage in the north and east, linked up the Moscow-held river routes to the new fur empire.

It was evident that in the unsettled condition of the frontiers, control of the rivers in the central plain meant control of the land. For those great rivers flowed like immense canals, almost free from rapids, through the plain which was almost without mountains. And between them there remained the old Tatar post roads.

If more of those river routes could be linked to the Oka-Volga valley terminal, more of the plain could be won for the new Muscovite state.

Settlers on the Move

And now a new move was being made by some of the settlers in the northeast. They started to drift down through the forest belt, out of the extreme northern cold toward the line of the Kama River, once held by Tatar outposts, and opened up by the weakening of the Volga peoples. The hunters, homesteaders and land seekers were migrating south, through the wooded steppe toward more fertile ground. Curiously enough, they were now the roving and looting bands, while the Tatars had gathered into settlements. They were aided in this southward move by Muscovite troops in the lowlands around Nizhni Novgorod, and by the new defense cordons of block-houses.

This drift of people, leaving huddles of cabins deserted in the dense forest, could not be checked or diverted to a planned destination. It tended directly south, toward warmer lands, beyond which lay the open prairies of the Ukraine.

It was the first advance to conquer the steppe.

The Flowering Culture of the Ming Dynasty

Madge Huntington

In the second half of the thirteenth century, the Mongolian conqueror Kublai Khan invaded China and established the ruling Yuan dynasty. In 1368 a Buddhist monk named Zhu Yuanzhang (best known as Taizu) led an army of peasants to victory against the Mongols and established the Ming dynasty, which brought a period of great economic, cultural, and social growth.

By the fifteenth century, the Ming dynasty was in full flower. The new Yongle emperor, who ruled from 1403 to 1424, moved the capital from Nanjing to the city of Beijing, which was rebuilt on an astonishing scale. The centerpiece of the emperor's capital was the massive Imperial Palace known as the Forbidden City, which still stands today. The Yongle emperor also expanded China's power over much of the known world (except Europe) as his navy explored and traded in Indonesia, Japan, Southeast Asia, and the eastern coast of Africa.

In the arts, the painted porcelain developed during the Ming dynasty is considered some of the finest ceramic work ever made. The Ming dynasty ended in 1644.

Madge Huntington is an author and frequent traveler to China.

The Ming dynasty, founded immediately on the heels of the Yuan [dynasty], ruled from 1368 to 1644 under sixteen emperors. These Ming emperors were the last truly Chinese dynasts. Their cap-

Excerpted from Madge Huntington, *A Traveler's Guide to Chinese History*. Copyright © 1986 Madge Huntington. Reprinted with permission from Russell & Volkening as agents for the author.

ital was established first at Nanjing (Nanking), or "Southern Capital," and then at Beijing ("Northern Capital"). The monuments of Ming architecture still standing in and near Beijing—the Forbidden City, the Temple to Heaven, the great underground Ming tombs, the rebuilt Great Wall—symbolize the consolidation of Ming power.

Ming ("Bright") Taizu ("Grand Ancestor") is the posthumous title of the founder and first emperor of the Ming dynasty, who ruled from 1368 to 1398. Ming Taizu, sometimes nicknamed the Beggar King, came from a poor family and, as a youth, had been a Buddhist monk. His original name was Zhu Yuanzhang, and as such he joined the . . . rebellion against Yuan rule; he led the capture of Nanjing in 1356 and, twelve years later, chased the last Yuan emperor from Beijing. After declaring the new "Bright" dynasty, he pursued the Mongol forces far north of the Great Wall and, for the first time in Chinese history, took the lands of Manchuria along the Sea of Japan.

Ming Taizu devoted his reign to restoring Chinese political and cultural autonomy. He reestablished schools, libraries, and the examination system for the selection of civil servants—all of which had been neglected under Mongolian rule. Despite his fondness for Buddhism, he, like Tang Taizong, declared Confucianism the state doctrine. . . .

The Yongle Reign

Ming Taizu, shortly before his death at seventy-one, chose his young grandson, son of his deceased eldest son, as heir. He purposely passed over his other sons because he considered them ambitious to the point of disloyalty. This judgment was justified posthumously when the unfortunate grandson was displaced by one of his uncles, best known as the Yongle emperor.

The title Yongle ("Perpetual Happiness") is not the name of the emperor but the name of a reign, so we refer to the Yongle emperor or the emperor of the Yongle reign. . . .

The Yongle emperor (r. 1402–24), fourth son of Ming Taizu, succeeded, after a four-year struggle, in taking the throne from his teenage nephew. The deposed young man escaped, disguised as a Buddhist monk; he never recaptured his throne, and only years later was it known that he had lived out his life hidden in a series of remote monasteries.

In order to strengthen the newly acquired northern section of the empire, the Yongle emperor moved the capital from Nanjing to Beijing. The new Ming capital, completed in 1421, was built in part over the southern area of the old Yuan capital. It consisted of three walled rectangles, one inside the other, erected along a north-south axis. These were the Inner City, the Imperial City, where court officials lived, and the Forbidden City, or Imperial Palace. Directly south of and adjacent to the inner city was the walled-in outer city, whose principal features were the ceremonial altars to heaven and agriculture. Each of these cities was defined by massive walls, although today only those around the Forbidden City remain; the outer series of walls was destroyed during the [period in modern Chinese history known as the] Cultural Revolution in the 1970s. The Forbidden City is now called the Palace Museum and is open to visitors. . . .

The Grandeur of the Forbidden City

The Forbidden City, off limits to the common subject, embodied the total separation between ruler and ruled. There is no palace in the Western hemisphere which has quite the massive presence of this complex. The scale of its 250 acres makes the human figure shrink to insectlike proportions. Thirty-five-feet-high walls define a rectangle a thousand yards from north to south and eight hundred yards from east to west. (Outside these walls, no one was allowed to build any structure taller than the imperial buildings.) Each wall contains one gate, but the official gate, called Wumen ("Meridian Gate"), is centered in the south wall. Inside, moving north, one crosses a vast courtyard to another wall and gate. Beyond a second courtyard, this one large enough to hold ninety thousand officials and divided by an artificial river crossed by five bridges, rises the 115-foot-high Hall of Supreme Harmony. Here, and in the two slightly smaller halls to the north, each preceded by its own courtyard, the emperors held audiences and officiated at ceremonies. When not so occupied, they retreated into the imperial living quarters and gardens which occupy the northernmost half of the Forbidden City. The Ming emperors lived lives all but unseen; in some cases they did not set foot outside the Forbidden City for decades. They lived within walls within walls within walls, and the commoner outside knew only that inside was contained the power which inflexibly controlled his life. . . .

The Yongle emperor, the only effective emperor to succeed the dynastic founder, consolidated Chinese culture through the enormous project of collecting over seven thousand texts, which were reproduced and cataloged in his famous *Yongle Encyclopedia*. This massive work kept many scholars fully employed for a lifetime. It also saved many of these texts from oblivion, and we are indebted to the Yongle emperor for perceiving the necessity of this archival task. Since the Chinese characters cannot be arranged alphabetically, the materials are organized by phonetic rhymes.

The World's Largest Ships

The greatest, and really the only, navigational expeditions in Chinese history took place during the Yongle reign. These expeditions were led by Zheng He, a Muslim eunuch who became an admiral in the Yongle court.

One explanation given in traditional Chinese histories for this sudden and unique spurt of seabound exploration is that the Yongle emperor wanted to find his deposed nephew, who was said to have fled by boat to a Buddhist monastery on some island in the South Seas. Recent scholarship amends this theory by suggesting that these expeditions were inspired by the emperor's eagerness to let the world know of his supreme sovereignty and his interest in receiving valuable tributes from any would-be colonies. Zheng He's fleet consisted of sixty-three oceangoing junks, the largest of which were 440 feet long and 180 feet wide and carried over four hundred men each—easily the largest ships of their day. They sailed first to what is now Indonesia, where the admiral found not the emperor's nephew but a native king, whom he brought back to the Forbidden City to pay homage to the Yongle emperor. Zheng He made seven other long expeditions and got as far as the east coast of Africa. He brought back no further kings but did return with an immense amount of geographic information as well as animals never before seen in China: ostriches, zebras, and giraffes.

Rulers of All Under Heaven

Nothing that Zheng He brought back to court dissuaded the Yongle emperor from the traditional notion that the Chinese emperor was the ruler of "all that is under Heaven," including any lands reached by Zheng He. The only voice of dissent came from the Japanese, whose pirates operated in the Sea of Japan and along the coasts of the newly acquired Ming territories in Manchuria. When the emperor sent orders that they stop their ravages, they dared to reply that heaven and earth were not the monopoly of one ruler and that the world belonged to itself, not to any individual!

Zheng He's expeditions continued after the death of the Yongle emperor, till 1433. After that, the Chinese made no further attempts to explore, conquer, or even reconnoiter by sea. Since Zheng He's personal account of his expeditions was destroyed by rivals within the Ming court, we can suppose that the scholar-administrators close to the emperors disapproved of costly naval voyages to lands across the seas, giving priority to the traditional concerns of protecting the northern and western borders. Whether this was the case or not, China lost her one opportunity to beat the West to the colonization of the islands of the South Seas, and her inward focus made it impossible for her to hold her own as the West moved into the Chinese sphere of influence.

Everyday Life in the 1400s

PREFACE

While aristocrats, kings, and religious leaders invented reasons to go to war—and spent great sums of money to fight—the average citizen of the fifteenth century led a life of dire poverty. Most people lived in the most rudimentary hovels, owned only the clothes on their backs, and struggled to scratch a living from the earth in order to eat once a day.

Whenever a local nobleman decided to go to war against his weaker neighbor or a powerful king, men in the small villages were rounded up and conscripted into military service. These citizen-soldiers had to provide their own weapons, food, and whatever uniforms they could cobble together. Life was even worse for women, who were often treated as property, had no rights to own land, and had no rights to the custody of their own children.

As the century progressed, however, things began to improve for the average citizen. After the Black Death wiped out about one-third of Europe's population in the 1300s, peasants moved from farms to nearly empty villages, where a merchant class began to grow. With the growth of commerce, middle-class people could suddenly afford things that previous generations could only dream of. Travel became a popular pastime for these traders; they could visit the natural hot springs in Germany, journey to Venice to see the sights, or make a religious pilgrimage to the Holy Land in Jerusalem.

As the century closed, the life of the average citizen was slowly improving as the former agricultural economy moved toward international trade and commerce.

The Citizen Armies of England

Alice Stopford Green

Wars in the fifteenth century were often fought between powerful kings, countries, and city-states. But small towns and villages also engaged in battles with their neighbors or had to fend off large invading armies from far-off lands. As such, it was the duty of every male English villager to gather whatever weapons he could find and become a soldier for his town at a moment's notice. These fifteenth-century ragtag armies consisted of everyone from wealthy lords and nobles to farmers, butchers, and bakers.

Between battles, average citizens were expected to labor without pay to construct walls, dams, fortifications, and harbors for defense of the common good.

Alice Stopford Green was an English historian and author born in 1848.

The inhabitants of a mediæval borough were subject to a discipline as severe as that of a military state of modern times. Threatened by enemies on every side, constantly surrounded by perils, they had themselves to bear the whole charges of fortification and defence. If a French fleet appeared on the coast, if Welsh or Scotch armies made a raid across the frontier, if civil war broke out and opposing forces marched across the country, every town had to look to its own safety. The inhabitants served under a system of universal conscription [compulsory enrollment in the military]. At the muster-at-arms held twice a year poor and rich appeared in military

Excerpted from Mrs. J.R. Green, *Town Life in the Fifteenth Century* (New York: Macmillan and Co., 1893).

array with such weapons as they could bring forth for the King's service; the poor marching with knife or dagger or hatchet; the prosperous burghers [citizens of the town], bound according to mediæval ideas to live "after their degree," displaying mail [metal] or wadded [padded] coats, bucklers [shields], bows and arrows, swords, or even a gun. At any moment this armed population might be called out to active service. "Concerning our bell," say the citizens of Hereford, "we use to have it in a public place where our chief bailiff [deputy] may come, as well by day as by night, to give warning to all men living within the said city and suburbs. And we do not say that it ought to ring unless it be for some terrible fire burning any row of houses within the said city, or for any common contention whereby the city might be terribly moved, or for any enemies drawing near unto the city, or if the city shall be besieged, or any sedition shall be between any, and notice thereof given by any unto our chief bailiff. And in these cases aforesaid, and in all like cases, all manner of men abiding within the city and suburbs and liberties of the city, of what degree soever they be of, ought to come at any such ringing, or motion of ringing, with such weapons as fit their degree." At the first warning of an enemy's approach the mayor or bailiff became supreme military commander. It was his office to see that the panic-stricken people of the suburbs were gathered within the walls and given house and food, that all meat and drink and chattels were made over for the public service, and all armour likewise carried to the Town Hall, that every inhabitant or refugee paid the taxes required for the cost of his protection, that all strong and able men "which doth dwell in the city or would be assisted by the city in anything" watched by day and night, and that women and clerics who could not watch themselves found at their own charge substitutes "of the ablest of the city."

Protecting the Coast

If frontier towns had periods of comparative quiet, the seaports, threatened by sea as by land, lived in perpetual alarm, at least so long as the Hundred Years' War protracted its terrors. When the inhabitants, had built ships to guard the harbour, and provided money for their victualling [stocking with food] and the salaries of the crew, they were called out to repair towers and carry cartloads of rocks or stones to be laid on the walls "for defending the town in resisting the king's enemies." Guns had to be carried to the church or the Common House on sleds or laid in pits at the town gates, and gun-stones, saltpetre, and pellet powder bought. For weeks together watchmen were posted in the church towers with horns to give warning if a foe appeared; and piles of straw, reeds and wood were heaped up on the sea-coast to kindle beacons and watch-fires. Even if the townsfolk gathered for a day's amusement to hear a play in the Court-house a watch was set lest the enemy should set fire to their streets—a calamity but too well known to the burghers of Rye and Southampton.

Village Fighting Village

Inland towns were in little better case. Civil war, local rebellion, attacks from some neighbouring lord, outbreaks among the followers of a great noble lodged within their walls at the head of an army of retainers, all the recurring incidents of siege and pitched battle rudely reminded inoffensive shopkeepers and artisans of their military calling. Owing to causes but little studied, local conflicts were frequent, and they were fought out with violence and determination. At the close of the fourteenth century a certain knight, Baldwin of Radington, with the help of John of Stanley, raised eight hundred fighting men "to destroy and hurt the commons of Chester"; and these stalwart warriors broke into the abbey, seized the wine and dashed the furniture in pieces, and when the mayor and sheriff came to the rescue nearly killed the sheriff. When in 1441 the Archbishop of York determined to fight for his privileges in Ripon Fair he engaged two hundred men-at-arms from Scotland and the Marches at sixpence or a shilling a day, while a Yorkshire gentleman, Sir John Plumpton, gathered seven hundred men; and at the battle that ensued, more than a thousand arrows were discharged by them.

Provisioning Soldiers

Within the town territory the burghers had to serve at their own cost and charges; but when the King called out their forces to join his army the municipal officers had to get the contingent ready, to provide their dress or badges, to appoint the captain, and to gather in money from the various parishes for the soldiers' pay. . . . When they were sent to a distance their fellow townsmen bought provisions of salt fish and paniers or bread boxes for the carriage of their food, and reluctantly provided a scanty wage, which was yet more reluctantly doled out to the soldier by his officer, and perhaps never reached his pocket at all. Universal conscription proved then as now the great inculcator [enforcer] of peace. To the burgher called from the loom and the [cloth] dyeing pit and the market stall to take down his bow or dagger, war was a hard and ungrateful service where reward and plunder were dealt out with a [stingy] hand; and men conceived a deep hatred of strife and disorder of which they had measured all the misery. When the common people dreamed of a brighter future, their simple hope was that every maker of deadly weapons should die by his own tools. . . .

In the town communities of the Middle Ages all public works were carried out by what was in fact forced labour of the whole commonalty. If the boroughs suffered little from government interference neither could they look for help in the way of state aid or state loans; and as the burgher's purse in early days was generally empty he had to give of the work of his hands for the common good. In Nottingham "booners"—that is the burgesses themselves or substitutes whom they provided to take their place—repaired the highways and kept the streets in order. . . . When [the town of] Hythe in 1412 sent for a Dutch engineer to make a new harbour, all the inhabitants were called out in turn to help at the "Delveys" or diggings. Sundays and weekdays alike the townsmen had to work, dining off bread and ale provided by the corporation for the diggers, and if they failed to appear they were fined fourpence a day. In the same way [the town of] Sandwich engaged a Hollander to superintend the making of a new dyke for the harbour; the mayor was ordered to find three workmen to labour at it, every jurat [alderman] two, and each member of the Common Council one man; while all other townsmen had to give labour or find substitutes according to their ability. The jurats were made overseers, and were responsible for the carrying out of the work; and so successfully was the whole matter managed that in 1512 the Sandwich haven was able to give shelter to 500 or 600 hoys [small boats].

Forced labour such as this could of course only be applied to works where skilled artificers [craftsmen] were not necessary; but occasions soon multiplied when the town mob had to be replaced by trained labourers, and we already see traces of a transitional system in the making of the Hythe harbour, where the municipality had to engage hired labour for such work as could not be done by the burgesses. But undertakings for which scientific skill was needed sorely taxed local resources, and the burghers were driven to make anxious appeals to public charity. In 1447, when Bridport wanted to improve its harbour, collectors were sent all over the country to beg for money; indulgences of forty or a hundred days were promised to subscribers by archbishops and bishops, and a copy of the paper carried by one of the collectors gives the sum of the masses said for them in the year as amounting to nearly four thousand: "the sum of all other good prayers no man knoweth save only God alone."

Bridge Repair

The building and repairing of bridges as being also work that demanded science and skilled labour involved serious cost. When the King had allowed the bridge at Nottingham to fall into the river, he generously transferred its ownership and the duty of setting it up again to the townspeople; who appointed wardens and kept elaborate accounts and bore grievous anxiety, till finding its charges worse than all their ordinary town expenses they at last fell to begging also. So also the mayor of Exeter prayed for help in the matter of the bridge there, which had been built by a wealthy mayor and was "of the length or nigh by, and of the same mason work as London Bridge, housing upon except; the which bridge openly is known the greatest costly work and most of alms-deeds to help it in all the west part of England." Such instances reveal to us the persistent difficulties that beset a world where primitive methods utterly failed to meet new exigencies, and where the demand for technical quality in work was beginning to lead to new organizations of labour. Meanwhile the burghers had to fight their own way with no hope of grants in aid from the state, and little to depend on save the personal effort of the whole commonalty.

Fifteenth-Century Home Life

George Gordon Coulton

Even the wealthiest citizens of the fifteenth century tended to live in cold, dark, uncomfortable quarters. Furniture was scarce and even kings and nobility had little in the way of couches or easy chairs. The only artificial light was provided by candles or burning animal fat, which was rare and expensive. Those of lesser means lived with even fewer amenities. Meals were also simple and modest.

George Gordon Coulton was born in England in 1858 and taught at Cambridge University as Birkbeck lecturer in ecclesiastical history and English. As a leading authority on English history of the Middle Ages, he was made fellow of the British Academy in 1929.

The furniture we shall find to be very scanty. Here is an inventory of one of the wealthiest at Colchester. . . . The citizen had a trestle-table; this was the ordinary arrangement, so that the boards could be put away in a corner except at meal-times. . . . Nothing in the way of chairs; some sort of settles or stools was doubtless taken for granted, and not inventoried. Two silver spoons, a cup, a table-cloth and two towels, a brass cauldron, a brass dish, washing-basin and ewer, trivet, and iron candlestick, two beds, two gowns, a mantle, one piece of russet cloth (for making up into clothes some day); three pounds of wool, two barrels. So much for the household furniture. The man was a butcher, and thus he possessed pickling tubs, meat, fat, corn, hay, and a cart. . . . The general impression of scantiness, however, is entirely borne out by contemporary wills and inventories, which survive in

Excerpted from G.G. Coulton, *Medieval Panorama: The English Scene from Conquest to Reformation.* Copyright © 1938 Cambridge University Press. Reprinted with permission Cambridge University Press.

considerable numbers. The richer folk had hangings for their rooms, which might run to considerable expense, and feather-beds with valuable quilts. Even kings and popes had no easy chairs, but would often sit on their beds to receive ambassadors. Still, when all has been reckoned, these things were not only primitive according to our modern ideas, but comfortless and insanitary. The fork was not yet invented for meals; handkerchiefs were almost unknown; folk ordinarily slept either naked or in their day-clothes, and the rushes on the hall floor were changed quarterly or yearly. . . .

Cold and Dark

Many of the Colchester citizens had only one living room which served all purposes. . . . One of the things . . . which would [bother] us most immediately would be the cold; in rooms with ill-fitting doors and windows, which in the majority of cases were unglazed, so that there was no alternative between darkness and open air. The fire burned commonly in a brazier in the middle of the hall, the smoke escaping as best it could through the roof; but here again, in a great town like London, there was provision for stone chimneys. In Montaigne's *Voyages,* when he goes to Switzerland, he notes with a special emphasis how the rooms are so well warmed with porcelain stoves that one actually takes off one's hat and one's furs when sitting indoors! In mid-sixteenth-century France, as in England, warm clothes were needed even more indoors than in walking abroad. . . . To quote from Miss Abram [*English Life and Manners in the Late Middle Ages*] . . . "Carpets are seldom mentioned in wills and inventories until the close of the fifteenth century. Henry VII had one in his bedchamber, but some of his rooms were strewn with rushes, or straw." "It is probable that, as civilization advanced, reception-rooms were used more frequently, and bedrooms less frequently, for the purposes of hospitality. Nevertheless, we have come across two cases of men of good social standing (a canon of Wells, 1492, and a Sergeant at Law, 1500) who had beds in their parlours. . . . In one of Hoccleve's poems, *Jereslaus's Wife*, an earl and countess, their daughter and her governess, all slept in the same room.". . .

Artificial light . . . was extremely expensive. In its cheapest form it was a dim cresset [hanging lamp] of oil or a rushlight [small candle] of mutton-fat; and, winter fodder being so rare, the result was that a pound of fat [to fuel a lamp] cost four times as much as a pound of lean meat. There was thus a great temptation to sit up by the embers of the fire and drink into the night. . . .

Bread and Beer for Breakfast

Thus, to the very end, there were glaring contrasts between the cloths of gold and brocade of the greatest folk, the elaborate art lavished on all their buildings, their furniture and even the commonest domestic articles, their extraordinarily ceremonious manners (duly noted by the Venetian envoy in Henry VII's reign), and those other things in the background which strike us as strangely uncultivated. . . . The meals . . . showed the same contrasts. Here, for instance, is an extract from the famous *Northumberland Household Book*, regulating the castles of perhaps the greatest baron in England at the beginning of the sixteenth century:

"Braikfastis for my lorde and my lady. Furst a Loof of Brede in Trenchors* ij Manchetts [small loaves] j Quart of Bere a Quart of Wyne half a Chyne of Muton or ells a Chyne of Beif Boilid.

"Braikfastis for my Lorde Percy [aged 10] and Mr Thomas Percy. Item Half a Loif of household Breide. A Manchett j Potell [4 pints] of Bere a Chekynge or ellse iij Mutton Bonys boyled.

"Braikfastis for the Nurcy for my Lady Margaret and Mr Yngram Percy. Item a Manchet j Quarte of Bere and iij Muton Bonys boiled.

"Braikfastis for my Ladys Gentylwomen. Item a loif of Household Breid a Pottell of Beire and iiij Muton Bonys boyled or ells a Pece of Beif Boilid.

"Braikfastis for my Lords Breder his Hede Officers of Houshold and Counsaill. Item ij. Loofs of Houshold Briede a Manchet a Gallon of Bere ij Muton Bonys and ij Peces of Beif Boilid."

The Percy meals were the same in Lent, except that (1) it was only the children who then breakfasted daily; the rest, only four times a week; (2) fish was substituted for flesh; e.g. the nurse and the babies had a piece of salt fish, a dish of sprats, or three white herring. . . . If the amount of beer seems startling, we must remember in the first place that our ancestors were under no temptation to drink water. It was only in a few towns of the later Middle Ages, and then almost entirely through the monasteries or friaries, that aqueducts were brought in. Again, practically no hot drinks were known, except alcoholic or medicinal. Thus ale and beer not only supplied very considerable calories from the strictly dietetic point of view, but comforted the stomach after the fashion of modern tea and coffee. The monastic allowance, where we find it specified, is seldom less than a gallon of ale a day. A priceless record from Coventry in 1520, which gives both the population of the city and its consumption of malt and wheat, points to a consumption of a quart of ale per diem per soul, man, woman and child. Thus, the men's average would run at least to two quarts.

---

* Trenchers were slices of bread which [people] used as plates, eating their meal upon them and leaving them as remnants for the poor or for their dogs.

Women in the Middle Ages

Marjorie Rowling

Society in the Middle Ages viewed the role of women in two opposite extremes. On one hand, the concept of romantic love and gallantry had recently come into fashion. On the other hand, women—because of the biblical Eve—were blamed for original sin and for causing humankind to be evicted from the Garden of Eden. In any case, women were widely considered by men to be inferior creatures and were thus treated as second-class citizens. They were not allowed to own property, had no legal claims to their own children, and were not permitted to attend schools.

As the fifteenth century progressed, the cultural enlightenment of the Renaissance alleviated some of the prejudices against women. In most places, however, men continued to treat women as little more than property, and their lot did not improve for hundreds of years.

Marjorie Rowling is an expert on English country life and medieval history whose books include *Everyday Life of Medieval Travellers* and *The Folklore of the Lake District*.

[In the Middle Ages] the Church's view, when broadcast by monks, clergy and friars preaching the ascetic ideal [of self-denial], was that woman was an instrument of the Devil, the supreme temptress, and as such must necessarily be both evil and inferior to man. How then did this teaching react in the sphere of everyday life? Here, from necessity, women's actual condition varied not only from century to century but, much more, from class to class. The well-born woman's lot differed from that of the rich merchant's wife, and both even more from

Excerpted from Marjorie Rowling, *Everyday Life in Medieval Times*. Copyright © 1968 Marjorie Rowling. Reprinted with permission from Salamander Books.

PUYALLUP PUBLIC LIBRARY

the position of villeins [feudal farmers] and serfs. Yet most men—theoretically at least—agreed that women were inferior beings. This gave them the right to inflict corporal punishment upon them.

There is ample proof of this attitude. A Dominican, Nicolas Byard, declared in the thirteenth century: 'A man may chastise his wife and beat her for correction, for she is of his household, therefore the lord may chastise his own.' Canon Law also stated: 'It is plain that wives should be subject to their husbands and should almost be servants.' Even the kindly and affectionate Goodman of Paris told his wife in the fourteenth century to

> copy the behaviour of a dog who always has his heart and his eye upon his master; even if his master whip him and throw stones at him, the dog follows, wagging his tail. . . . Wherefore for a better and stronger reason, women ought to have a perfect and solemn love for their husbands.

In Customary Law and Practice in the thirteenth century one clause of the statutes of a new town in Gascony asserted: 'All inhabitants of Villefranche have the right to beat their wives, provided they do not kill them thereby.' The Knight of La Tour-Landry, in his famous book written to give advice to his daughters, tells them of an aristocratic wife who, by scolding her husband in public, so incensed him that he 'smote her with his fist down to the earth, then with his foot he kicked her face and broke her nose . . . so that ever after she was shamed to show her visage, it was so foul blemished.'

At the opposite end of the social scale, village women who dared to rail against their husbands were doused in the ducking stool [a chair on a pole in which people were punished by holding them underwater] in the village pond. Court rolls show that villages were repeatedly threatened or fined for failing to provide these punitive instruments. . . .

Also Regarded with Gratitude

Womankind was also regarded with gratitude and pity in, at least some, male quarters. A French poem declares:

> Much ought woman to be held dear.
> By her is everybody clothed.
> Woman spins and makes our garments
> Of cloth of gold and cloth of silk.
> To all who read this story I say,
> Speak no ill of womankind.

A fifteenth-century writer sets out to champion the working woman:

> A woman is a worthy thing,
> They do the wash and do the wring.
> 'Lullay, lullay', she doth sing,
> And yet she hath but care and woe.
>
> A woman is a worthy wight,

She serveth man both day and night,
Thereto she putteth all her might,
And yet she hath but care and woe.

Arranged Marriages

Perhaps it was in the sphere of marriage that women's lot was the hardest, bearing on them more severely the lower their position in the social scale. Marriages were seldom a matter of choice but of arrangement by parents, guardians and overlords. The overriding consideration was financial gain or territorial aggrandisement. In the case of villeins their owners arranged for their early marriage since their offspring belonged to their overlord and their increase brought more workers for his estates.

The great lady, however, had not necessarily any better chance of a happy marriage than the bondwoman at her gates. Johann Busch, the fifteenth-century Saxon reformer, has drawn a pathetic picture of the Duchess of Brunswick on her death-bed:

> When her confession with absolution and penance was ended, I said to her, 'Think you lady, that you will pass to the kingdom of heaven when you die?' She replied, 'This believe I firmly.' Said I, 'That would be a marvel. You were bred in castles and for many years have lived with your husband the Lord Duke amid innumerable delights, with wine and ale, meat and venison, both roast and boiled; and yet you expect to fly away to heaven directly you die.'

> She answered, 'Beloved father, why should I not now go to heaven? I have lived in this castle like an anchoress [hermit] in a cell. What delights or pleasures have I had here, save that I have endeavoured to show a happy face to my servants and maidens? I have a hard husband, as you know, who has hardly any care or inclination towards women. Have I not been in this castle as it were in a cell?'

> I said to her, 'You think then that God will send his angels when you die, to bear your soul to Paradise?'

> 'This believe I firmly', she replied. Then said I, 'May God give you what you believe.'

The woman serf, however, fared worse, being regarded as little more than a beast. In 1411, on the manor of Liestal near Basle, it was prescribed that 'every year before Shrove Tuesday, when folk are accustomed to think of holy matrimony, the bailiff shall consider what boys and girls are of such an age that they may take wife or husband, so that he may allot to each his mate'.

Queen Blanche, mother of St Louis, pitied the serfs so much that she ordained that in many places they should be freed and pay some other due. She had most compassion for the young girls in serfdom, for men would not take them in marriage, and many of them were [not virgins]. . . .

On the other hand, on some estates a more humane attitude was taken towards bondwomen especially during their confinements, when they were sometimes excused the annual tribute of the Shrovetide hen, or received the gift of a load of firewood or fish from the lord's pond.

At Denchendorff in Germany each female serf received two measures of wine and eight white loaves at the christening of each of her children. As Christine de Pisan, a medieval woman writer, states, 'They received bread, milk, lard and potage, also some fish, and their life was often more secure and even more satisfying than that of better born women.'

Divorce Forbidden

The Church's attitude towards divorce did not make woman's lot more enviable. According to Canon Law a marriage, once made, was unbreakable. The furthest the Church would go was to make a marriage 'null and void', to say that a true marriage had never taken place. . . . So . . . a man, if tired of his wife, or for any other reason, could get rid of her, provided he could afford the expense of the necessary proceedings. . . .

The discovery of servile [having been a servant] ancestry in a wife was also a sufficient cause to annul a marriage; while some, having spent their wife's fortune, 'shamelessly deserted her, delighting in a prudent, handsomer and wealthier mate'.

Yet there is abundant evidence of happy marriages. The Goodman of Paris—an elderly French official of wealth and position—wrote a book of instructions for his child-wife, an orphan. Throughout the many pages, his sympathy and loving understanding for her keeps breaking through. He tells her that he writes the book

> for your honour and love and not for my service, since I had pity and loving compassion on you, who for long have had neither father nor mother to whom you might turn for counsel in your need, save me alone. . . . And know that I am pleased that you tend rose-trees and care for violets, and make chaplets and dance and sing. . . . As for the greater service you say you would willingly do me, if you were able and I taught it you, know, dear sister, that I am well content that you should do me such service as your good neighbours of like estate do for their husbands. . . . For I am not so overweening in my attitude to you that I am not satisfied with what you do for me. Provided there be no scorn or disdain. For although I know well you are of gentler birth than I, . . . yet in you I have no fear, I have confidence in your good intent.

Throughout his book the Goodman adopts this almost humble tone—'for to me belongeth none save the common service, or less'.

Marriage at a Young Age

Thomas Betson, a 40-year-old English merchant who traded in Calais [France], was deeply in love with his fiancée [and cousin] of 15, Katherine Riche, as we can plainly see from his letter to her in 1476:

> My own heartily beloved Cousin Katherine, I recommend me to you with all my heart. The token you sent is most welcome to me. Also a letter from your gentle squire telling me you are in good health and merry at heart. . . . If you would be a good eater of your meat alway, that you might grow fast to be a woman, you should make me the gladdest man of the world. . . .
>
> I pray you greet well my horse and beg him to give you four of his years to help you. And at my coming I will give him four of my years and four horse loaves. Tell him that I prayed him so. . . . And Almighty Jesus make you a good woman. . . .
>
> By your faithful lover and Cousin, Thomas Betson. I send you this ring for a token.

Thomas Betson continued to wish that his Katherine would make haste and grow to marriageable age, he wrote to her mother: 'I remember Katherine full oft, God knows. I dreamed once she was thirty winters of age, and when I woke I wished she had been but twenty, and so by likelihood I am sooner like to have my wish than my dream.' Soon after, Thomas married his Katherine and we know she proved a loving and helpful wife. For when, a year later, Thomas fell dangerously ill, Katherine, though but 16 and expecting the birth of her eldest son, not only nursed him faithfully, but looked after his business with all the competence to which the medieval women and the upper classes were trained from early childhood.

Keeping Clean

Philippe Braunstein

Before the fifteenth century, people had little use for bathing and cleanliness. In some regions with high incidence of disease, bathing was thought to lead to sickness and death, and people only bathed every six months or so. This problem was aggravated by religious leaders who preached that exposing the naked body—for any reason—was shameful and sinful. Many writers of medieval texts referred to the foul smell of unwashed humanity that they encountered in churches, markets, and public buildings.

Writer Philippe Braunstein reveals how these attitudes began to change, however, by the mid-1400s when standards of beauty, cleanliness, luxurious bathing, and stylish clothing came into fashion. Some cities that had been known for their public hot springs, such as Bath, England, and Baden, Germany, became gathering spots for locals and those who could afford to travel.

Cleanliness was important, but before the body could be cleaned it had to be rid of parasites. To remove lice, a person turned to the people he or she loved. In Montaillou [France] the chore was performed in the sunlight, on rooftops or doorsteps, by wives and mistresses. . . . Or consider . . . that extraordinary microcosm, the galley [ship] of pilgrims. Friar Felix Faber's [writings are] most informative. Parasites, he says, will flourish unless one takes precautions. "On a boat, too many people travel without a change of clothing; they live in sweat and foul odors, in which vermin thrive, not only in clothing but also in beards and hair. Therefore the pilgrim must not be lax; he must cleanse himself daily. A person who has not a single louse right now can have thousands an hour from now if he has the slightest con-

Excerpted from Philippe Braunstein, in *A History of Private Life,* vol. 2 (Cambridge, MA: The Belknap Press of Harvard University Press), edited by George Duby. Copyright © 1988 President and Fellows of Harvard College. Reprinted with permission from the publisher.

tact with an infested pilgrim or sailor. Take care of the beard and hair every day, for if the lice proliferate you will be obliged to shave your beard and thus lose your dignity, for it is scandalous not to wear a beard at sea. On the other hand, it is pointless to keep a long head of hair, as do some nobles unwilling to make the sacrifice. I have seen them so covered with lice that they gave them to all their friends and troubled all their neighbors. A pilgrim should not be ashamed to ask others to scour his beard for lice."

Filth, which carried with it epidemic disease, somehow had to be eliminated; on this point common sense and the general interest were in accord. Caring for the body not only preserved health but was also a pleasure. Heroes and heroines with fine hair and white or rosy complexions spent a good deal of time on their toilettes. Men and women of the late Middle Ages washed and had themselves massaged more frequently than their offspring, or so it seems, to judge by the abundance of sources dealing with the beautification and care of the body.

New Ideals for Beauty

For men beauty care was limited to athletic exertions followed by ablutions and massage; the comb and scissors served head and beard according to the canons of fashion, which, to judge by surviving portraits, changed as often as fashions in clothing. These attentions, coupled with various lotions for the body, were all that virility would tolerate. [Roman poet] Ovid [b. 43 B.C.], who remained the fifteenth century's arbiter of elegance, had long ago pointed out that men's bodies do not require much attention; the curled dandies of Venice and Florence, Bruges and Paris, carried things too far. Women took greater pains to make themselves seductive. Since [ancient Greek physician] Hippocrates insisted that a good physician should be able to answer any question about the body, [fifteenth-century] treatises on surgery included various methods of beautification, including cosmetics, depilatories [hair removers], breast creams, hair dyes, and even pommades [hair ointments] compounded of ground glass, astringents, and dyes. . . .

Thus, far from the world of sturdy peasant women . . . from the spinners and spoolers of the fabric-making towns, from the . . . Bohemian mines . . . where women were employed as washers and sorters—far from such places an artificial ideal of womanhood took shape in spite of criticism from the Church. This ideal was embodied in the pale complexion and plucked eyebrows of [some upper-class women]. . . .

Long hair connoted mourning, and in a mood of black melancholy [King] Charles the Bold allowed his nails to grow unchecked. Normally, however, people sought to restrain and curtail nature's exuberance. A construct of culture, a woman had to be smooth in order to be agreeable. Medical treatises explained that hair was the condensation of crude vapors and that excess feminine moisture which did not flow naturally was transformed into moss that should be trimmed. To remove hair women used strips of fabric dipped in pitch or destroyed hair follicles with hot needles; powerful depilatories were also used. . . .

Bathing Becomes Fashionable

Clean, smooth, brilliant skin was the result of repeated baths and much diligent care, capped by the application of creams. By the late Middle Ages monastic moralists had ceased to warn about the dangers of bathing. Bathing and steaming were so widespread at all levels of society that it no longer seemed appropriate to question the practice of washing the body frequently from head to toe. . . . The Dominican Felix Faber enthusiastically approved of bodily cleanliness and stressed the importance of regular changes of body linen. In the minds of many people frequent washing may have assumed the same spiritual value as frequent confession.

There were two ways of bathing: in bathtub or steam room, alone or with others. Baths at home were prepared in the bedroom, near the fire which was used to heat the water. Providing a bath for one's guests was one of the first duties of hospitality. . . .

The wealthy bourgeois typically disrobed and bathed at home, in private. In the home of Anton Tucher of Nuremberg, the master of the house undressed in a small room off his bedroom, where a tub was placed next to a brass cauldron on a tiled floor covered with wooden latticework. Fragrant herbs were allowed to steep in the bath water. [Some] recommended strewing rose petals over the bather. . . .

In the country bathing was no less common than in the city, to judge by the fabliaux [French fables written at the time]. Either inside the house or out, the bather crouched in a tub of hot water underneath a cover of taut fabric that kept in the steam. Sometimes two or more people bathed together in rituals of hospitality or sociability: for example, the bath after the grape harvest, or the baths that bride and groom took separately on the eve of the wedding, he with the friends of his youth, she with hers.

Hot Springs and Steam Baths

Both rural and urban areas contained public baths, sometimes administered by the community. Some were for therapeutic purposes as well as washing; the ancient tradition of bathing in hot springs survived in places noted for their healing virtues. In the fifteenth century thermal cures became fashionable, for example, at Bad Teinach in the Black Forest, where the *Wildbad* (or wild bath, meaning natural spring) attracted Duke William of Saxony accompanied by his physician in

1476, or at Hall in the Tyrol, where [Italian] ambassador Agostino Patrizi . . . paused to describe the sophisticated installations.

Watery pleasures were widely shared in the late Middle Ages. North of the Alps the steam bath had long been in wide use. *De ornatu*, an Italian treatise on female beauty care, indicates that the *stuphis*, the steam bath, is a German invention. . . . The sauna, one of the earliest descriptions of which is found in the writings of the geographer and diplomat Ibrahim ben Yacub, who visited Saxony and Bohemia in 973, was very common in Slavic and Germanic regions. In most villages the steam bath operated several days a week; its location was marked by a sign depicting a bundle of leafy branches.

[An] epic poem attributed to Siegrid Helbling describes with a wealth of detail all the phases of a steam bath shared by a knight, his valet, and various others. No sooner had the master of the bath sounded his trumpet than people flocked in, barefoot and beltless, carrying chemises or robes folded over their arms. They lay down on wooden benches in thick mists of steam that rose from heated stones upon which water was sprinkled regularly; the back, arms, and legs were kneaded by masseuses, and sweat was made to flow by flagellating the skin with branches. The body was rubbed with ashes and soap. Then a barber trimmed the hair and beard. Finally, the bathers donned their robes and went to rest in an adjoining room.

Medieval Medical Practices

Marzieh Gail

The average life expectancy in the fifteenth century was a little more than thirty-five years. Knowledge of germs, infection, viruses, and bacteria was unknown. As a result, medieval doctors specialized in magic, astrology, and religion, as well as bizarre practices such as draining pints of a patient's blood as a "cure."

Some of these medical practices began to dramatically improve during the late fifteenth century because of the intellectual and scientific knowledge disseminated during the Renaissance.

Marzieh Gail graduated from Stanford University and has a master of arts degree from the University of California at Berkeley. She is the author of a number of books on historical subjects.

Among all the subjects studied at a university, medicine, perhaps, showed the greatest advance. True, medicine still had one foot in the Middle Ages. Newer surgery and a better understanding of the human body were available, but many doctors held to old methods and remedies. Some cast their eyes heavenward in treating a disease, not in prayer but because they believed, along with astrologers, that every part of the body was governed by a planet. A doctor of that time might, for example, refuse to bleed a patient unless the moon was in its second quarter.

Bleeding was a favorite cure-all, and even those near death might be diligently bled. Doctors opened a vein to let out "bad blood," or

Excerpted from Marzieh Gail, *Life in the Renaissance*. All rights reserved under International and Pan-American Copyright Conventions. Reprinted by permission of Random House Children's Books, a division of Random House, Inc.

placed live leeches—as many as twenty at a time—on the patient to suck blood out. One treatment for madness included the taking of enough blood from a vein in the forehead to fill an eggshell. Insanity was a distressing ailment, then as now, but apparently did not make a man unfit for office; the chief officer of Castle St. Angelo, the Pope's stronghold in Rome, was intermittently mad, and so, for many years, was the reigning King of France.

People attributed healing powers to products that cost a great deal or came from far away. Thus pepper, ginger and other spices from the East were highly valued as medicines, and tobacco, newly discovered in America, found favor as a pain reducer. Sugar, a luxury, was believed to be a cure for lung congestion and was sometimes flavored with violets. Gold, taken internally, was supposed to arrest or at least to conceal leprosy.

Health hazards included birth. Many an infant and many a mother did not survive. Smallpox was also a great danger. Indeed, there was a saying that mothers counted their children only after they had had this disease. Wounds were an everyday affair. Ague, "the stone," that is, kidney and gall stones, gout, and various fevers were common. Bubonic plague was always erupting locally and changing everyone's plans, either for the moment or forever.

Healing with Herbs, Grease, and Plaster

Although we do not always know why, many strange cures of the time were effective. A wound might be treated with wormwood which had been thrown on a red hot tile and soaked in Greek wine. Bacon fat was rubbed into bruises. Open sores were plugged with lint and covered with a plaster. Doctors prescribed perfumes, powdered pearls, laxatives, lotions and unctions. One eye remedy was fleur-de-lis [flower of the lilies], including the entire plant, simmered over a slow fire. Borax and also white lead were recommended for pimples, and breath was sweetened with cardamon or licorice. Boiled toad was not unknown for heart disease, and, indeed, modern science has shown that a toad's skin contains something like the heart drug, digitalis. Worms were considered good for fevers. Even more bizarre were such cures as suspending a patient upside down, or preventing him from falling asleep.

So far as the healing arts were concerned, the superstitions of the past held the doctors back. They believed that the body was made of four elements: earth, air, fire and water. From these elements came four "humors": blood, phlegm, yellow bile and black bile. The amount and purity of these four humors in the body determined one's disposition and health. A man who had too much black bile was melancholy. If he had too much phlegm he was phlegmatic.

The selfishness of doctors also hindered the progress of medicine. A doctor who discovered a new remedy or successfully used a new operation often tried to keep the discovery to himself. A man hugged his knowledge to his bosom, or kept it in his family, which is one reason why there tended to be families of doctors.

Despite such backward attitudes and superstitions, the science of medicine did advance. Nature began to be referred to as a healer, and the study of medicinal herbs was widespread. The first printed book of such herbs came out in 1484, describing 150 different plants, and before the middle of the sixteenth century Pisa and Padua had botanical gardens for use in teaching medicine. Another school of healing relied on chemicals and a long war between mineralists and herbalists began. A noted Swiss doctor, Paracelsus, wandering about in search of knowledge, did not hesitate to collect medical information from barbers and executioners, bath-keepers, gypsies, midwives and fortune-tellers. . . .

People certainly knew that touching a sick person had something to do with catching his ailment. In plague time they would call out to one another: "Let us keep our distance!" Many shops would close, and if money was paid out, it would be received in a tray, not by hand.

Dissecting Bodies

Renaissance medicine owed most of its true progress to the revived interest in anatomy and in the human body. Corpses could be cut open and studied in all the medical schools of Italy. . . . But bodies for dissection were scarce. Some came from hospitals or from the gallows and occasionally a corpse would disappear from a cemetery. The bodies of criminals who died in prison might be taken to the dissection table if no relatives or friends intervened. The demand was great, particularly at Bologna, where one professor of anatomy cut up and examined a hundred cadavers. Leonardo da Vinci gained a detailed knowledge of the human body by dissecting more than thirty cadavers.

Besides increasing man's knowledge of how the different organs are affected by disease, all this study of the human structure enabled surgeons to improve their techniques and to invent new instruments. . . .

So informal was medical practice that one instrument was invented in mid-operation. A leading surgeon, with implements of coarse steel, was clumsily removing infected sections of a girl's finger bones; a goldsmith who was watching the proceedings begged the doctor to wait. He ran to his shop, and soon was back with "a little scalping-iron of steel, extremely thin and curved" which "cut like a razor." The operation was a complete success.

Even blood transfusion was tried. When [fifteenth-century] pope Innocent VIII lay dying, a doctor proposed introducing the blood of a ten-year-old boy into the Pontiff's veins. Attempts were made with three different boys, but the Pope was not revived and all the boys died.

Plastic surgeons had better luck. They repaired facial injuries with skin grafts taken from other parts of the patient's body, becoming so skilful that only faint lines showed where the edges of skin had been joined. Here was another "re-birth" since the art of plastic surgery had been practiced in ancient times but lost for centuries.

Renaissance Hospitals

Italian hospitals were the marvels of Europe. For one thing, they were exceptionally clean. They were also, in many cases, beautiful. Famous architects designed some of them and painters had their works hung in them. [In the sixteenth century] Martin Luther, the famous reformer, who visited Italy while still a priest, found the hospital system one of the few things he could praise. He spoke of the good food, and of "careful attendants and learned physicians." He told of the exact procedure when a patient entered the hospital: ". . . his clothes are removed in the presence of a notary who makes a faithful inventory of them, and they are kept safely. A white smock is put on him, and he is laid on a comfortable bed, with clean linen. Presently two doctors come to him, and servants bring him food in clean vessels."

Luther also told of how ladies of good family took turns as nurses. They stayed at the hospital for a few days, wearing a veil the entire time so that no one might learn who they were. As one completed her tour of duty, another took her place. All this shows a marked advance over the three basic kinds of hospitals in the Middle Ages— the leper hospitals, almshouses for old and infirm poor, and nursing homes with indifferent attendants and no resident doctor.

A hazard that faced doctors themselves was to be entrusted with too important a patient. A famous doctor, brought in to treat Lorenzo the Magnificent, leading member of the powerful Medici family of Florence, was unable to save him. When the doctor's body was later discovered in a well some thought he had committed suicide over his failure, but the more cynical decided he had been thrown there.

Close Government Supervision

Few believed in doctors completely. Sometimes a contract would be drawn up whereby the physician would receive no pay unless he cured a given ailment. City authorities tried hard to weed out quacks. Venice required doctors to swear that they would not delay a patient's recovery in order to collect a larger fee. No one was allowed to practice medicine in Venice unless he had completed a four-year course in a medical school. Physicians and surgeons were required to take a refresher course in anatomy at least once a year, and a later law obliged them to meet together and discuss cases every month.

Prescription druggists also came in for close supervision, as well they might, since they had many opportunities to substitute a cheap ingredient for a costly one. The government set a limit on how much could be charged for a prescription. Doctors were supposed to check on the accuracy with which their prescriptions were filled, and were forbidden to accept money from the druggist for sending business his way. An inspector came around regularly to check the files and observe the druggist in operation.

In those days, as now, druggists sold a variety of goods. Besides ointments, syrups and plasters of various kinds, they carried all manner of spices, as well as writing paper, candy, and even jewelry and varnish. In addition they had another sideline: they would sell the prescriptions of an especially able physician to other less skilled practitioners.

The surgeons of that day were divided into two classes: the "long robes" and the "short robes." The former had been to medical school and had learned current theories of treatment and procedure. They did not like to soil their long robes with blood and left the actual operating to barbers, executioners, and men like Ambroise Paré, an army doctor who is called the "father of French surgery." These surgeons wore short robes. There was still another kind of surgeon, but his work was scarcely professional. He was a migrant, travelling from place to place, operating and leaving town at once—which may be where we get the phrase "to cut and run."

Fashions of the Renaissance

Marzieh Gail

Although fashion and costume have long fascinated human beings, ostentatious displays of clothing were frowned upon by the medieval church. By the fifteenth century, however, style and fashion were once again central to the social lives of rich and poor, male and female. Silks, brocades, jewels, makeup, perfumes, and even platform shoes were all the rage in Europe—especially in Renaissance-era Italy.

Marzieh Gail graduated from Stanford University and has a master of arts degree from the University of California at Berkeley. She is the author of a number of books on historical subjects and is the daughter of a well-known Persian diplomat and scholar.

The Renaissance was an age of display, with every man his own showcase. Such an official as Venice's Doge [chief magistrate] had robes of cloth of gold and on state occasions put on a bonnet studded with jewels and valued at almost 200,000 ducats, or well over half a million dollars. Where eating too much had been one of the seven deadly sins in the Middle Ages, dressing too well now took its place.

Everybody wanted belts and buckles in constantly novel shapes, and a special guild was established to provide them. An ornamental belt clasp might be as large as a child's hand. For the Pope's cape-like outer garment, a button made by a master artist was the size of a small plate. Lace—which Venice is credited with inventing—was in demand even for gloves and shoes as well as for underwear and

Excerpted from Marzieh Gail, *Life in the Renaissance*. All rights reserved under International and Pan-American Copyright Conventions. Reprinted by permission of Random House Children's Books, a division of Random House, Inc.

nightgowns. . . . Women wore pattens, an early type of platform shoe, partly to keep their clothing out of the dirt, partly to look taller. The pattens were sometimes so high that their wearers, to avoid falling, had to teeter along leaning on the arm of a servant.

The Dogaressa, wife of the Doge . . . of Venice, might wear a gown of gold brocade lined with ermine and having a very long train, a gem-studded headdress with a light silken veil attached, enormous diamond and pearl brooches, and a gold belt that tied in front and hung to her feet. Sometimes, for drama, women would dampen down their blazing colors with an overall transparent veil of black.

Isabella d'Este, the brilliant and glamorous Marchesa of Mantua whom Italians called "The First Lady of the World," was so magnificent that the King of France sent word asking her for a wax doll dressed exactly as she was, to show his ladies at home. Just one of her ornaments was a bride's wedding belt that was worked in gold and silver and cost, in our money, well over two thousand dollars.

"We were . . . so magnificently dressed," wrote the famous noblewoman, Lucrezia Borgia, of a formal visit, "that we might have been said to have stripped Florence of all its brocade."

Rubies, Gold, and Wigs

Not only Italian but many other courts were splendid. England's King Henry VIII wore jewelled rings on both forefingers. He wore a plumed and jewelled hat cocked rakishly on one side, a huge, furred outer coat with great balloon sleeves, a white brocade tunic hung with rubies, and a scabbard heavy with gold for his dagger, to mention only part of his dress. His daughter, the great Queen Elizabeth, wore hoop skirts, huge ruffs [large crimped collars] stretched on wire, enormous sleeves, blinding jewels. One dress, described in detail by a French ambassador, was black taffeta with gold bands. Down the top of the arms it had sleeve openings (called *finestrelli*, little windows) which were lined with crimson. This dress was open in front all the way to the waist. . . . Elizabeth also had on a long red wig covered with pearls. About her arms were strands of pearls and bracelets of jewels.

One day when Robert Devereux, Earl of Essex—the Queen's favorite in her later years—had just returned from a journey, he burst into her apartments to surprise her. It was, however, Essex who was surprised. He found Elizabeth in the midst of her ladies; she was wearing a simple dressing gown, with no "beauty aids," no wig, and gray hair every which way about her face.

Wigs were much in demand. They were often made of real hair, bought from peasant women who let their hair grow long and then sold it. In Florence and Venice women wore false hair that was made out of white and yellow silk. Ordinary people also wore wigs. By way of a joke, a university student living at a boarding house in Paris advised a frequently beaten servant girl how to win her next battle with the landlady. "Next time," he said, "rip off her false curls and grab her hair." At supper time, hearing the noise of women fighting, he ran to separate the combatants. He found them struggling on the floor, ringlets to left of them, caps to right of them—and some floating tufts of the landlady's own hair.

Dress of the Average Citizen

Even the men who rowed gondolas went handsomely dressed. "I hold my sides," wrote Aretino, an Italian literary man who lived in a house overlooking Venice's Grand Canal, "when I listen to the boatmen shouting, jeering, and roaring at those who are rowed by servants who do not wear scarlet hose." Like leotards, such hose ran from a man's feet to his waist and were skin tight. The painter Carpaccio depicts them vividly in his most famous canal scene, where gondoliers in splendid garments glow with many colors from the famous Venetian dye-vats. Most elegant of the boatmen is a handsome young Negro, wearing a tight-fitting red cap with a white plume, a stylish red jacket with a touch of ermine at the shoulders, and patterned hose of silver and green.

Storing all of a noble's garments and other treasures was a problem in itself. Many palaces had an apartment or even a tower called the wardrobe—*guardaroba* in Italian—where clothing, costly plate, weapons, furniture and other valuables were kept. Nobles used to pass hours at a time in the wardrobe.

As for the [average] people, they copied, in much cheaper materials of course, the dress of society's leaders. Instead of pattens on their feet, they wore clogs. Their fans were of straw, with a small piece of looking glass for ornament, whereas those of the rich were of jewel-studded ivory or gold or tortoise-shell, and decorated with feathers, lace and drawings of current events. Some of the clothing commonly seen in Venice, such as the *cafetan,* a long gown with full sleeves, was Eastern in style and name. Whether the Venetians were arsenal workers, dock hands, or peasants at the market, their garments tended to be bright in color and were worn with an air.

Partly because it was felt that people should not dress beyond their station, the commoners were subject to laws which prohibited extravagance, particularly in dress. In Arezzo in 1568 a peasant woman was forbidden to wear any silk except a silk hairnet, a bonnet or some ribbons. The amount of gold cloth that could be used by the richer classes was also regulated. No boy under twelve was allowed to wear a belt made of pearls, and in 1562 a law was passed forbidding a woman who had been married ten years to wear any pearls at all. But in actual practice these laws were hard to enforce and were often flouted.

Raw Meat, Bread Crumbs, and Other Cosmetics

Other beautifiers were available. Cosmetics have probably been in use as long as there have been people. In ancient Greece, some women managed to disguise their appearance so well that officials stopped an epidemic of female suicide by decreeing that any woman who had killed herself would be carried naked through the market place. Searching for beauty, Renaissance women endured any agony, even cramming themselves into metal corsets that could be tightened by turning a key. The poet Petrarch said that they suffered as much from vanity as martyrs endure for faith. At night a Venetian belle might improve her complexion by applying a slice of raw veal that had been soaked in milk. Other skin aids included alum, extract of peach stones, lemon juice, bread crumbs, and vinegar distilled with dung. She also used a hair-remover (as did the ancient Greeks and Arabs) containing such ingredients as orpiment, lime, gum arabic and ant eggs.

The dressing table of a noble lady would be covered with comb cases, hair brushes with gilt backs, golden tweezers, dozens of rouge pots to color cheeks and bosom. A poet of the people wrote that ladies spent their whole day in front of the mirror, and complained that women of his class were beginning to imitate them. Women dyed their hair, preferring to be blonde, which in Venice often meant auburn. Fashionable men also appeared with dyed hair, and even with two different colors on successive days. Drying their hair, ladies would sit, mirror in hand, on the roof, wearing a loose dressing gown and a huge, crownless straw hat, with their hair spread out on the brim. They polished their nails, painted and plastered their faces, eyelids and even teeth. Among the cosmetics of the Marchesa of Mantua was a special recipe for washing the teeth that had been used by the Queens of Naples. Queen Elizabeth's teeth blackened as she aged, and she might have done well to send for this "toothpaste." Indeed, the lack of proper dentistry made people look old before their time, their faces shrunken, their noses and chins coming too close together.

Hiding Offensive Odors

Perfumes were a necessity. Foul smells, although doubtless not so harmful as our polluted air, tainted the Renaissance air. Pigsties, offal, urine, slaughterhouses, poulterers' and fishmongers' establishments, added their aromas. . . . A traveler might object to many smells, including those of English dining halls, where the floors were covered with none-too-clean rushes or straw. Among other smells, common enough in that age of no refrigerators, was that of salt fish. Venice was particularly smelly—especially when the canals were awash with garbage—and the Venetians were among the best customers for incense imported from the Orient. In the fifteenth century a still more expensive remedy was tried: someone got the idea of mixing spices with earth and packing this down on various paths and open spaces. During plague times the smell of sick and dead bodies and of medicines was such that people warded it off with flowers, fragrant herbs and other scents. When people in Rome were dying at the rate of at least one hundred a day a courtier wrote: "All I can do is to wash in vinegar, perfume my hands, and commend my soul to God—at home, not in church."

An Italian lady might make her own perfumes, putting them up in silver boxes for her friends. Everything, even to a roll of money, would be scented by those who could afford it. People carried prayer-beads of sweet-smelling amber or smelling bottles, and tucked about their persons a "pouncet-box," which had a perforated lid and was filled with perfumed unguents. For ceremonial processions, even the mules were rubbed with perfume. In the practice of witchcraft, precious scents were used to summon up demons and foul-smelling asafetida was used to repel them. Cinnamon and peppermint scents were added to bath water. Before and after a banquet, rose water from a silver ewer was poured on the hands of the guests. Although appealing first to the eye, Renaissance people wished to delight the other senses as well.

Sailing to the Holy Land

Louise Collis

Unlike in earlier centuries when only royalty and nobility could afford to travel, by the later fifteenth century touring foreign lands was a popular pastime for people of more modest means. One of the most fashionable journeys was a pilgrimage to the Holy Land of Jerusalem via the luxurious city of Venice, which at the time was a world power.

Margery Kempe was the deeply religious daughter of an English merchant who left her husband and fourteen children to make such a pilgrimage. When she returned to England, the illiterate Kempe dictated her memoirs to a priest. They have remained one of the most lucid and descriptive accounts of fifteenth-century life.

Kempe's words have been paraphrased in the following excerpt by Louise Collis, author of four novels and one book of historical essays.

Although pilgrim accounts of Venice remark on the enormous quantities of valuable merchandise to be seen in the city, none mention the fact that [the tourists], themselves, represented an important department of trade. The Venetian government were fully [aware of] this aspect of things and many enactments were passed to ensure the smooth passage of travellers to the Holy Land and back. The trouble they took was rewarded by an almost complete monopoly of the pilgrim traffic.

Specially licensed guides were on duty all day in the Piazza San Marco and at the Rialto. They must have been linguists and it was their business to help pilgrims in difficulties, finding lodgings, changing

Excerpted from Louise Collis, *Memoirs of a Medieval Woman.* Copyright © 1964 Louise Collis. Reprinted with permission from the author.

money, advising on the purchase of stores and provisions for the voyage and helping to bargain and make a fair contract with the ship's captain. It was their particular charge to see that pilgrims were not cheated. They were expressly forbidden to take commissions from money-changers, or shops. Their wages were regulated by statute. They were to receive whatever tips were offered gracefully and without trying to extort larger sums. . . .

Only registered captains could carry pilgrims. Ships must be seaworthy: newly painted alone would not do. Copies of contracts made with pilgrims must be deposited with the magistrates. The agreed date of departure was to be strictly adhered to. The captain was not to put into extra ports on the voyage for purposes of trade. The exact amount of merchandise that could be carried was laid down, along with the number of sailors, their equipment and pay. Clerks were to be employed to make careful notes of everything during the passage. The boats had a cross painted on the hulls at the waterline to prevent overloading. . . .

[Sleeping] berths were to be at least eighteen inches wide and long enough to accommodate the feet. All complaints were promptly attended to by specially appointed magistrates. Pilgrims could feel assured that in coming to Venice they were making the most sensible and economical arrangement. Even so, the expense was great. . . . On the Jerusalem journey, experienced travellers advised, one must be prepared to keep one's purse open.

The Pilgrims' Ships

Sailings were twice a year, in spring and autumn. When a sufficient number of pilgrims had gathered in the city, two banners would be set up in the Piazza San Marco. This meant the galley captains were signing on the crew and waiting on board to show prospective passengers over the ship, extolling its comfort, speed, seaworthiness, and the remarkably low price for which parties could be conducted even as far as Jordan, if necessary. For the contract was inclusive, covering all meals, hotel charges, entrance fees, guides and so on, from Venice back to Venice.

One hired a boat and rowed out to the galleys. The captain, who was also the owner, or part owner, received one affably, with drinks, if one seemed likely to pay extra for first-class accommodation and food. The ships were two- or three-masted and propelled by sails, except in harbour, when oars were used. At the bow was a [carved wooden] figurehead with a large beak. Aft, was a high [deck] where the captain lived in an expensively furnished cabin. Under this was a private hold, containing his money and plate, which also accommodated ladies travelling first-class.

The general cabin for pilgrims was the hold under the rowing deck. There were no portholes. Light and air came only through the hatchways. A berth consisted of a space big enough to lie down in chalked on the boards. This would be one's only private place during the voyage. Here, one spread one's mattress, piled one's luggage at its foot and tried to sleep through the noise of snoring, cursing, talking, the sailors running about overhead, the animals in pens on deck stamping, all the creaking and movement of a ship at sea. The heat and smell were horrible.

But this was in the future as the pilgrims surveyed the galley, noting what an excellent boat she was, as the captain said. He was an experienced seaman; had been to the Holy Land many times; . . . was acquainted with every port on the shortest route, there and back. The other galley was extremely inferior. He would not advise anyone to take passage in her. He spoke as a sailor and an honest man.

Signing a Contract

The next stage was to draw up a contract, in order to bind one's captain to observe certain elementary decencies. The guide books gave examples. One should try and get him to agree to a definite date of departure and the exact price for which he would undertake to sail to Jaffa, the port for Jerusalem, and conduct one round the necessary sights at a reasonable pace, so that one was not utterly exhausted by heat and continuous travel. One should insist on the full complement of mariners being taken, in particular the twenty crossbowmen stipulated by law in this very year, 1414, as a protection against pirates and Turkish war galleys.

It was a good thing to have it in writing that the meals were to be fit for human consumption and regularly served. Should the pilgrims wish to bring their own chickens, space must be reserved for coops on deck; and they must have the right to go into the cookhouse and do their own cooking, as there were those who couldn't stand Italian food day after day. Continual salads dressed with oil were found particularly unappetizing.

A further set of clauses could be inserted with advantage to restrain the captain from trying to combine pilgrims with merchandise, which was, in any case, forbidden by law. Chests of goods were not to be intruded into the pilgrims' cabin, taking up space already paid for dearly enough. Extra ports were not to be entered, unless the pilgrims especially wished.

On account of seasickness, overcrowding, rats, lice, fleas, maggots, foul air and general debility, travellers often fell ill. One should try to provide for such times: the captain must definitely concede the right to come up on deck for air at any hour and to remain there until revived. If the worst happened and one died, one's belongings were not to be seized from those to whom one had willed them. Also, a proportion of the passage money ought to be returned. It might not be possible to get him to agree to carry one's body to the nearest land for proper burial, because a corpse on a ship was considered unlucky by sailors. They preferred to pitch it overboard forthwith.

Lastly, the captain should be asked to give protection against violence from the crew, especially the oarsmen. These were not usually slaves in the fifteenth century, but a sort of conscript, notoriously rough, brutal and inclined to settle any argument in the most primitive manner.

These matters being all agreed and signed, the intending passenger took his contract and had it registered with the proper authorities in the city. There was now no more time for sightseeing or marvelling at shows. Much prudent shopping had to be done before embarkation. On this subject, also, the handbooks gave advice.

Gathering Provisions

Change your money into newly minted Venetian coins, they said; the Moors will accept nothing else. Go to the shop near St Mark's where you can buy 'a fedyr bedde, a matres, too pylwys, too peyre schetis and a qwylt' [a feather bed, mattress, two pillows, two pair of sheets, and a quilt] and sell them again for half-price on your return. A few pairs of linen drawers are recommended for coolness. On the other hand, it can be very chilly at sea and the careful traveller provided himself with a long warm overcoat.

Laxatives were necessary to combat unhealthy airs, such as those at Famagusta, in Cyprus, which were particularly deadly to English people. The captain should be prevented from putting in there, if possible. One needed a covered pail for the night and in case of seasickness. Although meals were included in the ticket, 'ye schal oft tyme have nede to yowre vytelys' [you shall oftentimes have need to your victuals] and it was wise to provide biscuit, bread, wine, water, cheese, eggs, fruit, sausages, sugar, sweetmeats and syrup of ginger to settle the stomach in emergencies. 'Also by yow a cage for half a dosen of hennys' [also buy you a cage for half a dozen hens], and a bag of millet for them.

Don't forget to lay in a good restorative, the pilgrim is urged, also rice, figs, raisins, . . . pepper, saffron, cloves and mace. Remember to take a saucepan, frying-pan, plates, cups, saucers, glasses, knives, 'a grater for brede and such nessaryes'. Above all, have a chest with proper lock and key. There is something about shipboard life that affects men's morals. As a result, it's not safe to leave anything down. Even one's own friends can't be relied on. . . .

At last the time came to hire a boat and row to the galley with one's bedding, pots and pans, food, medicine and hens. Fortified by having kissed a hundred relics and prayed to all the saints, one clambered aboard on the last leg of a journey which was to give one not only social status in the material world, but also a reserved seat in heaven. The flags of the Pope, the captain and the city of Venice were hoisted. The pilgrims sang an appropriate hymn. The sailors chanted orders and responses. The oarsmen sang their rowing song as the ship moved out of the harbour and caught the wind in its sails.

Visiting Port Cities

The course was southward along the Dalmatian coast, east through the Greek archipelago, Crete, Rhodes, Cyprus, the shores of the Holy Land. It took about a month. Numerous ports were entered in order to take on fresh provisions and to trade. Sometimes the pilots were not as skilful as they ought to have been and the ship struck rocks, or sandbanks, and had to be repaired. Or a sudden storm might come up and split the sails. These adventures were very frightening for the pilgrims, many of whom had never been to sea before. They could not judge how dangerous the situation was, nor had the crew time to explain. Margery and her companions, however, were experienced voyagers in that they had crossed the Channel, at least.

Although it delayed the journey, everyone was glad to put into harbour for a short break. The various cities seemed marvellously beautiful as they approached over the water. The walls were so fine, they thought, the churches so magnificent, the people delightful, the flags and banners welcoming. It was reassuring to feel the solid ground under one's feet again. There was a rush to land, even for an hour or two, in spite of the enormous fares charged by small boatmen who rowed out and offered to ferry them to the quay.

The stay might be extended to a few days. In that case, passengers took the opportunity of lodging in the town to recover health and spirits away from the communal cabin which, for those not fortunate enough to obtain a berth near the hatchways was 'ryght smolderyng hote and stynkyng' [right smoldering hot and stinking]. When the ship dropped anchor, 'be ye sped afore other', advises the practical William Wey, or else the best rooms will be taken and the freshest provisions already bought before you get there. In some places, it was well to be suspicious of fruits, as these were not suited to the English constitution and might cause serious illness. In others, especially Rhodes, the wine is particularly recommended as cheap and good. . . .

Shipboard Life

Life on board ship got on people's nerves at the best of times. The days were long and empty for the passengers who had no work to do. At dawn there were short prayers before a picture of the Virgin, held up by a sailor. These over, trumpets sounded and the crew began the day's tasks. The pilgrims had to try and think of some distraction. The oarsmen all had jars of wine for sale under their benches. Some bought a good supply and drank all day. Many gambled with dice and cards. The younger and more light-hearted danced, sang, lifted weights, turned somersaults, ran up the rigging, played on bagpipes, flutes, zithers, lutes and whatever other musical instruments they had in their luggage. The serious-minded read improving books, meditated, wrote memoirs, prayed and exhorted their fellows to use this unique opportunity to turn over a new leaf.

At about midday, the boatswain's whistle sounded for prayers again. This time, a chest was converted into an altar near the mast and mass was said, except for the actual sacrament, which was not given at sea, for various practical reasons: the ship did not carry an official priest; the host would not keep fresh in damp weather; there might be a sudden lurch of the ship at the most solemn moment and everything be pitched on to the deck; a worse omen for the voyage than that could scarcely be conceived of; there was not a single inch of space on board that could be dedicated as a holy place; people had sworn, quarrelled, and perjured themselves everywhere, and the sailors could be relied on to kick altar, priest and holy vessels out of their way if an emergency arose; in rough weather, one might sick up the holy sacrament, a thing to be avoided at all costs.

Food and Meals

Meals provided a welcome interlude. On the trumpets sounding, everyone rushed to the poop [deck] at full speed and sat down, the first comers in the best seats, no matter what their rank in life. Those not quick enough had to dine on the rowers' benches, unprotected from sun, wind or rain, as the case might be. First there was an aperitif. Then salad, mutton, or fish on fast days, pudding, cheese, bread, or biscuit, followed in rapid succession. The various courses, uniformly stale and adulterated, were planked down in front of the diners with the greatest celerity and, as soon as they had swallowed them, trumpets blew and the tablecloths were snatched off.

Dinner for the captain, senior officers and first-class passengers was served immediately afterwards. This was a more stately affair, brought in silver dishes, though the helpings looked smaller. The captain's wine was tasted by a servant before he drank, as if he were a prince. The inferior members of the crew cooked their own food and gnawed it brutishly on deck. Women did not come to table, which must have been a great joy to Margery's companions. They ate at their berths.

As only two meals a day were provided for in the ticket and as one sometimes couldn't face Italian cooking for a bit, the pilgrims often had recourse to their own provisions. Getting out their frying pans and the eggs which were keeping cool in the ballast sand under the cabin floorboards, they would go to the cookhouse where the cooks were cursing, swearing and falling over each other in the small, hot space.

It was not easy to obtain permission to do a little private frying from these irate beings. Substantial tips were necessary.

After eating, one might doze for a time, being careful to secure one's money to one's person; it was unsafe to lay down even a pen on board ship, if one hoped to see it again. There were days when everyone seemed to be in a happy dream and an almost celestial harmony to descend on the decks. On other days, tempers were lost on the smallest provocation, knives snatched up and damage done. The crew did not intervene in really fierce fights. It was not wise to do so. Never make enemies at sea, advise experienced travellers, the memory of these fatal disputes before them as they write. Never occupy another man's place unless he has expressly allowed it, or you will be taken for a thief and dealt with accordingly. Make yourself agreeable even to slaves, for you can't tell when you may have need of help. The prudent man, who hopes to survive the perils of the sea, is always watchful, not sitting down anywhere without first testing for soft pitch, keeping away from ropes, above all, not fancying his skill as a sailor and offering to help during storms. On the other hand, one should be manly and not spend one's days miserably taking every medicine recommended by the doctors and poking suspiciously at food in the fear of being poisoned. Moderation and tact are the supreme virtues in these circumstances. One wonders that Margery came through alive.

After Sunset

At sunset, the last public prayers were said. After the first part, the passengers were wished goodnight and sent below. The service then continued in Italian for a further quarter of an hour, ending with a prayer to the parents of St Julian. No one knew what connected this venerable couple with a seafaring life, but the crew could not safely face the night without having addressed them.

Indeed, night contained many trials besides the dangers of sudden shoals and rocks. Everyone was struggling in the hot dark space to lay down his mattress. Perhaps the ship was heeling sharply under a stiff breeze. A shouting match about sheets, such as Margery records, was a mild occurrence. Blood might be shed over accusations of theft, or of taking up more than one's allotted space. Some pilgrims were drunk. Others wouldn't stop talking, or put out their lights until the contents of chamber pots were poured over them. Even then sleep was difficult for anyone of sensitivity. The noises of the sea and wind were almost drowned by snoring, chattering nightmares, the smell, the heat, the vermin, the rats methodically feeding on the cheese and biscuits, bread and sweets with which the passengers hoped to assuage their hunger on succeeding days.

With regard to the vermin, however, there was one interesting point, duly noted in memoirs of the period: none were poisonous. Every known kind of horrible worm and biting creature could be counted in idle moments, except scorpions, toads, vipers and snakes.

Can one wonder that on those glorious days when the anchor dropped at some Calypso isle, people thumbed the phrase books eagerly and practised stuttering Greek for: 'Beautiful maiden, come and sleep with me'? In these places, all the inns were brothels. Women leaned invitingly from every window and beckoned from the doors. Of course, they would rob one, if they could. There was even a chance of being murdered, as these same books remarked. One did not care. One had escaped. Later, at the holy places, on one's knees, one could obtain remission of all sin in perpetuity.

Rules for Clergymen

Denys Hay

In the fifteenth century, the Catholic Church was the most powerful institution in Europe. But the church had a difficult time maintaining control over its priests. Corruption was widespread: Some priests skimmed money from church coffers and even broke their vows of celibacy to father children. In light of this, the synod of Paris issued the following rules, called canons, for priests to follow in 1429.

Denys Hay is a professor of history at Edinburgh University in Scotland and the editor of several volumes on European history.

C lergy are forbidden to gossip or laugh in church, or to play foolish and unbecoming games on holidays, at any rate during divine service.

Canons and prebendaries will only share in alms if they have been present at matins, mass and vespers. . . .

No canon or prebendary of a cathedral will leave it on a feast day for another church where he has a prebend on the grounds that the latter is more valuable.

The sacred vessels and appointments will be kept clean; dancing, profane songs, games and markets will not be held in sacred precincts.

Bishops will not ordain any clerk not of good life, who does not know the Epistles and Gospels, who cannot read and sufficiently understand the rest of the service. Some who wish to have the subdiaconate are unaware that this involves continence: they must be

Excerpted from Denys Hay, *Europe in the Fourteenth and Fifteenth Centuries.* Copyright © 1966 Longman Group Limited. Reprinted with permission from Pearson Education Limited.

told in advance. No one shall be inducted into a cure of souls without previous examination, with particular reference to the administration of the sacraments and his own morals.

When prelates ride abroad they will wear their proper hats; in church they shall wear below their vestments (which shall never be ornamented with velvet or silk) a linen rochet, neither too long nor too short.

The officers of episcopal courts extort money and perpetrate every kind of irregularity; bishops will reform their courts . . .

Abbots and monks will not dwell outside their monasteries. They will follow exactly the old rules for costume. In particular they are forbidden to wear short tunics, long cloaks, silver belts etc.

Entrance fees will not be charged by monasteries from those who wish to enter an Order, though gifts may be accepted.

Bishops and rectors will ensure the complete compliance with the legislation concerning the life and conduct of clergy and especially in regard to the prohibition of clerics frequenting inns, involving themselves in temporal matters, trade, dealings in wine and cereals, playing ball in public . . .

Blasphemy and perjury among the clergy should be punished twice as severely as among laymen.

Concubinage is so common among the clergy that it has given rise to the view that simple fornication is not a mortal sin. No bishop will tolerate any clerk living in concubinage, still less will he allow his connivance to be purchased.

The Renaissance in Music, Art, and Literature

PREFACE

With their strategic location on the Mediterranean Sea, the city-states of Italy such as Venice, Florence, and Milan were some of the most powerful and wealthy urban centers in Europe. Venice, at the center of Asian, African, and European trade, was a glittering city of canals and astounding churches and public buildings, and its navy was the most powerful in the world. Florence was famous for its gold and silver jewelry, leatherwork, fashionable clothing, and agricultural products such as wine, olive oil, and herbs. The city-state was ruled by the Medici family, bankers and industrialists who contributed vast sums of their wealth to public art and architecture.

This abundant and creative atmosphere provided a perfect incubator for the talents of skilled artisans, musicians, and craftsmen. By the end of the 1400s, artistic luminaries such as Leonardo da Vinci, Sandro Botticelli, Michelangelo, and others were busy creating immortal works of art that are today considered priceless.

The poets, painters, and musicians of the Renaissance based their work on the pre-Christian philosophies of the ancient Romans, which valued human rights over religious dogma. This focus on the joy, pain, beauty, and wisdom of human beings became known as humanism. Even though the artists of the Renaissance remained devout Christians and the church retained its awesome political power, the study of humanities was one of the driving forces of the Renaissance.

Travels in Fifteenth-Century Venice

Arnold von Harff

Situated in Italy on the Adriatic Sea, Venice was a hub of commerce between China, the Middle East, and Europe in the fifteenth century, and it possessed one of the most powerful navies in the world. The city square known as the Piazza San Marco was the location of Saint Mark's Basilica and was then, as it is today, a center of world tourism. People journeyed to Venice from all over Europe to sightsee and enjoy the international splendors and comforts that the city had to offer.

Arnold von Harff was a fifteenth-century German nobleman who was widely known for travel writing. His writings included descriptions of southern Europe, the Near East, and his pilgrimages to the Holy Land.

To describe first this trading house. As I stayed there for some time I was able to see daily much traffic in spices, silks, and other merchandise packed and dispatched to all the trading towns, since each merchant has his own counting house there—from Cologne, Strassburg, Nuremberg, Augsburg, Lubeck, and other German cities of the Empire. The merchants told me that the counting houses paid daily to the lords of Venice a hundred ducats free money, in addition to which all merchandise was bought there and dearly paid for. From this German house one goes over a long wooden bridge on the right hand.

Excerpted from Arnold von Harff, *The Pilgrimage of Arnold von Harff,* translated by Malcolm Letts (London: The Hakluyt Society, 1946). Reprinted with permission from The Hakluyt Society.

Then one reaches a small square called the Rialto. Here the merchants assemble daily about nine or ten o'clock for their business, so that each one can be found without delay. . . . Close by the square sit the money-changers [bankers] who have charge of the merchants' cash, which they keep with the money-changers so that they may have less money to handle. When a merchant buys from another he refers him to the bankers, so that little money passes between the merchants. Leading from the Rialto are long streets where the merchants have their shops, such as goldsmiths and jewellers selling pearls and precious stones. One street contains tailors, cobblers, rope-sellers, linen and cloth dealers, and others, trading there without number. Above the shops is a place like a monastery dormitory, so that each merchant in Venice has his own store full of merchandise, spices, rare cloths, silk draperies, and many other goods, so that it can be said that the wealth of Venice lies in this square.

Churches and Palaces

From here we went to the chief church of St Mark through many narrow streets, in some of which were apothecaries, in some bookbinders, in others all kinds of merchants driving a thriving trade. St. Mark's is a very beautiful but low church, above which are many round vaults covered with lead. This church, below and above and on both sides, is covered with marble stones, and in addition above and on both sides it is covered with gold. As one enters the church from the square there is, on the left hand, an altar enclosed with a railing against a pillar, upon which stands a wooden crucifix which was struck by a disappointed gambler and which has performed many miracles. . . .

Close by St. Mark's Church, southwards, stands the Doge's [chief magistrate's] Palace, which is very fine and is daily being made more beautiful by the Doge Augustin Barbarigo, who is now having the palace covered with marble and gilt. He was also building a whole marble staircase with beautiful carving, which at this time was not half complete, the half having cost ten thousand ducats. As one first enters the palace, stand two four-cornered marble columns carved with flowers, on the left close by St. Mark's Church These two columns, so placed that an iron bar can be laid on them, are called the Doge's Gallows. If he does evil, he is forthwith hanged between the two columns, and I was told as a truth that within a hundred years one person has been hanged there. As one first enters on the right hand one climbs a staircase to a round hall in which justice is administered. Also in this hall hangs an innumerable collection of arms of pilgrims who have been to the Holy Land. From this hall one ascends by a stone staircase to a very large hall which is the council chamber of the lords of Venice. In this council are seven hundred persons who are nobles called gentlemen, and I counted them at one time in this hall. . . .

The Doge of Venice

In this council chamber there are pictures . . . of all who have been doges of Venice. I asked a gentleman and told him that it seemed to me that there were a great number of councillors on the day when I counted them. He answered and said that if there were as many councillors as the land and people [could send] there would be seven thousand in the council. But the seven hundred who went daily to council were gentlemen—that is, nobles, all fine men, handsomely dressed in long gowns to the feet, the heads all shaved and on the head a small bonnet; all usually wear grey beards. They wear generally girdles round the gown. The sleeves of this gown are narrow at the hand, but behind they hang down about an ell wide, like a sack, just as we make clothes for jesters in our country. The gentlemen have to wear these cloaks and to go about like this.

Venice is a very beautiful city with many inhabitants. It lies in the middle of the salt sea, without walls, and with many tidal canals flowing from the sea, so that in almost every street or house there is water flowing behind or in front, so that it is necessary to have little boats, called barks, in order to go from one house, from one street, or from one church to another, and I was told as a fact that the barks at Venice number more than fifty thousand. . . .

In order to travel within the city, fifteenth-century Venetians used small boats called barks.

The doge at this time was Doge Augustin Barbarigo, an old man of more than seventy years. I saw him going in state to St. Mark's Church in this manner. First they carried before him eight golden banners, of which four were white and four brown. Then came a picture which was borne on a golden standard. Next was carried a golden chair with a cushion which was made of golden stuff. Next they carried his hat with which he is made a doge, which is valued at a hundred thousand ducats. Then came the doge, most gorgeously dressed. He had a long grey beard and had on his head a curious silk hat shaped like a horn behind, reaching upwards for a span's length. . . . This hat must be worn by every doge. Before the doge was carried also a white lighted candle in a silver candlestick.

There preceded him also fourteen minstrels, eight with silver bassoons, from which hung golden cloths with the arms of St. Mark, and six pipers with trumpets, also with rich hangings. Behind the doge was carried a sword with a golden sheath. There followed him the eleven chief lords with the other gentlemen richly attired, fine stately persons.

On Ascension Day the doge celebrates a festival each year before the haven on the high sea. He then throws a golden finger ring into the wild sea, as a sign that he takes the sea to wife, as one who intends to be lord over the whole sea. The ship in which he celebrates is a small stately galley, very splendidly fitted out In front of this ship is a gilt maiden: in one hand she holds a naked sword and in the other golden scales, a sign that as the virgin is still a maid, so the government is still virgin and was never taken by force. The sword in the right hand signifies that she will do justice: for the same reason the maiden holds the scales in the left hand.

The City's Arsenal

This lordship of Venice has inside the city a great house of weapons called the arsenal. . . . First at the entrance, travelling with the sun, we ascended some stairs to a great hall thirty feet wide and quite a hundred long which is full of arms hanging on both sides in three rows, one above the other, very orderly disposed, with everything that belongs to a soldier, such as a coat-of-mail, a sword, a dagger, a spear, a helmet, and a shield. In addition, as part of the arrangement of this hall, there are stored there more than three or four thousand swords, daggers, and innumerable numbers of long pikes, with many more accoutrements for war, and above in the roof are crossbows hanging side by side, touching each other, six rows deep. We were taken higher, up still another staircase, to a fine hall which was also arranged like the first and was no smaller. From these halls we went out and came to a large high building which has thirty arches under one roof, each arched space being one hundred and fifty paces long and ten broad, beneath which they build the great ships. Also close by stands another building with arches, in which they also build ships. Between the two runs deep water, and when the ships are ready they are rolled on round wooden wheels into the water. We went further into another building in which were very fine cannon, namely five main pieces of copper. They measured by one of my feet twenty-four feet long, and each cannon had three pieces which could be screwed into each other. As we were about to look into one of them, out crept a boy with a vegetable basket, who had hidden himself in it. I was told that each piece had cost seven thousand ducats and that each piece discharges a stone of a thousand pounds. . . . I was told as a fact by a gentleman who had made an inventory that . . . in every town under their dominion was more artillery than we saw there, since in his opinion Venice did not need so much, as she had only to arm the ships. And I can say in truth that having seen many armaments in such towns as Brescia, Verona, Padua, Treviso, Mestre, Vienna, Modon, Corfu, Roumania, Candia, Cyprus, and in many other towns, I had not seen even a part.

The Renaissance Rulers of Florence

Olivier Bernier

Florence was the heart of Renaissance Italy, and the city was ruled by a famous dynastic family named Medici, who derived its wealth from banking, trade, and industry. The Medicis, particularly Cosimo and his grandson Lorenzo the Magnificent, were among the great supporters of Renaissance artists. Although incredibly wealthy by fifteenth-century standards, Cosimo was much beloved by working-class Florentines and after his death in 1464 was called *Pater Patriae*—the father of his country.

When he came to power, Lorenzo the Magnificent created a court composed of brilliant poets, philosophers, painters, and musicians. Some of these well-known artists included Sandro Botticelli, Domenico Ghirlandaio, Leonardo da Vinci, and Michelangelo. Unfortunately, Pope Sixtus IV was jealous of Lorenzo's power and supported an assassination plot, known as the Pazzi Conspiracy, against him. Lorenzo survived, but his brother Giuliano was killed. Afterward, Lorenzo organized a deadly reprisal against his opponents. Despite this bloody outcome, Lorenzo remained a popular and beloved ruler among his Florentine subjects.

Olivier Bernier is a historian and author of several books that address the way people lived in centuries past.

Europe in 1469 numbered many ancient realms and countless noble families; but few kings were as rich or powerful as Piero de' Medici—an unassuming banker who, along with his friends, ran the government of Florence. And when Piero's son Lorenzo began to cel-

Excerpted from Olivier Bernier, *The Renaissance Princes* (Chicago: Stonehenge Press, 1983).

ebrate his betrothal in February 1469, the festivities were as splendid as anything the greatest monarch could devise.

Preceded by nine trumpeters, three pages, two squires, twelve nobles on horseback, and his younger brother Giuliano—who was wearing a brocade tabard [tunic], a doublet [sleeved, belted garment] embroidered with pearls and silver, and jeweled feathers in his velvet cap—Lorenzo de' Medici himself arrived, a picture of splendor. Introduced by a corps of drummers and fifers, he rode into the Piazza Santa Croce—the square where jousts and games were held—on a magnificent horse caparisoned [decorated] in red and white velvet embroidered with pearls. Lorenzo himself wore a fortune in gold thread, pearls, rubies, and diamonds. After a carefully organized tournament, the judges proclaimed Lorenzo the victor and awarded him a silver helmet that bore the figure of Mars, the Roman god of war. But the celebration was only just beginning; the bride had yet even to leave Rome. After she arrived in Florence, the Medici staged a feast for eight hundred of the citizens of the city, a banquet of many courses for some two thousand guests, and rejoicings for another three days.

A Renaissance Man

The center of this extravaganza, the twenty-year-old Lorenzo, was not inherently attractive, having an awkward, ill-proportioned figure and a remarkably ugly face with small eyes, a bilious complexion, and a curiously flattened nose. But never have appearances been so deceptive. Lorenzo was friendly, outgoing, and full of zest and energy. Under his father's thoughtful guidance, he had grown up in the museumlike atmosphere of the new Medici palace—a bold, innovative piece of architecture that broke with the traditional medieval style. Lorenzo's grandfather Cosimo, who died when Lorenzo was fifteen, had been the first Medici to rule Florence and, despite his extreme generosity to charities, had made a fortune for the family. But Cosimo's greatest contributions to the life of his family and of Florence touched the artistic and scholastic worlds; he patronized numerous artists, and he founded the Medici library as well as an academy for Greek studies.

Piero sought to continue Cosimo's example and make Lorenzo into a prototype of the new Renaissance man—someone who could draw on the cultures of ancient Greece and Rome, as well as that of medieval Italy; appreciate and write poetry; discuss philosophy with the greatest scholars; understand and finance the most talented artists; grasp politics and rule effectively, smoothly, even justly.

These were great expectations, but Florence provided the perfect setting for the making of such a Renaissance man. The city was in the midst of a dazzling cultural explosion during which interest in painting and architecture revived, scholars rediscovered the glories of Greece and Rome, sailors charted the world. Piero's library held more volumes than any other, and he opened it to all. His gardens were adorned with antique sculptures that provided inspiration for such great sculptors as the young Michelangelo.

The Medici family was both rich and intelligent. To choose Lorenzo's fiancée, the Medici went outside the city for the first time in order to form an alliance, just as other ruling families did. Clarice Orsini, Lorenzo's bride, was the daughter of a great Roman noble family, whose power would now work to enhance Piero's: a remarkable achievement in a highly class-conscious world.

Scholars Flee to Florence

Politically, the world was in a state of flux. The Eastern Roman Empire, with its capital in Constantinople, had endured for over a thousand years. Now, after resisting a variety of enemies, the once-powerful empire, weakened by its own internal dissensions, found itself confronted by a fearless warrior-people, the Turks, who swept in from the steppes of Asia. In 1439 the emperor John Paleologus, accompanied by the patriarch of Constantinople, had attended a council in Florence in an attempt to reunite the Eastern and Western Churches so that the West would be more likely to help him.

His mission failed, for in 1453 Constantinople fell to the Turks. But Paleologus did succeed in an unintended mission. He had brought books and learned men with him to the council, and after the fall of Constantinople, scholars migrated en masse to Florence. They had a powerful influence on the Florentines. Greek had for years been a dead, undecipherable language. But now, for the first time since the onset of the Middle Ages, the Italians learned enough Greek to read the works of Plato and Aristotle—the chief philosophers of Athens— and they rediscovered the great Roman authors in copies that had not been disfigured by the centuries or by careless, ignorant copyists.

Young Lorenzo was immediately influenced, for not only did he study Italian literature and Latin, but he also developed a devouring interest in Neoplatonism—the new philosophy taught by his tutor, Marsilio Ficino. Combining the Platonic cult of ideas with mystical longings and Christian precepts, Neoplatonism provided the perfect philosophic blend for the times. It also provided the perfect rationale for the kind of oligarchic rule the Medici had already established. Ficino taught Lorenzo the importance of classical cultures along with the brilliance of the new Italian achievements.

Financing the Renaissance

The Florentines needed money for their pursuits, and two great innovations had already provided the necessary wealth: banking and the use of credit. European trade in the fifteenth century consisted of two main commodities: spices and cloth—mostly wool, but also silk. Venice, with its maritime empire, supplied the spices: but Florence organized the trade routes across northern Europe to take wool from England to the Netherlands (today's Holland and Belgium), where it was spun and woven; then to France; and on to Italy. To facilitate these complex transactions—and to get around the need to send bags of gold from one end of Europe to another—the Italians invented the letter of credit. A merchant might sell his cloth in Florence but then collect the money in Gent, for example, from the local branch of the Medici bank. Since the Church prohibited the charging of interest, the bankers made their profit by taking a premium on the exchange from one currency to the other. By 1450 Florence had emerged as the major banking city in Europe and thus the richest. Consequently the Medici, the leading banking family in Florence, made staggering yearly profits.

Lorenzo de Medici

The city also had its industries. It produced fine woolen cloth and silk of extraordinary quality. Florence's goldsmiths and jewelers ranked among the finest in Europe. As a result Florence (with Milan, Venice, Rome, and Naples) reigned as one of the five great Italian powers—the Big Five. The word "Italy," in fact, usually referred to no more than a geographic location. Politically the peninsula contained a variety of independent countries: city-states such as Florence, Genoa, or Venice; duchies such as Milan, Ferrara, or Urbino; one kingdom, Naples; and in and around Rome, the Papal States—governed directly by the pope. Wars were frequent, though generally bloodless since the armies primarily consisted of mercenaries who valued their own lives. The smaller states constantly struggled to avoid being swallowed up by the five major ones. Each of these, in turn, engaged in a balancing act with the others to prevent any one competitor from growing too large and powerful. . . .

Possessing a Treasure Trove

If Italy was divided and unstable, so was Florence. Hereditary monarchs ruled most European countries, but Florence was an oligarchic republic: the rich citizens, in effect, controlled the government with a constitution so complex as to be unworkable. A variety of governing boards—none of which could rule without the others—made sure

that no one man would ever take over. In fact by the mid–
fifteenth century, the various governing boards were composed
largely of Medici followers. Thus, while Piero's status was that of
an ordinary citizen, everyone knew he acted—like Cosimo before
him—as the effective head of state. Still, his situation was inherently
unstable and required a good deal of finesse.

In this uncertain political atmosphere the Medici gathered a treasure trove of rare and beautiful objects: cups, boxes, pots of gold-
mounted alabaster, onyx, and other semiprecious stones. Tapestries
deep with colors covered their walls. The silks, brocades, and vel-
vets for the family's clothing and their beds boasted unparalleled
magnificence. Abundant, delicate, but sumptuous jewelry—rings,
bracelets, necklaces, brooches—adorned men and women alike.

But the new spirit reached outside the palace as well, to the vil-
las surrounding it and to the Medici-financed convent of San Marco,
where the walls shone brilliantly with frescoes by the Dominican
friar Giovanni da Fiesole, known as Fra Angelico. A new kind of
garden, more open and closer to nature, developed: vistas replaced
the small, wall-enclosed world of the medieval garden; sculpture (often antique) adorned the paths; water splashed in fountains.

But the Medici held all these wonders in a tenuous grasp. They
had as many enemies as friends, and for all their love of philosophy,
the men of the Renaissance could be singularly ruthless. Assassinations, plots, intrigues, invasions all played their parts in contemporary politics. Any sign of Medici weakness attracted predators ready
to exploit it. So, early on, Lorenzo needed to master the political
skills necessary for success in such an environment. His father not
only explained to him the intricate workings of the Florentine government and the Italian balance of power, but he also took him in as
a junior partner. Consequently, when Piero died, Lorenzo was ready
to take over as head of the family. At twenty Lorenzo assumed his
place as one of the most powerful men in Europe.

Medici's Troubles

Everything was quiet at first. An alliance among Naples, Florence,
and Milan provided stability. The Florentine councils' favor weighed
heavily toward the Medici. The city still prospered. But then, in
1471, trouble started. Florence looked to the neighboring city of
Volterra for its supply of alum—an ore necessary to the dyeing of
fabrics—and Volterra threatened to close off access to the mines.
Lorenzo unhesitatingly behaved with the required ruthlessness. He
ordered his army to attack Volterra, take it, sack it, and reduce it to
unquestioning obedience.

Even so, political stability did not last for long. In 1471 a new
pope, Sixtus IV, had been elected. In these days people almost ex-

pected the Holy Father to be greedy and self-seeking, but Sixtus exemplified these characteristics to an unusually high degree. A good family man, he fully intended to advance his nephew Girolamo Riario's career. But mere riches would not do for Girolamo. Sixtus was determined to find him a throne.

For several years the pope had been at odds with Lorenzo, who proved unwilling to cooperate in papal schemes. To be archbishop of Pisa, the pope had appointed a man whose corruption was extreme, even by the standards of the time. Seeing an opportunity to go against Sixtus, Lorenzo had refused to let the appointee take over the archdiocese. Further, the pope saw Lorenzo as a deterrent to the extension of the power of the Papal States. Lorenzo maintained a balance of power; once he vanished, the pope and his new ally, King Ferrante of Naples, might extend their sway indefinitely. Also, if the Medici could be removed from power, their fortune would become available to whoever eventually took over in Florence.

The Pazzi Conspiracy

Since, for the sake of public opinion, the plot had to seem purely internal, the pope and his nephew got in touch with the Pazzi family, wealthy Florentine bankers who envied and resented the Medici. The Pazzi agreed to do most of the footwork; their reward would be dominance over Florence. Thus the scheme has gone down in history as the Pazzi conspiracy.

For the actual assassinations, their plan was simple. The pope and his nephew would remain in Rome while a member of the Pazzi family, Francesco, and the archbishop-designate of Pisa traveled to Florence on an ostensibly friendly visit. While there they would attend Mass one Sunday along with Lorenzo and his brother Giuliano and would murder them both in church. The day arrived and just as the Mass began, a disturbance erupted. Giuliano, across the cathedral from Lorenzo, found himself surrounded by men with drawn swords who attacked him with such fury that they eventually pierced his body with nineteen wounds. Two priests armed with daggers attacked Lorenzo, who had to defend himself.

Since he had hardly expected to be murdered at Mass, Lorenzo was at a disadvantage, but he drew his sword and fought, and soon his friends were able to surround him. Together they battled their way into the sacristy and slammed its bronze gates in their assailants' faces. From there Lorenzo, who did not yet know that his brother had been murdered, escaped safely to the Medici palace.

Several hours elapsed before he learned of the death of Giuliano—a young man, handsome and brilliant, of whom Lorenzo had been deeply fond. But the people of Florence had already rallied behind the Medici. By the end of the day, all but a few of the murderers had been caught and hanged, including the appointed archbishop of Pisa.

A Clever Statesman

As soon as Sixtus found out that the plan had failed, he excommunicated Lorenzo and placed Florence under interdict: no Mass could be celebrated, no sacrament administered. The official reason he gave for these disciplinary measures was the execution of the archbishop-designate of Pisa. He fooled no one, least of all the king of Naples, who proceeded to implement stage two of the plan. The king sent troops to a valley sixty miles south of Florence. For the next two years war continued in a rather desultory way, as was then the custom. The Neapolitans won one battle but failed to take a little town that they besieged for several months. Nevertheless, Florence's position looked shaky, especially as her only ally, Milan, had been reduced to impotence by the murder of her duke a few years earlier.

But in 1479 a new duke of Milan—Lodovico Sforza—took over. When Lorenzo appealed to him for help, Lodovico advised trying for a reconciliation with Naples and added that he would use his influence with Ferrante; his sister had married Ferrante's son. In a gesture of incredible daring, Lorenzo left Florence secretly and sailed to Naples, gambling that his years of friendship with the notoriously treacherous Ferrante would guarantee his safety. When Lorenzo returned about three months later with a peace treaty, the Florentines received him as the savior of the city.

In that short time Lorenzo had proved himself the cleverest of Italian statesmen. Further, within a year Lorenzo had reorganized the government, creating an obedient new council called the Seventy, which would subjugate all others. On December 3, 1480, the pope, admitting defeat, received a Florentine embassy and lifted the interdict. Once again the old alliance of Milan, Florence, and Naples stabilized Italy; and this time Lorenzo could take full credit.

A Cultural Explosion

Although Lorenzo's political achievements were far-reaching, probably none alone would have done much for posterity's memory of him. In fact he founded his fame and that of Florence on the great cultural explosion he fostered. Most patrons simply bought paintings and sculptures; at best, they gave certain writers salaries. But Lorenzo, more than just generous, proved also to be accessible, interested, enthusiastic. Anyone, regardless of birth, could join his circle—made up of Ficino; the scholar-lecturer Angelo Poliziano, known as Politian; and Leon Battisti Alberti, the author of a key treatise on architecture—as its members discussed the nature of art, the best kind of government, the highest form of human development.

Such discussions and the resultant new opinions and ideas influenced the artists working in Florence; Sandro Botticelli, for example, translated Ficino's philosophy into paintings of genius. Botticelli's *Birth of Venus* and *Primavera* are works of incredible grace and beauty made more poignant by a touch of melancholy. The complex Neoplatonic symbols that make these works almost dissertations on the true nature of love have long been forgotten, but the paintings themselves remain masterpieces celebrating the rebirth of Florence under Lorenzo. Additionally, the artist known as Ghirlandajo produced portraits and paintings, in the guise of religious subjects, that showed the life-style of wealthy Florence. And under Andrea del Verrocchio's hand, sculpture reached a new degree of realism so that a bronze face seemed to breathe like that of its model.

Along with his support of the dazzling production of artworks, Lorenzo steadily and generously supported research and teaching. He founded a new university at Pisa and expanded the one at Florence—encouraging, in particular, the study of Greek. He also promoted the sciences. Some people believe that Lorenzo's workshop in the garden of San Marco constituted the first art academy—and was possibly the place where Lorenzo discovered the young Michelangelo modeling a bit of clay.

The Fall of the Medici

When Lorenzo died, in 1492, his eldest son, Piero, succeeded him as automatically as if Florence had been a kingdom instead of a republic. Another son, Giovanni, was already a cardinal—and would become Pope Leo X. The Medici moved their wealth from trade into real estate at an opportune moment, and Lorenzo's system seemed set to endure.

But without Lorenzo to keep the peace, the bickering rulers of Italy invited French intervention. Charles VIII appeared determined to reassert his rights over Naples, and in 1494 he invaded Italy. Piero, faced with the powerful French army, made an abject surrender, giving the king the right of passage through Florence as well as turning over to him the Florentine fortresses. Furious at this disgrace, the Florentines rebelled, and Piero and his brothers were forced to flee into exile.

Upon the Medici's departure a fanatical monk who had for several years been preaching against Lorenzo and the new hedonism seized the chance to gain influence over the Florentines, making use of the vacuum created by Piero's capitulation. The monk, Girolamo Savonarola, had gained notoriety some years before for his fiery sermons and his often uncanny predictions. Savonarola had actually forecasted Charles's invasion of Italy, and now he managed to convince the Florentines that Lorenzo and Piero had led them into a hedonistic, sinful way of life. From 1495 to 1498 the monk was the spiritual ruler of Florence, dominating the Florentine councils during the crisis that followed the Medici fall from favor. Savonarola urged the Florentines to change their sinful ways, and they followed him, turning away from the pleasure-seeking world of Lorenzo—a world that soon vanished.

Nevertheless, Lorenzo in his time had succeeded in his efforts to become Plato's philosopher-king incarnate. He had set a cultural example for other princes, who remembered him as Lorenzo the Magnificent. He had forever attached to his name an aura of discernment and intelligence, the aura of a prince whose treasures have transcendent value. Those fortunate enough to live in Florence and to be in Lorenzo's circle had experienced, in all its heady joys, the very spring of the Renaissance.

Leonardo da Vinci

Will Durant

Leonardo da Vinci is one of the most important artists of the Italian Renaissance. His *Mona Lisa* and *The Last Supper* are among the most well known paintings in modern history. While admired for his artistic skill for many centuries, his amazing understanding of science and invention is a more recent discovery. Da Vinci wrote his thoughts about engineering, biology, anatomy, astronomy, and other sciences in voluminous notebooks that have only been published and widely circulated in the twentieth century. Leonardo drew up plans for helicopters, military hardware, and submarines centuries before they were invented.

Will Durant was born in 1885 and, after teaching college in New York, began working up to fourteen hours a day in order to write the definitive ten-volume "History of Civilization" series with the help of his wife Ariel. Beginning in 1927, the Durants traveled around the world for forty years until the last volume was completed in 1967.

The most fascinating figure of the Renaissance was born on April 15, 1452, near the village of Vinci, some sixty miles from Florence. His mother was a peasant girl, Caterina, who had not bothered to marry his father. [The child's father], Piero d'Antonio, was a Florentine attorney of some means. In the year of Leonardo's birth Piero married a woman of his own rank. Caterina had to be content with a peasant husband; she yielded her pretty love child to Piero and his wife; and Leonardo was brought up in semiaristocratic comfort without maternal love. . . .

He went to a neighborhood school, took fondly to mathematics, music, and drawing, and delighted his father by his singing and his playing of the lute. In order to draw well he studied all things in nature

Excerpted from Will Durant, *The Renaissance: A History of Civilization in Italy from 1304–1576 A.D.* Copyright © 1953 Will Durant. Reprinted with permission from Simon & Schuster.

with curiosity, patience, and care; science and art, so remarkably united in his mind, had there one origin—detailed observation. When he was turning fifteen his father took him to [the studio of the famous artist] Verrocchio . . . in Florence, and persuaded that versatile artist to accept him as an apprentice. . . .

Meanwhile Ser Piero prospered, bought several properties, moved his family to Florence (1469), and married four wives in turn. The second was only ten years older than Leonardo. When the third presented Piero with a child Leonardo eased the congestion by going to live with Verrocchio. In that year (1472) [Leonardo] was admitted to membership in the Company of St. Luke. This guild, composed chiefly of apothecaries, physicians, and artists, had its headquarters in the hospital of Santa Maria Nuova. Presumably Leonardo found there some opportunities to study internal as well as external anatomy. Perhaps in those years he . . . painted the gaunt anatomical *St. Jerome* ascribed to him in the Vatican Gallery. And it was probably he who, toward 1474, painted the colorful and immature *Annunciation* of the Uffizi.

A week before his twenty-fourth birthday Leonardo and three other youths were summoned before a committee of the Florentine Signory to answer a charge of having had homosexual relations. The result of this summons is unknown. On June 7, 1476, the accusation was repeated; the committee imprisoned Leonardo briefly, released him, and dismissed the charge as unproved. Unquestionably he was a homosexual. As soon as he could afford to have his own studio he gathered handsome young men about him; he took some of them with him on his migrations from city to city; he referred to one or another of them in his manuscripts as *amantissimo* or *carissimo*—"most beloved," "dearest.". . . Leonardo might reasonably doubt why he and a few others had been singled out for public accusation when homosexuality was so widespread in the Italy of the time. He never forgave Florence for the indignity of his arrest.

Leonardo's First Commissions

Apparently he took the matter more seriously than the city did. A year after the accusation he was invited, and agreed, to accept a studio in the Medici gardens; and in 1478 the Signory itself asked him to paint an altarpiece for the chapel of St. Bernard in the Palazzo Vecchio. For some reason he did not carry out the assignment; Ghirlandaio took it over; Filippino Lippi completed it. Nevertheless the Signory soon gave him—and Botticelli—another commission: to paint . . . full-length portraits of two men hanged for the conspiracy of the Pazzi against Lorenzo and Giuliano de' Medici. Leonardo, with his half-morbid interest in human deformity and suffering, may have felt some fascination in the gruesome task.

But indeed he was interested in everything. All postures and actions of the human body, all expressions of the face in young and old, all the organs and movements of animals and plants from the waving of wheat in the field to the flight of birds in the air, all the cyclical erosion and elevation of mountains, all the currents and eddies of water and wind, the moods of the weather, the shades of the atmosphere, and the inexhaustible kaleidoscope of the sky—all these seemed endlessly wonderful to him; repetition never dulled for him their marvel and mystery; he filled thousands of pages with observations concerning them, and drawings of their myriad forms. When the monks of San Scopeto asked him to paint a picture for their chapel (1481), he made so many sketches for so many features and forms of it that he lost himself in the details, and never finished *The Adoration of the Magi*.

Leonardo the Military Engineer

There was nothing hesitant . . . only youth's limitless ambitions fed by burgeoning powers, in the letter that Leonardo, now thirty, sent in 1482 to Lodovico, regent of Milan. He had had enough of Florence; the desire to see new places and faces mounted in his blood. He had heard that Lodovico wanted a military engineer, an architect, a sculptor, a painter; well, he would offer himself as all these in one. And so he wrote his famous letter:

> Most Illustrious Lord, having now sufficiently seen and considered the proofs of all those who count themselves masters and inventors of instruments of war, and finding that their invention and use of the said instruments does not differ in any respect from those in common practice, I am emboldened without prejudice to anyone else to put myself in communication with your Excellency, in order to acquaint you with my secrets, thereafter offering myself at your pleasure effectually to demonstrate at any convenient time all those matters which are in part briefly recorded below.
>
> 1. I have plans for bridges, very light and strong and suitable for carrying very easily. . . .
>
> 2. When a place is besieged I know how to cut off water from the trenches, and how to construct an infinite number of . . . scaling ladders and other instruments. . . .
>
> 4. I have plans for making cannon, very convenient and easy of transport, with which to hurl small stones in the manner almost of hail. . . .
>
> 5. And if it should happen that the engagement is at sea, I have plans for constructing many engines most suitable for attack or defense, and ships which can resist the fire of all the heaviest cannon, and powder and smoke.
>
> 6. Also I have ways of arriving at a certain fixed spot by caverns and secret winding passages, made without any noise even though it may be necessary to pass underneath trenches or a river.

7. Also I can make covered cars, safe and unassailable, which will enter the serried ranks of the enemy with artillery, and there is no company of men at arms so great as not to be broken by it. And behind these the infantry will be able to follow quite unharmed and without any opposition.

8. Also, if need shall arise, I can make cannon, mortars, and light ordnance, of very beautiful and useful shapes, quite different from those in common use.

9. Where it is not possible to employ cannon, I can supply catapults, mangonels, traps, and other engines of wonderful efficacy not in general use. In short, as the variety of circumstances shall necessitate, I can supply an infinite number of different engines of attack and defense.

10. In time of peace I believe that I can give you as complete satisfaction as anyone else in architecture, in the construction of buildings both public and private, and in conducting water from one place to another.

Also I can execute sculpture in marble, bronze, or clay, and also painting, in which my work will stand comparison with that of anyone else whoever he may be.

Moreover, I would undertake the work of the bronze horse, which shall endue with immortal glory and eternal honor the auspicious memory of the Prince your father and of the illustrious house of Sforza.

And if any of the aforesaid things should seem impossible or impracticable to anyone, I offer myself as ready to make trial of them in your park or in whatever place shall please your Excellency, to whom I commend myself with all possible humility.

We do not know how Lodovico replied, but we know that Leonardo reached Milan in 1482 or 1483. . . . He made portraits of Lodovico, Beatrice, and their children, of Lodovico's mistresses Cecilia Gallerani and Lucrezia Crivelli; these paintings are lost. . . .

The Famous Paintings

Perhaps Cecilia was Leonardo's model for *The Virgin of the Rocks*. The painting was contracted for (1483) by the Confraternity of the Conception as the central part of an altarpiece for the church of San Francesco. The original was later bought by Francis I and is in the Louvre. . . . The colors have been darkened by time, but possibly the artist intended a darkling effect, and suffused his pictures with a hazy atmosphere that Italy calls *sfumato*—"smoked." This is one of Leonardo's greatest pictures, surpassed only by *The Last Supper*, *Mona Lisa*, and *The Virgin, Child, and St. Anne*.

The Last Supper and *Mona Lisa* are the world's most famous paintings. Hour after hour, day after day, year after year, pilgrims enter the refectory [monks' dining hall] that holds [*The Last Supper*] Leonardo's most ambitious work. In that simple rectangular building the Dominican friars who were attached to Lodovico's favorite church—Santa

Maria delle Grazie—took their meals. Soon after the artist arrived in Milan Lodovico asked him to represent the Last Supper on the farthest wall of this refectory. For three years (1495–8), on and off, Leonardo labored or dallied at the task, while Duke and friars fretted over his incalculable delays. The prior . . . complained to Lodovico of Leonardo's apparent sloth, and wondered why he would sometimes sit before the wall for hours without painting a stroke. Leonardo had no trouble explaining to the Duke—who had some trouble explaining to the prior—that an artist's most important work lies in conception rather than in execution, and . . . "men of genius do most when they work least." There were in this case, said Leonardo to Lodovico, two special difficulties—to conceive features worthy of the Son of God, and to picture a man as heartless as Judas; perhaps, he slyly suggested, he might use the too frequently seen face of the prior as a model for Iscariot. Leonardo hunted throughout [the streets of] Milan for heads and faces that might serve him in representing the Apostles; from a hundred such quarries he chose the features that were melted in . . . his art into those astonishingly individualized heads that make the wonder of the dying masterpiece. Sometimes he would rush from the streets or his studio to the refectory, add a stroke or two to the picture, and depart. . . .

Leonardo the Inventor

It is hard for us to realize that to Lodovico . . . Leonardo was primarily an engineer. Even the pageants that he planned for the Duke of Milan included ingenious automata. "Every day," says [sixteenth-century art historian Giorgio] Vasari, "he made models and designs for the removal of mountains with ease, and to pierce them to pass from one place to another; and by means of levers, cranes, and winches to raise and draw heavy weights; he devised methods for cleaning harbors, and for raising water from great depths." He developed a machine for cutting threads in screws; he worked along correct lines towards a water wheel; he devised frictionless roller-bearing band brakes. He designed the first machine gun, and mortars with cog gears to elevate their range; a multiple-belt drive; three-speed transmission gears; an adjustable monkey wrench; a machine for rolling metal; a movable bed for a printing press; a self-locking worm gear for raising a ladder. He had a plan for underwater navigation, but refused to explain it. He revived the idea of Hero of Alexandria for a steam engine, and showed how steam pressure in a gun could propel an iron bolt twelve hundred yards. He invented a device for winding and evenly distributing yarn on a revolving spindle, and scissors that would open and close with one movement of the hand. Often he let his fancy bemuse him, as when he suggested inflated skis for walking on water, or a water mill that would simultaneously play several musical instruments. He described a parachute: "If a man have a tent made of linen, of which the

Leonardo da Vinci's sketch of a catapult. In addition to being a gifted artist, da Vinci also possessed an amazing understanding of science and invention.

apertures have all been stopped up, and it be twelve cubits across and twelve in depth, he will be able to throw himself down from any great height without sustaining any injury."

Dreams of Flight

Through half his life he pondered the problem of human flight. Like Tolstoi he envied the birds as a species in many ways superior to man. He studied in detail the operation of their wings and tails, the mechanics of their rising, gliding, turning, and descending. His sharp eye noted these movements with passionate curiosity, and his swift pencil drew and recorded them. He observed how birds avail themselves of air currents and pressures. He planned the conquest of the air:

> You will make an anatomy of the wings of a bird, together with the muscles of the breast, which move these wings. And you will do the same for a man, in order to show the possibility of man sustaining himself in the air by the beating of wings. . . . The rising of birds without beating their wings is not produced by anything other than their circular movement amid the currents of the wind. . . . Your bird should have no other model than the bat, because its membranes serve as . . . a means of binding together the framework of the wings. . . . A bird is an instrument working according to mechanical law. This instrument it is within the power of man to reproduce with all its movements, but not with a corresponding degree of strength.

He made several drawings of a screw mechanism by which a man, through the action of his feet, might cause wings to beat fast enough to raise him into the air. In a brief essay *Sul volo, On Flight,* he described a flying machine made by him with strong starched linen, leather joints, and thongs of raw silk. He called this "the bird," and wrote detailed instructions for flying it.

> If this instrument made with a screw . . . be turned swiftly, the said screw will make its spiral in the air, and it will rise high. . . . Make trial of the machine over the water, so that if you fall you do not do yourself any harm. . . . The great bird will take its first flight . . . filling the whole world with amazement and all records with its fame; and it will bring eternal glory to the nest where it was born.

Did he actually try to fly? A note in the *Codice Atlantico* says: "Tomorrow morning, on the second day of January, 1496, I will make the thong and the attempt"; we do not know what this means. Fazio Cardano, father of Jerome Cardan the physicist (1501–76), told his son that Leonardo himself had essayed flight. Some have thought that when Antonio, one of Leonardo's aides, broke his leg in 1510, it was in trying to fly one of Leonardo's machines. We do not know.

Leonardo was on the wrong tack; human flight came not by imitating the bird, except in gliding, but by applying the internal combustion engine to a propellor that could beat the air not downward but backward; forward speed made possible upward flight.

Leonardo's Ideas on Flying

Leonardo da Vinci

Leonardo da Vinci is rightfully remembered for his timeless paintings such as the *Mona Lisa*. But Leonardo was a true Renaissance man who excelled at many talents: He was a military engineer, a biologist, an astronomer, a cartographer (mapmaker), and a geologist. He invented dozens of machines that were centuries ahead of their time, including a helicopter, submarine, and machine gun. Leonardo filled thousands of pages with scientific theories, anatomical drawings, stories, and other thoughts from his ever-inventive mind. Hundreds of those pages have survived into the modern era.

Leonardo was fascinated with flying from the time of his childhood, and he spent many years attempting to perfect a flying machine. In the following excerpt, the Italian master makes notes to himself on theories of flight.

Man when flying must stand free from the waist upwards so as to be able to balance himself as he does in a boat so that the centre of gravity in himself and in the machine may counterbalance each other, and be shifted as necessity demands for the changes of its centre of resistance.

Remember that your flying machine must imitate no other than the bat, because the web is what by its union gives the armour, or strength to the wings.

If you imitate the wings of feathered birds, you will find a much stronger structure, because they are pervious; that is, their feathers are

Excerpted from Leonardo da Vinci in *The Notebooks of Leonardo da Vinci,* edited by Jean Paul Richter (New York: Dover Publications, 1970).

separate and the air passes through them. But the bat is aided by the web that connects the whole and is not pervious.

To Escape the Peril of Destruction

Destruction to such a machine may occur in two ways; of which the first is the breaking of the machine. The second would be when the machine should turn on its edge or nearly on its edge, because it ought always to descend in a highly oblique direction, and almost exactly balanced on its centre. As regards the first—the breaking of the machine—, that may be prevented by making it as strong as possible; and in whichever direction it may tend to turn over, one centre must be very far from the other; that is, in a machine 30 braccia long the centres must be 4 braccia one from the other.

Bags by which a man falling from a height of 6 braccia [about 25 feet] may avoid hurting himself, by a fall whether into water or on the ground; and these bags, strung together like a rosary, are to be fixed on one's back.

An object offers as much resistance to the air as the air does to the object. You may see that the beating of its wings against the air supports a heavy eagle in the highest and rarest atmosphere, close to the sphere of elemental fire. Again you may see the air in motion over the sea, fill the swelling sails and drive heavily laden ships. From these instances, and the reasons given, a man with wings large enough and duly connected might learn to overcome the resistance of the air, and by conquering it, succeed in subjugating it and rising above it.

A Renaissance in Music

Yehudi Menuhin and Curtis Wheeler Davis

Although the Renaissance was more famous for its poetry, art, and architecture, music also underwent changes during the period. Around 1400, English composer John Dunstable wrote music that introduced harmony based on intervals of the third and sixth notes of the musical scale. In the 1420s, Guillaume Dufay developed a polyphonic style that included a focus on the human voice, which fit nicely with the humanistic theories that guided the Renaissance.

Yehudi Menuhin is a violinist, conductor, and composer who first appeared on the concert stage at the age of seven. His music is widely played throughout the world. Curtis Wheeler Davis is a television writer and producer who has won three Emmy and two Peabody Awards.

A fter A.D. 1400, the Renaissance was in its glory. . . .

Two Renaissance musicians brought stability to composed music in the West. John Dunstable (c. 1400–1453) in England and Guillaume Dufay (c. 1400–1474) in France achieved order and logic in the writing of music for multiple voices. They felt that accidental clashes between independent lines [of music] should not be tolerated. They formulated rules of harmony, not for scholarly reasons, but out of sheer necessity, avoiding dissonances except where they might lend greater force of expression. There is great poise in works such as Dunstable's motet Veni Sancti Spiritus and Dufay's Lamentation for Constantinople (the city had fallen to the Turks in 1453),

Excerpted from Yehudi Menuhin and Curtis W. Davis, *The Music of Man.* Copyright © 1979 Yehudi Menuhin and Curtis W. Davis. Reprinted with permission from The Random House Group Ltd.

a new stability and control which impressed their contemporaries. The sound we now recognize as Western music was finally taking shape. The extent of this musical reform is made clear by these words written in 1474, the year of Dufay's death, by the composer and theorist Tinctoris: "There is no music not written within the past forty years that is considered by the learned as worthy of hearing." But the overriding reason why flexibility was giving way to order was not the growing Western sensitivity to harmony, but something which constitutes the major difference between Western music and that of most of the rest of the world: musical writing.

By the time of Dufay and Dunstable, the system of putting notes on paper had finally become dependable. Its evolution cannot be traced without a short step back to Charlemagne's day and the curious squiggles which comprise the earliest Western musical notation, called neumes [which] began to be attached to sacred texts around the ninth century. One, in the Bodleian Library at Oxford, is a melody to a Latin "Song to the Muses" whose words date from the fifth century, one of the oldest notated examples of secular music in existence. These neumes were developed mainly in the monasteries. . . .

Music's Great Leap Forward

During the Renaissance, music became far less incidental, and more a part of the display of learning, power and wealth. Court choirs and instrumental groups became the rule, and composers were taken into residence to write for them, as painters were to adorn the palaces of nobility. Older music was quickly swept aside, and the musician was no longer considered an artisan like the builders of Gothic churches: he was an honored artist. Skills in instrumental manufacture took great leaps forward alongside those of performance, as noble patrons demanded higher quality.

What this means for the Western musician is the forging of the music we know and love out of the extraordinary stress of the period. To most, the Renaissance means painting, sculpture, drama, literature, architecture, and finally music. This cultural explosion was hardly noticed by the majority of people, who could hardly afford such products. But printed music could travel as the minstrels once had done, becoming part of even the humblest home.

Up to now, formalized attitudes toward the nature of the world had been largely the responsibility of the church, which continued to insist that the world was flat, and the sun circled the earth. Mariners taking part in long ocean voyages launched by Vasco da Gama and [Ferdinand] Magellan began to think otherwise, and so did the scientists. Music now made another vital contribution to our process of thought. When man first transformed sound into music, advances were made by the method of trial and error, a process which science now adopted.

Science may not have been within the reach of all, but music sharpened the analytical sense in imperceptible ways. Singing to improvised accompaniments at home was a great achievement for Western man; he was becoming a tester and measurer of his own artistic capacities.

The open challenge to the status quo arose first not from science or exploration, but within the ranks of the church itself. In 1517 Martin Luther nailed his Ninety-Five Theses on the door of his church at Wittenberg, accusing the Roman Catholic church of corruption. The Reformation was born. Luther, himself a fine musician, threw out much old church music and wrote new hymns of which "A Mighty Fortress Is Our God" is the best known among dozens. Luther was a sort of Master Singer, and was even called that, inventing melodies which were then framed in the learned art of polyphony thanks to his adviser and collaborator Johann Walter. These four-part settings were not as complex as the part writing developed by Dufay and others, for Luther intended these hymns to be sung by the people, the entire congregation, giving fresh voice to their growing sense of power, of individual rights, while at one and the same time they could learn to master the elements of harmony previously reserved for the specialists.

The First High-Quality Instruments

Artists are often the first to anticipate social change. The cultural fact that marks the Renaissance more than any other was the rediscovery of the classical Greek conception of the ideal human form. The works of Leonardo [da Vinci] and Michelangelo reflect this, and Europe gained a fresh sense of continuity with its own distant past. The heroic quality in the Greek spirit accorded perfectly with a time when man would be seen as "the measure of all things." The violin is a symbol for man the measurer, and by the mid-1500s it had evolved into the instrument we know. Before the Renaissance the design and use of instruments was haphazard, parts would be taken by any players at hand, and the voice was still supreme. The violin is a natural leader, the ultimate musical match for man himself, and craftsmen whose skills were a match for the ideals of beauty of ancient Greece made it the king of instruments. All the instruments were improving and multiplying in a dizzying variety, [with names such as] shawms and sackbuts, bombards and rauschpfeife, krummhorns, lutes, bandoras and virginals. We can date only a few to a time prior to 1500, but hundreds after that. Musicians may have taken less care in the Middle Ages, or worn out the ones they had through hard use. Workmanship now assured quality with quantity, and princes collected instruments as the basis of house ensembles; they did not, in fact, belong to the musicians who played them.

The Printing Press Changes the World

E.R. Chamberlin

The great thinkers of the fifteenth century searched monastery libraries and private collections for handwritten books from ancient Greece and Rome. These dusty old tomes would have been read by only a few if it were not for a mechanical invention invented around 1450: the printing press. Before the invention of the printing press, books were rare and expensive items individually copied by hand. Only the very rich could afford them, and the only books copied were well-known works such as the Bible (few scribes would undertake the effort to hand-copy the writings of individual scholars or authors). The distribution of books on philosophy, rhetoric, math, astronomy, religion, and other less weighty subjects radically changed the world and helped fuel the Renaissance.

The first printing presses relied on the use of single letters—called movable type—that could be used interchangeably with other letters. The Koreans and Chinese had both experimented with movable type made from clay, wood, bronze, and iron in the eleventh century, but their alphabets were so complicated that the printing press was impractical.

Around 1453, Johannes Gutenberg invented a method of casting movable type from a melted lead alloy poured into an adjustable mold. The type was then secured in a large plate that was moved up and down onto pieces of paper with a large metal screw. Gutenberg's invention was so successful that it remained an unchanged standard of typecasting and printing until the late nineteenth century.

E.R. Chamberlin is an expert on Renaissance history and an author of several books.

Excerpted from E.R. Chamberlin, *Everyday Life in Renaissance Times*. Copyright © 1965 E.R. Chamberlin. Reprinted with permission from Salamander Books.

The art of printing came full formed into the world at the precise moment that it was needed. Printing was a result, not a cause, of the intellectual ferment at work within Europe but without it that ferment would have been limited, for men would have been forced to continue to work in small, isolated groups. Before the invention, every book in the world was a handwritten work. There was an army of copiers in each centre of learning, at each great court, and a book deemed valuable could be assured of reproduction into hundreds of copies. But such reproduction was done without overall plan; a scholar desiring a work would have to locate a copy, commission a copier and pay him for the scores of hours the task would occupy. The chance of error through ignorance or negligence on the part of the copiers would multiply with each successive edition of a work, so that eventually the establishing of a correct text became a major problem. The great works of history, such as the Bible, were ensured a continued existence for there was always someone, somewhere, who desired his own copy. But the works of unknown men were limited to the few copies circulated among friends, and, if immediate interest ceased, then the book would disappear for years or perhaps for ever. As a result, men again and again tackled problems which had been solved by others in distant places and times. Printing opened a channel of communication of a kind which had never before been seen. The work of the few was swiftly available to the many, and among the many were those who could take the work a stage further and, in their turn, publish the results to an even wider audience.

Details in a Law Suit

The controversy regarding the true inventor of printing is very nearly as old as the art itself. In 1499 the Chronicler of Cologne firmly stated that it was the work of 'a burgher of Mainz, born at Strasburg, called Junker Johan Gutenberg'. The Chronicler was bitterly attacked by those anxious to claim the honour for their own country, but all available evidence substantiates him. Gutenberg was born sometime between 1394 and 1399. Typically, most of what is known of him is gleaned from a series of law suits which he seems to have conducted with an aggressive verve. In 1439 he was brought to court by the brothers of a man who had been his partner but who had died before the object of their partnership was achieved. The brothers sought to obtain details of a 'secret process' which the partners had been working upon; their law suit failed, but from it arose the first indications of printing in Europe.

The details of the case were necessarily kept vague; there was no patent law to protect a new invention and it suited all concerned to keep the facts to themselves. But the disputed process almost certainly related to the making of a [printing] type-mould. There was further talk of a 'press' which had been in the dead man's possession, but that was a common object. Variants of a screw with a handle which, when pulled down, would exert great pressure upon a plate were already in wide use. Gutenberg's unique contribution to the great inventions of the world was not printing, as such, but the means of producing thousands of movable letters all exactly alike. Printing—the transferring of marks from a raised surface to a flat one—was already very old. Gutenberg must have been familiar with the crude playing-cards of his day, produced from woodcuts to which coloured inks were applied and printed on paper. There was even a method to print the titles of books upon the covers by means of large letters carved in brass, and during Gutenberg's lifetime the principle of carving a whole page of text upon a single block of wood was introduced into Europe. These block-books enjoyed wide popularity but their use was limited to the reproduction of short, popular texts for which there was a steady demand. It required many hours' work to produce a single block which could be used only for the specific book for which it was carved. Mass-production of lengthy works required one vital component: movable letters which could be swiftly arranged in the innumerable combinations which make up words.

Simple but Costly

The scant evidences of Gutenberg's early life show that, at various periods he was associated with the manufacture of small, metal objects. Mainz was well known for the precision of its workers in precious metals, and Gutenberg's own family long had connections with the Archbishop's mint. He was therefore familiar with the problems of casting and stamping metal to a high degree of precision. This was to be the key to the problem. Wooden letters each had to be carved by hand and the most skilled woodcarver would introduce variants in each, which accumulated as they were placed together. Metal can be melted and poured into a mould, thus providing a swift and simple method of producing thousands of identical shapes; the material can also be used again when the shape is blurred. Gutenberg's invention brought together two familiar objects; a punch and a mould. The punch was in hard metal and on its head was carved the letter . . . required. On being struck into a piece of soft metal—the matrix—the punch would transfer an exact impression of the letter. . . . The matrix was then inserted into the base of a rectangular mould . . . , hinged to allow extraction of the finished type, and molten metal poured in. The principle was simple but its application was costly. Gutenberg had to bear all the heavy costs of an ordinary printer, and at the same time have reserves in hand to meet the scores of problems which any new process encounters. He succeeded in perfecting his invention but he lacked business ability; even as he entered history through a law suit, so he left, being sued by Johan Fust, a goldsmith who had put up capital for a certain major production. Gutenberg was unable to pay and his entire equipment passed into the hands of another man.

Printing was an accepted fact by at least 1460. Two years after this date civil war broke out in Mainz and the little group of printers established there were forced to leave, and settled throughout Europe. In 1465 printing had reached Italy; five years later a press was established in France. The Low Countries [present-day Netherlands, Luxembourg, and Belgium] followed and there, in the city of Bruges, an Englishman named William Caxton learned the new art and later founded his own press 'at the sign of the Red Pale', near Westminster Abbey in London.

Producing Paper

The rapid growth of printing depended upon the supply of a cheap and abundant material to print upon. Parchment and vellum had been used in the learned world for hundreds of years, but they were so expensive as writing materials that it was a common habit to scrape a manuscript clean and use the material again for a new work. A cheap, durable and easily produced material was required to match the mass-production capabilities of the printing press, and the printers found it in paper. It had first been introduced into Europe during the twelfth

Johannes Gutenberg's invention of the printing press allowed the widespread distribution of books during the Renaissance.

century in response to the demand arising from the growth of universities; printing boosted that demand, making large-scale paper-manufacture an economic proposition. The common ingredient was linen rags, boiled to a pulp and beaten to a creamy consistency. A shallow wooden frame, with a bottom of closely woven wires, was dipped into the pulp and, when lifted out, surplus water would drain away, leaving a thick residue in the tray. The workman would give the tray a shake to cause the fibres to interlock, and the page of wet paper would be dumped out to dry. It later became common to weave some device into the wire bottom which would imprint itself upon the pulp, thereby forming a watermark. This simple method produced an attractive material so durable that books made from it exist today, 500 years later, with little or no deterioration. Paper was supplied to the printer in pages and not in rolls, each sheet being precisely the size of the tray in which it was made.

Casting Type

The vital typecasting section of a printing works had the simplest of equipment; a furnace, bellows, ladle and a supply of the precious moulds. The cutting of the punches and the preparation of the matrixes would already have been done by a skilled man, probably a goldsmith by training. The typecasters' work was largely mechanical. A minute quantity of the molten metal was poured into the mould; it would set almost immediately and a twist of the fingers released the gleaming new type. Examined for imperfections, the rough edges would be filed off and it would join the rest in a basket. The letters would be sorted and passed on to the compositor. The earliest known illustration of a printing press occurs in a [woodcut made in] 1499. . . . All the essential details are clearly visible; the compositor with his case of type, the unwieldly press itself where . . . the pressman . . . is about to pull the great lever, and a workman wielding the inkballs with which the type was inked. A page of manuscript is propped up before the compositor and he is in the act of picking up type. These will be slipped into the composing stick in his left hand and then transferred to the two-page forme beside him on the bench. In its turn, the full forme was transferred to a stone bed on the press itself, where it was inked. The sheet of paper to be printed was placed upon a hinged container and an outer leaf—the tympanum—brought down upon it. The tympanum was covered with a sheet of vellum with an area cut in the centre precisely the size of the type area. This was to protect the margins of the sheet from any dirt or ink which might lay upon the surrounding equipment which held the type. As soon as the sheet was in position, type and paper were slid under the plate of the press, the screw tightened and the plate brought into contact with the paper, exerting a heavy but smooth pressure.

The Gutenberg Bible

In spite of the slowness of this work the most ambitious projects were successfully undertaken. The earliest pieces of printed work were indulgences—simple, one-sheet productions, but very shortly afterwards work began on a book which, even today, would rank as a major publishing project. This was the great '42-line Bible'—so called from the numbers of lines on each page—which was probably begun by Gutenberg in partnership with Fust. Judged by any standard, this first of the world's printed books remains one of the most beautiful. The object of the first typefounders was exactly to copy the existing fashion in manuscript writing, and so successful were they that it takes a trained eye to detect a difference between a manuscript and an early printed book. It long remained the custom to add illuminated initials and rubrics by hand. The new craft did not at once cause the collapse of the copying industry; wealthy scholars were at first prejudiced against the use of print, deeming it an unworthy method to enshrine the thoughts of the great. But increasingly, scribes and copiers found themselves employed only for special, luxurious works. The demand for cheap, duplicated books grew with the supply, for Europe was hungry for learning.

Life in the Americas

In the 1400s, the leaders of Europe engaged in power struggles with one another while the artists and thinkers of the day fomented a cultural Renaissance. Unbeknownst to them, half a world away the people of the Aztec and Inca empires were building kingdoms and creating art and architecture that equaled or surpassed any in Europe.

The tribes that made up the Aztecs were poverty-stricken nomads as late as the 1300s. Then through a series of intermarriages, palace intrigues, and small-scale wars, the Aztecs solidified their power over the local tribes who inhabited the region around present-day Mexico City. By the middle of the 1400s, the Aztecs ruled one of the mightiest empires in the Americas, second only to the Incas in present-day Peru.

As the Aztecs built a glittering city on the shores of Lake Texcoco, in southern Mexico, Guatemala, and Belize, the classic period of Mayan culture had come to an end. The great pyramids of cities such as Chichén Itzá still remained but were abandoned and overgrown by jungle. By this time, the main center of Mayan activity was the city of Tulum, whose dazzling white buildings were first sighted by Spanish conquistadors in 1517.

To the south, the Inca kings ruled over the mightiest kingdom in the Americas. The Inca empire stretched over a wide array of ecological regions, from the towering peaks of the Andes Mountains, through the tropical rain forests in the valleys below, and down to the long coastal strip along the Pacific Ocean. The capital of the empire lay in the valley of Cuzco near the now-famous ruins at Machu Picchu.

As the fifteenth century ended, the rulers of the Aztec and Inca empires were poised to reign in their respective regions for centuries. When the Spanish conquerors arrived in the early sixteenth century, however, the cultures that had taken so long to build were quickly destroyed in a matter of a few years.

The Building of the Aztec Empire

Stuart J. Fiedel

In the twelfth century, the Aztecs were a small, disorganized tribe wandering through central Mexico. Within one hundred years they had managed to conquer all the other tribes in the region and become one of the most powerful kingdoms in the Americas. Their capital city, Tenochtitlán (present-day Mexico City) was a stunning jewel on the shores of Lake Texcoco filled with awe-inspiring stone pyramids and other dazzling architecture. The homes of the wealthy were filled with art treasures, gold, silver, and precious stones.

Aztec civilization was at its zenith at the end of the 1400s. When the Spanish conquistadors (conquerors) led by Hernán Cortés arrived in 1519 they systematically looted the city and reduced the empire to rubble within two years. Over 100,000 Aztecs were killed in the process, and by the mid–sixteenth century hundreds of ships, called galleons, were returning to Spain overloaded with plundered Aztec treasure.

Stuart J. Fiedel is an author and expert on pre-Columbian American history.

In the [14th] century Toltec [Mayan] refugees and Chichimec [Aztec] immigrants streamed southward into the Basin of Mexico, where they intermarried with the local inhabitants. In the process, the rustic Chichimecs learned the more civilized ways of central Mexico. The newly merged populations formed more than 50 tiny statelets, whose ruling dynasties claimed descent from the Toltecs and adopted the Toltec

Excerpted from Stuart J. Fiedel, *Prehistory of the Americas.* Copyright © 1987, 1992 Cambridge University Press. Reprinted with permission from Cambridge University Press.

ideology of divinely authorized kingship. The statelet centers were generally built in areas that had been virtually uninhabited in earlier times.

Arrival on Lake Texcoco

The last of the Chichimec immigrants to arrive in the Basin were the Tenochca or Mexica, whom we know as the Aztecs. They seem to have begun as a semi-civilized agricultural tribe, forced by drought or overpopulation to leave their home town of Aztlan, which was probably located in western Mexico. By the time the Aztecs arrived in the Basin, there was not much vacant land left to be colonized, and they settled as squatters at one spot after another, only to be driven off by the landowners, who were repelled by their savage ways. The people of Colhuacan allowed them to remain in their territory as serfs; but when the Aztecs sacrificed a Colhuacan princess who had been offered as a wife for their chief, and her father, arriving for the marriage ceremony, beheld a priest dressed in his daughter's flayed skin, the Aztecs were expelled from Colhuacan too. They resumed their wandering until they came to some uninhabited swampy islands near the western shore of Lake Texcoco. It was here, according to Aztec legend, that they saw an eagle, with a snake in its beak, sitting on a cactus—the prophesied marker of the site where they should establish their capital. The twin Aztec towns of Tenochtitlán and Tlatelolco were founded on the islands in 1325 or 1345. In 1367, the Aztecs started serving as mercenary soldiers for Tezozomoc, the ruler of the Tepanec city-state of Azcapotzalco, who was competing against the rulers of Texcoco for recognition as paramount lord of the new Chichimec states. Also in 1367, Acamapichtli was appointed as *tlatoani* ("speaker," or ruler) of Tenochtitlán. He and his successors collaborated with the traditional tribal council, composed of lineage elders and priests. About 1400, Tezozomoc rewarded the Aztecs of Tlatelolco for their support by giving them his son as their first king, and he gave one of his daughters in marriage to Acamapichtli's son. The Aztec cities grew larger and more wealthy. The Aztecs were delegated more responsibility for the administration of conquered states, and they were awarded a share of the land and tribute won by Tezozomoc when he finally defeated the Texcocans in 1418.

Following Tezozomoc's death in 1426, his eldest son, Maxtla, seized the throne of Azcapotzalco from his half-brother, who had been chosen by their father to succeed him. Maxtla then murdered the Aztec rulers, who had supported his rival. This provoked a rebellion by the Aztecs, who, with the aid of the Texcocans, destroyed Azcapotzalco in 1428. The victorious tlatoani, Itzcoatl, carried off an internal power play at Tenochtitlán, depriving the lineage heads of any significant role in decision-making or the administration of conquered lands. In 1434, the rulers of Tenochtitlán, Texcoco, and the less powerful city of Tlacopan formed the Triple Alliance. The rulers of the other small states in the Basin were induced to become tribute-paying vassals of the Alliance through a combination of interdynastic marriages, offers to share in the tribute from newly conquered areas, and occasional threats or applications of force. Most of the agricultural tribute collected from the vassal lords was kept by the tlatoani, but the rest was distributed to high-ranking nobles who had distinguished themselves in battle. After securing control of the Basin, the rulers of the Triple Alliance began large-scale water control and construction projects and embarked on the conquest of outlying areas. Toward the end of his reign, Itzcoatl ordered construction of a causeway that linked Tenochtitlán to the towns on the shore of Lake Xochlimilco, and he conquered towns in Morelos and northern Guerrero, 62.5 miles to the south. His successor, Moctezuma I (1400–1469), undertook renovation of the temple of the Aztecs' patron god, Huitzilopochtli; he also ordered construction of a great palace, a 10-mile-long dike across Lake Texcoco, a canal leading to Tlatelolco's market area, and an aqueduct that brought fresh water to Tenochtitlán from the springs at Chapultepec. His armies achieved numerous conquests in areas to the south and east of the Basin. By 1500, the Triple Alliance controlled a territory of about 125,000 square miles and a population of as many as 10 million. . . .

An Enormous City

Tenochtitlán by this time covered 5 square miles, with a resident population of 150,000 to 200,000. The city proper was linked by canals and causeways to nearby provincial centers and suburbs, forming a "Greater Tenochtitlán" with 400,000 inhabitants. An additional 600,000 people lived in centers, villages, and hamlets in the rest of the Basin of Mexico. It is not surprising that the Spaniards who arrived in 1519 were awestruck by their first glimpse of Tenochtitlán, for it was bigger than most European cities of the time—five times the size of contemporary London, for example. The Spaniards compared the Aztec capital to Venice [Italy], for Tenochtitlán's "streets" were canals. The canals, laid out in a north-south grid pattern, were filled with a steady traffic of canoes laden with passengers or cargo. Much of Tenochtitlán itself, and the surrounding farm plots that produced food for its inhabitants, had been created by an enormous drainage and land reclamation project. The canals functioned not only as thoroughfares but as drainage ditches, which reduced the water content of the swampland around the original islands to the point where it could be farmed. Mud from the lake bed and rotting vegetation were piled on top of the drained plots, raising them higher and thereby lessening the danger of flooding. Defense against rainy-season floods was also provided by the dike that had been built across a narrow neck of Lake Texcoco; the dike also prevented the salty waters of the eastern lake from polluting its western third, which the Aztecs had filled with fresh water, piped in by their aqueduct. Chinampa agriculture was highly productive: 1 acre could provide enough food for six to eight people.

Temples and Palaces

At the center of Tenochtitlán was a sacred precinct, dominated by a 200-foot-tall pyramid, on which stood the twin temples of Tlaloc, the rain god, and Huitzilopochtli, the sun god. Smaller temples were devoted to Tezcatlipoca, Xipe Totec, and other gods. The precinct also included the priests' quarters, a large ball court, and a tzompantli on which the skulls of tens of thousands of sacrificial victims were displayed. The buildings of the central precinct were torn down by the Spaniards, and the buildings of colonial Mexico City rose upon their ruins. Only in 1978 did Mexican archaeologists begin to excavate the giant twin temple pyramid. The archaeologists moved in after workers laying in an electric cable stumbled upon a huge circular stone, which bore a carved relief depicting the dismembered goddess, Coyolxauhqui. This stone lay in the plaza where the corpses of sacrifices landed after rolling down the steps of the Great Temple. Excavation has revealed 11 construction stages, and more than 50 rich offering caches that had been buried within them. Among the 200 objects found in a typical cache were human skulls, flint and obsidian blades, and stone sculptures; in addition, many hundreds of stone beads were generally included.

Surrounding the sacred precinct were the palaces of Tenochtitlán's rulers. Moctezuma II's palace contained his luxurious private residence and pleasure gardens, which included an aviary, a zoo, and apartments for human freaks. It was also an administrative center, with a council room, law courts, a treasury, storerooms for tribute, a jail, an arsenal, guest rooms, a hall for music and dance performances, and quarters for 3,000 servants and workmen.

There were two major marketplaces, one located near the temple precinct, the other in Tlatelolco (the twin city that was finally absorbed around 1500). Spanish observers reported that the Tlatelolco market was bigger than those of Rome and Constantinople. All manner of exotic imports, food, even slaves, were offered for sale in the markets. The Aztecs used cacao beans, cotton cloaks, and quills filled with gold dust as standard units of value in their commercial dealings.

Classes and Clans

Aztec society was stratified into classes, yet it seems to have retained a few traces of an earlier kinship-based organization. The highest class, the nobles or *pilli*, were all relatives of the king; they may have comprised 5% of the population. The nobles had their own inherited estates, as well as tribute-paying lands that were granted to them by the tlatoani as rewards for the services they rendered him as administrators or warriors. Most of the population were commoners, or *macehuales*. Each of them belonged by birth to one of 20 clans, or *calpultin*. Members of a *calpulli* occupied their own ward in the city, jointly owned and farmed chinampa plots in the suburbs, maintained their own temple, set up schools for the military education of their young men, and went to war as a combat unit. The calpulli members were often not just kinsmen, but also practiced the same specialized craft. Each calpulli was internally ranked, on the basis of closeness to the founding ancestor of the lineage. Calpultin of different rank together comprised each of the four quarters into which Tenochtitlán was divided. The lowest class were the *mayeques,* displaced and conquered farmers who, having no rights to calpulli land, worked as tenants on the estates of the nobles. Also occupying the lowest rungs of the social ladder were porters and slaves, who were usually recruited from among the ranks of captives and debtors. There were two groups who were able to achieve some upward mobility in the Aztec hierarchy: Long-distance traders in exotic goods, the *pochteca*, could amass great wealth, but they avoided public displays that might provoke the nobles' enmity; and warriors who distinguished themselves in battle might be granted estates of their own and waivers of tribute payments.

Large-Scale Human Sacrifice

The Aztecs were almost incessantly at war. One aim of this warfare was to conquer other peoples and force them to pay tribute. About one-third of Tenochtitlán's food needs was satisfied by the 7,000 tons of maize and 4,000 tons each of beans, sage seed, and amaranth, that were received yearly as tribute from the provinces. More exotic items, such as cloth, metal, jade, quetzal feathers, cacao, and the like were also required as tribute. When subject peoples rebelled against the heavy payments imposed upon them, the Aztec army, more than 100,000 strong, would take the field against them. Some groups, notably the Mixtecs, Tarascans, and Tlaxcalans, successfully resisted the Aztecs. When Cortés arrived in Mexico, the Tlaxcalans became his allies in battles against the Aztecs.

The Aztecs also had a less obviously pragmatic reason for waging war, which was to obtain captives who would be sacrificed to their gods. So important was this motivation that during the reign of Moctezuma I (1440–1469), a series of prearranged battles were fought by the armies of the Triple Alliance against those of Tlaxcala and Huexotzingo; the sole purpose of these "Flowery Wars" was for each side to capture sacrificial victims from the other (flowers and blood were poetic equivalents for the Aztecs).

Human sacrifice was not an Aztec innovation in Mesoamerican religion; the Toltecs and Maya had certainly practiced this custom, and it may have originated in the time of the Olmecs or even earlier. However, the scale of Aztec sacrifice seems to have surpassed anything that came before. Basing [an] estimate on the figures given in several post-Conquest sources . . . each year about 2,000 people were sacrificed at Tenochtitlán, and another 8,000 to 18,000 in the other cities and towns of the Basin of Mexico. To celebrate the dedication of the renovated Great Temple in 1487, sacrifices went on for 4 days straight. A steady stream of prisoners, probably numbering about 14,000, was led up to the pyramid's summit. There, four priests grabbed each victim's arms and legs, bent his body backwards over a stone, and a fifth priest slit the victim's chest open with a flint knife and pulled out the heart, which was burnt as an offering to the gods. War captives were the most common sacrifices, but slaves and children were also killed. The highlight of some ceremonies was the sacrifice of a privileged young man or woman who had been pampered for a year as the impersonator of a god or goddess. These sacrificial victims were flayed, and their putrid skins were worn for 20 days by priests or penitents, in imitation of the god of spring, Xipe Totec.

The Aztecs believed that to prevent the destruction of the universe, which had already occurred four times in the past, the gods must be supplied with a steady diet of human hearts and blood.

Quetzalcoatl: The Great God of the Aztecs

C.A. Burland and Werner Forman

Quetzalcoatl, the Feathered Serpent, was the Aztecs' most important god. The Aztecs believed Quetzalcoatl was their creator who traveled to the underworld to collect bones, which he sprinkled with his own blood, in order to form human beings.

In the following excerpt, C.A. Burland and Werner Forman detail the legends of Quetzalcoatl, often referring to particular codices, such as the *Codex Laud* and the *Codex Vienna*. Codices were sacred picture books of ancient Mexico called "thought paintings." Since so many languages were spoken in the sprawling Aztec empire, communication was achieved with these picture books rather than with an alphabet. The codices, made from fine strips of deer skin and painted with vegetable and mineral dyes, detailed the lives and legends of dozens of Aztec deities.

C.A. Burland worked at the British Museum for thirty-six years and has written numerous books about the indigenous people of North, Central, and South America. Werner Forman has collaborated on more than fifty books and is a renowned photographer and an authority on ancient civilizations.

Quetzalcoatl, the Feathered Serpent, Lord of Healing and magical herbs, the symbol of learning, of poetry and of all things beautiful, the Lord of Hope and the brilliant Lord of the Morning Star, was

Excerpted from C.A. Burland and Werner Forman, *Feathered Serpent and Smoking Mirror.* Copyright © 1975 Orbis Publishing Limited, London. Reprinted with permission from Little, Brown and Company (UK).

the spirit who brought up the sun in the morning and thus brought the beneficent [beneficial] power of the sun god to all humans, animals and vegetation. One of the most important figures in the religion of pre-Columbian [before Columbus arrived in the New World] Mexico, Quetzalcoatl was . . . both a real person and a myth. The King Quetzalcoatl was the founder of an empire, and of a way of life which differed from that of other Mexican societies mainly by being more deeply religious. His greatest success was to form a confederation of tribal groups under the domination of the Toltec families, who supported a sequence of divine kings, each one of whom was called the Quetzalcoatl, though they also had their own personal names.

The story of the first great king Quetzalcoatl relates how he came from heaven to earth and founded a dominion among the people of Mexico where he lived as a celibate, holy priest, until a dispute among the gods led to his destruction. While at a great ceremony, Quetzalcoatl was plied with strong drink laced with the magic [psychoactive psilocybin] mushroom. Tempted by the demonic goddess who inhabited the mushrooms, he seized her and copulated during the feast. On awakening from his poisoned sleep he realized that he had condemned himself. Giving up all his palaces, he travelled across Mexico until he arrived naked on the shores of the Caribbean Sea. There he embarked on a raft of serpent skins, and sailed far away, towards the sunrise, until the tremendous heat ignited the boat and his heart arose, flying up to join the sun. . . .

A Fertilizing Breath of Life

A series of nine Toltec kings, each of whom was called Quetzalcoatl, followed the first great ruler. Each is depicted making fire on his accession and is credited with the erection of temples and sweat baths. Each royal succession is very carefully recorded, so that it has been possible to date the whole line of Toltec kings, ending with the fall of Tula under the last Quetzalcoatl, in the final decade of the tenth century.

In the stories of his adventures on earth, Quetzalcoatl is shown as a sexually potent being, whose energies were pent up until he was tempted by the goddess Tlazoteotl. In all descriptions of his personality, he is said to have been active and vigorous, and to have had an enormous penis. He wore a special loin-cloth with a rounded end, apparently as a bag in which to stow this marvellous organ. In a painting in the *Codex Laud* in the Bodleian Library, Oxford, he is seen as a wind blowing in the waters; sitting within the water, displaying her open vulva to him, is the younger moon goddess. The implication is that the breath of Quetzalcoatl is the fertilizing breath of life, and that the goddess will be impregnated by it.

The god Quetzalcoatl was also the Lord of Life, who brought penitence, love, and exemption from the usual rituals of sacrifice and blood offering, and he was, therefore, a figure of divine wisdom and love. Thus he could be understood, even by the early missionaries from Spain, as a being not wholly demonic, even though he was often shown under the strange guise of a serpent clothed in the green feathers of the quetzal bird.

The Feathered Serpent

The Feathered Serpent is one of the great mysteries of ancient Mexican belief. In ancient times the quetzal, a native of the western mountains of Guatemala, also lived in Mexico. It was regarded as the most beautiful of all birds and its name, Quetzaltotolin, means the most precious, or the most beautiful bird. The symbol of the feathered serpent can well be called Quetzalcoatl, which means not just the 'feathered serpent', but the 'most precious serpent', though, to be iconographically correct the god Quetzalcoatl is not himself the feathered serpent, but the one who emerges from the serpent, just as the Morning Star rises from the horizon. The most beautiful images of the god illustrate this aspect: a limestone example in the National Museum in Mexico City shows the face of the god in the serpent's mouth, as he retires at sunset, and there is a remarkable jade statue in the British Museum in which the god is shown arising from the serpent like the sun rising at dawn.

The Aztec language often had words of the same sound, but with different meanings. The word 'coatl' not only means serpent, it also means a twin; in this case, the twins are the Morning Star and the Evening Star, Quetzalcoatl and Xolotl. The god referred to as the Feathered Serpent, should thus really be described as the Precious Twin, since 'quetzal' means both 'the bird' and 'precious'. A great confusion could have been avoided if more attention had been paid in the past to the meaning of the words, rather than to the appearance of the symbol, which was merely a literal representation.

Other representations indicate different aspects of the god. Occasionally, statues show him as a very great priest, the Lord of Penitence, his face painted with black strips beside the eyes, a red ring around the mouth, and large areas of blue on the forehead. As Quetzalcoatl Ehecatl, Lord of the Winds, he is shown wearing a mask that projects like a pointed snout covering the lower part of his face. This is known as the 'wind mask', and is usually painted a bright red. It was probably derived from the snout of the Mexican whistling toad, *Rhinophryne dorsalis*, and, by its shape, suggested to the Mexican mind the shape of the Earth Monster, a cross between an alligator and a toad. A temple dedicated to Ehecatl was circular in plan, for as a god of the wind he could blow or breathe in any direction and therefore could not be confined to a square structure facing only the four cardinal points. In

the Vienna Codex, Quetzalcoatl, as the wind god, is shown supporting the heaven with his hands. The heaven is the heaven of waters,
and, in effect, he is holding the rain clouds above the earth, and show-
ering out their waters as they are driven from place to place before the
wind. As god of the weather, the wind and the rain, Quetzalcoatl joins
the hierarchy of the vegetation gods. His function as the wind is to dry
the soil, and to prepare the earth for the coming of the rains.

At other times he is just a god of springtime and rising vegetation. . . . Quetzalcoatl, as a ruler on earth, also had to leave his wealth,
his garments, and finally his life, before he could be taken into the
heavens and made into the Morning Star. It is as this self-sacrificing
god who became the Morning Star that he is the god of springtime and
of rising life.

Aztec Human Sacrifice

Fray Diego Durán

By the 1400s the Aztecs ruled over a huge empire that was as rich and advanced as any in the world at that time. The Aztecs obtained their wealth through a decades-long program of tenacious war and conquest.

The Aztec religion stated that the gods of their world could only be appeased through bloody human sacrifice. To fulfill their commitment to their deities, the Aztecs slaughtered men, women, children, and enemies who had been captured in war. They did this by cutting their chests open and ripping out their still-beating hearts. This gory practice was at an apex in the fifteenth century at the height of Aztec power.

Fray Diego Durán was a Dominican friar and the first known Spaniard to have recorded Aztec history. Although Durán wrote about the Aztecs in the sixteenth century, it is assumed that he translated the following excerpts from the oral history of Aztec elders who were alive in the fifteenth century, before the Spanish conquest. Durán's work is the earliest and most thorough history available of pre-Columbian Mexico.

Many days had passed after the return of the Aztecs from the war in the land of the Huaxtecs. [The war hero] Tlacaelel then reminded King Motecuhzoma of the work on the temple they had begun to build, and said that a great stone should be carved to serve as an altar or table upon which sacrifice would be made. This Tlacaelel, in addition to being bold and cunning in the artifice of war, also invented devilish, cruel, and frightful sacrifices. Motecuhzoma gave orders that the stone be carved and that on it be sculpted the war of

Excerpted from Fray Diego Durán, *The History of the Indies and New Spain,* translated by Doris Heyden and Fernando Horcasitas. Copyright © 1994 University of Oklahoma Press. Reprinted with permission of University of Oklahoma Press.

liberation from Azcapotzalco, fought by their forebears, so that it be carved there in perpetual memory. Tlacaelel was pleased with this idea, so he gathered the stonecutters and sculptors, saying to them:

"Master craftsmen, our lord the king wishes you to cut a large round stone that we shall call *temalacatl*, which means 'stone wheel'. On the face of this will be inscribed our wars with the Tepanecs, since this sculpture must be an eternal reminder of that heroic event. I beg of you to excel in this work; let it be well carved and done as quickly as possible, and in this way your names will be glorified and you will be remembered forever." The craftsmen were happy to carry out his orders. They sought a large stone about a *braza* and a half wide; they then made smooth its surface and on it represented in their carving the war with Azcapotzalco. This was very finely done and was finished so swiftly that some days later they were able to notify the king that the sacrifice stone was ready. The king then ordered a base to be made for it to rest upon. And so a platform was made, slightly higher than a man, and the carved rock was placed upon it.

"The Skinning of Men"

Now that the stone had been set up, they called certain youths who lived in seclusion within the temples—some of those who were outstanding in their duties—and gave them the office of carrying out this sacrifice that the [Spanish believed the] devil had invented and taught them [but was actually a part of Aztec tradition]. They were told: "Take care that every day you prepare yourselves to perform this sacrifice, since the lords of all the neighboring cities and provinces will be invited to the festival and you must not put us to shame." The young men thanked Tlacaelel and the king and promised to practice and rehearse according to the instructions that were given to them. And so they did.

When the festival day and the beginning of the month called Tlacaxipehualiztli, "Flaying of Men," approached, the Aztecs invited the lords from the entire land: the rulers of Tezcoco and Tacuba, of Chalco and Xochimilco, those from the Marquesado, from Couixco and Matlatzinco, and the heads of the Mazahua people. Finally, they invited all the noblemen they could from the surrounding area so they would come and see what took place at that feast and realize what it signified.

Once the guests had arrived, the king had many fine things brought from his treasury and gave these as presents: handsome mantles and breechcloths, rich clothing exquisitely worked, feather-work, wide sashes, sandals, labrets of precious stones, gold ear ornaments, and nose pendants. A great feast followed, with quantities of fowl, meat from the hunt, different breads, chocolate drinks, and pulque. After the guests had eaten and drunk, they were assigned booths adorned with flowers and reeds, within which they could sit and watch. The visitors [sat in the decorated boxes and] awaited the ceremony, which had been unknown to them before that time.

The prisoners were brought out and lined up at a place called Tzompantitlan, which means something like "Place of Skulls." At this place there was a long low platform upon which stood a rack where the skulls of sacrificial victims were strung and where they remained permanently as reminders of these sacrifices, as relics. The prisoners were arranged in a file and were told to dance; all of them were there, dancing. And all the victims were smeared with chalk, their heads were feathered with down, and on top of the head each wore some white feathers tied to his hair. Their eyelids were blackened and around their mouths they were painted red. Then the men who were to perform the sacrifice came out and stood in a row, placed according to their rank. Each one was disguised as a god. One of them wore the garb of Huitzilopochtli, another was dressed as Quetzalcoatl, another as Toci [Our Grandmother]. Another represented Yopi, still another Opochtzin [the Left-Handed One]; another was Totec [Our Lord], and finally one wore the garments of Itzpapalotl [Obsidian Butterfly]. Then one warrior was disguised as a jaguar, another as an ocelot, and yet another as an eagle. All carried swords and shields, inlaid with gold and gems, and all these sacrificers were covered with featherwork and rich jewels.

For all these men an arbor, beautifully adorned with flowers and with paintings that bore the insignia of those gods mentioned, had been prepared. This arbor was made of branches and leaves of a tree called *tzapotl* [the sapodilla]; that is why the arbor was called Tzapotl Calli, "House of *Tzapotl*." Within it were seats also made of sapota wood, where all of them sat down according to age and rank. This arbor had been erected on the summit of the pyramid in a place called Yopico.

Ritual Battle

When the images of the gods who were to perform the sacrifice had been seated, then came the old priests called Tecuacuiltin and the temple singers. A drum was brought forth and to the rhythm of its beat they began to dance and sing. The high priest, in full dress for the rite, then came forth with tall feathers in his headdress, his arms covered with golden bands from which hung large, shining green and blue feathers. Carrying in his hand the great knife of black [obsidian], the knife called *ixcuahualli*, he went to be seated in a place especially arranged for him. After he was seated, they brought out one of the prisoners from the Huaxteca and with a rope that emerged from a hole in the middle of the great round stone tied his foot around the ankle. Thus tied to the stone, he was given a wooden sword and a shield; the sword was not equipped with blades but was feathered from top to bottom.

At this point the high priest, who for this day was called Yohualahuan [Drinker of the Night] and Totec [Our Lord], rose from his seat and slowly descended the steps until he reached the place where the prisoner was. He walked around the stone twice, sanctifying it, and, having again tied the victim who was upon it, he returned to his seat. Then one of the elderly men, dressed as a jaguar, appeared and gave the victim—or placed next to him—four wooden balls made of torch pine and told him to try to defend himself with them. He wrapped a cloth around the prisoner's body and gave him a little Divine Wine to drink. After this he withdrew, leaving the victim alone. One of the men disguised as a god then approached the stone, dancing, with his shield and sword in his hands, well protected by his [padded cotton] armor. He went up to the stone where the prisoner was tied. The poor wretch threw the balls at him, but these were repelled by the sacrificer (or executioner) if he was skillful. Thereupon the prisoner picked up his feathered sword and defended himself the best he could. Some of the victims possessed such ability that they tired out two or three attackers before others could wound them. But as soon as the victim was wounded—on his leg, on his arms, or on any part of his body—four priests, their bodies painted black, with long braided hair, dressed in garments like chasubles, ascended the stone and laid the wounded man on his back, holding him down by the feet and hands. The high priest then rose from his seat, went to the stone, and opened the chest of the victim with the knife. He took out the heart and offered the vapor that rose from it to the sun. As soon as the heart had cooled, he delivered it to the priest, who placed it in a vessel called the *cuauhxicalli* [eagle vessel], which was another large stone dedicated to the sun. In its center it contained a cavity that was also used for another type of sacrifice.

Human sacrifice was an essential element of Aztec religious practices.

Extracting the Hearts

These ceremonies were performed in the case of all the prisoners, each one in his turn. However, there were some who, on being given the shield and sword, felt the sword with their fingers. When they realized that the sword was not edged with knives but with feathers, they cast it away and threw themselves upon their backs on the stone. The priests then took hold of them, and the high priest opened their chests and extracted their hearts. Some of the victims, such as those mentioned here, were unwilling to go through so much ceremonial and they cast themselves upon the stone immediately, seeking a quick death. Whether one defended himself well or whether one fought badly, death was inevitable. That is why all those priests were required; when one was tired of sacrificing, another would take his place. At the most it means another half hour of life.

After all the sacrificial victims had died, the corpses were taken back to the place where, as live men, they had stood in a row, and the bodies were cast down there. Those who had taken part in the sacrifices entered certain rooms of the temple with the high priest, took off their ritual garb, and, with great reverence, put it away in a place reserved for this.

The lords from other cities and from the provinces who had come to observe the sacrifice were shocked and bewildered by what they had seen and they returned to their homes filled with astonishment and fright.

Dressed in the Skins

Motecuhzoma now called those who had performed the sacrifice and thanked them for their skillful work. He had them dressed in fine mantles, breechcloths, and sandals and commanded that they be given maize, beans, *chian* seed, and cacao in large quantities. This was done to encourage others to take part in these exercises, which the Aztecs felt were filled with virtue and honor.

By ancient tradition the feast was followed, the next day, by another celebration. At this time the king gave his noblemen the usual gifts: fine mantles, rich breechcloths, sandals, labrets, ear spools, shields, other weapons, and insignia that were both handsome and valuable. They also received little gold banners. All the men, according to their position and merit, received emblems and insignia, some of more importance than those given to others. In this way no one was excluded from participating in these feasts and ceremonies. Rewards of this type were given to all the noblemen—and even to those who were not of noble birth—who had distinguished themselves in war. Once the rewards had been distributed, those who had been sacrificed were flayed and the Tototectin put on the skins and wore them. Carrying their shields in one hand and rattle staffs in the other, they went from house to house. First they visited the houses of the nobility and chieftains and went to all the other houses after these, asking for alms, wearing the skins all the time. The rich gave them mantles, breechcloths, and waistbands; the common people gave them ears of corn and other edibles. For twenty days these men begged. At the end of this time they had gathered great quantities of clothing and food. The flayed skins had been worn in the manner the god [Xipe Totec] was portrayed.

When the twenty days had passed, they took off the reeking skins and buried them in a special room in the temple. In this way ended the feast and the sacrifice of the Huaxtecs, which had been made to solemnize the first use of the carved stone.

The Inca Empire

Michael A. Malpass

The Incas created the largest empire in the Western Hemisphere in the fifteenth century, controlling an estimated 12 million people in present-day Peru, Ecuador, and parts of Chile, Bolivia, and Argentina. The Incas gained their power in less than a century, conquering and assimilating many cultures that existed in a wide variety of environments from jungles to urban areas. The Inca agricultural system provided a wide variety of grains, vegetables, and other necessities and their economy was based on barter of tools, pottery, food, and jewelry. Indigenous Inca domination of the southern Andes Mountains ended abruptly in 1532 when Spanish conquistadors, led by Francisco Pizarro, invaded and destroyed the empire in order to plunder the native silver, gold, and other resources. Michael A. Malpass is associate professor of anthropology at Ithaca College in Ithaca, New York. He has been actively engaged in archaeological research in Peru since 1980.

The Incas built their empire in less than a century. This in itself was an extraordinary achievement, but other empires have expanded as rapidly or even more so. . . . Conquering people is a relatively straightforward thing to do; all one needs is many well-armed soldiers and effective military leaders. However, to integrate conquered peoples into a single empire that functions as a unit with central control is much more difficult. This is especially so when the conquered societies are spread out over a broad area of very rugged terrain, such as the [Inca Empire in the] Andes mountains. Perhaps the greatest achievement of the Incas is that they appear to have successfully organized all the groups they conquered into an empire that did function as a unit. This is not to say the empire ran smoothly; quite to the contrary, the history of the Inca empire is one of rebellions and conflict. It is also apparent that the Incas did not use a single policy of incor-

Excerpted from Michael A. Malpass, *Daily Life in the Inca Empire.* Copyright © 1996 Michael A. Malpass. Reprinted with permission from Greenwood Publishing Group, Inc., Westport, CT.

poration for every conquered group; rather, they tailored their policies to the particular circumstances of each group.

One of the reasons for the Incas' success was their use of the existing political and social structures of conquered people for ruling them. Instead of trying to change the people's lives, they tried to maintain continuity so the subjects' lives were disrupted as little as possible. The Incas saw their relationship to conquered peoples as one of *institutionalized reciprocity*. This means that the Incas expected the conquered people to work for them, but in return they provided them with services and goods, food and clothing, beer, coca, and even entertainment. They assigned conquered leaders positions of authority in the government, gave them high-status gifts, and honored their religious beliefs and practices. In return the Incas expected the conquered people to work hard for them, to produce, among other things, food, cloth, pottery, buildings, and other large and small items; and to be obedient and loyal subjects. How the Incas organized their empire to do this is the topic of this excerpt.

Military Organization and Warfare

Certainly one of the key reasons for the Incas' success in building their empire was their military organization. Their superior army, leaders, equipment, and tactics helped them to defeat their enemies. The highly disciplined army mainly comprised people recruited from already-conquered groups. Warfare in the Andes was basically hand-to-hand combat with clubs and spears, and the Inca army was very well armed by Andean standards. Bows and arrows were not a highland weapon, although the Incas employed tropical forest groups who did use them. A more common weapon that could be used from a distance was the sling. Moreover *bolas*, a group of leather straps tied together with rocks at their ends, were used for bringing enemies down: a warrior would throw his bola around the enemy's legs. Defensive weapons included shields and cotton armor.

One of the most important considerations of warfare is providing food and supplies for the soldiers. This was as true for the Incas as it is today. Given how rapidly the Inca armies expanded the empire, the problem of providing food to them as they advanced up and down the spine of the Andes must have been considerable. One of the keys to this success was the Inca road system. The Incas constructed roads to connect the different parts of their empire, and along the roads they placed major Inca cities where food and clothing were stored. . . .

The Incas' terms of conquest were relatively simple, but severe. Ownership of the lands of conquered people was claimed by the Inca king, although the people were allowed to use it. The land was divided into three parts: one for the Inca state, one for the Inca religion, and one for the conquered people's use. Local leaders were given positions in the Inca bureaucracy and left to rule as before. However, their sons were taken to Cuzco and trained in Inca policies. When the old leader died his son would replace him, bringing to the job his new knowledge and the Inca point of view. Finally, the Incas allowed conquered people to continue worshipping their own gods, but they had to acknowledge the superiority of the Inca gods. The Incas bestowed honor on the sacred objects of conquered people by setting up a shrine for them in Cuzco. Although this seems generous and noble, the Incas had a political reason for doing it: the objects were held hostage with the threat if the people rebelled, the Incas might damage or destroy them. . . .

A Barter Economy

It is important to note that the Inca economy was not based on money. There was no common standard of value, such as the dollar in U.S. society today. Goods were bartered between individuals, who negotiated the relative worth of each object. Items exchanged included surplus food and manufactured items—for example, tools, pottery, or objects of personal adornment such as jewelry. Because the Incas controlled trade between regions, everything exchanged was strictly local. Therefore the range of goods exchanged was relatively restricted.

Land was not owned by individuals. It belonged to a person's ayllu [clan]; one had the right to use the land but not to sell it. However, by official decree the Inca king owned all the land of the empire and gave each ayllu the use of its land. The only things a person actually owned were the personal objects she or he obtained, either by gifts or barter.

For the Incas, the main means of subsistence was agriculture, the sowing and reaping of domesticated plants and the breeding of domesticated animals. The Andes are one of the several places in the world where many plants and animals were originally domesticated as people learned their cycles of reproduction. An entire range of plants was grown by Andean people in the different environmental zones. The most important crop grown was corn, also known as *maize*. Corn beer, called *chicha*, was consumed in large quantities as a dietary drink and during important ceremonies.

A wide variety of other crops was also grown. including potatoes, *quinoa* (a mid-altitude grain with a high protein content), *oca* and *ullucu* (two high-altitude tubers, similar in use to potatoes but different in flavor and shape), many different kinds of beans and squash, sweet potatoes, *manioc* and *yuca* (both starchy, low-altitude tubers), tomatoes, chili peppers, avocadoes, and peanuts. Other non-edible plants were also grown, such as coca [the plant used as a base for cocaine] (chewed with lime to withstand cold and fatigue). cotton, and gourds. The two main domesticated animals were llamas and alpacas; the former was used as a pack animal, and the latter's soft wool was used for clothing. Ducks and guinea pigs were raised for food as well.

These plants and animals were exploited in different combinations in different environmental zones. The Incas used these zones very effectively, in terms of both the crops grown and the use of people to grow them. Farming implements were very simple: a footplow, hoe, and clod-breaker were used for preparing fields for planting. The footplow turned up large chunks of earth, which were then crushed with the clod-breaker, a club-like tool. The hoe, whose blade came straight out from the handle rather than at a 90-degree angle (like that of modern hoes), was used for weeding and breaking up clods as well. In the absence of draft animals, these were the only tools needed—and they were very effective. Even today it is common to see Andean people preparing fields with these same tools. Agriculture was done by both men and women, with men using the footplow and women the hoe. Harvesting also was done by both sexes working together, as it is today.

In addition to agriculture, the Incas used wild plants and animals to supplement their diet. Certain areas of each province were reserved as hunting grounds, although the inhabitants could request permission of the king to use them. Deer and guanaco, a wild relative of the llama, were the main prey. Vicuñas, another wild relative of the llama, were caught for their extremely soft wool; they were released after shearing. The wool was spun and woven into clothing. Birds were killed by snares, slings, or the use of the bola, a series of leather strips with stones tied at the ends.

Inca Artisans

As in many large-scale, complex societies, the Incas had a high degree of occupational specialization. Because of the exceptional skill indicated by many of the objects manufactured by the Incas, it is thought that the makers were fulltime specialists. Such specialization is also reflected in the presence of workshops at Inca sites where such individuals toiled. Three craft occupations deserve special mention: pottery, textiles (i.e., cloth), and metal working.

Inca pottery is highly distinctive and very well made. There are several different shapes, but the two most common are a plate and a large jar with a pointed base and elongated neck. The latter was used for storing liquids, such as chicha. The designs on Inca pottery are highly repetitive; geometric shapes are common, especially on storage jars. The designs on the pottery used at administrative centers for feeding the local workers were uniform. This is because the Incas wanted to make sure the people using the pottery recognized the source of their hospitality. Thus it was important that the pottery be made in a highly controlled way. The Incas actually set up communities of potters whose sole task was to do this. There are Spanish accounts of people being moved to a community to produce pottery for that province.

The importance of textile (woven fabric) production to the Incas cannot be overstated. Producing cloth was the second largest industry in the empire, after agriculture. Three grades of cloth were made, each serving a different purpose. The coarsest weave was used for making blankets only, and the medium weave was for basic clothing. The finest cloth, called *cumbi cloth*, was carefully woven and of exceptionally high quality.

Clothing of all sorts was made from a wide variety of materials—including cotton and the wool of wild vicuñas and domesticated alpacas and llamas. Cotton was utilized more often on the coast, where it grows readily and where it might have been domesticated during the late Preceramic Period. Several shades of color, ranging from brown to white, were grown and used on the coast. Wool textiles were more common in the highlands, because cotton does not grow well in the high altitudes and because camelids (llamas, alpacas, and vicuñas) are abundant there. The wool is easy to dye and spin; owing to its exceptional warmth and light weight, it is an ideal material for highland peoples.

Both cotton and wool must be spun into thread before being woven. This was done with a simple spindle and whorl. Starting with a ball of material attached to a stick, a woman (this was generally women's work) would twist some of it into a thread and wrap it around the spindle. The spindle whorl, attached to the end of the spindle, acted to keep the spindle rotating at an even rate to make the thread uniform in thickness. The spindle and whorl also acted as a weight to keep the thread taut. Women could spin thread while doing other activities, such as herding or visiting. The practice is still common in the Andes today. After spinning, the thread could be dyed or used in its natural color. . . .

The Importance of Style

Cloth in Inca society had five important uses, in addition to its use as clothing: (1) it was a form of identity by which to recognize where an individual was from; (2) it was an indicator of prestige; (3) it was used in ceremonial occasions as offerings; (4) it was given as official gifts to conquered people; and (5) it was a form of payment for members of the army. When one considers the many ways that cloth functioned in the empire, it is easy to understand its importance to the Incas.

One early Spanish writer, Bernabé Cobo, noted that the Incas required people to wear their native clothing wherever they were in the empire, and that they were severely punished if they did not. This indicates that the particular way of dressing was distinctive from group to group, as it still is in many remote regions of the Andes today. For instance, the kind of hat worn by individuals today mirrors Cobo's comments that the most important insignias of identity were worn on the heads of men.

The wearing of distinctive clothing allowed a person's place of origin to be recognized from a distance. Therefore it became much more difficult to leave one's group, because one would be immediately recognized by Inca officials. Being that the Inca mitima [clothing] policy was so extensive, the wearing of identifiable clothing became an important source of control over people's movements.

In a similar vein, designs were highly significant in the Inca prestige system. Certain patterns identified the wearer as a member of a royal panaca [elite], and other patterns identified other social groups. Thus not only could one recognize a person's place of origin by his or her clothing, but one could also determine his or her social status. Therefore one would immediately know how to act toward someone on sight.

Cloth had ceremonial and political uses as well. Virtually all sacrifices to Inca gods involved the burning of cloth, especially cumbi cloth. It is said that one hundred cloths of the finest quality were burned in sacrifice to the sun every morning in Cuzco. Why was cloth sacrificed? It had an important role in the society, and people typically sacrifice what has value to them.

Cloth was also used in a political sense. When a group was conquered, the Incas gave cumbi cloth to the vanquished leaders as a sign of respect for them. By accepting the cloth, the conquered leaders accepted their position of subservience to the Inca empire. Finally, soldiers in the army were given a specific amount of cloth as part of their pay, and there are accounts of rebellions when soldiers failed to receive their ration of clothing.

For the reasons just described, cloth production, like pottery manufacture, was carefully controlled. Cloth was frequently given as a reward for good service, so rulers and administrators had to have large quantities on hand. Therefore a large number of persons were employed by the Inca empire to make cloth. At the Inca city of Huánuco Pampa, one very large part of the site was dedicated almost exclusively to the production of cloth. In the provinces, apparently there were villages dedicated to the production of cloth as there were villages focused on pottery.

Gold and Silver

The Incas used metals for various purposes. Gold and silver were used extensively, but only for luxury items and ceremonial objects (e.g., llama figurines) that were often buried with sacrificial victims at the tops of mountains. The use of these two metals was restricted to the Inca nobility. The lower classes used copper, a soft metal that can easily be worked to achieve a variety of shapes, for items of personal adornment (e.g., large pins used for holding shawls closed), as additions to clothing, and for a variety of ceremonial objects such as sacrificial knives. On the other hand, because it is soft, copper is not good for making tools. The metal of choice for tools was bronze, a combination of copper and tin or arsenic. Bronze was used for axes, chisels, knives, tweezers, and war-club heads as well as jewelry and other objects.

There is surprisingly little written about native mining activities, perhaps because this activity was very quickly taken over by the Spaniards and converted to their own techniques. Gold, silver, and copper, the three main metals used, are abundant in Peru and Bolivia. Only gold is found in its pure form. . . . Stones and deer antlers were used as tools to break up the veins of ore, and sacks of animal hides or baskets were used to carry the material out of the mine.

Mines were worked only during the summer, to take advantage of the warmth, and the miners worked only from noon to sunset, to prevent exhaustion. Mine work for the Incas was done with m'ita labor [the forced labor of conquered people] drawn from settlements near the mines.

Silver and copper are found as ores (i.e., rocks with several kinds of materials mixed together). Once the ore was removed from the mine, the valuable metal had to be separated from the rest of the material. This was done by heating the ore. Different metals have different melting temperatures, and can be removed at different times during the heating process. Copper may also have been used without heating, as it is a soft material and is found in relatively pure deposits.

Because the use of silver and gold was restricted to the government, mining for these metals was carefully regulated. Copper was used much more widely and thus was unregulated. The ore deposits and mines were considered sacred places, and ceremonies were conducted in their honor.

The Incas were familiar with a variety of techniques for working metals, including simple hammering, casting, smelting, riveting, and soldering. (In fact, many metalworking practices preceded the Incas.) For the making of jewelry, the Incas utilized inlaying and incrustation to achieve intricate designs. They often employed the finest craftsmen in Cuzco to make the luxury items.

Growing Up in Inca Society

Ann Kendall

The Inca Empire ruled over a widely diverse area that included coastal deserts, rich agricultural valleys, tropical forests, and the towering peaks of the Andes Mountains in present-day Peru. In order to oversee such a large region, the rulers of the empire maintained control over the way administrators and bureaucrats raised their children. Upon reaching puberty, select boys and girls of the ruling class were taken from homes and trained for various duties and services.

Ann Kendall is an anthropologist and author whose specialty is the Incan culture of Peru.

Before the child was born the mother was supposed to confess and pray for an easy delivery, while the husband was meant to fast during the delivery. Although midwives as such were unknown, mothers of twins were considered to have special powers and were sometimes present to help with the birth. Many women delivered without assistance and were able to take themselves and the baby to the nearest water source to wash. The mother then resumed normal household tasks, usually immediately. If she bore twins, however, or the baby had some defect, the family considered it a bad omen and fasted, performing certain rituals to counter-act this. On the fourth day after birth the baby was put in a *quirau* (cradle), to which it was tied, and its relatives were invited around to see it and drink chicha [a fermented grain drink]. A commoner carried her child in a cradle

Excerpted from Ann Kendall, *Everyday Life of the Incas*. Copyright © 1973 Ann Kendall. Reprinted with permission from Salamander Books.

on her back, which was supported with a shawl tied over the chest when she went out and wished to take the child with her.

[Seventeenth-century author El Inca Garcilaso De La Vega], who was himself brought up by his Palla mother in the Inca tradition, gives an interesting account of the upbringing of children under Inca regime:

They brought up their children in a strange way, both Incas and common folk, rich and poor, without distinction, with the least possible pampering. As soon as the baby was born it was washed in water and wrapped in shawls. Every morning when it was wrapped up it was washed in cold water, and often exposed to the night air and dew. When the mother wanted to pamper her child, she would take the water into her mouth and then wash it all over, except the head, and especially the crown, which was never washed. It was said that this accustomed the babies to cold and hardship, and also that it strengthened their limbs. Their arms were kept inside the swaddling clothes for more than three months, because it was thought that if they were loosened earlier, they would grow weak in the arm. They were kept lying in their cradles, which were sort of rough benches on four legs with one leg shorter than the others so that they could be rocked. The bed on which the baby reclined was a coarse net which was only a little less hard than the bare boards: the same net was used to hitch the baby to the sides of the cradle and tie it up so that it could not fall out.

The mothers never took the babies into their arms or on their laps either when giving suck or at any other time. They said it made them crybabies, and encouraged them to want to be nursed and not to stay in the cradle. The mother bent over the baby and gave it her breast. This was done thrice a day, in the morning, at midday, and in the evening. Except at these times no milk was given, even if they cried. Otherwise it was thought they would get used to sucking all day long and develop dirty habits with vomiting and diarrhea, and grow up to be greedy and gluttonous men. . . . The mother reared the child herself, and never gave it out to nurse, even if she were a great lady, unless she were ill.

. . . When the child was old enough to be moved from the cradle, Garcilaso says, a hole was made in the ground for it to jump about and play in. The hole came up to the child's armpits and was lined with a few rags and contained some toys for its amusement. This device may have been used in special circumstances as a sort of play pen, perhaps in the Incas' gardens, but Garcilaso does not elaborate on the whereabouts of this pit. . . .

Naming Ceremony

The child was named later at a special ceremony called *Rutuchico* meaning the 'cutting of the hair'. This was performed when the child was weaned, at one to two years old. All the relations attended this ceremony and sometimes friends of the family. After a feast the eldest, or most important, male relative started off the haircutting by removing a lock of the child's hair. Each person who cut a lock offered the child a gift. The hair and nails were thus cut and carefully preserved.

When this ceremony was performed on the Emperor's son, each noble, in order of importance, cut off a lock of the prince's hair and offered him rich gifts of fine clothes and jewellery of gold and silver, revering him as a grandson of the Sun.

The names given to children at the Rutuchico were used only until they reached maturity. During this period most children followed their parents about and learnt by copying them and helping them in their daily tasks. Unproductive play was not encouraged, and from childhood everyone learned all the crafts required for their everyday needs, such as making simple clothes, shoes and utensils, cooking and agriculture. Male children helped their parents in looking after their animals, chasing birds and pests from their fields. Girls helped their mothers with the new babies and there were always plenty of simple household tasks requiring attention, such as sewing, cooking, washing and cleaning.

Rigors of Education

There was no formal education available for most of the sons of the commoners, except for the trades that they learnt from their parents. The following quote from an Inca ruler's sayings sums up the attitude of the nobility:

> It is not right that the children of plebians should be taught knowledge that is only suitable for nobles, lest the lower classes rise up and grow arrogant and bring down the republic: it is enough that they learn the trades of their fathers, for governing is no matter for them, and it is discreditable to power and to the state that these should be entrusted to the common people.

Some of the girls, daughters of commoners, might however be selected for education in the provincial *Acllahuasi*, the House of the Virgins. These were convents in which the Chosen Women—*Mamacunas* (Consecrated Women) and *Acllas* (Virgins) lived. In each province an agent, the *Apupanaca*, was appointed by the Emperor to select the girls and be responsible for organizing their keep in the Acllahuasi. He travelled to all the villages choosing the 'prettiest, of best appearance and disposition' from amongst girls aged nine to ten years old. These girls lived in the provincial capitals under the care of the Mamacunas—nuns dedicated to teaching—who prepared them for their future. The Mamacunas taught the girls religion and womanly chores: to dye, spin, and weave wool and cotton to a high standard; to cook food and to make fine chicha, especially chicha prepared for sacrificial rites. When the girls reached the age of 13–14 they were taken to Cuzco by the Apupanaca for the Inti Raymi, Festival of the Sun.

In Cuzco the Acllas were presented to the Emperor who was then responsible for deciding on their future. The most beautiful girls became the servants or concubine wives of the Inca [Emperor] himself, or were given by him to those he wished to honour or reward for their services, usually Incas [ruling family] and curacas [administrators]. Others were kept for special sacrifices, to serve in the shrines or to live in the convents where they instructed future generations of Acllas.

Educating Upper-Class Males

All the sons of Incas and curacas were obliged to attend the *Yachahuasi* (House of Teaching) in the capital, Cuzco. In the case of the latter, the privilege of attendance was double-edged. On the one hand they had the advantage of living in the Inca court all the year round and of receiving an education in the Inca culture. This, however, also served as indoctrination, and created in them favourable attitudes to Inca policies for the time when they inherited posts from their fathers. . . .

Of life in the schools Garcilaso writes:

> As they had no book-learning, the teaching was done by practice, daily use, and experience, and in this way they learned the rites, precepts, and ceremonies of their false religion and came to understand the reason and basis of their laws and privileges, the number of them, and their true interpretation. They attained the knowledge of how to govern and became more civilized and better skilled in the art of war. They learnt about the times and seasons of the year and could record and read history from the knots. They learned to speak with elegance and taste, and to bring up their children and to govern their houses. They were taught poetry, music, philosophy, and astrology, or such little as was known of these sciences. The masters were called amautas—'Philosophers' or 'Wise men'—and were held in high esteem.

. . . Discipline was kept by beatings of up to ten blows on the soles of the feet—though teachers were restricted to meting out one beating a day!

Rites of Puberty

Puberty rites were held for girls and boys, called *Quicochico* and *Huarachico* respectively.

There was no formal collective ceremony for the girls, with the possible exception of the participation of the daughters of the nobility on the occasion of the boy's Huarachico. Quicochico, a family affair, was celebrated when a girl had her first menstruation. In preparation she remained at home fasting for three days, while her mother wove her a new outfit. She emerged on the fourth, was washed, her hair was braided, and she was dressed in the fine new clothes and sandals of white wool. Meanwhile her relatives had gathered for a two-day feast to celebrate the occasion, at which it was her duty to serve them. Afterwards, everyone gave her gifts and she received a permanent name from her most important male relative, who gave her good advice and told her to obey and serve her parents to the best of her ability.

Women's names suggested qualities admired and considered suitable for a female to have, so that a girl might be named after an object or an abstract quality—such as Ocllo (Pure) or Cori (Gold). An unusual name was given one of the Coyas who was called Mama Runto (Runto meaning Egg) because she had a lighter complexion than most Andean women, and the comparison was considered an elegant figure of speech. Boys were given titles and names evocative of qualities or characteristics of animals: Yupanqui (Honoured), Amaru (Dragon), Poma (Puma), Cusi (Happy), Titu (Liberal).

The boys took part in the puberty ceremony called Huarachico when they were about 14, give or take a year. This was one of the most traditional of the Inca rituals, held each year for the sons of noblemen in Cuzco. Although at its most ceremonious and important in Cuzco, puberty rites were also held at the same time in the provincial capitals under the direction of Inca governors, for the sons of local nobles. Similarly, a simpler celebration also marked the puberty of the commoners, at which the boys were given their first breechcloths made for them by their mothers. . . .

[Seventeenth-century Spanish writer Bernabé] Cobo . . . describes elaborate ceremonies, sacrifices, rituals and dancing, while sports, athletics and military games play a very secondary role. . . .

Preparing for the Ceremony

Preparations for Huarachico were begun well in advance [of the ceremony]. Special outfits were woven by the women for their sons: narrow shirts made from fine vicuña wool, and narrow white mantles which fastened at the neck by a cord from which hung a red tassel. Meanwhile the candidates went to the shrine of Huanacauri, about six-and-a-half kilometres (four miles) from Cuzco, where they made sacrifices to the idol, asking permission to enter the knighthood. The priests gave each boy a sling and drew a line on his face with the blood of the llama that had been sacrificed. The boys then collected ichu grass for their parents to sit on. Upon returning to Cuzco, everyone prepared for the coming festivities by making vast quantities of chicha.

On the first day of the month the nobles presented their sons to the Sun, their ancestor, in the Temple of the Sun. The boys were dressed in their special home-made outfits and so were their kinfolk. Next, they all went to Huanacauri, taking with them a sacred white llama. The following morning more sacrifices and rituals were performed at the Huanacauri shrine before the return to Cuzco. During the return a curious ritual was enacted: the parents whipped the boys' legs with slings. Upon arrival in Cuzco they made sacrifices to idols and the mummies of ancestors in the central square.

After a few days' rest, during which the boys probably fasted, the families reassembled in the central square, this time in the presence of the [royal] Sapa Inca, for more celebration and ritual, which would eventually lead to the awarding of the knighthoods. The boys—and the girls—who were to serve in the festivities, were given outfits from the storehouses of the Sun by the high priest. The boys' clothing consisted of striped red and white shirts and a white mantle which had a blue cord and red tassel; they also wore special usuta sandals, made of ichu grass for the occasion by their male kin. At this point everyone moved towards Huanacauri, for the hill of Anahuarque, where after more sacrifices the Incas danced their special Taqui dance. This was followed by the ritual of a foot race. The boys, watched and cheered on by their relatives, raced for a distance of about 1,000 metres, (1,100 yds) down a dangerous slope. They were met at the finishing post at the bottom of the slope by the girls, who waited upon them with tumblers of chicha.

Next, after returning again to Cuzco, they set out for the hills of Sabaraura and Yavira, where further sacrifices and dances were performed. Here the boys were given their insignia of maturity, the breechcloth and gold ear-plugs, by the Sapa Inca. After again dancing the Taqui, everyone returned to Cuzco, repeating the ritual of whipping the boys' legs, to do homage to the gods. After these numerous ceremonies, the new knights went to bathe in a fountain called *Calipuquio*, behind the fortress of Cuzco, where they placed the clothes which they had worn for the ceremonies and put on other clothing called *nanaclla*, which was coloured black and yellow. Finally, on returning to the central square of Cuzco, the Huacapata, they were given presents by their families, including weapons from their godfathers, and lectured on how they should comport themselves as adults and were told to be brave and loyal to the Emperor and revere the gods.

The Age of Exploration

PREFACE

Throughout most of the fifteenth century, Europeans had no way of knowing what bounty and riches lay across the oceans in the Americas. Their small sailing ships were only suitable for sailing on the warm, calm Mediterranean Sea.

During this period, the economy in Europe grew more dependent on trade with India and the Orient, where spices, silks, cottons, and other goods were in abundance. To bring these items such a great distance overland from the east using pack animals was expensive, time-consuming, and dangerous. Thus the Europeans set out to find an alternative sea route to India and the East.

Prince Henry of Portugal correctly believed that the shortest water route to India was south around the African continent. Unfortunately, the Atlantic coast of Africa was a mariner's nightmare. Headwinds, rocky shoals, and hostile natives took the lives of hundreds of sailors determined to sail to India. The Portuguese struggled for decades before Vasco da Gama finally sailed into Calicut, India, in 1498.

Celebration of da Gama's long, difficult voyage, which cost the lives of two-thirds of his men, was eclipsed by an Italian sea captain named Christopher Columbus. Columbus, sailing under the Spanish flag, had sailed west to the country he believed was India. Although Columbus had actually reached the Bahamas, he went to his grave believing that he had discovered a water route to India.

The Spanish discovery of America brought incredible wealth to Spain, while the Portuguese excursions into Africa brought riches to that small country. These explorations of commerce, however, were disastrous for the native inhabitants of the conquered lands. The Portuguese began trading in African slaves in 1440 and continued to do so for four hundred years. This trade, along with that conducted by other European nations, would decimate the cultures of Africa. As for the natives in the Americas, they too would be nearly wiped from the face of the earth by European diseases and greed.

What began in the late 1400s as a few men searching for a trade route to India would lead to the conquest of the African and American continents and—within a few hundred years—the eventual growth of the United States into the world power that it is today.

The Exploits of the Chinese Dragon Fleet

Louise Levathes

Although European explorers could not find a sea route to India until the late 1400s, the Chinese ruled the Indian Ocean basin from 1405 to 1433 with more than three hundred treasure ships manned by twenty-eight thousand sailors, known as the Dragon Fleet. In fact, when Portuguese explorer Vasco da Gama first sailed down the African coast and offered cheap trinkets to the natives, they scoffed at his meager offerings, having already seen the riches of the Orient that included silks, porcelain, and other goods. Chinese leaders, however, had little interest in ruling the world with their powerful navy. By the mid-1400s, China turned toward development at home, and the once-mighty Dragon Fleet faded into history.

Louise Levathes is a journalist who has worked for the New York *Daily News, National Geographic*, and others. She was also a reporter for WNET-TV. In 1990 she was a visiting scholar at the Johns Hopkins Center for Chinese and American Studies at Nanjing University, in Jiangsu, China.

A larm spread quickly through the East African town of Malindi. Across the sea, beyond the coral reef, strange storm clouds appeared on the horizon. Fishermen hastily dragged their outriggers to

Excerpted from Louise Levathes, *When China Ruled the Seas.* Copyright © 1994 Louise E. Levathes. Reprinted with permission from the author.

safety on dry land. As the clouds gathered, it suddenly became clear that they were not clouds at all but sails—sails piled upon sails, too numerous to count, on giant ships with large serpent's eyes painted on the bows. Each ship was the size of many houses, and there were dozens of these serpent ships, a city of ships, all moving rapidly across the blue expanse of ocean toward Malindi. When they came near, the colored flags on the masts blocked the sun, and the loud pounding and beating of drums on board shook heaven and earth. A crowd gathered at the harbor, and the king was summoned. Work ceased altogether. What was this menacing power, and what did it want?

The fleet moored just outside Malindi's coral reefs. From the belly of the big ships came small rowboats and men in lavish silk robes. And among the faces were some the king recognized. These men he knew. They were his own ambassadors, whom he had dispatched months ago on a tribute-bearing mission. Now emissaries of the dragon throne were returning them home, and they brought wondrous things to trade. But had so many men and so many ships come in peace, or had they come to make the citizens of Malindi subjects of the Son of Heaven?

The year was 1418.

The Largest Armada in History

The largest of the ships moored off Malindi were four-hundred-foot-long, nine-masted giant junks the Chinese called *bao chuan* (treasure ships). They carried a costly cargo of porcelains, silks, lacquerware, and fine-art objects to be traded for those treasures the Middle Kingdom [China] desired: ivory, rhinoceros horn, tortoiseshell, rare woods and incense, medicines, pearls, and precious stones. Accompanying the large junks on their mission were nearly a hundred supply ships, water tankers, transports for cavalry horses, warships, and multi-oared patrol boats with crews numbering up to 28,000 sailors and soldiers. It was a unique armada in the history of China—and the world—not to be surpassed until the invasion fleets of World War I sailed the seas.

In the brief period from 1405 to 1433, the treasure fleet, under the command of the eunuch admiral Zheng He, made seven epic voyages throughout the China Seas and Indian Ocean, from Taiwan to the Persian Gulf and distant Africa, China's El Dorado. The Chinese knew about Europe from Arab traders but had no desire to go there. The lands in the "far west" offered only wool and wine, which had little appeal for them. During these thirty years, foreign goods, medicines, and geographic knowledge flowed into China at an unprecedented rate, and China extended its sphere of political power and influence throughout the Indian Ocean. Half the world was in China's grasp, and with such a formidable navy the other half was easily within reach, had China wanted it. China could have become the great colonial power, a hundred years before the great age of European exploration and expansion.

But China did not.

A Short-Lived Era

Shortly after the last voyage of the treasure fleet, the Chinese emperor forbade overseas travel and stopped all building and repair of oceangoing junks. Disobedient merchants and seamen were killed. Within a hundred years the greatest navy the world had ever known willed itself into extinction and Japanese pirates ravaged the China coast. The period of China's greatest outward expansion was followed by the period of its greatest isolation. And the world leader in science and technology in the early fifteenth century was soon left at the doorstep of history, as burgeoning international trade and the beginning of the Industrial Revolution propelled the Western world into the modern age.

In 1498, when Vasco da Gama and his fleet of three battered caravels rounded the Cape of Good Hope and landed in East Africa on their way to India, they met natives who sported embroidered green silk caps with fine fringe. The Africans scoffed at the trinkets the Portuguese offered—beads, bells, strings of coral, washbasins—and seemed unimpressed with their small ships. Village elders told tales of white "ghosts" who wore silk and had visited their shores long ago in large ships. But no one knew anymore who these people had been or where they had come from. Or even if they had really come at all. The treasure fleet had vanished from the world's consciousness.

Zheng He and Vasco da Gama missed each other in Africa by eighty years. One wonders what would have happened if they had met. Realizing the extraordinary power of the Ming navy, would da Gama in his eighty-five to a hundred-foot vessels have dared continue across the Indian Ocean? Seeing the battered Portuguese boats, would the Chinese admiral have been tempted to crush these snails in his path, preventing the Europeans from opening an east-west trade route? . . .

China rose as a maritime power and . . . after the wide-ranging voyages of the treasure ships, it systematically destroyed its great navy and lost its technological edge over Europe. At the heart of the matter is China's view of itself and its position in the world, which has changed little to the present day. Today there is still the same ambiguity toward foreigners and foreign influence. The opening and closing of doors. The sullen refuge in isolation.

Far from being the landlocked people they are often portrayed as in history, the Chinese have been skilled and adventurous boatmen since the dawn of their civilization. Even before we can speak of

"China" or the "Chinese," Neolithic people from the mainland of Asia were the ancestors of the diverse peoples of Oceania, who conquered both the Indian Ocean and the Pacific in the first millennium B.C. Little doubt remains that there were Asian people in the New World before Columbus, and the evidence points to not one but several periods of contact.

Portuguese Explorations in Africa

J.H. Parry

The Portuguese began to explore Africa's western coast in 1419, driven by the vision—and financial backing—of Prince Henry, the third son of Portugal's King John I. Although he was later called Prince Henry the Navigator, he never explored himself. Instead he sponsored expeditions, and Henry's captains—Gil Eanes, Nuno Tristão, and others—each managed to advance Portuguese interests a little farther south along the coast, exploring well-known African geographical landmarks such as Cape Branco, the Senegal River, Cape Verde, and elsewhere.

These men were followed by dozens of other Portuguese explorers, who inched their way down the coast battling harsh winds, rough seas, rocky coasts, and an often hostile native population. The conditions for exploration were so difficult that it took more than fifty years—until 1488—for the Portuguese to round Africa's southernmost point. And it would take another decade before Vasco da Gama finally made the journey to India, where a wealth of silks, spices, and other desirable trading goods could be obtained.

J.H. Parry was born in England in 1916 and educated at Cambridge University. He later became a professor of modern history at the University College of the West Indies. Parry is a Member of the Order of the British Empire and a distinguished author of several books.

Excerpted from J.H. Parry, *The Age of Reconnaissance.* Copyright © 1963 J.H. Parry. Reprinted with permission from University of California Press.

The far-reaching plans and hopes attributed by the chroniclers to Prince Henry of Portugal have attracted more attention than his actual achievements. The exploration of the West African coast appears as a mere preliminary, a rehearsal for the opening of the India trade forty years after the Prince's death. Yet the two enterprises were separate and distinct. [The African country of] Guinea is not on the way to India; not, certainly, for a sailing ship. The Guinea trades had a value of their own, independent of the lure of India. The discovery of a coast where gold could be obtained from the same sources which supplied, by desert caravan, the cities of Morocco, was a geographical and commercial achievement of great significance in its own right.

The chroniclers . . . concentrated their attention on voyages sponsored by the Prince and recorded the achievements of his captains: of Gil Eannes who in 1434 first rounded Cape Bojador with its dangerous shoals stretching far out to sea; Nuno Tristao, who sighted Cape Branco in 1442, who two years later landed on Arguim island, within the curve of the cape, which was to become the first European slaving-station in Africa, and who in 1444 discovered the mouth of the Senegal [River]; Dinis Dias who, also in 1444, reached Cape Verde with its high, rounded hill visible far to seaward, and explored Palmas island where the . . . slave [trading stations] of Gorée were later to be established; Nuno Tristao again, who explored the wide mouth of the Gambia where (probably) he was killed in 1446; Cadamosto, the Venetian, whose expedition in 1455 was probably the first to visit the Cape Verde Islands; Diogo Gomes, who disputed Cadamosto's claim and who certainly in the following year found the mouths of the Geba and the Casamance rivers; and Pedro da Sintra, who about 1460 sighted the mountains of Sierra Leone and gave them their name because—it was said—of the thunderstorms that growled and roared, as they still do, about Mount Auriol. These, however, were only the most famous among many fishing, sealing and trading voyages of which no record now remains. The fisheries off the Mauretanian coast were valuable enough in themselves to have attracted Portuguese and Andalusian [Spanish] skippers. Prince Henry and his brother Prince Pedro, by placing gentlemen of their households in command of some of the ships and demanding from them longer voyages, more detailed reports, more captives to be converted or enslaved, and higher returns, gave energy and direction to a movement of maritime expansion which probably would have taken place in any event, but which might for many years have been confined to fishing and casual slaving.

Ivory, Gold, and Slaves

The Mauretanian coast was and is sandy, monotonous and sparsely inhabited . . . inhospitable and dry. Apart from fish, sealskins and seal oil, either taken directly or bought from the coastal people, and a few slaves, the country had little of commercial value to offer. . . . The coastline is broken by several big rivers, of which the Senegal and the Gambia are the chief, descending from the Futa Jallon mountains. Villages at the mouths of these rivers were to become in time major centres for the trans-Atlantic slave trade, and ivory, gums and a little gold dust were to be had. [Venetian explorer] Cadamosto describes the country vividly; its inhabitants—Muslims in their white gowns, and naked [Africans]; its animals—elephant, hippopotamus, monkeys; its markets, where one could buy, besides the ordinary commodities of the trade, ostrich eggs and skins of baboon, marmot and civet; its tree-lined estuaries. From just south of Gambia, however, to just south of Freetown—the coasts of Portuguese and French Guinea and Sierra Leone—the shallows are full of islands, rocks and shoals, and the whole stretch from Iles de Rhos to Cape St Ann is marked on modern Admiralty charts 'all approach dangerous'. . . . About Cape Three Points, however, there is a change, to an open sandy coast with occasional rocky headlands. The coast is readily approachable, except for a heavy surf. This was the Mina de Ouro [Mine of Gold], the Gold Coast which in recent times has appropriated the name of Ghana, [the name of] an unconnected medieval empire far inland. The *Mina* was not, of course, a gold mine (though some envious Spaniards seem to have thought so) but a stretch of coast where gold was traded in considerable quantities, some worked into ornaments, but most in the form of dust washed from streams inland. East of the Volta there is another long stretch of low-lying coast, with a few good harbours, particularly Lagos, with lagoons and mangrove creeks stretching as far as the Niger delta. This, the largest mangrove swamp in the world, is a vast sodden sponge into which the waters of the Niger pour, to seep out to the Gulf through tortuous innumerable creeks. At the western edge of the delta is the Benin river, which gave access to the most powerful and most developed of the coast kingdoms, the kingdom of Benin. Benin, besides numerous slaves captured in its constant wars, produced—and still produces— pepper of a ferocious and lasting pungency, comparable in quality with pepper imported into Europe overland from India.

Exploring Africa's Coast

Prince Henry's death in 1460 removed an incentive to explore. The explorers had reached a difficult and dangerous stretch of coast, with no evident prospect of improvement; and some of them were alarmed by the probability that . . . the North Star [their guide to navigation], barely visible above the horizon at Sierra Leone, would disappear if they went further. The merchants were content to develop their modest but prospering trade at the mouths of the Senegal and the Gambia. The Crown, to which Prince Henry's African rights reverted, was willing enough to encourage discovery, but unwilling to incur expense, especially since Henry had left a load of debt. . . . No official action was taken on Guinea until 1469, when [Portuguese king Alfonso V] agreed to lease the whole enterprise . . . to a private individual. The lessee, Fernão Gomes, [agreed] to pay an annual rent and to explore 100 leagues of coast annually during the five-year period of his lease. Little is known of Gomes as a person; but he was clearly a man of energy, a good organizer and a good judge of men, and his story is one of success. He carried out his obligations, and more; he made a fortune from his highly speculative investment; spent much of it serving his king in arms in Morocco; and was knighted for his pains.

In 1471 Gomes' captains reached Sama, near Cape Three Points, the first village of the Mina de Ouro, and in the next four years the coast was explored as far as Benin. Whether Gomes' people investigated the Cameroons coast is uncertain . . . but certainly during this period Fernando Po discovered the fertile island which bears his name. . . .

During the years of [Gomes' exploration] nearly two thousand miles of coastline had been roughly explored, the Guinea trade had assumed roughly the form which it was to retain for more than a century, and its commercial value had been clearly demonstrated. No doubt with that value in mind, the King, after the expiry of the lease, entrusted responsibility for the affairs of Guinea to his son, the future John II. . . .

The Guinea Trade

The new king immediately turned his attention to the problems of regulating and defending the Guinea trade. . . . Adequate defence was the most urgent need; and this was provided in 1482 by the construction of the factory-fort of São Jorge da Mina. This famous fortress [called Elmina Castle] was built by Diogo d'Azambuja, diplomat, engineer and soldier, of dressed stone shipped from Portugal, on a site acquired by negotiation with the local chiefs. It had a garrison of sixty soldiers—not always up to strength—and soon gathered round it a native village inhabited by labourers and fighting auxiliaries. Its provisioning was difficult: the water supply was poor, and food, other than local fish, and fruit and vegetables brought from the island of Sao Thomé, came out from Portugal; but interlopers kept away from it, and it served its purpose well for a hundred and fifty years.

The trade which Elmina Castle defended was chiefly in gold, slaves and pepper, with minor dealing in ivory, gum, wax, palm oil, occasional ostrich eggs and similar curiosities. The principal exports were cloth and hardware. . . . Slaves were valuable, though not very numerous; perhaps 500 a year at the end of the century. . . . The Portuguese factory at Gató on the Benin river exported slaves not only to Portugal, but also to Mina, where the local up-country traders needed carriers and would pay for them in gold. . . . All in all, some twelve or fifteen Portuguese ships annually traded on the Coast at the end of the century; as Vasco da Gama, according to Barros, informed the ruler of Calicut. In the early decades of the sixteenth century the trade, especially the slave trade, steadily increased. . . .

John II prudently developed the Guinea trade which he already possessed, while simultaneously but separately pursuing coastal exploration. He sent out a series of expeditions at Crown expense, in caravels [ships] equipped for discovery, not for trade, commanded by extremely capable professional navigators. Among their equipment they carried stone columns [called padrãos], which they were to erect at prominent points on newly-discovered land. . . . In 1483 Diogo Cão set up his first *padrão* at São Antonio do Zaira at the mouth of the *rio poderoso*, the Congo; explored the river for some distance; and pushed on down the coast as far as Cape Santa María in 13°S, where he erected a second *padrão*. He returned to Portugal in 1484, bringing several Congolese natives with him to be instructed in the Christian faith and taught to wear clothes. Cão's reception was more than usually enthusiastic; his Congolese were fêted in Lisbon and taken into the King's household for education; and Cão was knighted. . . .

Sighting the Cape of Good Hope

The increasing length of the African voyages posed difficult problems in victualling [supplying] the small caravels employed in the work. Wood and water could be taken in here and there on the coasts of Angola and South-West Africa, but no food was to be had there. Cão's successor, the equally capable and still more famous Bartolomeu Dias, took a store-ship in addition to his two caravels on the expedition which left Lisbon in 1487. He provisioned the caravels from the store-ship in Angra Pequeña . . . and left the store-ship there with a small party on board, about Christmas. From there they beat against wind and current until . . . the caravels stood out from the coast to seek a better wind. They sailed south-west or sou'-sou'-west for many days until, about latitude 40°S, they at last picked up the prevailing westerly wind. They ran east for some days, hoping to regain the coast, until well east of the longitude of Cape Voltas, then stood to the north, and eventually fell in with the land about Mossel Bay. They had [passed] the Cape [of Good Hope] without sighting it. . . . The current there sets to the south-west and the water is warm, corroborative evidence that the way to India lay open; but Dias' people, tired and anxious about their provisions, persuaded him to turn back. There was no mutiny; the habit of submitting major decisions to a general meeting was deeply ingrained in all seamen during the Age of Reconnaissance, and few commanders far from home ventured to override if they could not over-persuade. It was on the return passage that Dias sighted the great cape he had been seeking. . . . Dias had discovered . . . the way to India. . . . At Angra Pequeña he found his store-ship, with only three of the ship-keepers still alive. He set up a *padrão* at the point now known as Point Dias, put in briefly at Elmina on his passage home, and finally reached Lisbon in December 1488.

African Kingdoms in the 1400s

Margaret Shinnie

When the Portuguese first began to explore the coast of western Africa in the mid-1400s, the African continent had been the site of many great civilizations for thousands of years. The gold and other riches of the continent had attracted Arab traders from the north since at least the eighth century, and the religion of Islam had gained prominence among many people in the northwestern African kingdoms of Mali, Ghana, and Songhai. Cities such as Timbuktu in Songhai were famous throughout the world as trade and learning centers.

By the 1300s, a Mali king named Mansa Musa was known throughout the Mediterranean and Europe. Mansa Musa's fame was a result of his pilgrimage to Mecca, which was preceded by five hundred slaves bearing staffs of gold. On the way home, Musa's army captured Gao, the capital city of Songhai, but by the fifteenth century, the city was ruled by an Islamic king named Sonni Ali.

Margaret Shinnie is a British author with intense interest in precolonial African history.

The Songhai people lived on the banks of the middle Niger, as they still do, and in the seventh century, a Berber tribe, called the Dia, came down and imposed political control over them. The Songhai were farmers and fishermen, and the Dia ruled over them and gradually extended the area of land under their control. They also developed commerce and trading activities, as had the other big states of the Sudan, and exchanged goods with Ghana, Egypt and the countries of the

Excerpted from Margaret Shinnie, *Ancient African Kingdoms* (New York: St. Martin's Press, 1965).

North African coast. In the eleventh century they adopted the faith of Islam, probably because of influence from the Muslim countries with whom they traded, but the Songhai themselves were not much affected by Islam. At about the same time, a capital city was established at Gao, and judging by [the King of Mali] Mansa Musa's delight at the capture of this city by his army, it must have been a wealthy and important place. . . . Songhai became a tributary state of Mali for a time, from 1325 until 1335 when Ali Kohlen . . . restored his people to independence. It was a perpetual struggle for the Songhai to maintain their independence for they were pressed on all sides [by hostile tribes], all of whom were anxious to extend their dominion.

Capturing Timbuktu

About 1464, there came to the throne of the Songhai a king called Sonni Ali. He was an able and ambitious man, if a little ruthless, and hearing of some quarreling and enmity amongst the rulers of Timbuktu, he decided to take advantage of this and set out with his army to capture that city. He entered Timbuktu in 1468, and took it, killing many of the citizens. Then he decided to attack Jenné, a town, like Timbuktu, celebrated for its trade and learning. Jenné had had a rather more peaceful existence than Timbuktu as it lay in a well watered, even marshy, area, and was more difficult to attack. It took Sonni Ali some years to realize this ambition, but Jenné finally fell to him, probably about 1473. After this victory, he was much occupied with keeping the Mossi out of his kingdom, but by the time he died in 1492, he had established a fairly stable empire over much of the middle and upper reaches of the Niger. An Arab writer, Mahmud el Kati, describes him: 'He was always victorious. He directed himself against no country without destroying it. No army led by him in person was put to rout. Always conqueror, never conquered, he left no region, town or village . . . without throwing his cavalry against it, warring against its inhabitants and ravaging them.' In spite of his achievements, Sonni Ali had not been particularly liked by his people, for he was too cruel and too much of a dictator. When he died, the throne went to his son for only a few months, and was then usurped by one of Sonni Ali's generals with the support of the people. This general was a Muslim, called Mohammed Touré, and he took the title of Askia, being known as Askia Mohammed.

Centres of Learning

Sonni Ali had been a man of war and had forced allegiance to the Songhai kingdom over a wide area, and now Askia Mohammed set about organizing this kingdom into a properly administered state. He divided his kingdom into provinces and put a governor, often a member of his own family or a trusted friend, in charge of each province.

He created a number of central offices, almost like the Ministries of a modern government, to look after justice, finance, agriculture, and other matters of importance in the running of a state. He instituted a system of taxation whereby each town or district had its own tax collector, and he made some improvements which were designed to benefit trade, as for example putting an inspector in charge of each important market, and making weights and measures the same all over the kingdom. Apart from this kind of administrative reform, as a Muslim, he was sympathetic to the work of Muslims within his state, and encouraged them—the traders, and especially the learned men. Timbuktu, Jenné, and Walata flourished as centres of religion and learning; and as always when the Muslim population was settled and at peace trade flourished also and brought added wealth to Gao and Timbuktu. Sudan gold continued to flow northward, together with slaves, ivory, ebony and ostrich feathers, and in exchange came manufactured goods of copper and iron, brassware, sword blades from Spain and Germany, cloth, and . . . salt. Timbuktu became a great centre, and its University, one of the first in Africa, was so famous that scholars came to it from all over the Muslim world.

Princely Palaces and Stately Temples

[Fifteenth-century Moroccan writer] Leo Africanus tells us much about the Western Sudan at this time. He was himself a most interesting person with a remarkable history. Born a Moor, he was captured by pirates when journeying on the Mediterranean sea as a young man; and the pirates, finding that he knew a great deal about African countries which seemed very remote to most people, gave him to Pope Leo XI in Rome as a present. The Pope was much impressed with his knowledge and set him free so that he could describe his travels and record what he knew. As a special favour he also gave him his own name—Leo.

He tells us of his journey to Walata, at that time the most northerly of the Songhai possessions, and of his pleasure at meeting such friendly people. "These people are black", he says, "but most friendly unto strangers." He visited Timbuktu, and after the fine Arab architecture of the North African states, he found the buildings rather poor and mean, "cottages built of chalk and covered with thatch", but evidently the buildings which Es-Saheli put up for Mansa Musa still stood, for Leo says: ". . . there is a most stately temple still to be seen, the walls whereof are made of stone and lime; and a princely palace also built by a most excellent workman from Granada." He tells us something about the town: "Here are many shops of artificers [artisans] and merchants, and especially of such as weave linen and cotton cloth. And hither do the Barbary (North African) merchants bring the cloth of Europe. All the women of this region except maid-servants go with their faces covered, and sell all necessary victuals. The inhabitants, and especially strangers there residing, are exceeding rich, insomuch that the king that now is, married both his daughters to two rich merchants. Here are many wells containing most sweet water. . . . Corn, cattle, milk and butter this region yields in great abundance; but salt is very scarce here, for it is brought hither by land from Taghaza which is five hundred miles distant.'

King Askia's Riches

At the time of Leo's visit, Askia Mohammed and his court happened to be at Timbuktu also and received Leo in audience. He must have been dazzled by the wealth and pageantry at the court and tells us:

> The rich king of Timbuktu has many plates and sceptres of gold, some whereof weigh 1300 pounds; and he keeps a magnificent and well-furnished court. When he travels anywhere, he rides upon a camel which is led by some of his noblemen: and so he does likewise when he goes to warfare, and all his soldiers ride upon horses. . . . They often have skirmishes with those that refuse to pay tribute, and, so many as they take, they sell unto the merchants of Timbuktu. Here are very few horses bred, and the merchants and courtiers keep certain little nags (horses) which they use to travel upon; but their best horses are brought out of Barbary. . . .
>
> Here are a great store of doctors, judges, priests and other learned men, that are bountifully maintained at the king's cost and charges. And hither are brought divers manuscripts of written books out of Barbary, which are sold for more money than any other merchandise. The coin of Timbuktu is of gold without any stamp or superscription: but in matters of small value they use certain shells (cowrie shells) brought hither out of the kingdom of Persia. . . .

This was Timbuktu at the height of its prosperity, and other towns such as Jenné and Walata would have made a similar impression. After leaving Timbuktu, he travelled about the country and then came to Gao, Askia Mohammed's capital city. This was a great town, unwalled, where Leo tells us: 'The houses thereof are but mean, except those wherein the king and his courtiers remain. Here are exceeding rich merchants. . . . It is a wonder to see what plenty of merchandise is daily brought hither, and how costly and sumptuous all things be. Horses bought in Europe for ten ducats, are sold again for forty and sometimes for fifty ducats a piece. There is not any cloth of Europe so coarse, which will not be sold here. . . . A sword here is valued at three or four crowns, and so likewise are spurs and bridles with other like commodities, and spices also are sold at a high rate; but of all other commodities salt is the most extremely dear.' It is clear that Askia Mohammed was ruler of a wealthy land, which had wide contacts for trading, and which was renowned for its distinguished scholars and centres of learning.

Pilgrimage to Mecca

As soon as he assured himself of the prosperity and well-being of his kingdom, Askia Mohammed set out on a pilgrimage to Mecca, arriving in the holy city in 1497. There he gave 10,000 gold pieces as alms for the poor, and for the establishment and upkeep of a hostel for other pilgrims from the western Sudan. He also received official recognition of his position as king of the Songhai, a matter of some importance to him since . . . he was a usurper to the throne.

On his return from Mecca, he set about extending his kingdom, and subdued peoples to the west and the south, taking in all the land that had once belonged to Mali, and reaching almost to the shores of the Atlantic. Next he tackled the Hausa states to the east, which had previously been left in peace by the rulers of the great kingdoms of the Sudan.

Culture Clash in Black and White

Brian M. Fagan

For centuries, Europeans had looked to the East to the Holy Land and Constantinople for their cultural guidance. The continent of Africa, which lay to the south, was a mysterious unknown land to the average European Christian. When the explorers of Western Europe first made contact with the black natives of Africa in the fifteenth century, a chasm of misunderstanding that lay between the two races erupted into a clash of cultures that would last for centuries.

Brian M. Fagan is a professor of anthropology at the University of California, Santa Barbara, who has written several books on anthropology.

Western Europe was born three thousand years ago. For millennia it had been a geographical outpost of Asia, on the fringes of civilizations and empires based on the Near East and Mediterranean lands. Twenty-five centuries ago it became a western peninsula with a consciousness and identity all its own. This consciousness was born of Greek civilization . . . and matured still further in later European victories against the Huns, Turks, and Moors. Europe faced eastwards, its intellectual and political frontiers terminating at . . . Constantinople (Byzantium). The philosophies and thoughts of the Greeks had spread from the Mediterranean deep into Western Europe, creating a European spirit that was opposed to Asia, but looked towards it. Part of this philosophy was [Greek philosopher] Aristotle's famous notion that the world was divided into Greeks and barbarians, those people who were by nature free, and those who were destined to be slaves.

Excerpted from Brian M. Fagan, *Clash of Cultures.* Copyright © 1984 W.H. Freeman and Company. Reprinted with permission from the author.

This attitude towards other societies was one of the forces that gave Europeans a curious ambivalence about the outside world. One part of their psychology filled them with a sense of hostility and rejection towards foreigners, and a need to protect themselves against intruders. Yet at the same time, Judeo-Christian doctrines taught that one should love one's neighbor—even one's enemy—as oneself. In time, the same Christian teachings encouraged a deep sense that the individual was as important as the state, and fostered leanings towards justice and equality that were ultimately to revolutionize Europe's relationships to its non-Western neighbors. An increasing sense of individualism and adventure bred an intense curiosity about the outside world. What peoples lived south of the endless wastes of the Sahara Desert? Were there distant lands beyond the boundless horizons of the western ocean?

As late as the fourteenth century, the European world was a relatively small and familiar place, bounded by the shores of the Mediterranean, limited by the eastern steppes [of Russia] and the unknown Sahara, by the limitless wastes of the Atlantic to the west. . . .

Paradise Beyond the Horizon

For most Europeans, the center of the medieval world was thought to be Jerusalem, the biblical city of the Holy Land set "in the midst of the nations and countries that are round about." The unknown lay without, a teeming wilderness of land and water peopled by giants, monstrous birds and fierce sea serpents.

For centuries, long before classical times, people had looked back over the tumultuous millennia of history with nostalgia towards a Golden Age, to a mythical past when the earth gave of its plenty and everyone lived lives of ease and luxury. A deeply felt belief that all humanity had fallen from grace in the Garden of Eden permeated European consciousness. The angel with the flaming sword who guarded the gates of the garden shut the door of paradise to a civilization condemned to live with the knowledge of its fall from grace. This sense of degeneration was to dominate Western thinking until the sixteenth century and beyond. It also fuelled an intense curiosity about the world beyond. Had all humanity suffered in the Fall? Were there still people living in a natural state, untrammeled by the burdens of civilization? Was paradise still to be found on earth?

At first the notion of paradise had no founding in contemporary reality, lying only in the teachings of Christianity and the past. But the Crusades and the travels of the Venetian Marco Polo and his ilk had drawn up the curtain on a dazzling and tantalizing world all around, a world of gold and jewels, of rich spices and dazzling fabrics. As Europe's horizons widened, a new myth was born—that of paradise on earth. One prime candidate was Ethiopia, the strange African land where the Nile had risen, the blessed kingdom of the elusive King Prester John, who ruled from East Africa to the Indus. Thus, paradise was thought to lie in the east, perhaps between the Nile and the Indus, the Tigris and the Euphrates (Genesis 2:11–15). One of the principal aims of Portuguese exploration of the West African coast was to open a channel of communication with Prester John. So pervasive was the belief in this paradisial kingdom that Vasco da Gama, who opened the route to India [in 1498], actually carried letters from the king of Portugal to the fabled monarch.

New and Unsettling Worlds

The Age of Discovery dawned in [the second decade of] the fifteenth century, when Prince Henry the Navigator of Portugal and other monarchs of his age were motivated to exploration. For the most part their motives were commercial and political—to find spices and new markets, to search for fresh allies against the forces of Islam. They had high-minded motives, too—to perform great deeds for the glory of God and a profound wish to propagate the Faith. But however practical their motives, they were also moved by an irrational, psychological urge to make great discoveries, to find places known in myth and legend.

By the middle of the sixteenth century, European seamen had sailed most of the great oceans of the world in search of these golden lands. As the Portuguese voyaged southwards around Africa and eastwards towards Asia and the Spaniards explored the New World, they discovered a new and unsettling world, a world densely settled not with godlike, paradisial beings, but with a new and confusingly diverse heathen humanity engaged in "dayly tumultes, fears, doubts, suspitions, and barbarous cruelties." The ethnocentric teachings of Aristotle and others cast most of these peoples in bestial modes as people without civilization, social order, or religion. A few societies, like the West African kingdoms, were described as orderly; "Monarchical, living under Laws, Order, and Princes," wrote John Ogilby in his *Africa*. The remainder were "sway'd on all occasions like tumultuous Herds, and at other times like tame Cattel feeding, and following their idle pleasures." These were far from paradisial images, but descriptions penned out of ignorance, superstition, and a widespread belief that most savages were little more than beasts. These were the "bad savages," the counterpoint to the magnificent human societies that still flourished beyond human ken. It was only in later centuries that the tendency to equate the primitive with the bestial gave way to more humanitarian viewpoints that saw non-Westerners as childlike human beings, but at least human.

The Myth of the Noble Savage

It was from these early discoveries that the diverse Western images of savages and barbarism were forged. Eventually it became clear that Prester John was a fable, and that paradise did not exist on earth.

So the quest for paradise became a search for a utopian kingdom where people were still high-minded and filled with brotherly love. Slowly, the Golden Age turned from a nebulous dream into a detailed, idealistic image of a society where primitive children of nature inhabited a heavenlike country beyond the seas. The explorer no longer searched for paradise, but for utopia, for a nostalgic place where the pressures of Western civilization could be forgotten.

The myths of paradise and utopia, of lands of gold, were to persist for centuries, part of the elaborate tapestry of fables and idealistic stereotypes that were to evolve into tales of the [idealized] Indian braves and dusky maidens so beloved of nineteenth-century American novelists. Such myths were fabricated at home, far from the remote shores and islands where explorers confronted hostile tribes and ravaged local villages for gold and slaves. All that was needed was for a few romantic, imaginative travelers to return home, and rumors were born—of lands rich in gold, of great kings, cannibals, and vast, rich cities, of people living simple lives untrammeled by the degenerate cares of Western civilization. The myth of the noble savage was born, which was to color European thinking about the non-Western world right up to [the twentieth] century.

For five centuries, Westerners have looked at non-Europeans with a curious ambivalence. Philosophers extolled the virtues of primitive children of nature living in a perfect state of happiness only twenty days' sailing from Europe. This was the world of myth and illusion, the realm of the conquistador, the sea captain, and the missionary; that of harsh reality—massacres, land grabbing, forced conversion, and forced labor. There was always a duality about the non-Western world: on the one hand it was a physical world that could be of practical use, on the other an ideal, nostalgic world where Europeans could project their idealism, vent their dissatisfactions, and dream of unattainable paradise. This outside world was to remain infinitely variable, ever susceptible to different interpretation, the victim of our ever-changing, ever-convoluted thought about other societies.

First Contact

The realities of the outside world first struck home at the very beginning of the Age of Discovery, when Europeans first sailed around the west coast of Africa. During the 1420s and 1430s, Henry the Navigator, prince of Portugal, organized annual voyages southwards from Europe deep into tropical latitudes. His captains claimed [islands known as] the Azores, Madeira, and the Canaries. They coasted down the west coast of Africa and rounded the great western bulge in 1433. The rich gold and ivory markets of tropical Africa were opened up to commercial enterprise. The same adventurous voyages brought Europeans into their first direct contact with tropical Africans, not only with the relatively sophisticated West African kingdoms of what are now Ghana and Nigeria, but with people who were "all Blacke, and are called Negroes, without any apparell, saving before their privities." They also encountered the Khoikhoi, the notorious "Hottentots" of the Cape of Good Hope, who were to become the very epitome of everything that was savage, evil, and primitive. The Khoikhoi were soon classified as evil savages, having little in common with the rest of humankind.

The untutored seamen who frequented quayside taverns embellished the practical realities of Africa with tales of cannibalism and the fantastic, of mysterious apelike creatures, and of "libidinous" [sexually active] blacks. The Portuguese and Spanish had been in close contact with North Africa for centuries. The impact of the black people of the southern tropics was perhaps less powerful in their minds than in that of northerners and particularly Englishmen. Yet many chroniclers marveled at the astounding diversity of skin colors in Africa and the New World. "One of the marveylous thynges that god useth in the composition of man, is colour: whiche doubtlesse can not bee consydered withowte great admiration in beholding one to be white and an other blacke, being coloures utterly contrary," wrote one Spanish observer in 1555. One thing was clear: the Africans were no paradisial "Ethiopians," but an alien people of a color that was repulsive in European eyes. . . .

Continent of Mystery

Blackness did not necessarily make the Africans repulsive savages, but it did make them the object of intense curiosity. How had they acquired their black color? Was it because of the torrid African climate? . . . The Africans' black skins started off as a scientific mystery. It was only later, in the days of the slave trade, that it became a social fact. But from the very beginning the Africans' black skins set them apart as people from a distant, pagan continent. And their apparent lack of religion isolated them from the mainstream of Christian civilization. Some English writers went as far as to link their paganism with savagery and blackness. They were, wrote one observer, "A people of beastly living, without a God, lawe, religion, or common wealth."

The Africans were set apart not only by their color, but by their entire way of life and morality, which differed dramatically from that of Europeans. They were discovered at a time when Europeans had an insatiable interest in the wonderful and the exotic, in the adventurous and often miraculous world that lay beyond the Mediterranean and the Western Ocean. African savagery was not so much an issue (as it was to become at the height of the slave trade) as an observed and accepted fact that set blacks apart as radically different kinds of people. They were frequently described as "brutish," "bestial," or "beastly." Pages and pages of early travelers' tales abound with stories of cannibalism, warfare, horrible diets, and dreadful tortures. Perhaps this is hardly surprising, for Africa was a continent of mystery, teeming with savage beasts and exotic monsters. . . .

The virtual avalanche of geographical discoveries during the fifteenth and sixteenth centuries not only transformed the known world, but led scholarship in new directions. Increasingly, scholars turned away from a preoccupation with their own salvation towards a curiosity about the outside world and about human diversity. As time went on, the physical differences between people assumed heightened significance. How was one to create order out of human diversity? How had humanity risen above bestiality? Were there lesser orders of humans below the Westerner? The question was to fascinate European thinkers for centuries.

Da Gama Navigates to India

Gaspar Correa

After a long and treacherous journey around the tip of southern Africa, Vasco da Gama finally managed to reach the city of Calicut, on India's Malabar coast, on May 20, 1498. Da Gama and his crew waited aboard their ship until the local ruler, Zamorin, welcomed the Portuguese. Although da Gama was unable to sign a treaty or commercial agreement with the Indians, he returned to his homeland with a load of valuable spices.

The following account of da Gama's arrival in Calicut was written by Portuguese author Gaspar Correa, who first traveled to India in 1514 when he was very young. Correa later obtained a diary written by Joam Figueira, a priest who accompanied da Gama on his first voyage to India. Sometime around 1561, Correa wrote a history of da Gama's exploits in India. At the author's request, the work was not published until after his death. The book was not widely circulated until 1790 but today is considered one of the most accurate descriptions of da Gama's voyages to India.

The ships continued running along the coast close to land, for the coast was clear, without banks against which to take precautions; and the pilots gave orders to cast anchor in a place which made a sort of bay, because there commenced the city of Calicut. This town is named Capocate [located six miles from Calicut], and on anchoring there a multitude of people flocked to the beach, all dark and naked, only covered with cloths half way down the thigh, with which they concealed their nakedness. All were much amazed at seeing what they

Excerpted from Gaspar Correa, *The Three Voyages of Vasco da Gama and His Viceroyalty* (New York: Burt Franklin, 1969). Reprinted with permission from The Hakluyt Society.

had never before seen. When news was taken to the King he also came
to look at the ships, for all the wonder was at seeing so many ropes
and so many sails, and because the ships arrived when the sun was almost set; and at night they lowered out the boats, and Vasco da Gama
went at once for his brother [Paula da Gama] and Nicolas Coelho, and
they remained together conversing upon the method of dealing with
this King. . . .

Meeting of the Cultures

The next day at dawn a great many skiffs came out with fishing nets,
passing near the ships, and Vasco da Gama told the Moorish pilots to
call the fishermen to sell some fish, since they knew the language of
the country. When they heard themselves called by the pilots they
came at once and entered the ship, and gave a quantity of fish like sardines, which they called *canalinhas*, and they gave a great many for a
vintin [silver coin], which they bit with their teeth to see if it was silver. Vasco da Gama told the pilots to say, if the fishermen asked, that
they came from Melinde, and had arrived there parted company, and
were going in search of other ships of their company which they
thought they might find there. When the fishermen returned on shore
many people asked questions of them, as they had seen them go on
board the ship. They related what had been said to them, and shewed
the coin which had been given them for the fish. All this was related
to the King, who waited for our people to send [go] to him. The King
was very desirous that the Portuguese should send on shore, and he
ordered the fishermen to go to the ships to sell their fish, or anything
they liked, and to inquire about everything. This they did, and brought
many fowls, figs, and cocoa-nuts, and there came many of them.
Vasco da Gama ordered that no one should buy except the pilots and
Moors, whom he ordered to pay according to the will of the owners,
and to offend them in nothing. . . . The Moor and the pilots said to the
captain-major, that he should send on shore; he replied, that he should
not land in a foreign country without leave from its owner, as he had
acted in Melinde. At this conjuncture there came a boat full of wood
to sell; and as there was much wood in the ship they did not take it,
and as they were going away the captain-major ordered them to be
called, and there were six men came in the boat, and he ordered a
vintin to be given to each man, and that they might go their way, as
there was no need of the wood. The Moor asked why he gave them
money, since they did not take the wood. And the captain-major
replied, "They are poor men and come to sell their wood, and as it was
not bought they were going away discontented, and on that account
he had ordered money to be given them, that their labour might not
have been in vain; for he was thus accustomed to pay well all those
who did good to him." At this the Moor and the pilots were surprised;

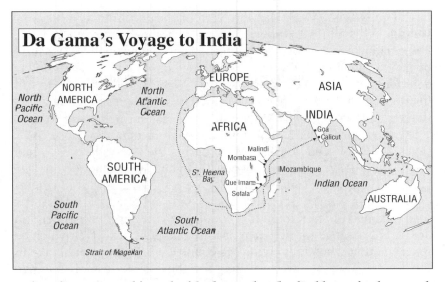

Da Gama's Voyage to India

and so they repeated it to the black people who had brought the wood, so that they went ashore very much pleased, and related this as a great wonder. It was at once told to the King, who, in talking with his own people, vaunted much the liberality and goodness of the Portuguese; on the King's questioning the fishermen about everything, they told him all that they had heard from the pilots, and that they did not venture to come out on shore because they had not got the King's leave to do so, and that they came from Melinde, and were going about lost in search of their company, which they had expected to find here; and as they had not found them they were intending to go away.

Sending a Message to the King

Thus things remained for three days; and as the fishermen, who came back again, said that they had related everything to the King; and as the captain-major saw that the King sent no message, he asked the Moor his opinion of what they ought to do, because they did not know the customs of these people. The Moor told him that he ought to send a message to the King and say what he wanted. This seemed good, and the Moor was ordered to get ready to go on shore; and at this time there came from the shore a large boat in which there was a servant of the King, a gentleman of birth, whom they call Nair: he came without clothes, except a white cloth which covered him from the middle to half the thighs; he had a very thin round shield, with slings of wood and vermilion, which glittered very much, and a naked sword with an iron hilt: the sword was short, of an ell's length [27 inches], and broad at the point; his hair was pressed down upon his head; he was a very dark man, and very well made. On reaching the side of the ship, without coming on board, he asked for the captain; and the captain-major answered him that he was the person he wanted; that he was the captain. The Nair then said that the King had sent him to say that they should send word who they were, and what they wanted in his port. The captain-major answered that he had not sent his message because he had not yet had the King's leave to do so, but now that he had ordered it he would do so. Then the Moor went with the Nair with full instructions as to what he was to say. The King, on seeing the messenger, and that he was a Moor, imagined that our men were so also. The Moor said to the King, "Sire, the captain-major of those ships says: 'I did not send you a message during these days because I had not got your leave to do so;' but now that you have sent it by your servant, he has sent me, and he says that he is the [servant] of the greatest Christian King in the world; who had sent a fleet of fifty ships which he had ordered to go to a country to take cargo of pepper and drugs, in exchange for rich merchandise and gold and silver which he sent; and that when they found the country where they could take in the cargo which they were seeking for, they should establish a firm peace and good relations with the king of it, which should last for ever; and he was the ambassador who was to go on shore, because the captain-major would not leave the ship to go ashore. And after their setting out on their voyage a storm at sea had separated them from the rest of the fleet, and they knew nothing of it and had been going about to many places for two years like lost people; and they had been to Melinde, where there is a very noble king to whom they had related this fortune of theirs. As he had taken compassion upon them, he had said that he would give them pilots who would bring them to the country where the pepper grew, and there were many drugs, for which we thanked him very much; and the pilots brought us here where we now are; and we have come with great hopes that since in this city of yours there are pepper and drugs, we should fall in with our fleet; and since we have not found it we are sorrowful, for we do not know what we are to do; and this is the reason of our coming and what we seek." When the King heard all this message he was much surprised; and in talking of it with his own people, he said that it would be well, since our people had put into port, to know what merchandise they wished to buy, and what merchandise they had brought to sell? . . .

Establishing Peace and Friendship

The King felt a great longing to obtain as much from our people . . . [and] as to the cargo which he was going in search of, he would fill his ships with as much pepper and drugs as they wished for, and would give him on payment whatever there was in the city; and in the meantime they might do what they pleased. The King also sent the Moor in a boat with many figs, fowls, and cocoa-nuts fresh and dry. The good brothers were much pleased on hearing the King's message, and gave great praise to the Lord. Having taken counsel together, they sent many thanks to the King for his reply, and for the refreshments, and said that they accepted it out of courtesy, but that they could neither accept, nor buy, nor sell anything without first establishing peace and friendship; because if they did not first make that agreement they could do nothing, for such were the regulations received from their King, and if they did not act in that manner he would order their heads to be cut off: for that reason they would do nothing and would return thence if they did not first establish peace, for their King did not wish to trade except with his friends.

Christopher Columbus: Admiral of the Ocean Sea

Desmond Wilcox

For decades, Italian-born explorer Christopher Columbus dreamed of finding an ocean route to India by sailing west. He took the plans for the voyage to kings and queens across Europe, hoping for monetary backing, but received only ridicule and scorn. He was finally given ships and supplies by the king and queen of Spain.

Columbus seriously miscalculated the circumference of the earth and believed that he could easily reach India in a matter of weeks. The Italian explorer was the first known European to voyage to the Americas, landing in modern-day Hispaniola. During his lifetime, however, Columbus continued to believe that he was near India and had no idea he was on an entirely different continent.

Desmond Wilcox is the head of BBC Television's general features department in England and a former reporter and foreign correspondent for the *Daily Mirror*.

He was born in Genoa in 1451, the son of a weaver. We know him as Christopher Columbus, though it wasn't the name he later gave himself. His early years are obscure. According to his son, Ferdinand, he studied astronomy, geometry and cosmography at the University of Pavia. According to his own account, he went to sea when he was 14. Certainly in his early 20s he was sailing the Mediterranean, and

Excerpted from Desmond Wilcox, *Explorers*. Copyright © 1975 Desmond Wilcox. Reprinted with permission from BBC Worldwide Limited.

at 25 he was aboard a Genoese ship when she was attacked and sunk off Cape St. Vincent by the Franco-Portuguese fleet. He was fortunate to escape drowning. He reached the Portuguese mainland and settled in Lisbon.

At the time, Lisbon was the center of a large colony of Genoese merchants and seamen. Its cosmopolitan atmosphere suited Columbus. In 1477, he joined a voyage to the north, visiting Bristol [England] and possibly Ireland and Iceland. It might well have been this voyage and what he learned on it that helped to crystallize the ideas that had been forming in his mind.

Ambition began to press him. He had the drive for power, riches and status that characterized [explorer Francisco] Pizarro and so many other Renaissance Europeans. He set up a map-making business in the Portuguese capital with Bartholomew, a brother ten years his junior.

Then, at the age of 28, he married. It was a surprising match, giving him a taste of that status he craved. He was an attractive young man, tall, blond and blue-eyed, and with his drive and sense of purpose any young woman might have been taken by him. Nevertheless, he was hardly in the same social stratum as Felipa Perestrella de Moniz. Her father had been governor of Porto Santo, one of the Portuguese possessions in the Atlantic, and her family had connections with Prince Henry the Navigator. Yet she married him, despite his background, and introduced him to a world of ideas and culture which he found, greatly to his taste. A year later she gave him a son, Diego.

Seeking Gold and Glory

The marriage served as yet another spur to his ambition. He wanted not the modest wealth he might have earned from map-making, but great riches. Two voyages to West Africa had shown him that gold could be had for the taking—if one knew where to look for it. He conceived the idea that since it existed in Africa it must exist elsewhere in tropical climates. Marco Polo, years before, had written about the vast wealth of the east. He had painted a lavish picture of Cathay, the land known to us as China. Marco Polo had talked of Japan—Cipangu, he called it—as an island of silks, spices, ivories, gems and golden temples.

But the talk among the most ambitious of the merchants and seafarers in Lisbon wasn't of Africa or the east. The east was owned by the [Mongol ruler the] Grand Khan. The voyage there was long and difficult. Africa, what was known of it, was already largely under the control of Portugal. What the visionaries talked of lay to the west, beyond the vast Atlantic. Despite the popular belief of the day, most mariners had little doubt that the earth was round, not flat. The classical geographers had also believed that there was only a short ocean distance between Spain and India. Between them, to the west, there might be unknown lands full of gold and treasure beyond imagination. If not, they calculated a voyage would establish a direct sea route to the eastern seaboards of Cipangu and Cathay and the spice islands of the Indies.

The idea caught the imagination of Columbus. And there was another aspect to it now. Besides gold, he sought glory. If he sailed westwards and discovered new lands, if he penetrated the great empire of the Khan, he could carry with him the gospel of Christ and convert millions of heathen to the one true religion. Where Pizarro was later in history to see himself as a conqueror, who had made a business arrangement with the state, Columbus saw himself as the very instrument of God. He wrote later: "In the New Heaven and Earth which our Lord made He made me Cristoval Colon [Christopher Columbus] the messenger and showed me where to go."

Wrongly Measuring the Miles

He began to prepare for the enterprise. He read widely and made a particular study of geography. He needed a sponsor, and the sponsor would require facts and convincing arguments before he would provide the ships and stores that Columbus required.

Sixteen hundred years earlier, Eratosthenes had made a very accurate calculation of the size of the earth. Since then, cosmographers had gradually reduced that size. Medieval map-makers had gone even further, pulling the eastern extremity of Asia increasingly to the west. It seemed to Columbus that contemporary map-makers bore out his growing belief that the way to the riches of the Indies lay to the west. His own calculations not only confirmed this, but showed the route to be very much shorter than anyone had dreamed. On one of his voyages to West Africa he estimated that a degree of longitude was 45 2/3 miles. Using that figure as the basis of his calculations, he concluded that Japan lay just beyond the Azores. The discovery was immensely exciting. It was also immensely inaccurate. He calculated that Japan lay a mere 2,400 nautical miles west of the Canaries, and China no more than 3,550. In fact the distances are 10,600 and 11,766 respectively.

At this time, Columbus' wife, Felipa, died and left him with a young son to bring up. He took it calmly. It made little difference to his plans. The dream of "gold, God and Cathay" dominated his mind. All his efforts were directed to making it a reality. He managed to examine the correspondence of Paola da Toscanelli, a Florentine scientist who had approached King Alfonso V of Portugal with a similar project 25 years earlier. He saw a copy of the map that Toscanelli had made. It tallied very much with his own view of the world. His study of Toscanelli simply reinforced the vision that Columbus already had. He put his project to Alfonso's successor, King John II of Portugal. It was rejected by a committee of experts. Quite simply, they couldn't accept Columbus' estimate of the distance to the Indies by the western route he proposed. More importantly, King John was committed to the idea of the route via the Cape [of Good Hope in Africa].

But Columbus had the kind of personality that is stiffened by rejection. His determination to mount an expedition that would reach the Indies from the west grew stronger. His conviction that Cathay lay at the far side of the Atlantic became unshakable. If King John's committee had doubts about his calculations, they were fools. He turned from Portugal to Spain.

Frustrated and Ridiculed

It wasn't easy. From 1485 to 1489, Columbus spent his time building influential friendships, sounding court opinion, finding individual backers. He took a mistress, Beatriz Enriquez, who bore him a son, Ferdinand. He sent his brother Bartholomew to sound out the French and English courts, but the young man had no success.

Increasingly Columbus was becoming the butt of court ridicule. "From the age of 28, I served in the enterprise and conquest of the said Indies," he wrote. He was now 38. For ten years he had peddled his scheme in all the centers of European influence, without success.

Then in 1489, the sovereigns of Spain, Ferdinand and Isabella, agreed to see him. Again his hopes rose. Again they were shattered. Their Majesties wouldn't—couldn't—support him. The Moors in Granada were being crushed. It was an expensive business. Even if the sovereigns had wished to back him, there was no money to spare for him.

For Columbus it was another setback. But it wasn't the end. His single-mindedness became little less than obsession. The more his vision of the Indies grew and strengthened, the more he was frustrated and ridiculed.

Actually, Isabella liked the scheme. In particular she liked the missionary aspect that Columbus had taken care to stress. It would give her great satisfaction to think that, through her, millions had been saved from darkness—shepherded into the bosom of the true church. She didn't forget. In 1492, when the last stronghold of Islam had been crushed in Granada, Columbus was recalled to court. Ferdinand and Isabella agreed that a small expedition of three ships could sail west in search of the Indies.

But the terms Columbus wanted for himself were unacceptable. He asked for the hereditary title of Admiral of the Ocean Seas. He wanted to be made Viceroy and Governor-General of all territories he claimed in their Majesties' names. He wanted a tenth of the profits from the ex-

Standing before the Royal Court of Spain, Christopher Columbus explains his plan for reaching the Indies.

pedition, and to be a major investor in any subsequent expeditions. It was too much. Columbus was adamant. He hadn't waited 13 years to give way now. Reluctantly, the sovereigns withdrew their offer.

The Queen Supports Columbus

Columbus knew he was right, though it didn't take the edge off his disappointment. It began to seem that the whole thing was going to remain a dream for ever. Then suddenly the Queen's confidante told him that Isabella had changed her mind. She and Ferdinand would accept all his conditions. He couldn't believe that it had finally happened, after the long years of ridicule and disappointment. He could only conclude that God himself had interceded on his servant's behalf. He wrote:

"When there was incredulity among all men, He gave the Queen, my Lady, the spirit of understanding and great courage. I went to take possession of the New World in her Royal Name. The rest of them sought to cover their ignorance, concealing their small knowledge by harping upon obstacles and the expense. But Her Highness on the contrary approved the Enterprise and supported it the best she could."

By April 17, the agreement between the sovereigns and Columbus had been completed and signed. His terms were accepted. He was given a letter of introduction from the Spanish court to the Grand Khan of Cathay. By the middle of May he was in Palos, near Cadiz, awaiting the arrival of the ships and stores. The town was to provide two of the vessels in payment of a debt it owed the Crown.

Columbus carried a letter addressed to one of the town dignitaries, Diego Rodriguez Prieto, from Ferdinand and Isabella:

"Know ye that whereas for certain things done and committed by you to our disservice you were condemned and obligated by our Council to provide us for a twelve-month with two equipped caravels at your own proper charge and expense . . . we command that within 10 days of receiving this our letter . . . you have all ready . . . to depart."

Ships and Supplies

Ten days was to prove far too optimistic as an estimate of the amount of time necessary to provide the vessels. In the end, it took 10 weeks. The time wasn't wasted. There was a great deal for Columbus to do. A third ship had to be found, lists of stores [supplies] and equipment drawn up and assembled, a crew sworn in. The Crown, now that the decision to mount an expedition had been taken, was unstinting in putting its whole authority behind the enterprise. Apart from the letter to the town of Palos, three other royal letters were issued. They instructed all timber merchants, carpenters, ship's chandlers, bakers and provision merchants in Andalusia [Spain] to provide Columbus with everything he needed at reasonable prices. The articles he bought were to be free from local taxes. In addition, if anyone who agreed to sail with Columbus had a civil or criminal action pending against him, such action was to be suspended.

The two ships eventually provided by Palos were caravels, a type of vessel that had already been used for the successful exploration of the West African coast. Their names were *Pinta* and *Niña*. They were single-decked craft with a low forecastle for stowage of cables and sails. The raised quarter-deck had a toldilla on it, a construction that housed the captain's and master's cabins. Caravels drew about six feet of water and had a hold some nine feet deep. The overall length was 70 feet and the beam a little over 20.

The third ship, when she arrived, was a disappointment to Columbus. Her name was *Santa Maria*, and she was a [slow, heavy ship called a] não. He had asked for three caravels. Instead for his flagship, he had to make do with this heavier, slower, more rounded vessel, rarely seen outside the Mediterranean. She drew no more water than the caravels, though she weighed almost 90 tons against their 60. The one thing in her favor was the great size of her hold.

Setting Sail

The fleet left Palos on August 3, 1492. There was modest rejoicing at the departure, though Palos itself was in a state of some confusion: Spain had decided to expel its Jewish population [only days before] and the quayside was full of wretched emigrants.

The *Santa Maria* turned southwesterly and began to run down the African coast, the *Niña* and *Pinta* holding station behind her.

Despite the support that Ferdinand and Isabella had given Columbus, their actual financial involvement in the expedition was slight. Most of the funds came from friends of Columbus at court and from Genoese financiers operating in Spain. Additionally, many of the men on board the three ships had investments in the enterprise. The three owners of the ships were present, Juan de La Cosa of the *Santa Maria*, Cristobal Quintero of the *Pinta* and Juan Nino of the *Niña*. La Cosa and Nino were also masters of their vessels. . . .

Spirits were high. The voyage so far had gone almost exactly to plan. The intention now was to turn westwards into the open Atlantic, in the hope of picking up a favorable northeast trade wind that would carry them all the way to Cathay. In the meantime there were last-minute repairs and adjustments to be carried out, and the final load of stores to be taken aboard. It was vital to carry all the provisions necessary to meet every eventuality.

It was usual at that time to carry fresh meat, in the form of live pigs and chickens, in pens and coops on deck. The rest of the food was carried in barrels. There was salted meat and sardines, flour, rice and biscuits, chick-peas, lentils, beans, almonds, raisins, honey, cheese and vinegar. Wine and water were carried in casks, olive oil in great earthenware jars.

A ship at sea, in the midst of an unknown ocean, had to be totally self-sufficient. If planks were sprung in a storm they had to be replaced or repaired. If sails ripped or rotted, there had to be stores from which new ones could be made, and sailmakers to make them. Apart from food and drink, stores had to include wood, bolts, nails, pitch, whale oil, tallow and sulphur. There had to be supplies of sailcloth, yarn, ropes, cord, and sheets of copper and iron, together with the tools for using them.

Apart from Columbus' own inspired, but totally inaccurate calculations, there was no way of knowing how long the journey west might take, nor what strange monsters or human enemies might be met with on the way. No one aboard seriously thought they might sail off the edge of the earth and fall into the bottomless pit. But there were few without some lingering fear of running into seas of boiling water, or coming face to face with three-legged men and one-eyed fiends [as spelled out in the legends of the day].

Each ship was armed. There were iron cannon and falconets [small cannon]. The cannon were mounted on wooden carriages with wheels, and fired through ports in the ships' sides. They weighed half a ton each and could throw a four-pound stone ball up to 1,000 yards. The falconets were mounted on the bulwarks [vessel sides] on swivels. They had a caliber of a little under two inches, and were more usually loaded with pieces of scrap iron than with ball. In case of a boarding attempt, the artillery could be backed up by arquebuses [muskets] carried by some of the crew.

The armament required its own specialist stores. There were stone balls for the cannon, scrap for the falconets and barrels of powder. There were wadding and matches for the artillery and arquebuses, bolts for the crossbows, arrows for the bows. Bucklers, swords and lances had to be carried for use by the crew.

The range of additional stores necessary to make the expedition self-sufficient was enormous. There were copper cauldrons, three-legged iron cooking pots, copper ladles, measuring vessels, bowls, candles and snuffers, lamps and oil and wicks to go with them. There was tinder and firewood for the cooking stove, and steel and flint to fire it. There were boat-hooks, sweeps, wooden buckets and tubs, mats, baskets, fish hooks, lines, sinkers, nets and harpoons. For disciplinary problems, there were manacles and leg irons, and for trading with the subjects of the Great Khan there were brass hawks' bells, tambourines and strings of colored glass beads. Each ship was a microcosm of late 15th Century Spain.

Proceed or Return?

On September 6, the fleet left the Canaries. Three days later, land finally disappeared from view. The weather remained calm, the sea was a magnificent greenish blue, full of leaping flying fish. The men worked together well enough, but even then Columbus could sense an underlying discord. He wrote in his journal: "I decided at this point to reckon less [mileage] than I made, so that if the voyage were a long one the people would not be frightened and dismayed." He was making, in fact, an average of 110 miles a day. . . .

On the 25th, Martin Alonso Pinzon rushed to the poop [deck] of the *Pinta* and shouted across to the *Santa Maria* and the *Niña*, "Tierra, Tierra!" He claimed the reward offered by the sovereigns to the first man who sighted land—an annuity of 10,000 maravedis, equal to ten months of an able seaman's pay. But investigation showed nothing. On October 7, it was Vincente Yanez Pinzon's turn to raise a flag at *Niña*'s masthead. Land, he declared, lay dead ahead. Once more, it was a false alarm.

On the 10th, mutiny broke out on the *Santa Maria*. The men refused to go any farther. "I calculate landfall at Cathay at any hour," said Columbus. "But the men fear we have sailed too far south and missed Asia altogether." There were disagreements between Columbus and the Pinzon brothers as to whether they should proceed or return. Columbus promised the crews that if the Indies weren't sighted within the next two or three days he would turn back. In his journal there is no hint of a compromise: "I will continue until I find them," he wrote. . . .

Then, at 2 A.M. on Friday, October 12, 1492, Rodrigo de Triana, lookout on the *Pinta*'s forecastle, saw the New World.

Columbus had covered 3,066 miles in 33 days. As far as he was concerned, the island that lay revealed ahead of them when the sun rose was part of the Great Khan's Cathay. It was a view he held until his death. He landed that same afternoon, dressed in his scarlet doublet and carrying the royal standard. Once on the beach, with inhabitants watching from the shelter of palm groves, he knelt and prayed:

"O Lord, Almighty and Everlasting God, Thou hast created the Heaven and the Earth, and the Sea, blessed and glorified by Thy Name, and praised be Thy Majesty which hath used Thy Humble servants, that Thy Holy Name may be proclaimed in this second part of the Earth."

Looking for Khan

Columbus named the place San Salvador and claimed it in the name of Spain. Then he turned to the task of finding the court of the Great Khan. He had with him a "converso," a converted Jew by the name of Luis de Torres. De Torres spoke Hebrew and Arabic and was to act as interpreter for the expedition. It was believed that through one or other of the two languages, de Torres would be able to communicate with the Khan's representatives.

De Torres called to the natives in Arabic, then Hebrew. The Indians—Arawaks of the Taino tribe—came forward tentatively, showing curiosity and no sign of aggression. Neither did they show any understanding of what de Torres was saying. Columbus gave them trinkets, "so that these people might be well disposed toward us—to be delivered and converted to our Holy Faith by love rather than by force.". . .

Columbus concluded that he had landed on one of the islands in the archipelago that was thought to lie east of Japan. It was understandable that the Indians there should be so poor. Many that he saw bore the scars of battle, yet none seemed warlike. The most reasonable explanation to Columbus was that the Khan's warriors made periodic raids, stole the Indians' gold and took them away as slaves. . . .

There were just enough signs of gold in San Salvador to whet the expedition's appetite. A Taino with a gold ornament in his nose pointed southwards when he was questioned about it. It simply confirmed what Columbus was already thinking. The mainland, with the vast treasure houses, lay in that direction. Taino guides agreed to show him the way. He wrote to his king and queen:

"I here propose to leave to circumnavigate this island until I may have speech with this King and see if I can obtain from him the gold that I heard he has, and afterwards to depart for another much larger island which I believe must be Japan according to the description of these Indians whom I carry, and which they call Colba, in which they say that there are ships and sailors both many and great; and beyond this is another island which they call Bofio, which also they say is very big; and the others which are between we shall see we pass, and according as I shall find a collection of gold or spicery, I shall decide what I have to do. But in any case I am determined to go to the mainland and to the city of Quinsay, and to present your Highnesses' letters to the Grand Khan, and to beg a reply and come home with it."

Colba turned out to be Cuba, not Japan, though Columbus was never aware of it. He dropped anchor in the large bay of Puerto Gibara, which he called Rio de Mares, at the end of October. The pressure on him to find gold was increasing. The Pinzons in particular were becoming restive. They had travelled 3,000 miles to see the fabled city of Quinsay, which Marco Polo had described as being built of gold. So far they had seen nothing but empty beaches and naked Indians. . . .

Bitter Disappointment

Cuba was beautiful. "I never beheld so fair a thing," said Columbus. Yet still there was no gold. He wondered how much further he had to go to find the treasures Marco Polo had seen. The men had become troublesome, accusing him of having misled them. For a moment he had a vision of himself returning to Spain empty-handed. It was unthinkable. Then he heard the words he had been waiting for so long. A naked Taino was standing before him and pointing south. He was saying "Cubanacan"; it was the name of an inland village. Columbus mistook the words for "El Gran Khan."

An expedition was mounted at once. De Torres collected his impressive credentials bearing the signatures of the sovereigns of Spain. He was to "carry gifts and letters of credence from your Highnesses to the mighty Emperor of that city where seven palaces are roofed entirely with gold." The prospect filled de Torres with apprehension. He expected a scene of such monumental magnificence that he wondered if he could handle it.

Cubanacan turned out to be a bitter disappointment. It was a village of 50 thatched huts, a few large and rectangular, most small and circular. The inhabitants, Taino Indians, were little more than subsistence farmers, living on manioc, corn and potatoes and smoking rolled tobacco through their nostrils. De Torres couldn't make himself understood in either Arabic or Hebrew. The few trinkets of gold that the Tainos wore hardly matched Marco Polo's description of Cathay. Taino Caciques, the provincial ruler, was kind and courteous to the visitors; his subjects kissed their hands and feet, believing them to have come from heaven. But the conquerors from Andalusia had expected gold. Obeisance was not a satisfactory substitute. . . .

Returning to Spain

Columbus left Hispaniola in the *Niña* on the morning of January 16, 1493, for Spain. He carried a few Indians with him and a little gold.

His intention was to return as soon as possible with reinforcements. Gold lay somewhere at the back of Hispaniola, he was convinced. He would have it whatever the cost. It had become the driving passion of his life: "O most excellent gold! Who has gold has a treasure which gives him power to get what he desires, it lets him impose his will on the world and even helps souls into paradise.". . .

Columbus' reception in Barcelona, where the court was sitting, was ecstatic. The town went wild about the hero who had reached Cathay and claimed so much of it for Spain. He pointed to the group of Taino Indians and the pile of gold artifacts he had brought, and said: "The humble gifts which I bring to your Highnesses will give you some idea of the wealth of these regions. Doubters may say I exaggerate the amount of gold and spices to be found, and, in truth, we have only yet seen a hundredth of the splendor of these kingdoms. . . . I know that huge mines of gold will be found if your Highnesses allow me to return." (It was not known then that as well as the "humble gifts" he was displaying to their Catholic Majesties, his expedition was carrying syphilis from the New World and introducing it into Europe for the first time.)

His plea to Ferdinand and Isabella for continued support was successful. He was allowed to return to Hispaniola. This time it was to be no mere voyage of exploration, but a full-scale conquest. Seventeen ships and 1,500 men went with him, including noblemen, courtiers and priests. The Indians were to be converted to Christianity, a trading colony was to be established, and Columbus was to explore Cuba and find out whether it was mainland as he believed, or simply another island.

Columbus Describes the New World

Christopher Columbus

On October 12, 1492, when Italian-born navigator Christopher Columbus's three ships landed on the island known today as Hispaniola, the explorer thought he was on the coast of India, and so he called the natives "Indians." As was typical of the times, Columbus gave no heed to the property rights of the indigenous people who lived there and claimed all lands for Ferdinand II and Isabella I, the king and queen of Spain who had financed his trip.

In order to gain support for another journey to the New World, Columbus wrote the following letter in March 1493 after returning to Spain. In the letter, Columbus repeatedly described vast gold deposits that he had never seen and in fact did not exist. The exaggerations worked, however, and Columbus returned to the New World in 1493— this time with seventeen ships and almost fifteen hundred men.

Julian Mates was associate professor of English at C.W. Post College and the author of several books on music and drama. Eugene Cantelupe was also associate professor of English at C.W. Post College and the author of books on Renaissance poetry and painting.

Sir, forasmuch as I know that you will take pleasure in the great triumph with which Our Lord has crowned my voyage, I write this to you, from which you will learn how, in twenty days I reached the

Excerpted from Christopher Columbus, "Letter to the Keeper of the Privy Purse," in Julian Mates and Eugene Cantelupe, eds , *Renaissance Culture: A New Sense of Order* (New York: George Braziller, 1966).

Indies with the fleet which the most illustrious King and Queen, our lords, gave to me. And there I found very many islands filled with people without number, and of them all have I taken possession for Their Highnesses, by proclamation and with the royal standard displayed, and nobody objected. To the first island which I found I gave the name *Sant Salvador*, in recognition of His Heavenly Majesty, who marvelously hath given all this; the Indians call it *Guanahani*. To the second I gave the name *Isla de Santa María de Concepción*; to the third, *Ferrandina*; to the fourth, *La Isla Bella*; to the fifth *La Isla Juana*; and so to each one I gave a new name.

When I reached Juana, I followed its coast to the westward, and I found it to be so long that I thought it must be the mainland, the province of Catayo. And since I found neither towns nor cities along the coast, but only small villages, with the people of which I could not have speech because they all fled forthwith, I went forward on the same course, thinking that I should not fail to find great cities and towns. And, at the end of many leagues, seeing that there was no change and that the coast was bearing me northwards, which was contrary to my desire since winter was already beginning and I proposed to go thence to the south, and as moreover the wind was favorable, I determined not to wait for a change of weather and backtracked to a certain harbor already noted, and thence I sent two men upcountry to learn if there were a king or great cities. They traveled for three days and found an infinite number of small villages and people without number, but nothing of importance; hence they returned.

Claiming Islands for Spain

I understood sufficiently from other Indians, whom I had already taken, that continually this land was an island, and so I followed its coast eastward 107 leagues [one league equals three miles] up to where it ended. And from that cape I saw toward the east another island, distant 18 leagues from the former, to which I at once gave the name *La Spañola*. And I went there and followed its northern part, as I had in the case of Juana, to the eastward for 178 great leagues in a straight line. As Juana, so all the others are very fertile to an excessive degree, and this one especially. In it there are many harbors on the sea coast, beyond comparison with others which I know in Christendom, and numerous rivers, good and large, which is marvelous. Its lands are lofty and in it there are many sierras and very high mountains. . . . All are most beautiful, of a thousand shapes, and all accessible, and filled with trees of a thousand kinds and tall, and they seem to touch the sky; and I am told that they never lose their foliage, which I can believe, for I saw them as green and beautiful as they are in Spain in May, and some of them were flowering, some with fruit, and some in another condition, according to their quality. And there were singing the nightingale and other little birds of a thousand kinds in the month of November, there where I went. There are palm trees of six or eight kinds, which are a wonder to behold because of their beautiful variety, and so are the other trees and fruits and plants; therein are marvelous pine groves, and extensive meadow country; and there is honey, and there are many kinds of birds and a great variety of fruits. Upcountry there are many mines of metals, and the population is innumerable. *La Spañola* is marvelous, the sierras and the mountains and the plains and the meadows and the lands are so beautiful and rich for planting and sowing, and for livestock of every sort, and for building towns and villages. The harbors of the sea here are such as you could not believe it without seeing them; and so the rivers, many and great, and good streams, the most of which bear gold. And the trees and fruits and plants have great differences from those of La Juana; in this [island] there are many spices and great mines of gold and of other metals.

Sharing, Loving Natives

The people of this island and of all the other islands which I have found and seen, or have not seen, all go naked, men and women, as their mothers bore them, except that some women cover one place only with the leaf of a plant or with a net of cotton which they make for that purpose. They have no iron or steel or weapons, nor are they capable of using them, although they are well-built people of handsome stature, because they are wondrous timid. They have no other arms than arms of canes, [cut] when they are in seed time, to the ends of which they fix a sharp little stick; and they dare not make use of these, for oftentimes it has happened that I have sent ashore two or three men to some town to have speech, and people without number have come out to them, and as soon as they saw them coming, they fled; even a father would not stay for his son; and this not because wrong has been done to anyone; on the contrary, at every point where I have been and have been able to have speech, I have given them of all that I had, such as cloth and many other things, without receiving anything for it; but they are like that, timid beyond cure. It is true that after they have been reassured and have lost this fear, they are so artless and so free with all they possess, that no one would believe it without having seen it. Of anything they have, if you ask them for it, they never say no; rather they invite the person to share it, and show as much love as if they were giving their hearts; and whether the thing be of value or of small price, at once they are content with whatever little thing of whatever kind may be given to them. I forbade that they should be given things so worthless as pieces of broken crockery and broken glass, and lace points, although when they were able to get them, they thought they had the best jewel in the world; thus it was learned that a sailor for a lace point received gold. . . .

They Believe I Came from the Sky

They even took pieces of the broken hoops of the wine casks and, like animals, gave what they had, so that it seemed to me to be wrong and I forbade it, and I gave them a thousand good, pleasing things which I had brought, in order that they might be fond of us, and furthermore might become Christians and be inclined to the love and service of Their Highnesses and of the whole Castilian [Spanish] nation, and try to help us and to give us of the things which they have in abundance and which are necessary to us. And they know neither sect nor idolatry, with the exception that all believe that the source of all power and goodness is in the sky, and they believe very firmly that I, with these ships and people, came from the sky, and in this belief they everywhere received me, after they had overcome their fear. And this does not result from their being ignorant (for they are of a very keen intelligence and men who navigate all those seas, so that it is wondrous the good account they give of everything), but because they have never seen people clothed or ships like ours.

And as soon as I arrived in the Indies, in the first island which I found, I took by force some of them in order that they might learn [Castilian] and give me information of what they had in those parts; it so worked out that they soon understood us, and we them, either by speech or signs, and they have been very serviceable. I still have them with me, and they are still of the opinion that I come from the sky, in spite of all the intercourse which they have had with me, and they were the first to announce this wherever I went, and the others went running from house to house and to the neighboring towns with loud cries of, "Come! Come! See the people from the sky!" They all came, men and women alike, as soon as they had confidence in us, so that not one, big or little, remained behind, and all brought something to eat and drink, which they gave with marvelous love. In all the islands they have very many *canoas* [canoes] like rowing *fustes* [boats], some bigger and some smaller, and some are bigger than a *fusta* of eighteen benches. They are not so beamy, because they are made of a single log, but a *fusta* could not keep up with them by rowing, since they make incredible speed, and in these they navigate all those islands, which are innumerable, and carry their merchandise. Some of these canoes I have seen with 70 and 80 men on board, each with his oar.

Gold Mines and Trade

In all these islands, I saw no great diversity in the appearance of the people or in their manners and language, but they all understand one another, which is a very singular thing, on account of which I hope that Their Highnesses will determine upon their conversion to our holy faith, towards which they are much inclined.

I have already said how I went 107 leagues in a straight line from west to east along the coast of the island Juana, and as a result of that voyage I can say that this island is larger than England and Scotland together; for, beyond these 107 leagues, there remain to the westward two provinces where I have not been, one of which they call Avan, and there the people are born with tails. Those provinces cannot have a length of less than 50 or 60 leagues, as I could understand from those Indians whom I retain and who know all the islands. The other, *Española*, in circuit is greater than all Spain . . . since I went along one side 188 great leagues in a straight line from west to east. It is a desirable land and, once seen, is never to be relinquished; and in it, although of all I have taken possession for Their Highnesses and all are much richly supplied than I know or could tell, I hold them all for Their Highnesses, which they may dispose of as absolutely as of the realms of Castile. In this *Española*, in the most convenient place and in the best district for the gold mines and for all trade both with this continent and with that over there . . . where there will be great trade and profit, I have taken possession of a large town to which I gave the name *La Villa de Nauidad*, and in it I have built a fort and defenses, which already, at this moment, will be all complete, and I have left in it enough people for such a purpose, with arms and artillery and provisions for more than a year, and a *fusta*, and a master of the sea in all [maritime] arts to build others; and great friendship with the king of that land, to such an extent that he took pride in calling me and treating me as brother; and even if he were to change his mind and offer insult to these people, neither he nor his people know the use of arms and they go naked, as I have already said, and are the most timid people in the world, so that merely the people whom I have left there could destroy all that land; and the island is without danger for their persons, if they know how to behave themselves.

Cannibals and Warrior Women

In all these islands, it appears, all the men are content with one woman, but to their *Maioral*, or king, they give up to twenty. It appears to me that the women work more than the men. I have been unable to learn whether they hold private property, but it appeared true to me that all took a share in anything that, one had, especially in victuals.

In these islands I have so far found no human monstrosities, as many expected, on the contrary, among all these people good looks are esteemed; nor are they Negroes, as in Guinea, but with flowing hair, and they are not born where there is excessive force in the solar rays; it is true that the sun there has great strength, although it is distant from the Equator 26 degrees. In these islands, where there are high mountains, the cold this winter was severe, but they endure it through habit and with the help of food which they eat with many and excessively hot spices. Thus I have neither found monsters nor had report of any, except in an island which is the second at the entrance to the Indies, which is inhabited by a people who are regarded in all the islands as very ferocious and who eat human flesh; they have many canoes with which they range all the islands of India and pillage and take as much as they can; they are no more malformed than the others, except that they have the custom of wearing their hair long like women, and they use bows and arrows of the same stems of cane with a little piece of wood at the tip for want of iron, which they have not. They are ferocious toward these other people, who are exceedingly great cowards, but I make no more account of them than of the rest. These are those who have intercourse with the women of *Matremomio,* which is the first island met on the way from Spain to the Indies, in which there is not one man. These women use no feminine exercises, but bows and arrows of cane, like the above said; and they arm and cover themselves with plates of copper, of which they have plenty. In another island which they assure me is larger than *Española,* the people have no hair. In this there is countless gold, and from it and from the other islands I bring with me *Indios* as evidence.

Slaves and Spices

In conclusion, to speak only of that which has been accomplished on this voyage, which was so hasty, Their Highnesses can see that I shall give them as much gold as they want if Their Highnesses will render me a little help; besides spice and cotton, as much as Their Highnesses shall command; and gum mastic, as much as they shall order shipped, and which, up to now, has been found only in Greece, in the island of Chios, and the Seignory sell it for what it pleases; and aloe wood, as much as they shall order shipped, and slaves, as many as they shall order, who will be idolaters. And I believe that I have found rhubarb and cinnamon, and I shall find a thousand other things of value, which the people whom I have left there will have discovered, for I tarried nowhere, provided the wind allowed me to sail, except in the town of Navidad, where I stayed [to have it] secured and well seated. And the truth is I should have done much more if the vessels had served me as the occasion required.

This is enough. And the Eternal God, Our Lord, Who gives to all those who walk in His way victory over things which appear impossible; and this was notably one. For, although men have talked or have written of these lands, all was conjecture, without getting a look at it, but amounted only to this; that those who heard for the most part listened and judged it more a fable than that there was anything in it, however, small.

So since our Redeemer has given this triumph to our most illustrious King and Queen, and to their renowned realms, in so great a matter, for this all Christendom ought to feel joyful and make great celebrations and give solemn thanks to the Holy Trinity with many solemn prayers for the great exaltation which it will have, in the turning of so many peoples to our holy faith, and afterwards for material benefits, since not only Spain but all Christians will hence have refreshment and profit. This is exactly what has been done, though in brief.

Done on board the caravel off the Canary Islands, on the fifteenth of February, year 1493.

At your service.   The Admiral.

1337–1453

The Hundred Years' War is periodically fought between England and France.

1347–1351

The Black Death, or bubonic plague, sweeps across Europe. In Italy alone, the plague strikes again in the years 1400, 1422–1425, 1436–1439, 1447–1451, and 1485–1487.

1378–1417

The Great Schism divides the Christian church as the Eastern Orthodox and Western Roman churches each elect their own pope.

1415

Henry V of England crushes the French in the Battle of Agincourt, beginning the last phase of the Hundred Years' War; Catholic reformer Jan Hus is burned at the stake as a heretic.

1419

Prince Henry, the third son of Portugal's King John I, sponsors several mariners to explore Africa's rocky and inhospitable coast.

1420–1433

The Hussite Revolution is fought in the modern-day Czech Republic between followers of John Hus who want to reform the church and soldiers loyal to Pope Martin V who want to persecute the Hussites for heresy.

1428

Aztec warriors win decisive battles against their rivals and become the most powerful people in the Valley of Mexico.

1429

The French, led by Joan of Arc, defeat the English at Orleans and begin to reverse English advances in the Hundred Years' War.

1434

Portuguese captain Gil Eanes sails two hundred miles south of the Canary Islands to name the wind-swept Cape Bojador in Africa.

1440

Explorers sell a dozen African slaves in Portugal, marking the beginning of a four-hundred-year slave trade run by Portuguese sailors; the most powerful king in the Americas, Montezuma I begins a twenty-eight year reign over the Aztec people.

1449

The French retake most of the lands formerly lost to the English in the Hundred Years' War.

ca. 1450

Utilizing movable type cast from metal alloy, Johannes Gutenberg invents the printing press in Germany.

1452

Renaissance painter and inventor Leonardo da Vinci is born.

1453

The Islamic Ottoman Turks conquer the city of Constantinople, ending one thousand years of Christian rule in that city; the Hundred Years' War finally ends when the French take the Bordeaux region from the English.

1455–1485

The War of the Roses, a civil war in England, is waged as two ruling dynasties compete for power.

1456

The Gutenberg Bible, the first European book printed with movable type, is printed.

1469–1492

The powerful Lorenzo de Medici rules Florence, ushering in an age known as the Renaissance.

1474

King Ferdinand and Queen Isabella rule over a newly united Spain.

1475

Renaissance artist Michelangelo is born.

1480

The Inquisition is formally initiated in Spain. Jewish people, heretics, and other non-Catholics are tortured and burned at the stake.

1488

Portuguese exploration down the West African coast is expanded when Bartolomeu Dias sails around the southern tip of Africa and names it the Cape of Good Hope.

1492

Christopher Columbus sails across the Atlantic Ocean and becomes the first European to travel to modern-day San Salvador, Cuba, Hispaniola, and the Bahamas.

1498

Portuguese explorer Vasco da Gama sails around Africa and opens the first European sea route to India; Columbus makes his third transatlantic voyage and sights the Orinoco River along the present-day Venezuela-Brazil border in South America.

FOR FURTHER RESEARCH

Christopher T. Allmand, ed.. *Society at War: The Experience of England and France During the Hundred Years' War*. New York: Barnes & Noble, 1973.

Abraham Arias-Larreta, *Pre-Columbian Masterpieces: Popul Vuh, Apu Ollantay, Chilam Balam*. Kansas City, MO: Editorial Indoamerican Library of the New World, 1967.

Olivier Bernier, *The Renaissance Princes*. Chicago: Stonehenge Press, 1983.

Fernand Braudel, *Capitalism and Material Life 1400–1800*. New York: Harper and Row, 1973.

C.A. Burland and Werner Forman. *Feathered Serpent and Smoking Mirror*. New York: G.P. Putnam's Sons, 1975.

E.R. Chamberlin, *Everyday Life in Renaissance Times*. London: B.T. Batsford, 1967.

Geoffrey Chaucer, *The Canterbury Tales*. Trans. Frank Ernest Hill. New York: Longmans, Green, 1960.

Louise Collis, *Memoirs of a Medieval Woman*. New York: Thomas Y. Crowell, 1964.

Gaspar Correa, *The Three Voyages of Vasco da Gama and His Viceroyalty*. New York: Burt Franklin, 1969.

George Gordon Coulton, *Medieval Panorama: The English Scene from Conquest to Reformation*. New York: Meridian Books, 1955.

Joseph Dahmus, *The Middle Ages: A Popular History*. Garden City, NY: Doubleday, 1968.

Georges Duby, ed., *A History of Private Life: Revelations of the Medieval World*. Cambridge. MA: Belknap Press of Harvard University Press, 1988.

Fray Diego Durán, *The Aztecs: The History of the Indies of New Spain.* Trans. Doris Heyden and Fernando Horcasitas. London: Cassell, 1964.

Will Durant, *History of Civilization, Part V: The Renaissance.* New York: Simon & Schuster, 1953.

Editors of Time-Life Books, *Voyages of Discovery: Timeframe AD 1400–1500.* Alexandria, VA: Time-Life Books, 1989.

Brian M. Fagan, *Clash of Cultures.* New York: W.H. Freeman, 1984.

Stuart J. Fiedel, *Prehistory of the Americas.* Cambridge, England: University of Cambridge Press, 1992.

Marzieh Gail, *Life in the Renaissance.* New York: Random House, 1993.

Alice Stopford Green, *Town Life in the Fifteenth Century.* New York: Macmillan, 1907.

Ralph A. Griffiths, *The Reign of King Henry VI.* Berkeley and Los Angeles: University of California Press, 1981.

Victor Wolfgang von Hagen, *The Ancient Sun Kingdoms of the Americas.* Cleveland, OH: World Publishing, 1961.

Frederick Hartt, *History of Italian Renaissance Art.* New York: Harry N. Abrams, 1987.

Denys Hay, ed., *Europe in the Fourteenth and Fifteenth Centuries.* 1966. Reprint, London: Longman, 1989.

George Hodges, *Saints and Heroes: To the End of the Middle Ages.* 1911. Reprint, Freeport, NY: Books for Libraries Press, 1973.

Madge Huntington, *A Traveler's Guide to Chinese History.* New York: Henry Holt, 1986.

Ann Kendall, *Everyday Life of the Incas.* New York: Dorset Press, 1973.

Margaret Wade Labarge, *Medieval Travelers.* New York: W.W. Norton, 1983.

Harold Lamb, *The March of the Muscovy: Ivan the Terrible and the Growth of the Russian Empire 1400–1648*. Garden City, NY: Doubleday, 1948.

Leonardo da Vinci, *The Notebooks of Leonardo da Vinci*. Vol. 2. New York: Dover, 1970

Louise Levathes, *When China Ruled the Seas: The Treasure Fleet of the Dragon Throne 1405–1433*. New York: Simon & Schuster, 1994.

Jon E. Lewis, ed., *The Mammoth Book of Eye-Witness History*. New York: Carroll & Graf, 1998.

Barnet Litvinoff, *1492*. New York: Charles Scribner's Sons, 1991.

William Manchester, *A World Lit Only by Fire: The Medieval Mind and the Renaissance*. Boston: Little, Brown, 1992.

Julian Mates and Eugene Cantelupe, eds., *Renaissance Culture*. New York: George Braziller, 1966.

Yehudi Menuhin and Curtis Wheeler Davis, *The Music of Man*. New York: Methuen, 1979.

Robin Neillands, *The Hundred Years' War*. London: Routledge, 1991.

J.H. Parry, *The Age of Reconnaissance*. Cleveland, OH: World Publishing, 1963.

C.W. Previté-Orton, *The Shorter Cambridge Medieval History*. Vol. 2. Cambridge, England: Cambridge University Press, 1952.

Werner Rösener, *Peasants in the Middle Ages*. Chicago: University of Illinois Press, 1992.

James Bruce Ross and Mary Martin McLaughlin, eds., *The Portable Renaissance Reader*. New York: Viking Press, 1953.

Cecil Roth, *The Spanish Inquisition*. New York: W.W. Norton, 1964.

Marjorie Rowling, *Everyday Life in Medieval Times*. New York: Dorset Press, 1968.

Kirkpatrick Sale, *The Conquest of Paradise: Christopher Columbus and the Columbian Legacy.* New York: Penguin, 1991.

Margaret Shinnie, *Ancient African Kingdoms.* New York: St. Martin's Press, 1965.

Robert Warnock and George K. Anderson, *Centuries of Transition.* Glenview, IL: Scott, Foresman, 1967.

Desmond Wilcox, *Ten Who Dared.* Boston: Little, Brown, 1977.

2-15-02

SE

349c

PUYALLUP PUBLIC LIBRARY